MEASURING
COMMERCIAL
DAMAGES

**Subscriber
Update
Service**

BECOME A SUBSCRIBER!
Did you purchase this product from a bookstore?

If you did, it's important for you to become a subscriber. John Wiley & Sons, Inc., may publish, on a periodic basis, supplements and new editions to reflect the latest changes in the subject matter that you *need to know* to stay competitive in this ever-changing industry. By contacting the Wiley office nearest you, you'll receive any current update at no additional charge. In addition, you'll receive future updates and revised or related volumes on a 30-day examination review.

If you purchased this product directly from John Wiley & Sons, Inc., we have already recorded your subscription for this update service.

To become a subscriber, please call **1-800-225-5945** or send your name, company name (if applicable), address, and the title of the product to:

mailing address: **Supplement Department**
                                John Wiley & Sons, Inc.
                                One Wiley Drive
                                Somerset, NJ 08875

e-mail: **subscriber@wiley.com**
fax: **1-732-302-2300**
online: **www.wiley.com**

For customers outside the United States, please contact the Wiley office nearest you:

Professional & Reference Division
John Wiley & Sons Canada, Ltd.
22 Worcester Road
Rexdale, Ontario M9W 1L1
CANADA
(416) 675-3580
Phone: 1-800-567-4797
Fax: 1-800-565-6802
canada@jwiley.com

John Wiley & Sons, Ltd.
Baffins Lane
Chichester
West Sussex, PO19 1UD
ENGLAND
Phone: (44) 1243 779777
Fax: (44) 1243 770638
cs-books@wiley.co.uk

Jacaranda Wiley Ltd.
PRT Division
P.O. Box 174
North Ryde, NSW 2113
AUSTRALIA
Phone: (02) 805-1100
Fax: (02) 805-1597
headoffice@jacwiley.com.au

John Wiley & Sons (SEA) Pte. Ltd.
2 Clementi Loop #02-01
SINGAPORE 129809
Phone: (65) 463-2400
Fax: (65) 463-4604; (65) 463-4605
wiley@singnet.com.sg

MEASURING COMMERCIAL DAMAGES

PATRICK A. GAUGHAN

JOHN WILEY & SONS, INC.

New York • Chichester • Weinheim • Brisbane • Singapore • Toronto

Copyright © 2000 by John Wiley & Sons, Inc. All rights reserved.

Published simultaneously in Canada.

Library of Congress Cataloging-in-Publication Data:
Gaughan, Patrick A.
    Measuring commercial damages / Patrick A. Gaughan.
        p.   cm.
    Includes index.
    ISBN 0-471-35730-8 (alk. paper)
    1. Lost profits damages—United States. 2. Business losses—
United States. 3. Damages—United States. I. Title.
KF1250.G35   1999
658.15′5—dc21   99-38747

Printed in the United States of America.

10 9 8 7 6 5 4 3 2 1

CONTENTS

Preface   **xi**

1 Introduction   **1**

Development of Litigation Economics   1

Commercial Damages Analysis Compared to Personal Injury
    and Employment Litigation   2

Qualifications of a Damages Expert   4

Interdisciplinary Nature of Commercial Damages Analysis   5

Difference Between Economics and Finance   7

Finding a Damages Expert   8

Getting the Damages Expert on Board Early Enough   15

Court's Position on Experts   16

Standards for Admissibility of Expert Testimony   18

Expert Reports   21

Defense Expert as a Testifying Expert   21

Quantitative Research Evidence on the Benefits
    of Calling a Defense Expert   23

Types of Commercial Damages   24

Treatment of the Relevant Case Law   24

Legal Damage Principles   25

Contract-Related Damages   28

Commercial Damages in Personal Injury   31

Summary   33

References   34

2 Economic Framework for Estimating Lost Profits   **37**

Foundation for Damages Testimony   37

Approaches to Proving Damages   39

Causality and Damages   43
Using Demonstrative Evidence to Help the Client
    Understand Its Losses or Lack of Losses   49
Causality and Loss of Customers   50
Graphical Sales Analysis and Causality   51
Economists and Other Damage Experts: Role of Causality   53
Causality and the Special Case of Damages Resulting
    from Adverse Publicity   53
Length of Loss Period: Business Interruption Case   54
Case of Postinterruption Growth Exceeding Preinterruption Growth   56
Disaggregating Revenues by Product Line to Prove Causality   57
Disaggregating Revenues to Show Spillover Losses   59
Length of Loss Period: Plaintiff Goes Out of Business   60
Length of Loss Period: Breach of Contract   61
Methodological Framework   62
Summary   64
References   65

**3 Macroeconomic Analysis
    for Measuring Commercial Damages**   **67**
Macroeconomics   67
Measuring Economic Growth and Performance   68
Using More Narrowly Defined Economic Aggregates   75
Overstatement of Inflation Statistics   82
Other Measures of Inflation   84
Caution on Using Economic Growth Rate Data Too Directly   88
International Economic Analysis   91
Macroeconomic and Regional Economic Analysis
    and the Before and After Method   93
Summary   94
References   95

4 Industry Analysis   **96**
Government Sources of Industry Data   96
Standard Industrial Classification Codes   100
New North American Industry Classification System   106

Private Sources of Industry Data												107
Retaining an Industry Expert												114
Conducting an Industry Analysis												115
Relating Industry Growth to the Plaintiff's Growth												117
Measuring the Strength of Association: Industry versus Firm												119
Yardstick Approach and Industry Analysis												122
Summary												126
References												126

**5 Projecting Lost Revenues												128**

Projections versus Forecasts: Economic
   versus Accounting Terminology												128
Using Graphical Analysis as an Aide in Forecasting												129
Methods of Projecting Lost Revenues												131
Understanding Regression Output and Diagnostics												138
Common Problems Affecting Regression Models												140
Confidence in Forecasted Values												144
Frequency of the Use of Econometrics Techniques
   in Commercial Litigation												147
Seasonality and Forecasting												149
Capacity Constraints and Forecasts												151
Sensibility Check for the Forecasted Values												152
Projecting Lost Sales for a New Business												153
Projecting Losses for an Unestablished Business												156
Case Study: *Lightning Lube, Inc. v. Witco*												158
Summary												159
Appendix												160
References												166

**6 Cost Analysis and Profitability												169**

Presentation of Costs on the Company's Financial Statements												170
Measures of Costs												171
Profit Margins and Profitability												172
Burden of Proof for Demonstrating Costs												173
Fixed versus Variable Costs												173
Using Regression Analysis to Estimate Costs												175

Capacity Constraints and Fixed versus Variable Costs 181
Limitations of Using Unadjusted Accounting Data
    for Measuring Incremental Costs 182
Treatment of Overhead Costs 183
Unprofitable Businesses and Recovery of Damages 186
Mitigation of Damages 187
Cash Flows versus Net Income: Effects
    on the Discounting Process 190
Recasted Profits 192
Case Study: Profits That Are Not Really Profits 195
Firm-Specific Financial Analysis 195
Cross-Sectional versus Time Series Analysis 199
Summary 199
References 200

7 Time Value of Money Considerations 203

Interest Rates and Securities Markets 204
Prejudgment Losses 214
Cost of Capital 218
Discounting 226
Summary 231
References 232

8 Business Valuations 235

Measures of Business Value 239
Equity Valuation Models 240
Earnings-Based Models 243
Estimating Cash Flows 250
Estimating Discount Rates 257
Market Comparable Models 262
Asset Valuation Models 267
Summary of Valuation Models 268
Discounts and Premiums 270
Valuing Other Financial Assets 274
Summary 278
References 278

9   Intellectual Property   **282**

Patents   282

Royalty Arrangements   288

Computer Software   293

Copyrights   293

Trademarks   299

Trade Secrets   303

Summary   306

References   307

10   Securities Damages   **310**

Fraud on the Market   310

Mergers-Related Damages   330

Churning   335

Summary   345

Appendix A: Case Study:

  In Re Computer Associates, International, Inc.   346

Appendix B: Cases Setting Holding Periods   351

References   352

11   Antitrust Concerns   **355**

Antitrust Laws   355

Antitrust Enforcement   358

Monopolization and Attempts at Monopolization   365

Market Power   370

Common Types of Antitrust Cases   373

Summary   382

References   383

Glossary   **385**

Index   **391**

PREFACE

Over the past few decades the field of litigation support has grown dramatically. It includes a wide variety of experts and support specialties. One field within that group that has become more prominent in recent years is damages estimation. For certain types of litigation, such as personal injury litigation (where in the methodology of measuring the loss of wages and benefits is applied) an established methodology and a large quantity of literature exists. However, in spite of its obvious importance, little has been written on commercial damages—particularly methodological works. This book seeks to provide a methodological framework for the field of commercial damages.

The goal of *Measuring Commercial Damages* is to set forth a standard methodology for the measurement of the most common type of commercial damages—lost profits. The anticipated audience is a combination of accountants, attorneys, and economists. The range of different types of commercial damages covered is quite broad, extending from basic lost profits analysis to particular types of losses that may occur in intellectual property, securities, and antitrust litigation. The book initially sets forth a standard methodology, while later sections delve into the more unique damages issues that can arise in the aforementioned types of cases. Given the breadth of the audience, a detailed analysis of particular specialties is not attempted. Rather, an overview of these special topics is provided. The reason for this is that the goal of the subsections is to provide the reader with an introduction to these areas. It is assumed that the reader does not have an in depth familiarity with many of the issues in these areas.

As is mentioned numerous times throughout this book, the knowledge and skills required to do a competent and expert job at measuring commercial damages is quite broad. Few experts will possess strengths in all required areas. For this reason, experts who are strong in one area, say accounting, may find the introduction to the relevant economic topics useful in attempting to do some of this analysis as well as for working with economists in a team paradigm. Conversely, readers who are economists will repeatedly find that the strengths of accountants are touted throughout the book (and vice versa). Readers who are attorneys working with experts will gain a better understanding of how these different experts can interact and what each can and cannot do. Attorneys will also learn how damages should be measured so as to arrive at a nonspeculative opinion.

This book is organized so that readers who seek to efficiently learn more about a particular topic do not have to read the entire book or preceding chapters to gain an understanding from the selected readings. However, the cost of presenting more "self contained" chapters is some repetition. Readers who read the entire book may note that some topics that have been covered are briefly discussed a second time. While this is done to a limited extent, it is done by design, allowing readers of selected chapters to gain the most they can from the time they invest in the book. Clearly, the professional audience has very high time costs and this format may be helpful.

It is hoped that *Measuring Commercial Damages* will add to the limited literature that exists in the field of commercial damages, and will spur further developments as others build on what has been done in this book. It is readily acknowledged that this book is a start to the development of a standard methodology and that in time others practitioners will further advance this development.

1

INTRODUCTION

This book is designed to provide a methodological framework for measuring commercial damages. Its goal is to discuss some of the more important issues within this framework. The discussion is presented with an emphasis on the interdisciplinary nature of commercial damages analysis. Depending on the type of case, the expert who values damages of a company in litigation may need to have a well-rounded knowledge of the research and practices in the related disciplines of macroeconomics, microeconomics, econometrics, and finance, including investment analysis, capital market theory, corporate finance, and, last but not least, accounting. Given the broad range of expertise that may ultimately be needed, combined with the fact that few individuals would be experts in all of these fields, a team of experts, such as economists working with accountants, is often the optimal solution.

This book is not meant to present an exhaustive review of all the issues relevant to commercial damages analysis. Rather, it is meant to discuss the most important and fundamental issues. However, each case brings with it its own set of unique factors and these need to be considered on an individual basis. No broad-based book, such as this one, can anticipate all of the unique circumstances that may be encountered. For this reason, this book focuses on the more commonly encountered circumstances and presents a general damages evaluation framework capable of handling all of them.

DEVELOPMENT OF LITIGATION ECONOMICS

Litigation economics, sometimes also referred to as forensic economics, has developed significantly over the past two decades, during which the National Association of Forensic Economics (NAFE) was formed (http://nafe.net). A national body of economists who work in the field of litigation economics and who may provide expert testimony in court proceedings, the organization is composed of mainly Ph.D. economists, many of whom have academic affiliations, as well as other members with different backgrounds. In addition to the creation of NAFE, three well-received, refereed, academic journals devoted to the field of litigation economics—*Journal of Forensic Economics, Journal of Legal Economics* and *Litigation Economics Digest*—have begun publication. These journals have given litigation economics an academic stature similar to other subdisciplines in the field of economics. In addition to there being a forum for respected scholarly work in this area, most of the major meetings and the leading professional conferences of economists in the United States, including the American Economics Association and the Western Economics Association annual meetings, now have several sessions devoted exclusively to litigation economics. Such conferences have allowed the exchange of ideas that has further developed the methodologies in the field. There are also now two on-line exchange forums. The first, sponsored by the National Association of Forensic Economics and called NAFE-L, features the exchange of ideas on a variety of litigation economics topics but is mostly geared to personal injury litigation. The second, called Business Damages Forum, features an exchange of ideas on various issues related to commercial damages and business valuations.

At present, the leading use of damages experts, often economists, tends to be in personal injury and wrongful death litigation. This is not surprising, because this type of litigation is clearly the most common. Although there are some similarities between commercial damages analysis and the estimation of damages in personal injury and wrongful death litigation, major differences cause them to be two separate fields, often including different groups of practitioners. In general, economists who do personal injury damages analysis tend to have a background in labor economics, but may not have a background in finance. Many of these experts are sole practitioners who often have a full-time academic position. Experts in commercial damages analysis, instead, tend to be a more diverse group. Many of them work for large firms, including some public companies. They come from a variety of backgrounds, with the most common being accounting, economics, and finance.

COMMERCIAL DAMAGES ANALYSIS COMPARED TO PERSONAL INJURY AND EMPLOYMENT LITIGATION

Economists are often called upon to provide testimony on damages in personal injury and wrongful death litigation. These cases utilize a more or less standard methodology that does not vary significantly among cases. This methodology has been well developed in the forensic economics literature. In addition, a concise statement of many of the generally accepted steps in the damages measurement process for personal injury cases has been set forth in *Economic Expert Testimony: A Guide for Judges and Attorneys.*[1] The methodology usually involves projecting lost earnings and fringe benefits (net of mitigation in personal injury cases) over the work-life expectancy of the plaintiff, as well as a valuation of lost services over a time period that may approach the plaintiff/decedent's healthy life expectancy. The work life is the generally accepted standard for the terminal date of lost earnings estimates while the life expectancy is often used as a guide to establish the length of the loss period to measure the value of lost services (the life expectancy may be reduced to reflect the diminished ability to provide services due to the aging process).[2] Both the life expectancy and the work-life expectancy are based on statistical data that establish averages from demographic and labor market characteristics, as contrasted with commercial damages analysis where the loss period is usually determined by a different set of circumstances, such as what may be set forth in a contract.

In personal injury litigation, the monetary amount presented is usually derived from the historical earnings of the plaintiff or decedent. For those who have not yet had much of an earnings history, lost earnings may be derived from government statistics that set forth earnings as a function of age, sex, and education. Where appropriate, historical compensation data may allow the expert to measure the value of fringe benefits. Once the total compensation base has been established, the expert constructs a projection by selecting a proper growth rate. The projected values are then brought to present value terms by applying an appropriate discount rate.

In employment litigation, the expert may project damages using methods similar to those employed in personal injury cases. However, the role of the economist can be expanded when there are claims of bias or other discriminatory practices. Here, in addition to possibly measuring the damages of the plaintiff, the economist may be called upon to utilize his or her econometrics and statistical background to render an opinion on the liability part of the case.[3]

Commercial damages cases tend to vary considerably. Although some of the evaluation techniques used may be similar, the circumstances tend to vary more

---

[1] Thomas Ireland, Stephen M. Horner, and James Rodgers, "Reference Guide for Valuing Economic Loss in Personal Injury, Wrongful Death and Survival Actions," in *Economic Expert Testimony: A Guide for Judges and Attorneys* (Tucson: Lawyers and Judges Publishing Co.) 1998, 1–108.

[2] Michael Brookshire and Frank Slesnick, "A 1990 Survey Study of Forensic Economists," *Journal of Forensic Economists,* Spring/Summer 1991, IV (2), 125–149.

[3] Michael Piette, "Economic Methodology and the Analysis of Employment Discrimination," *Journal of Forensic Economics,* Fall 1991, IV (3), 307–316.

widely from case to case. In addition, the industries involved can be very different and may each present unique issues. Given this wide variability and the necessary industry analysis, commercial damages cases present a greater degree of complexity and typically result in greater time demands being placed on the expert in order to conduct a thorough analysis. The time demands often tend to be significantly greater than those associated with a typical personal injury or wrongful death loss analysis, thereby making a commercial damages loss analysis a more expensive proposition.

Another important difference between commercial damages analysis versus personal injury and wrongful death loss analysis is the role of cost analysis. The losses of a worker are typically wages and benefits, with job-related expenses usually not as significant a factor. In commercial damages analysis, costs related to lost revenues are generally quite important. Here the skills of an accountant may be most useful in measuring the appropriate costs that would have been incurred in order to realize certain lost revenues.

QUALIFICATIONS OF A DAMAGES EXPERT

It is important that the commercial damages expert possess a well-rounded background to measure the damages reliably and to withstand the criticisms that come from cross-examination. Although courts are generally somewhat lenient in what they accept as an expert, the "expert must possess requisite skill, training, education, knowledge, or experience from which it can be assumed that the opinion is reliable."[4] Given that these attributes are generic, it is important to focus on the specific credentials relevant to measuring economic damages.

The desirable qualifications of an economic expert witness are set forth in various publications in the field of litigation economics. Examples can be found in Stuart Speiser's *Recovery For Personal Injury and Wrongful Death,* Michael Brookshire and Stan Smith's *Economic/Hedonic Damages,* Gerald Martin's *Determining Economic Damages,* and Gary Baker and Michael Seck's *Determining Economic Loss in Personal Injury and Death Cases.*[5] The qualifications set forth in these publications focus on applications in personal injury and wrongful death

---

[4] *Mattott v. Ward,* 48 N.Y. 2d 455, 423 N.Y.S. 2d 645 (1979).

[5] Speiser, Stuart, *Recovery For Wrongful Death and Injury: Economic Handbook,* 2nd ed. (New York: West Group) 1998; Brookshire, Michael L. and Stan V. Smith, *Economics/Hedonic Damages, The Practice Book for Plaintiff and Defense Attorneys* (Cincinnati: Anderson Publishing Company) 1990; Martin, Gerald, *Determining Economic Damages* (James Publishing Inc.) 1995; Baker, W. Gary and Michael K. Seck, *Determining Economic Loss in Personal Injury and Death Cases* (New York: Shephard's/McGraw Hill) 1987.

litigation. The requisite qualifications to competently estimate commercial damages and render an *expert* opinion are similar, however, the qualifications tend to be broader. These have also been set forth in the forensic economics literature.[6]

Desirable qualifications of an economist who could provide expert witness testimony on commercial damages include:

- Doctorate in economics, finance, or accounting
- Background in finance or financial economics
- University teaching position—preferably at the graduate level
- Scholarly publications in economics, finance, or accounting
- Professional presentations in economics, finance, or accounting
- Experience in industry analysis and forecasting
- Experience in commercial damages analysis

The qualified witness may not possess all of the foregoing, but may have clear strengths in one area that may outweigh possible deficiencies in others.

In lost profits litigation, the courts have consistently ruled that economists and accountants are appropriate expert witnesses to testify on damages. Attorneys sometimes hire accountants to do lost profits analysis, but CPAs generally have a limited background in economics and finance and lack the expertise to conduct a thorough economic analysis. However, accountants may provide valuable expertise on certain issues such as cost analysis and preparation of pro forma financial statements. For some commercial damages cases an interdisciplinary approach combining the expertise of economics, finance, and accounting, perhaps through the use of more than one expert, may be useful. This may mean that just one expert testifies and that the testifying expert relies on the work of other experts.

INTERDISCIPLINARY NATURE OF COMMERCIAL DAMAGES ANALYSIS

Most commercial damages analysis tends to be performed by experts from one discipline, such as economics, finance, or accounting, without the expert drawing on the expertise of those outside of his or her discipline. This situation is unfortu-

---

[6] Patrick A. Gaughan, "Economics and Financial Issues in Lost Profits Litigation," in *Litigation Economics,* Patrick A. Gaughan and Robert Thornton, eds. (Greenwich, Conn.: JAI Press) 1993.

nate because in many commercial damages cases the necessary skills and expertise tend to transcend traditional discipline boundaries. The skills of an economist
may be invaluable to analyze the relevant economic environment, do an industry
analysis, and construct reliable projections. A finance expert may be necessary to
analyze relevant variables from financial markets, such as rates of return. An accountant may be useful to conduct a costs analysis or to perform other work,
such as the reconstruction of financial statements, including cash flow statements. The needs just described are in general not part of the training that one ac-
quires in any one of these disciplines. However, it is common to see experts from
one field try to conduct the entire damages analysis for a given case. In such instances, they may do a competent job on the part of the analysis within their expertise, while failing to do a competent job in that portion of the analysis that is
outside of their expertise. A preferable approach is to use a team of experts, with
one leading expert providing the methodological structure and performing the
part of the analysis within his or her expertise. Other experts then provide their
own specific expertise upon which the leading expert relies to put forward the
loss measure.

Although it is acceptable for one expert to rely on the opinions of other experts when putting forward an expert opinion, it may be useful to have more than
one expert on the team testify. In this manner, each expert stays within his or her
own expertise and is capable of handling the cross-examination on the various
relevant issues that might arise.

Relative Strengths of Economists versus Accountants

Economists have training in various forms of macroeconomic and microeconomic analysis. Often they have extensive training and expertise in statistical
techniques and econometrics, techniques that may be invaluable in forecasting.
However, unless they have separately acquired a background in finance, many
economists have limited familiarity with financial statements and are not involved in the preparation of such statements. This is the bailiwick of accountants
who may have specialized training in areas such as cost accounting, which can
be most useful when determining profit ratios to apply to forecasted revenue levels. Some accountants have a Masters in Business Administration (MBA) degree
and others have an undergraduate degree in accounting and a CPA. It is important to note that even though an MBA is a graduate degree, most MBA programs
provide only general business training. The economics and forecasting courses in
MBA programs are usually fairly elementary and provide the student with limited training. These courses are not comparable to the training that a Ph.D. econ-

omist would normally receive. Some accountants have doctoral degrees and may possess such training. However, one of the strengths of accountants is their experience in the field, which can be quite useful particularly if it is in the industry that is being considered in the lawsuit.

An example of the court's reaction to opposing experts who possessed some of the strengths and shortcomings just discussed can be found in *Digital & Analog Design Corporation v. North Supply Company*. The plaintiff introduced an expert who had a doctorate and who held himself out to be an expert in economics and business finance. Although the court seemed a little confused about the forecasting methods employed by the economist, they were notably impressed.

> In this regard DAD's economic expert is in the field of economic analysis, with a large number of publications and professional activities to his credit. The evidence would reasonably support his technique of cost-profit analysis, the so-called "time series analysis and projection."
>
> NSC, by comparison did not produce a comparable expert. Instead, NSC relied upon the testimony of a certified public accountant, an employee controller of NSC, a Mr. Simon, neither of whom it appears had as extensive training or expertise in the time series analysis method as had Dr. Zinser, and neither of whom utilized a competing method of analysis to calculate a lesser amount of profits.[7]

Although impressed by the economist's forecasting abilities, the court found his cost analysis wanting. The economist merely applied the gross margin to projected lost sales without more carefully measuring incremental costs as discussed in Chapter 6. A solution that neither side attempted would have been to have an economist do the lost revenue projection and an accountant conduct the analysis of the costs associated with the forecasted lost revenues. Such an approach, when appropriate, is advocated throughout this book.

DIFFERENCE BETWEEN ECONOMICS AND FINANCE

Attorneys are more aware of the relative skills and strengths of economists versus accountants than they are when comparing specialists in economics versus finance, partly because the fields are somewhat interrelated. Many economists consider finance to be a subfield of economics. Indeed, there is a field called financial economics that applies economic analysis to financial markets. However,

---

[7] *Digital & Analog Design Corporation v. North Supply Company,* 44 Ohio St. 3d 36; 540 N.E. 2d 1358 (1989).

there are several differences between a doctorate in economics and a doctorate in finance. For one, finance degrees are often conferred by a college of business within a university whereas economics degrees may be offered by the university outside of the college of business. This difference is not important. What may be more relevant is the different training of the individuals.

The training of Ph.D.s in economics and finance have several differences. One of them is that a Ph.D. in finance may have some training in accounting and may have taken certain courses taught in the business schools that economists are not required to take. Many economists lack any knowledge of finance and financial statements. It is possible, for example, to get a doctorate in economics without ever having seen a financial statement (as shocking as this sounds). Indeed, many economists do analysis on many complicated and esoteric areas and consider topics such as the analysis of financial statements simplistic. Nonetheless, it is important that the economists in commercial damages analysis have a more broad knowledge base that may involve going beyond the initial training received in graduate school. For example, those who write their dissertation on a financially related topic may get this background as part of their thesis research.

FINDING A DAMAGES EXPERT

There are many ways for an attorney to find a damages expert. One of the most often used is word-of-mouth and referrals, whereby an attorney consults with colleagues he or she respects and gets the names of experts who have successfully performed for them. If this process is not successful, other methods must be employed.

Certain types of media, including regional legal publications and legal reference diaries, advertise the services of experts. It is important that references be gathered and checked, particularly in cases where initially the attorney does not have any additional information on the expert other than what the advertisement supplies. This review process can be enhanced by a verdict search, which may reveal the names of cases in which the expert has testified.[8] Both the attorneys who retained the expert in the past and the attorneys who cross-examined the expert in prior matters can be consulted for feedback. Keep in mind, however, that an adversarial attorney, particularly one who may not have done as well as he wanted to in the case in question, may fail to give an objective review.

---

[8] *Verdict Search,* Moran Publishing Company, East Islip, New York. (www .verdictsearch.com)

Other sources for obtaining information on experts are the expert referral companies. These firms maintain names and *curricula vitae* (CVs) of experts in many different specialties which they refer to attorneys for a fee.[9] A CV is a document that lists an expert's credentials. The fee that these companies charge may include an initial charge as well as a built-in hourly charge that is incorporated into the expert's fee. This may cause the expert's fee to be different than what it otherwise would be if she were contacted directly without a referral intermediary. However, referral agencies can greatly speed up the process of finding an expert—particularly if one is looking for unique expertise such as a specialist in a certain narrowly defined industry.

Another source of experts can be local universities. A professor in a nearby university may have a certain appeal to a jury from the same community. In addition, professors may possess the ability to explain complicated concepts clearly. However, attorneys have to be very careful if they are hiring an academic who lacks litigation and testimony expertise. It takes a certain personality to withstand the rigors of the adversarial litigation process in the United States. Furthermore, the way one voices arguments and positions in an academic environment is very different from how opinions may be expressed in an adversarial litigation environment. As obvious as this sounds, many would-be litigation experts who are pure academics may find this difficult to comprehend. Therefore, attorneys need to exercise caution in using untested experts whose testimony may be somewhat unpredictable. The role of experience is discussed later in this chapter.

Several economic consulting firms, ranging from small "boutiques" to large national firms, offer litigation-related services. Some specialize in commercial matters while others offer a variety of damages-related services. Many possess well-qualified individuals but attorneys still need to give the specific experts working on their case careful scrutiny.

Still another source of experts is the major consulting arms of accounting firms and other larger litigation companies. In recent years, accounting firms have aggressively expanded their consulting operations after they discovered the profit margins on traditional accounting work, such as auditing, shrank because of competitive pressure and corporate cost cutting. These firms can bring larger quantities of personnel to a project. However, although it may seem comforting that such a firm can apply many professionals to a given project, usually one specific expert ends up testifying. The fact that an army of accountants may be employed at a given firm may be of limited benefit when that expert testifies on his personal credentials and on the analysis that was performed and the opinions that

---

[9] Technical Advisory Service for Attorneys, Blue Bell, Pennsylvania. (www.tasanet .com)

were developed. Therefore, when it comes to actual testimony the specific credentials and track record of the expert are more important than the quantity of staff that a firm employs. This should not be construed to imply that larger firms are inferior to small ones. Rather, the expert selection process is individualistic and should be focused on the specific expert or team of experts that will ultimately testify.

Critically Reviewing a Potential Expert's Curriculum Vitae

Many attorneys seem to take at face value the content of a potential or opposing expert's CV without applying careful scrutiny. Some attorneys merely give the CV a cursory scan and conclude from the length of the CV that the expert possesses impressive credentials. Sometimes a closer review of the listings included on the CV can expose the misleading nature of the items. For example, in lieu of quality publications, an expert may list presentations made before attorneys, which are nothing more than marketing appeals and sales pitches. Other publications may include very general articles in legal newspapers and magazines. These articles do not go through the scrutiny that a refereed journal article or book would. Sometimes what is listed as a publication is a paper or article that has not even been published.

Degrees

One of the most fundamental characteristics of a degree as it relates to litigation is the degree's relevance. It is very common for experts to want to testify in an area that is outside of their expertise. Courts have been supportive of objections to experts testifying outside of their expertise.[10] In the area of commercial damages, many individuals put themselves forward as experts. Courts are often liberal in accepting such individuals and rely on the voir dire process and cross-examination to expose any deficiencies. However, at a minimum, attorneys should be aware that doctoral degrees in some fields such as engineering or operations research provide little or no training in the areas that would be relevant to most types of commercial damages analysis. Attorneys should be very wary of the mail-away Ph.D. These are doctoral degrees that one can earn at home. Several institutions offering such degrees have sprung up and some even advertise in major publications. If the degree-granting institution is unknown, the attorney should get its catalog and review the criteria it employs for issuing degrees.

---

[10] *Wright v. Williams,* 47 Cal. App. 3d 802, 121 Cal Rptr. 194 (1975).

When encountering opposing experts with such degrees, this area of inquiry can be very fertile.

Published Books

Published books can be an impressive credential for an expert to have. These books are even more impressive if they are published by major publishers who tend to be selective. Books that have received acclaim or won awards for their quality are even better. Books that have been used as textbooks may also provide the author with certain credentials that other experts who have not published any books may lack. In addition, books in the area in which the expert is testifying can be invaluable. It is great to use as an expert the person "who wrote the book" in the area.

Beware of books published by vanity publishers. These are publishers who publish a book for an author for a fee. They are not unlike photocopy houses as opposed to the more traditional publisher. Having such a published book implies that none of the many publishing houses that exist considered the work worthy of publication. It also implies that the book in question has a very limited readership and may not be regarded as authoritative by anyone in the field.

Refereed Journal Articles

In addition to published books, another important standard used for evaluating scholarship in academia is *refereed* journal articles. A refereed journal is one that utilizes a group of experts in specific specialities to blindly review articles submitted to the journal in their speciality. A journal's editors allocate the articles to the relevant referees and ensure that the process is completed without revealing the names of the authors or the referees. These referees judge the quality of the article and decide if it is worthy of publication. This peer review process is very different from articles that are reviewed by an editor who simply decides whether a piece is of interest to the readers.

There are three refereed journals in the field of litigation economics. the *Journal of Forensic Economics, Journal of Legal Economics,* and *Litigation Economics Digest.* Although many of the articles in these journals focus on areas other than commercial damages, a certain quantity of articles on commercial damages have been published in each of these refereed journals. Other refereed journals that may feature articles in the area of commercial damages can be found in the closely related field of law and economics. This is a subfield of economics, in which someone getting a doctorate in economics can specialize. The three leading journals in that field are the *Journal of Law and Economics,* the *Journal of Legal Studies,* and the *Journal of Law, Economics and Organization.* In finance, there are many refereed journals, including *Journal of Finance, Journal of Fi-*

nancial Economics, Journal of Applied Corporate Finance, Financial Manage-
ment, Financial Analysts Journal, Journal of Accounting and Economics, and
many others. In econometrics there are several quality journals such as *Econo-*
metrica, Journal of Econometrics, and *Journal of the American Statistical Asso-*
ciation in addition to others. In the field of accounting, *Accounting Review* and
Accounting Horizons are two leading refereed journals. *Accounting Horizons* is
published by the American Accounting Association. While not a refereed journal,
the *Journal of Accountancy* is published by the American Institute of CPAs and
is widely distributed to all members of the Institute.

Presentations

An expert's CV often contains lists of presentations. In the academic world the
publication process often begins with a refereed presentation to one's peers in the
specific area of the article. Refereed presentations are those that are accepted after a Call for Papers has been announced and various submitted articles are reviewed by the organizers of paper sessions at various academic conferences. The
standards for acceptance vary widely but are usually higher than nonrefereed
presentations. Attorneys should be wary of presentation listings that are merely
promotion sales presentations made before potential clients.

Testimony Lists

Some experts list their prior testimony experience on their CV. When this is done
along with other valid credentials it may serve a purpose. However, if this is the
bulk of the CV, questions about the individual's expertise need to be raised. Perhaps the true expertise of the expert is selling his services to attorneys.

Concluding Comments on Contents of CVs

The expert witness arena has become quite crowded as professionals from many
fields have discovered that they can earn impressive fees by serving as experts in
litigated matters. They have learned that they may be better able to get the assignment if they have a long CV filled with impressive sounding contents. Therefore, it is incumbent on the attorneys to carefully review the listed items and ascertain their quality. When reviewing the contents of an opposing expert's CV,
one's own expert can be invaluable. For example, it has been observed on many
occasions that experts who lack publications may try to compile a list of alternative credentials that may take up several pages. As previously noted, one tactic
employed by such witnesses is to list testimonies. The retaining attorney must
then decide if a list of court appearances as an expert witness is truly a credential, particularly if there is little else on the CV. Another example that is really a

form of misrepresentation is what may be listed under the heading of publications. Experts who lack legitimate publications often list various items that range from papers that were never published to names of speaking appearances. A cross-examining attorney can have a field day with such misrepresentations. Therefore, it is the retaining attorney's responsibility to review the contents of an expert's CV carefully.

Credentials versus Experience in Litigation Analysis

Attorneys need to be aware that litigation-related analysis is a specialized field and not all highly credentialed experts can perform well in it. One classic example of an expert who possessed extremely impressive credentials but who lacked a familiarity with litigation analysis occurred in a recent antitrust case where the class action plaintiffs hired the Nobel Prize winning economist Dr. Robert Lucas.[11] With respect to his credentials, the court had the following comments:

> We next come to Dr. Robert Lucas and the opinions he expressed, particularly as regards to the alleged collusion engaged in by all of the Defendants. First, it is proper to recognize Dr. Lucas' eminent and distinguished credentials. He is affiliated with the University of Chicago, indisputably one of the finest educational institutions in the world. He is also a past recipient of the Nobel Prize in Economics, an award without equal in recognition of scholarship and contributions in his chosen discipline. It was with high expectation that the Court anticipated his testimony and denied requests from the defendants to preclude his testimony or to conduct a separate Daubert hearing out of the presence of the jury.

However, with respect to his analysis the Court was not as complementary.

> Sad to say, Dr. Lucas' testimony did not measure up to his unique qualifications. Among other things, his testimony showed the following:
>
> (a) he abdicated entirely the concept of the independence of the expert witnesses and simply became the sponsor for the Class Plaintiff's theory of the case;
> (b) he was ignorant of material testimony and other evidence;
> (c) his essential opinions were not only based on the evidence, they were inconsistent with it;

---

[11] *In Re Brand Name Prescription Drugs Antitrust Litigation,* 1999 U.S. Dist. Lexus 550, January, 19, 1999 (decided and docketed).

> (d) his opinions were offered without any scientific basis or having been sub-
> ject of economic methodological testing.
>
> Dr. Lucas reached his conclusions within 40 hours of his engagement and be-
> fore he undertook any substantial or detailed study of the prescription drug indus-
> try. Most of the facts upon which he based his opinions and conclusions were sup-
> plied by Class Plaintiffs' counsel, although he admitted he did not expect Class
> Plaintiff's counsel to have a balanced presentation. His expert's report was re-
> drafted by Class Plaintiff's counsel in its entirety and included what counsel
> wanted. In Dr. Lucas' own words: "I don't think there is a single sentence in this af-
> fidavit that's intact from the first draft that I proposed."

The lesson derived from the above case is that a variety of skills and abilities
are needed in order to be a competent expert witness in the field of commercial
damages. Impressive academic credentials can be a major plus in a courtroom.
These lofty credentials may cause a judge or jury to attach greater weight to the
testimony of the expert. However, the value of experience in the courtroom cannot be overestimated. Professors are used to lecturing with few challenges from
the student audience who are dependent upon the professor for their grades. Stu-
dents tend to be more in awe of highly regarded professors than cross-examining
attorneys who may believe that the testimony of the professor stands between
him and a high verdict. The expert must be familiar with the aggressive challenges that can occur during a cross-examination or a long deposition. With such
challenges in mind the expert prepares his report. Without such experience it is
difficult to anticipate the nature of the challenges. Simple factors that the expert
may take for granted can be the source of persistent cross-examination. Experience allows the expert to prepare properly. It is difficult to substitute a reputation
derived from writing journal articles and conducting research studies for such an
experience. The optimal solution is to find an expert who has impressive credentials in the form of degrees, publications, and awards, but who also has substantial experience in a litigation environment. Unfortunately, such experts are hard
to find.

Reviewing the Expert's Publications

Publishing books and articles in refereed, scholarly journals can be a major plus
for an expert. Such qualifications can add weight to the expert's opinions, particularly when the publications are related to the subject of the testimony. Attorneys
should be aware of the content of these publications, making sure that the content of the publications does not contradict the opinions being offered at trial.

Even the expert himself must review his publications for any potential inconsistencies. Such inconsistencies can be used to impeach the expert. Such was done to Dean Schmalensee, the economic expert put forward by Microsoft in its recent antitrust trial. Dr. Schmalensee, who opined on the lack of monopoly power by Microsoft, was confronted with the following quote from a *Harvard Law Review* article he wrote which addressed the relationship between persistent excess profits and long-run market power.

By Mr. Boies:

Q. Let me ask you to look at page eight, if I could, Dean Schmalensee, and the protion I want to direct your attention to is the paragraph right above the heading "Patterns of Conduct." As you can tell from the fact that I have highlighted the next paragraph, I'm going to want to direct your attention to that, too.

But right now I want to direct your attention to the paragraph that says, "Even if all measurement problems are solved, therefore, profitability is an unreliable measure of short-run market power. Nevertheless, persistent excess profits provide a good indications of long-run power. They show clearly that there is some impediment to effective imitation of the firm in question. The deadweight loss caused by such a breakdown in competition, and the resulting market power available to individuals firms, can be roughly estimated from the observed excess profits."

When you have had a chance to look at this paragraph in context, I have a couple of questions about it.

After a pause, where the witness may have considered how to reconcile this quote from one of his own publications with Microsoft's impressive record of profitability, the witness responded with a classic quote:

A. I have had a chance to look at it. It, of course, appeared 16 years ago, and my immediate reaction is, "What could I have been thinking?"

GETTING THE DAMAGES EXPERT
ON BOARD EARLY ENOUGH

One of the errors that attorneys sometimes make in commercial and other types of litigation, such as personal injury and employment litigation, is not retaining the damages expert early enough in the process. Attorneys often devote much of their time to the liability side of their case while paying relatively less attention to the damages aspect. Sometimes, when they focus on damages, such as when they gather necessary damages-related documents, they may attempt do so without the aid of a damages expert. This may result in important documents not being gathered or important questions not being asked in depositions.

This error may occur for a variety of reasons. One is that the attorney may think he knows enough to gather the necessary damages-related materials and to conduct a complete deposition. Another reason is that there may be cost constraints driving the litigation where the client is trying to control litigation expenses and the attorney does not want to add to the client's costs by hiring an expert until the very last moment when it cannot be put off any longer. This often comes when deadlines for naming experts are near and the client either must incur this cost or go without an expert. While the attorney may believe that he has gone to great lengths to keep his client's costs down, putting off retaining the damages expert may cause the damage side of the case to suffer. In this case, the apparent cost consciousness may in the long run be a disservice to the client.

In commenting on the failure to bring an economic damage expert on early enough, one expert noted:

> A typical disaster scenario. The damage expert gets hired two days before the deadline for expert disclosure. A pile of documents and depositions arise at the expert's office a week later. When the expert calls the attorney to ask for key data that was not in the pile, the litigator says "It looks like we never asked for that in the document request or at depositions. Oh, by the way, they want to take your deposition next week." The expert must do a damages analysis that makes assumptions about key facts and then alter those assumptions depending on trial testimony. This often results in a poorer analysis and increases expert's costs by a factor of 2 or 3.[12]

COURT'S POSITION ON EXPERTS

Courts have underscored the importance of expert testimony on economic damages. In fact, in *Larsen v. Walton Plywood Company,* the court stated:

> Respondents point out that a reasonable method of estimation of damages is often made with the aid of opinion evidence. Experts in the area are competent to pass judgement. So long as their opinions afford a reasonable basis for inference, there is a departure from the realm of uncertainty and speculation. *Expert testimony alone is a sufficient basis for an award for loss of profits.*[13]

---

[12] James Plummer and Gerald McGowan, "Ten Most Frequent Errors in Litigating Business Damages," *Association of Business Trial Lawyers,* 5(1), November 1995.

[13] *Harold Larsen et al., Respondents, v. Walton Plywood Company et al., Appealants,* Washington Plywood Company, Inc. No. 36863, Supreme Court of Washington, Department One, 65 Wash. 2d 1; 190 P. 2d 677; Wash. (1964).

The *Federal Rules of Evidence* are quite broad regarding what is considered acceptable expertise in an expert witness. Rule 702 states that "A witness may be qualified as an expert by *knowledge, skill, experience, training or education.*" With such general criteria, a wide variety of individuals may serve as experts. However, an individual who possesses some of the necessary criteria set forth in Rule 702 may still be objectionable if opposing counsel can demonstrate to the court that the expertise is not specific enough to the areas in which the expert is testifying.

Not all states, however, have adopted standards similar to the federal rules. Some states, such as California, are quite liberal and allow many individuals to testify if their testimony will assist the jury in reaching its decision. Even in the face of such broad rules, opposing counsel may be able to exploit the weakness in an expert's credentials on voir dire, which may reduce the weight that a jury would place on the expert's testimony.

Using Management as Experts

In some cases attorneys have tried to use management and the company's officers as experts at trial. Courts have accepted such testimony. In *Aluminum Products Enterprises v. Fuhrmann Tooling,* the court allowed the plaintiff's president to testify based on his personal knowledge of the business and the industry.[14] The disadvantage of such testimony is that the witness is an interested party in the litigation. However, the witness brings firsthand knowledge from working in the industry every day. Depending on the facts of the case, if such knowledge is helpful, a combination of internal fact/expert witnesses and outside experts may be very effective. This may be the case when internal financial witnesses, such as a company controller, are used to authenticate and describe the collection of data, such as cost data, upon which the outside damages expert is relying. It also is helpful when the expert lacks a significant background in the industry. The internal expert can be used to testify on trends and practices in the industry. Such an expert can also confirm numerical trends that the external expert may testify that he has found when analyzing industry data. The internal expert may be able to verify that those quantitative trends, such as reduced sales of distributors caused by manufacturers selling directly to retailers, were experienced by those who worked in the industry.

---

[14]*Aluminum Products Enterprises v. Fuhrmann Tooling,* 758 S.W.2d 119 112 (Mo. Ct. App. 1988).

Using an Expert as a Consultant

A damages expert can be invaluable to an attorney even if the expert never testifies. An experienced expert can assist the attorney in understanding an opposing expert's report and opinions. Often an attorney may not have specialized training in the field in which the opposing expert is testifying. The fields of economics, finance, and accounting are very specialized and it is difficult for an attorney to be knowledgeable in the law and also have expertise in these other related areas. In addition, like many other scientific fields, disciplines such as economics, finance, and accounting have their own set of jargon and notations that may require some interpretation. Having a knowledgeable and experienced expert to rely on can be of great benefit. Such experts can be used in a variety of ways from interpreting the opposing expert's report to preparing detailed lines of cross-examination for deposition and trial. The expert-consultant may also be able to check for the presence of errors in the opposing expert's report. Without a quantitative background, the opposing attorney may not be able to do such a careful quantitative review of the opposing expert's analysis. Attorneys should be aware, however, that such work can sometimes be surprisingly time consuming, because an opposing expert's report may intentionally be cryptic and may not fully reveal how the expert arrived at the various numerical values. Sometimes the term "reverse engineering" is used to describe this process. The consulting expert may have to invest considerable time figuring out exactly how the numbers were computed. In addition, once the method used by the opposing expert is exposed, counsel may want to run different scenarios using more favorable factual and economic assumptions to see their impact on the loss estimates. This is a very thorough way of pursuing the damages part of the case. However, such work may be time intensive and may require the consulting experts to invest more time than even the opposing expert.

STANDARDS FOR ADMISSIBILITY OF EXPERT TESTIMONY

For approximately 70 years, between 1923 and 1993, the standard applied in Federal Court for admissibility of expert testimony was the *Frye test*. This standard was based on the 1923 criminal case *Frye v. United States* in which expert testimony on the results of a lie detector test was ruled inadmissible.[15] The *Frye* test focused on whether the analysis and testimony was based on generally ac-

---

[15] *Frye v. United States,* 293 F. 1013 (D.C. Cir. 1923).

cepted methods and standards within the given field. Whether the Federal Rules of Evidence superceded the *Frye* test was decided by the U.S. Supreme Court in 1993 in the *Daubert v. Merrill Dow* case.[16] In this case, having to do with damages claims resulting from a mother ingesting Bendectin, the Supreme Court ruled that Rule 702 of the Federal Rules of Evidence is inconsistent with and supercedes the *Frye* test. The court stated that it did not find anything in the Federal Rules that requires general acceptance. The Supreme Court indicated that one should look to the Federal Rules to determine whether testimony is admissible.

The court stopped short of putting forward a checklist of characteristics to which expert testimony must adhere.[17] Nonetheless, the court enumerated a list of four factors that expert testimony should possess:

1. **Testing.** This factor is more applicable to the physical sciences.[18] However, insofar as testimony on statistical issues involve various forms of statistical analysis, such as hypothesis testing, this factor could become relevant.

2. **Peer Review and Publication.** Another factor that the U.S. Supreme Court highlighted was peer review and publications. This is particularly relevant for unique methodologies. If they have been subject to peer review, such as through the publication process in refereed journals, there may be a greater degree of reliability.

3. **Known Rate of Error.** If the analysis has a known rate of error, then this may be an indicator of its reliability. This rate can be applied to the case of statistical analysis which, for example, provides confidence levels for the value of a coefficient generated by a regression analysis, which is used to project lost revenues.

4. **General Acceptance.** Although the Supreme Court did not explicitly rule that general acceptance is required, it did point to such acceptance within the relevant community as one factor that a trial judge could use when evaluating such proposed testimony. The various components of the loss measurement process set forth in this book are standard components of various related disciples and do not have a problem of general acceptance.

---

[16] *Daubert v. Merrill Dow,* 509 U.S. 579 (1993).

[17] Robert Dunn, *Expert Testimony: Law and Practice,* Vol. I (Westport, Conn.: Lawpress Corp.) 1997, 195–201.

[18] Lawrence Spizman and John Kane, "Defending Against A Daubert Challenge: An Application in Projecting the Lost Earnings of a Minor Child," *Litigation Economics Digest,* Spring 1998, III (1), 43–49.

However, to reinforce this point, various commonly used textbooks are cited throughout so as to emphasize this issue.

The *Daubert* standard is new and its applicability to damages testimony will be developed over time. There have been some examples of *Daubert* being used to deny economic expert testimony in the areas of hedonic damages, which is the use of certain research studies in labor economics to value a human life or the loss of the enjoyment of life.[19] However, in the commercial damages arena, many of the techniques that are used, such as certain forecasting methods or cost accounting methods, are quite standard and not controversial. Therefore, the fact that *Daubert* has replaced the *Frye* test may be less relevant to economic damage testimony than it is for other areas of expert testimony.

Daubert Standards Do Apply to Commercial Damage Experts

The *Daubert* decision was directed at scientific experts. While many believed that it should apply to all expert testimony, it was not until the *Kuhmo Tire* decision that the court made clear that *Daubert* standards apply to all expert testimony. *Kuhmo* was the third of three related decisions that clarified this process. *Daubert* was the first and it was followed by *General Electric v. Joiner.*[20] In *Joiner,* the court held that a trial court's decision on a *Daubert* motion should be reviewed by an appellate court under a traditional abuse of discretion criteria. *Joiner* also said that motions to exclude expert testimony based on *Daubert* should be made, where possible, prior to the trial. In *Kuhmo Tire,* the Supreme Court reversed the 11th Circuit of the Court of Appeals and held that *Daubert* standards apply to all expert testimony.[21] Both *Daubert* and *Kuhmo* were later applied to the calculation of damages in a price fixing case, *Coastal Fuels of Puerto Rico v. Caribbean Petroleum Corp.*[22] In this case, the First Circuit reversed and remanded a $4.5 million verdict. In reaching its decision the First

---

[19] *Hein v. Merck & Co.,* 868 F. Supp 203 (M.D. Tenn 1994) and *Ayers v. Robinson,* 887 F. Supp. 1049 (N.D. Ill. 1995).

[20] *General Electric v. Joiner,* 118 S. Ct. 512 (1997).

[21] *Kuhmo Tire Company v. Carmichael,* 119 S. Ct. 1167, 1999 U.S. Lexus 2189 (March 23, 1999).

[22] *Coastal Fuels of Puerto Rico v. Caribbean Petroleum Corp.,* No. 98 1652, 1999 U.S. App. LEXIS 7249 (1st Cir. April 14, 1999).

Circuit cited *Daubert* and *Kuhmo* in ordering a new trial and encouraging the trial court to exercise its gatekeeping role as set forth in *Daubert*.

EXPERT REPORTS

The Federal Rules of Civil Procedure, Rule 26 (a) (2) require that the expert provide a signed expert report. This report should set forth all of the opinions that the expert may put forward at trial, including relevant exhibits in support of the opinions. The qualifications of the expert should also be disclosed as part of the report or as an attachment provided separately. In addition, the expert must provide a list of all the cases he/she has testified in, either at trial or in a deposition, within the past four years. In addition to exchanging an expert report, the Federal Rules also require the disclosure of the identity of all experts who may give expert testimony at trial. States vary in their report disclosure requirements. Some follow the Federal Rules and some do not.

Although the Federal Rules require more disclosure in reports, a fair amount of leeway can still be applied in determining how detailed reports can be. One school of thought put forward by attorneys is to provide a very detailed report to show the other side that the analysis is very thorough and well thought out and that the damage estimates are firm. Armed with such a report, attorneys may think that the case is more likely to settle. Another reasoning in support of more abundant disclosure is to provide extra details so that there is no opportunity for opposing counsel to object on the grounds that the proper pretrial disclosure was not made. The other school of thought is to provide only the minimum required under the Rules so as to avoid providing fodder for cross-examination. Both approaches have pros and cons.

DEFENSE EXPERT AS A TESTIFYING EXPERT

One view within the defense bar is that the defendant should not put his own expert on the stand for damages. The idea is that if the defendant puts on alternative damages testimony, even though that testimony may put forward a lower damages value, such testimony might give credence to the idea that there really are measurable damages. There is also the concern that if a jury hears two damages amounts, a higher one from the plaintiff and a lower one from the defendant's expert, then they may simply average the two, particularly if they cannot decide which is more appropriate. On the other hand, the strategy of failing to call a defendant's damages expert can really backfire. One of the classic examples of that was the *Texaco v. Pennzoil* case where the defense decided not to put on his own damages expert and relied on attacking the plaintiff's damages analysis.[23] When the jury found the defendant Texaco liable, there was no damages testimony for the jury to consider other than the plaintiff's presentation. The huge award that resulted underscored the drawbacks of this strategy.

> Our problem in reviewing the validity of these Texaco claims is that Pennzoil necessarily used expert testimony to prove its losses by using three damages models. In the highly specialized field of oil and gas, expert testimony that is free of conjecture and speculation is proper and necessary to determine damages. (cite omitted) Texaco presented no expert testimony to refute the claims but relied on its cross-examination of Pennzoil's experts to attempt to show that the damages model used by the jury was flawed. Dr. Barrows testified that each of his three models would constitute an accepted method of proving Pennzoil's damages.

Another good example where the court highlighted the failure of the defendant to present alternative damages testimony occurred in *Empire Gas Company v. American Bakeries Co.*

> A great weakness of American Bakeries' case was its failure to present its own estimate of damages, in the absence of which the jury could have no idea of what adjustments to make in order to take into account American Bakeries' arguments. American Bakeries may have feared that if it put in its own estimate of damages the jury would be irresistibly attracted to that figure as a compromise. But if so, American Bakeries gambled double or nothing, as it were; and we will not relieve it of the consequences of its risky strategy.[24]

The success of the defense's use of an expert was underscored in *Associated Indemnity Co. v. CAT Contracting Inc.* where the court followed the analysis of the defense's expert in molding its damages award.[25] The Court of Appeals of Texas reversed a prior seven figure award and instead awarded an amount that was a fraction of the original award put forward by the defense's expert. In this case, a construction joint venture sued a surety. The court was more impressed by the defense's expert argument that the plaintiff's own financial history should be used to measure losses rather than just the industry averages used by the

---

[23] *Texaco Inc. v. Pennzoil Co.*, 729 S.W. 2d 768 (Tex. App. 1987), cert. dismissed, 485 U.S. 994 (1988).

[24] *Empire Gas Company v. American Bakeries Co.*, 840 F. 2d 1333, 1342 (7th Cir. 1988).

[25] *Associated Indemnity Co. v. CAT Contracting, Inc.*, 918 S.W. 2d 580 (Tex. App. 1996).

plaintiff's damages expert. The defense's expert testified as to what the lost incremental revenues were and what the profit margins associated with these revenues would be. The court then used these amounts, rather than the plaintiff's expert's computations, to arrive at a damages award.

In cases where the defendant believes that the plaintiff has mitigated his damages and, therefore, the plaintiff has not really incurred any net damages, it is best for the defense to put on his own damages expert to demonstrate the point. In these cases, if the analysis is sufficiently thorough and convincing the court may ignore the plaintiff's damages presentation and deny an award based on the defense's expert's testimony. The defendant may be able to reduce the effectiveness of the plaintiff's damages presentation if the defendant can show that while his actions may have resulted in some lost profits, the plaintiff was able to substitute other business that resulted in his profits being essentially unchanged from prior years. Such a result occurred in *Alcan Aluminum v. Carlton Aluminum of New England.*[26]

QUANTITATIVE RESEARCH EVIDENCE ON THE BENEFITS OF CALLING A DEFENSE EXPERT

Robert Trout, of Economatrix Research Associates, Inc. and Lit-Econ, conducted a study that measured the impact of economic testimony on damages awards. His 1991 study found that when only the plaintiff called a damages expert, the average award was $418,355.[27] However, when the defendant also presented his own damages expert to counter the plaintiff's damages expert, the average award was less than a quarter of the plaintiff's only expert alternative—$98,567. Trout summarized the results of his analysis as it relates to the benefits of the defendant calling his own damages expert as follows:

> The findings concerning the use of economists suggest that a reasonable strategy for the defense counsel should be to use an economic expert whenever the plaintiff uses an economic expert, except in cases where the defense's economic expert testimony might increase the chance that liability would be found against the defendant or support the testimony of the plaintiff's economist.[28]

---

[26] *Alcan Aluminum v. Carlton Aluminum of New England, Inc.,* 35 Mass. App. 161, 617 N.E. 2d 1005 (1993) *review denied,* 416 Mass. 1105, 621, N.E. 2d 685 (1993).

[27] Robert R. Trout, "Does Economic Testimony Affect Damage Awards," *Journal of Legal Economics,* 41 (March, 1991), 43–49.

[28] Robert Trout, 1991, 47.

TYPES OF COMMERCIAL DAMAGES

There are several different reasons why a business may incur damages. For example, damages can arise from a breach of contract, tort, antitrust violation, fraud, or condemnation. The economic methods used to value these damages may be similar even though the law may be very different. However, depending on the particular cause of action, additional types of economic analysis may be employed. For example, in the case of an antitrust violation, a market analysis may be conducted using methods from the field of microeconomics known as industrial organization. These nondamages-related economic issues are briefly discussed in Chapter 11.

Commercial damages may arise in the form of either lost profits or a loss of asset value. Chapter 6 defines what is meant by lost profits in a litigation context. Under certain circumstances, lost profits may not coincide with the more traditional accounting measure of profits. Lost asset value can occur when the value of an asset, such as a brand name or even a complete business, has declined due to reasons that are the subject of the litigation. Even when the lost asset value is the measure of loss, the method of measuring the diminution in value is often similar to the method that would be used in the lost profits approach. If the future cash flows to be derived from the asset are expected to be lower, the present valuation of this reduction can be used as the measure of loss.

TREATMENT OF THE RELEVANT CASE LAW

This book focuses on the methods of conducting a damages analysis. It does not focus on the relevant case law. This does not imply that this issue is not important. Clearly, the case law provides the framework within which losses can be presented in court. Readers, however, are directed to other fine works in this area for a discussion of the issue. One of the leading books in this field is Robert Dunn's *Recovery of Damages for Lost Profits*.[29] Another is William Cerillo's *Proving Business Damages*.[30] These works are relied on in this book to provide guidance on the court's position on the methods of measuring damages. They are regularly updated through supplements, which include recent cases on various damage-related issues.

---

[29]Robert Dunn, *Recovery of Damages for Lost Profits,* 5th ed. (Westport, Conn.: Lawpress Corp.), 1998.

[30]William A. Cerillo, *Proving Business Damages,* 2nd ed. (New York: John Wiley & Sons), 1991.

LEGAL DAMAGE PRINCIPLES

In measuring damages, experts should be familiar with the basics of legal damage principles. This section touches on some of the relevant major principles. For a more in-depth discussion, readers are encouraged to pursue the abundant sources that are available in this area.

Proximate Causation and Reasonable Certainty

In order for damages to be recoverable, they must be *proximately caused* by the wrongful acts of the defendant. In addition, damages must be proved within a *reasonable degree of certainty*. A key word in the latter phrase is "reasonable." By applying the modifier reasonable, the courts have acknowledged that it may not be possible to compute damages with 100% certainty. Therefore, some degree of certainty less than 100% is acceptable. Here the opinion testimony of an expert can be used to establish the reasonable limits of acceptability. In allowing some level of certainty less than 100%, courts recognize that, even for historical damages, the actions of the defendant may have permanently changed events so that one may never know exactly what would have transpired in the absence of such actions. For future damages, the course of events clearly can never be known with certainty. If a 100% standard were adopted, damages might never be awarded. In addition, the defendant would be able to take advantage of the fact that, through the wrongful acts, it moved the plaintiff to a situation where it may never know the exact magnitude of its damages.

Occurrence of versus the Amount of Damages

It is important to distinguish between establishing the fact of damages within a reasonable certainty and the actual measurement of those damages.[31] The reasonable certainty is applied to the fact that the damages actually occurred. However, a lesser standard is applied to the actual measurement of the magnitude of the damages themselves. Here the courts have recognized the particularly difficult problem that arises in the measurement of damages that may have or will occur after the actions of the defendant may have permanently changed the course of events. The courts do not allow the defendant to benefit from the fact that its cau-

---

[31] Dunn, 1997, p. 1.3.

sation of the plaintiff's damages may render such damages incapable of being proved within a 100% degree of certainty. However, if the occurrence of the damages themselves is uncertain, then the plaintiff may not be able to recover such damages.

This reasoning is clearly articulated in *Story Parchment Co. v. Paterson Parchment Paper Co.*[32] In this case, in which the plaintiff sought damages for antitrust violations of the defendant, the Supreme Court stated the following:

> Where the tort itself is of such a nature as to preclude the ascertainment of the amount of damages with certainty, it would be a perversion of fundamental principles of justice to deny any relief to the injured person, and thereby relieve the wrongdoer from making any amend for his acts. In such case, while the damages may not be determined by mere speculation or guess, it will be enough if the evidence shows the extent of the damages as a matter of just and reasonable inference, although the result is only approximate. The wrongdoer is not entitled to complain that they cannot be measured with exactness and precision that would be possible if the case, which he alone is responsible for making, were otherwise.

Reasonable Basis for the Damages Calculation

There must be a *reasonable basis* for the damages put forward. This basis is sometimes referred to by other terms such as a *rational standard.*[33] The courts may try to serve as a filter through which speculative presentations are prevented from being used by the jury to arrive at a damages award. The range of acceptability is still quite broad and the expert is allowed to adopt the damages methodology to fit the unique requirements of each case. As the Supreme Court of Kansas stated in *Vickers v. Wichita State University:*

> As to evidentiary matters a court should approach each case in an individual and pragmatic manner, and require the claimant furnish the best available proof as to the amount of loss that the particular situation admits.[34]

Foreseeability

Another important legal principle in the field of commercial damages is the *foreseeability rule.* In order to be recoverable, the damages must be foresee-

---

[32] *Story Parchment Co. v. Paterson Parchment Co.,* 282 U.S. 555, 563 (1931).

[33] *Vickers v. Wichita State University,* 213 Kan. 614, 620, 518 P.2d 512, 517 (1974).

[34] See Robert Dunn, *Recovery of Damages for Lost Profits,* 5th ed. (Westport, Conn.: Lawpress Corp.) 1998, 391–392.

able by the defendant at the time the defendant acted in a way that resulted in the damages. For example, in a breach of contract, the defendant must be able to foresee that when it breached the contract with the plaintiff, the defendant was going to cause the plaintiff to incur damages. This legal principle arises out of the very famous *Hadley v. Baxendale* English case.[35] This case is similar to many business interruption claims that occur today. It involves a mill owner who sued a shipper for lost profits due to the late shipment of an iron shaft necessary to run the mill. The court concluded that the lost profits were not recoverable, as they were not within the contemplation of the parties.

Foreseeability can become clear when the plaintiff explicitly communicates its anticipation of damages to the defendant at the time of the defendant's actions. In the absence of such direct communications, the courts are put in the position of determining what was *within the contemplation of the parties*. This can be interpreted to mean that if the defendant is capable of understanding how its actions might have an adverse effect on the plaintiff, then they are within the contemplation of the defendant. For example, if the defendant has contracted with the plaintiff to provide certain services or products, the defendant may know of the use to which the plaintiff may be putting such services or goods. The defendant may be further able to anticipate the impact on the plaintiff if he would have to do without such services or goods. In such cases, the actual contract between the parties may provide some useful information for determining what is within the contemplation of the parties. Other evidence can come from testimony or knowledge of communications between the parties, where the use to which the plaintiff was putting the goods and services provided by the defendant was communicated to the defendant. The plaintiff would ease its burdens of proof if, at the time he entered into the contract, he explicitly advised the defendant of the anticipated damages if the defendant failed to complete his contractual obligations.

A clue to the reasonable foreseeability should be the fact that a given transaction was commercial in its nature. Continuing with the contract example, the court may conclude that the defendant knew in advance that the plaintiff was using the goods or services for some commercial purpose in the hopes of generating profits. Accepting this, a court may conclude that it would be reasonable that there may be a loss of profits if the contract was breached. It may be even clearer if both parties were unambiguously aware of the purpose to which the goods or services provided by the defendant were put by the plaintiff.

---

[35] *Hadley v. Baxendale*, 156 Eng. Rep. 145 (1854).

Collateral Transactions

A party may claim damages from a *collateral transaction,* a transaction that is contingent upon another transaction. A party may claim that the failure of the defendant to perform the first transaction resulted in losses in another transaction that was itself contingent on the performance of the first transaction. Damages resulting from such transactions may not be recoverable unless it can be demonstrated that they were foreseen and within the contemplation of the parties at the time of the agreement. The plaintiff may have a clearer case if she can demonstrate that the second transaction flows directly from the first, as opposed to a more indirect route where the plaintiff might argue that if she had been able to enjoy the proceeds from the first contract, then she would have pursued another venture which, in turn, would have generated additional profits which she claims as damages. The plaintiff's argument is stronger if she can show that she gave the defendant notice of the dependence of the second transaction on the first. Such notice, however, may not be necessary in the case of a reseller where the seller knows the nature of the buyer's (reseller) business. Here foreseeability is presumed given by the nature of the buyer's business.

CONTRACT-RELATED DAMAGES

Parties to a contract can incur damages in a number of ways. A buyer may lose profits due to the failure of a seller to deliver. Such a failure may cause the buyer to incur *incidental* and/or *consequential* damages. Incidental damages are those expenses that the buyer may incur from having to secure replacement goods. Consequential damages are those which the plaintiff may have incurred as a consequence of the defendant's failure to perform. Once again, the defendant must have been able to foresee these damages and the plaintiff must not have been able to avoid such damages by securing performance from other parties. This alternative performance is sometimes referred to as *cover.* The plaintiff, however, may be able to cover the transaction by securing the goods or services elsewhere but still incur damages. This would be the case if the cover price were higher than the contract price. Here the damages would be the price difference as well as any incidental damages.

The law carries with it a requirement that the plaintiff make efforts to mitigate its damages from securing alternative sources or cover. The situation becomes more problematic when the goods or services in questions are unique and not readily available in the marketplace. Mitigation of damages is discussed in Chapter 6.

Contractually Related Liability Limitations

The seller may include provisions in the contract to limit its liability to the buyer. In a sale of goods, such as machinery, these provisions may limit the seller's obligations to repair the goods without any allowance for the recovery of consequential damages, including any lost profits. Courts have concluded that if the limitations are very extreme, they may be found *unconscionable.*

Warranty-Related Damages

A breach of warranty is a contract-related claim. Under the Uniform Commercial Code, there are two types of warranties: express and implied. In an express warranty, the seller clearly delineates which characteristics of the goods that he sells are guaranteed. In an implied warranty, the promise is less clearly stated and a more general guarantee is given, such as general merchantability. The normal standard of warranty-related damages is the difference between the value of the goods as warranted and the value of the goods that were accepted. Although this area of commercial damages is important, it is not the focus of this book, which is more directed to the measurement of lost profits, such as those that might arise in contract-related consequential damages.

Other Types of Damages Cases

A complete listing of all of the different types of cases in which there is a claim for commercial damages is well beyond the scope of this section. However, it may be useful to highlight a few of the more common types that may give rise to a lost profits claim.

Distributor, Manufacturer's Representative, and Franchisee Relationships

A variety of contract cases arise involving the various representations by a manufacturer or another goods or service provider. A *distributor* is similar to a *manufacturer's representative.* Both represent the manufacturer, but a distributor often takes possession of the goods and maintains an inventory of the products whereas a manufacturer's representative augments the seller's sales force without physically storing an inventory. Each may or may not have exclusive territories. A *franchisee* may be given the right to market a company's products within an exclusive territory. Disputes often arise from the termination of these agreements with the terminated party claiming damages for lost profits under the agreement. These disputes may be caused by the franchisee or distributor failing to perform or the franchisor failing to live up to its obligations such as by failing to provide agreed upon marketing support for the product. The franchisor may contend that it terminated the franchisee because it did not properly market the product.

Despite the wide variety of these lawsuits, the methodology used to measure damages can be found within the framework set forth later in this book. The method usually involves constructing revenue projections and applying costs ratios to derive profits from projected revenues. In other instances, such as in the case of terminated franchisees, the damages analysis may involve employing business valuation techniques to place a value on a terminated franchisee that no longer exists.

Contracts to Provide Services

Other types of contract-related damages can arise from a failure to provide the contractually agreed upon services. When these cases involve major figures in high-profile businesses, they tend to attract much media attention. For example, movie stars who walk out on film agreements or authors who fail to provide manuscripts are forms of these types of disputes. In the case of publishers, they may involve demands for a return of an advance. In the film industry, however, the analysis may be substantially more complicated, involving loss of invested capital or lost projected profits.

Construction-Related Contract Cases

Another common type of contract cases are construction cases. These often involve lawsuits for failure to complete construction on time or according to the specifications of the contract. Other construction cases have to do with who pays for certain costs and whether cost overruns can be passed on to the builder. Still another type of construction case is one that involves damages related to the loss of bonding capacity. The loss of such capacity may limit the volume of work that a contractor can bid for, which may give rise to a claim for lost profits on the additional work that the plaintiff claims he would have been awarded, had he had a certain bonding capacity.

Noncompete Agreement Cases

Still another common form of contract-related damages cases are those that involve covenants not to compete. This can come from provisions in a business sales agreement where an owner of a business agreed not to compete with the buyer for a period of time. Other cases involve professional service firms where individuals agreed not to compete for a period of time with an employer in exchange for certain consideration. The damages analysis can sometimes be complicated as it may involve measuring the damages that result exclusively from the illegal competition. An important part of this analysis is isolating these specific damages. Cases may be more straightforward where a personal service provider, such as an attorney or a broker, competed by stealing specific clients or customers than in a situation where a firm improperly competes and is one competitor among several in the market. In such cases, the industry analysis may be quite important in assessing the change in the level of competition and the resulting damages.

COMMERCIAL DAMAGES IN PERSONAL INJURY

Economists play a prominent role in measuring damages in personal injury. These damages often involve projections of lost earnings over a work-life expectancy or a valuation of the services that an injured party or a decedent would have provided.[36] In a personal injury lawsuit, a business generally cannot claim damages due to the injuries of an employee. However, in cases where the employees were largely responsible for the profits of the business, such as in a small business with few employees and where the plaintiff was the prime force behind the generation of the business' profits, the profits of the business may become an important part of the damage measurement process.[37] An example could be a president of a small business who was involved in an accident that caused him not to be further involved in the business which, in turn, resulted in the closure of the business. Here the projected profits, along with other forms of compensation that the individual derived from the business, such as officer's compensation or other perks, might be relevant.[38]

The courts have usually drawn a distinction between cases where the profits of a business are a function of an individual's personal efforts and returns that are the product of the invested capital. In the latter case, where returns are more passive, the law of torts is less relevant.

---

[36] Thomas Ireland, Stephen M. Horner, and James Rodgers, op cit.

[37] *Ginn v. Penobscot Co.,* 334 A. 2d 874 (Me. 1975).

[38] Patrick Gaughan and Henry Fuentes, "Minimization of Taxable Income and Lost Profits Litigation," *Journal of Forensic Economics,* Winter 1990, IV (1), 55 – 64.

Personal Injury and Corporate Damages
Due to Loss of Key Man

It is not unusual that a company's rise to success can be largely caused by the efforts of one unique individual. This is sometimes referred to as the role of the *key man* in corporate finance. Corporate America is filled with examples of companies whose growth and success can be largely attributed to the efforts of one individual making a far greater contribution than any other member of the company. It is logical, then, that a company can be significantly damaged if that individual dies or is impaired as a result of injury so that he can not participate in the activities of the business. The courts have come to recognize this. Although the company itself may not be able to recover its lost profits, the injured party, who may be a controlling shareholder, may be able to individually recover such lost profits.[39]

Damages Resulting from Other Business Torts

A variety of tortious behaviors can cause recoverable damages in the form of lost profits. These can include tortious interference with business, fraud, and unfair competition. The varieties of each of these categories of business torts can be virtually limitless. While the case law is correspondingly voluminous, the methodology to measure damages, such as lost profits, can be found in the following chapters. Basically, however, courts have found that "lost profits in a tort action are limited to those damages proximately caused by the defendant's wrongful conduct."[40] Such profits usually can be measured through a projection of *but for* profits and a comparison of such projected profits with the actual and "projected actual" profits. This comparison is described in detail in the chapters that follow.

Punitive Damages

Punitive damages have increased dramatically over the past three decades. Punitive damage awards can be far higher than and bear little discernable relationship to the actual damages incurred by the plaintiff. For example, in *TXO Production*

---

[39] *Lundgren v Whitney's Inc.,* 94 Wash. 2d 91, 614 P. 2d 1272 (1980).
[40] *Horan v. Klein's-Sheridan, Inc.,* 62 Ill. App. 2d 455, 459, 211 N.E. 2d 116 (1965).

Corp. v. Alliance Resources Corp. (TXO), the court allowed a $10 million award of punitive damages even when the compensatory damages were only $19,000.[41] A very different set of factors are employed in arriving at an amount of punitive damages. For example, in *TXO,* the court considered the amount of harm caused by the defendant, the defendant's intent, and the amount of an award that would be necessary to prevent the defendant from engaging in this behavior in the future. The U.S. Supreme Court found that such factors can support an award of punitive damages that far exceeds the compensatory damages so that it bears no relationship to it as reflected by the multiple of 526:1.

Prior to *TXO,* the courts had been more intent on keeping some relationship between compensatory and punitive damages. In *Pacific Mutual Life Insurance Co. v. Haslip,* the court asserted that it would be difficult to derive a clear mathematical relationship between compensatory and punitive damages.[42] However, this court did caution against arriving at punitive damages amounts that were far out of proportion with the actual damages the plaintiff incurred.

This book does not focus on punitive damages but concentrates on compensatory damages in commercial litigation. Readers are referred to the abundant literature on this topic which sets forth some methods for arriving at such damages.[43]

SUMMARY

This chapter introduces the use of an expert to measure damages in commercial litigation. One of the first steps in this process is selecting the right expert. Given the diversified nature of the field of commercial damages, this expert needs to have a well rounded background in fields such as economics, econometrics, finance, and accounting. Given the fact that a wide range of expertise may be needed, it may be necessary to have a team of experts where one expert testifies but relies on the work of other experts. A common combination is an economist and an accountant. In some cases, more than one expert may testify

There are many sources of experts. The most often relied upon seems to be referrals from colleagues. If that is not a fertile source of experts, then other

---

[41] *TXO Production Corp. v. Alliance Resources Corp.,* 113 S. Ct. 2711 (1993).

[42] *Pacific Mutual Life Insurance v. Haslip,* 499 U.S. 1 (1991).

[43] Evert Dillman, "Punitive and Exemplary Damages," in *Litigation Economics,* Patrick Gaughan and Robert Thornton, eds. (Greenwich, Conn.: JAI Press), 1993, 91–106.

sources such as local universities or referral agencies may be needed. Particularly in cases where the expert is not referred by a colleague, attorneys need to carefully review the expert's credentials. These credentials should include a terminal degree in his field, a doctoral degree, and publication of books and refereed journal articles in the field. Care must be applied when reviewing experts' CVs to ensure that they are accurate and truly what they are purported to be. For example, what is listed as a publication should be verified as a published work.

There are several ways to use damages experts. One is to have the expert author a report and serve as a witness. Another is to use the expert purely as a consultant but not as a testifying witness. This latter strategy is often used by defendants who do not want to give credence to the plaintiff's damages claims. Instead, they may want to use the expert to help cross-examine the plaintiff's expert. Research results, as well as the experience of several notable cases, raises serious questions about this strategy. In some cases it works well and in others it can backfire. The strategy for each case varies and should be determined based on close consultation with the expert.

REFERENCES

Alcan Aluminum v. Carlton Aluminum of New England, Inc., 35 Mass. App. 161, 617 N.E. 2d 1005 (1993) *review denied,* 416 Mass. 1105, 621 N.E. 2d 685 (1993).

Aluminum Products Enterprises v. Fuhrmann Tooling, 758 S.W.2d 119 112 (Mo. Ct. App. 1988).

Associated Indemnity Co. v. CAT Contracting, Inc., 918 S.W. 2d 580 (Tex. App. 1996).

Ayers v. Robinson, 887 F. Supp. 1049 (N.D. Ill. 1995).

Baker, W. Gary, and Michael K. Seck, *Determining Economic Loss in Personal Injury and Death Cases* (New York: Shephard's/McGraw Hill, 1987).

Brookshire, Michael, and Frank Slesnick, "A 1990 Survey Study of Forensic Economists," *Journal of Forensic Economics,* Spring/Summer 1991, IV (2).

Brookshire, Michael L., and Stan V. Smith, *Economics/Hedonic Damages, The Practice Book for Plaintiff and Defense Attorneys* (Cincinnati: Anderson Publishing Company, 1990).

Cerillo, William, *Proving Business Damages,* 2nd ed. (New York: Wiley, 1991).

Daubert v. Merrill Dow, 509 U.S. 579 (1993).

Digital & Analog Design Corporation v. North Supply Company, 44 Ohio St. 3d 36, 540 N.E. 2d 1358 (1989).

Dillman, Evert, "Punitive and Exemplary Damages," in *Litigation Economics,* Patrick Gaughan and Robert Thornton, eds. (Greenwich, Conn.: JAI Press, 1993).

Dunn, Robert, *Expert Testimony: Law and Practice,* Vol. I (Westport, Conn.: Lawpress Corp., 1997).

Dunn, Robert, *Recovery of Damages for Lost Profits,* 5th ed., (Westport, Conn.: Lawpress Corp., 1997).

Empire Gas Company v. American Bakeries Co., 840 F. 2d 1333, 1342 (7th Cir. 1988).

Gaughan, Patrick A. "Economics and Financial Issues in Lost Profits Litigation," in *Litigation Economics,* Patrick A. Gaughan and Robert Thornton, eds. (Greenwich, Conn.: JAI Press, 1993).

Gaughan, Patrick A., and Henry Fuentes, "Minimization of Taxable Income and Lost Profits Litigation," *Journal of Forensic Economics,* IV (1), Winter, 1990.

Ginn v. Penobscot Co., 334 A. 2d 874 (Me. 1975).

Hadley v. Baxengdale, 156 Eng. Rep. 145 (1854).

Harold Larsen et al., Respondents, v. Walton Plywood Company et al., Appealants, Washington Plywood Company, Inc. No. 36863, Supreme Court of Washington, Department One, 65 Wash. 2d 1, 190 P. 2d 677 (1964).

Hein v. Merck & Co., 868 F. Supp 203 (M.D. Tenn 1994).

Horan v. Klein's-Sheridan, Inc. 62 Ill. App. 2d 455, 459, 211 N.E. 2d 116 (1965).

In Re Brand Name Prescription Drugs Antitrust Litigation, 1999 U.S. Dist. Lexus 550, January, 19, 1999 (decided and docketed).

Ireland, Thomas, Stephen M. Horner, and James Rodgers, "Reference Guide for Valuing Economic Loss in Personal Injury, Wrongful Death and Survival Actions," in *Economic Expert Testimony: A Guide for Judges and Attorneys* (Tucson: Lawyers and Judges Publishing Co., 1998).

Lundgren v. Whitney's Inc., 94 Wash. 2d 91, 614 P. 2d 1272 (1980).

Martin, Gerald, *Determining Economic Damages* (Costa Mesa, CA: James Publishing Inc., 1995).

Mattott v. Ward, 48 N.Y. 2d 455, 423 N.Y.S. 2d 645 (1979).

Pacific Mutual Life Insurance v. Haslip, 499 U.S. 1 (1991).

Piette, Michael, "Economic Methodology and the Analysis of Employment Discrimination," *Journal of Forensic Economics,* Fall 1991, IV(3).

Plumber, James, and Gerald McGowan, "Ten Most Frequent Errors in Litigating Business Damages," in *Association of Business Trial Lawyers,* 5(1), November 1995.

Speiser, Stuart, *Recovery For Wrongful Death and Injury: Economic Handbook,* 2nd ed., (New York: West Group, June 1998).

Spizman, Lawrence, and John Kane, "Defending Against A Daubert Challenge: An Application in Projecting the Lost Earnings of a Minor Child," *Litigation Economics Digest,* Spring 1998, III (1).

Story Parchment Co. v. Paterson Parchment Co., 282 U.S. 555, 563 (1931).

Technical Advisory Service for Attorneys, Blue Bell, Pennsylvania. (www .tasanet.com)

Texaco Inc. v. Pennzoil Co., 729 S.W. 2d 768 (Tex. App. 1987), cert. dismissed, 485 U.S. 994 (1988).

Trout, Robert R., "Does Economic Testimony Affect Damage Awards," *Journal of Legal Economics,* 41 (March) 1991.

TXO Production Corp. v. Alliance Resources Corp., 113 S. Ct. 2711 (1993).

Verdict Search, Moran Publishing Company, East Islip, New York (www .verdictsearch.com).

Vickers v. Wichita State University, 213 Kan. 614, 620, 518 P.2d 512, 517 (1974).

Wright v. Williams, 47 Cal. App. 3d 802, 121 Cal Rptr. 194 (1975).

2

ECONOMIC FRAMEWORK FOR ESTIMATING LOST PROFITS

This chapter discusses two preliminary and fundamental aspects of commercial damages analysis: causality and the methodological framework for measuring damages. The first section of this chapter examines the ways in which economic analysis can be used to provide evidence of causality in commercial damages litigation. Economists may employ certain statistical techniques to determine whether the plaintiff was responsible for the alleged damages of the defendant. Having established causality, the next step in the process is determining the loss period, which can be decided by many factors, including whether the losses have ended as of the trial date. Following this discussion, the methodological framework for measuring damages is introduced.

FOUNDATION FOR DAMAGES TESTIMONY

The experts may be provided with certain factual assumptions to serve as a basis for their testimony. This is clearly set forth in Rule 703 of the *Federal Rules of Evidence,* which states "The facts or data in the particular case upon which an expert bases an opinion or inference may be those perceived by or made known to the expert at or before the hearing." In the context of commercial damages analysis this may involve various facts, such as the assumed actions of the opposing party in the litigation. The expert is not a fact witness. Rather, the expert may be asked to compute what damages result from certain data and assumed facts. The methodology contained in this book attempts to set forth a systematic method to analyze the assumptions utilized by the expert.

Role of Assumptions in Damages Analysis

Economic damages testimony is typically based on a series of assumptions. It is important for the attorney retaining the expert to know all of the key assumptions as well as what the basis for each is. It is equally important for the opposing counsel to understand the role of these assumptions and to know how the damages would differ if other assumptions were employed. An expert may rely on three categories of assumptions:

1. *Factual Assumptions.* Factual assumptions are the various facts that the expert is asked to assume. Depending on the particular circumstances of the case, the expert may do some investigation of these facts to understand if there are any important differences between what the expert is told occurred and what in fact did occur. However, generally the expert is not a private investigator and does not necessarily verify all of the facts that he is asked to assume. These facts may be made known to the expert either by the retaining attorney or through documents that the expert reviews. These documents may include deposition testimony and trial testimony that may precede the expert's own testimony.

2. *Assumptions Involving the Opinions of Other Experts.* Additional experts may be employed to analyze certain other aspects of the damages claim. These experts can vary from appraisers who will determine the value of equipment or real estate assets to industry experts who may testify on the practices and standards of the industry or the existence of certain trends in the industry. The use of the opinions of other experts as a predicate for a damages calculation is very common in a variety of other types of damages analysis besides commercial damages. For example, in personal injury analysis, an economist may employ the findings of a vocational expert who may opine as to the expected future employability and earnings potential of an injured party.

3. *Economic and Financial Assumptions.* The assumptions that the expert brings to the analysis are the economic assumptions. Examples include the rate of inflation and the discount rate, which are applied to a projection of future lost profits. Such assumptions are usually the product of the expert's knowledge and of the analysis that may have been done for the case in question.

In cross-examining an opposing expert, it is important to focus on these various assumptions. The expert can be asked how the analysis would differ if the assumptions of the opposing party were employed. In some cases, it is possible for the expert to indicate how the damage value would differ if alternative assumptions were used. In other cases, the analysis may be fairly complicated and opposing counsel may have to settle for a basic response on the approximate magnitude of the revised loss. If this is the case, then opposing counsel must bring his own expert into court to provide an answer to such questions. Obviously, opposing counsel's expert may be asked about some of the same questions.

Hearsay

One of the ironies of trial testimony is that the expert is often able to testify relying on written or oral statements that in other contexts would be considered hearsay.[1] This often frustrates trial attorneys. Evidence that otherwise would not be admissible may be introduced through the expert who might simply say that he has heard or reviewed certain items that the attorney otherwise would not be able to introduce. Obviously, opposing counsel is still able to challenge the contents of the documents or statements that the expert is relying upon.

APPROACHES TO PROVING DAMAGES

Courts have accepted two broad approaches to proving damages: the *before and after method* and the *yardstick approach*. The methods are widely cited in the case law on damages so finding precedents in support of their application should not be difficult.

Before and After Method

The before and after method compares the revenues and profits before and after an event, such as a business interruption. A diminution in revenues or profits may be established based on the difference between the before and the after levels. This method assumes that the past performance of the plaintiff is representative of its performance over the loss period. It also assumes that sufficient historical data are available from which to construct a statistically reliable forecast. In

---

[1] Robert Dunn, *Expert Testimony: Law and Practice,* Vol. I, (Westport, Conn.: Lawpress Corp.) 1997, 160.

addition, it assumes that economic and industry conditions are similar during the loss period as they were in the before period so that the data are comparable.

While the before and after method has a certain appeal, it cannot be blindly applied without more rigorous analysis, such as that set forth in this book. If some of the factors upon which its successful application is dependent are not available, such as sufficient historical data, then the expert must utilize another methodology.

Failing to Give Consideration to Before and After Factors

In many types of business interruption cases it makes logical sense to compare the preinterruption period with the postinterruption period. Not to do so may imply that the expert assumes that the two periods are the same. If they are not, this can result in a major error. An example of the court's recognition of such oversight by an expert is found in *Katskee v. Nevada Bob's Golf*. In this case, a lessee sued a lessor for lost profits on sales of merchandise resulting from the failure of the lessor to allow the lessee the right to renew a lease.[2] The expert assumed that the location in question and the replacement location were the same in all relevant aspects except for their square footage.

> The witness called as an expert on the topic by Nevada Bob's testified that Nevada Bob's lost $130,455 in profits because it was not permitted to expand into the adjacent L.K. Company Space. The witness computed this figure by computing the yearly revenue produced per square foot at the location to which Nevada Bob's moved after vacating the L.K. Premises and multiplying that figure by the square footage of the adjacent space. . . . He then next multiplied this computation by gross profit margin and subtracted therefrom his estimate of the additional expenses incident to the increased square footage. He then divided this figure by 12 to obtain what he designated as lost profits per month and multiplied that figure by the number of months Nevada Bob's stayed at the premises after L.K. breach. . . .

In its criticism of this methodology the court stated:

> No studies and comparisons were made as to differences in customer bases, relative accessibility of the facilities, proximity to recreation areas or other shopping areas, parking or other external factors. *The witness also used sales figures from a different time period and made no study as to any changes in the relative market* (emphasis added). He did not evaluate whether there was any change in the number of competitors, whether there was any change in customer interest in the relevant products, or whether there were any changes in the products sold by Nevada Bob's.

---

[2] *Katskee v. Nevada Bob's Golf,* 472 N.W. 2d 372 (Nov. 1991).

Katskee v. Nevada Bob's is a good example of the court's rejection of an overly simplistic method and one that ignores differences in the before and after time periods. The court indicated that many important changes may have occurred and the expert simply ignored this possibility. The case is instructive in that it requires that a sufficiently detailed analysis, including an application of the before and after method, should be conducted when relevant.

Challenges to the Use of the Before and After Method

One of the ways a defendant may want to attack the use of the before and after method is by trying to prove that the after period may be different from the before period. The defendant may want to show that there is a good reason for such a difference and that this difference is not based on any actions of the defendant. For example, the defendant may try to prove that certain specific other factors, such as the plaintiff's own mismanagement, were responsible for a poorer performance in the after period. A weaker economic demand in the after period, such as one caused by a recession, could be another explanation that the defense may try to put forward. Under the circumstances, it would be reasonable to expect that firms like the plaintiff would do as well as before. In order to effectively make this argument, the defense may need to present its own analysis showing how the plaintiff had performed in the past relative to the performance of the economy. Having established this association, the defense can then present an analysis of the economic conditions during the after period and show how it is a weaker economic environment.

The weaker economic environment is but one of potentially many reasons why a plaintiff's performance during the after period could be expected to be worse. The circumstances of each case will differ and each may bring its own specific reasons. Other examples could include poor management decisions or changed industry conditions. In order to find such alternative explanations, defense counsel and the expert may need to devote sufficient time to learn the plaintiff's business and understand how the business, or the actions of the plaintiff, have changed over time.

Yardstick Approach

The yardstick approach involves a comparison with *comparable* businesses to see if there is a difference in the level of the plaintiff's performance after an event relative to that of the comparable businesses. This method can be used if there is an insufficient track record to apply the before and after method or it can be used to buttress the findings of the before and after method.

One of the key issues in applying the yardstick method is the issue of comparability. Each case is different and comparability may be defined differently depending on how the yardstick approach is being used. If the performances of other firms in the industry are being used to estimate how the plaintiff would have performed, then the expert needs to analyze these other firms to determine that they are truly comparable—that they service similar markets and sell similar products or services as the plaintiff's.

Challenges to the Use of the Yardstick Method

The defendant may want to challenge the use of this method by asserting that the so-called comparable firms are not really that comparable and that there would be a reasonable basis to expect these companies to perform differently from the plaintiff. This may involve an analysis of the comparable group to see if they are truly similar. In doing this analysis the services of an industry expert to work with the damages expert can be particularly helpful. An industry expert may be able to quickly alert the damages expert to important differences between the plaintiff and the comparable group that would explain differences in performance.

Lack of comparability can derive from many sources. It could be that the industry definitions used by the plaintiff's expert are inappropriate. Industries can have important subcategories and these subcategories can differ significantly from one another. For example, there may be a high-end or high-margin luxury category and there may be a low-end category that features significant discounting and price competition. If the competitive pressures have intensified in the low-end category, but not in the luxury category, then using one category to measure the profitability in the other may not be helpful. The high-end category will have very different profit margins while the low end with its lower margins may depend on volume to generate its profitability.

Using the Yardstick Approach for Newly Established Businesses

The before and after method often cannot be used effectively for a newly established business because it has not been around long enough to have sufficient before period data to compare with the after period ones. In these cases, a plaintiff may be restricted to using a yardstick approach. An example of the application of the yardstick method for a newly established business is provided by *PRN of Denver v. A. J. Gallagher* where the Florida Court of Appeals recognized that a standard before and after method would not be possible.[3]

---

[3] *PRN of Denver v. A.J. Gallagher & Co.*, 521 So. 2d 1001 (Fla. Dist. Ct. App. 1988).

Denver concedes that the usual predicate for a commercial business's claim of lost profits is a history of profits for a reasonable period of time anterior to the interruption of the business.

In citing the reasoning of another case involving a wrongfully evicted hotel coffee shop, the court stated:

The operator of a hotel coffee shop who is wrongfully evicted after a mere two weeks of operation may prove his loss of profits by establishing the profits of his business whose fifteenth month operation of a coffee shop was similar in every respect then, a fortiori, PRN of Denver, Inc. a successor whose operation and operators are the same as its predecessor, may prove its loss in the same manner, without running afoul of the rule prohibiting the recovery of purely speculative damages.

The issues related to measuring damages for unestablished and newly established business are revisited later in Chapter 5.

Concluding Comments on the Before and After and Yardstick Methods

Although these two methods are continually cited in the case law, they are only a general outline for two alternative ways of proving damages. This book attempts to go beyond these two methods and provide a broader methodological framework that the expert may adapt to a variety of damage circumstances. As the court said in *Pierce et al. v. Ramsey Winch Company,* a "plaintiff is not limited to one of these two methods. A method of proof specially tailored to the individual case, if supported by the record, is acceptable."[4]

The methodology presented herein encompasses both methods but goes beyond the bounds of either one to present a more complete methodological framework that can be more flexibly applied to a broader array of circumstances than what can be accomplished using just the before and after method or the yardstick approach.

CAUSALITY AND DAMAGES

The issue of causality is fundamental to commercial damages litigation. If the losses of the plaintiff are substantial, but it is not conclusive that the losses were

---

[4] *Pierce et al. v. Ramsey Winch Co.,* 753 F. 2d 416 (5th Cir. 1985).

caused by the actions of the defendant, the litigation may be pointless. When liability is questionable, the courts and both parties may save resources through bifurcation of the proceedings. The liability phase of the trial may, for example, focus on the obligations of the defendant under a contractual agreement. However, even in the liability phase, there can also be important economic and financial issues that the expert may provide evidence on.

Economists have long been asked to present evidence on liability in employment litigation. For example, economists are used in age, gender, or racial discrimination cases to ascertain if a defendant's employment policies are biased.[5] The economist might use statistical techniques, such as logit and probit analysis, to determine if age is a statistically significant explanatory variable in a equation in which employee termination is the dependent variable. The courts have long accepted such statistical or econometric testimony to help the trier of facts make these kinds of liability determinations in bias-related litigation.[6] Interestingly, the level of these courtroom presentations can be fairly sophisticated, with relatively complicated techniques normally reserved for advanced research, being brought to bear on an audience that generally lacks statistical training. This limitation, however, has not hindered the acceptance and reliance on such evidence.

Under certain circumstances, statistical analysis may be applied to investigate liability in a commercial lawsuit. On the simplest level, statistics can be employed to bolster economic theory used to establish how the sales of the plaintiff would have varied had it not been for a specific event, such as the actions of the defendant. This can be done by establishing the closeness of association between the sales of the plaintiff and various economic variables. For example, correlation or regression analysis could be used to show the historical degree of association between the plaintiff's sales and broad economic aggregates, such as national income, gross domestic product (GDP), retail sales, as well as more narrowly defined economic variables, such as industry sales.

Understanding Correlation Analysis in a Litigation Context

A basic step in applying correlation analysis is the computation of the correlation coefficient (r). In equation form, this is expressed as follows:

---

[5] Dolores A. Conway and Harry V. Roberts, "Regression Analysis in Employment Discrimination Cases," in *Statistics and the Law,* Morris H. DeGroot, Stephen E. Feinberg, and Joseph B. Kahane, eds. (New York: Wiley), 1986, 107–168.

[6] *Vuyanich v. Republic National Bank of Dallas* (D.C. Tex. 1980).

$$r = \frac{n \sum xy - (\sum x)(\sum y)}{\sqrt{n^2 [\sum x^2 - (\sum x)^2][\sum y^2 - (\sum y)^2]}}$$ (2.1)

where $\sum x$ = Sum of the x values
$\sum y$ = Sum of the y values
$\sum x^2$ = Sum of the squared x values
$\sum y^2$ = Sum of the squared y values
$(\sum x)^2$ = Sum of the x values squared
$(\sum y)^2$ = Sum of the y values squared
$\sum xy$ = Sum of the product of x and y for each paired observation
n = Number of x-y observations

The correlation coefficient can take on values between -1 and $+1$. A perfect negative correlation exists when we have a one-for-one negative relationship between two variables. Here the correlation coefficient is -1. (See Figure 2.1a.) The opposite is the case when there is a perfect one-for-one positive relationship between two variables, giving a correlation coefficient of $+1$. (See Figure 2.1b.) If there is absolutely no relationship between two variables, then we have a correlation coefficient equal to zero. (See Figure 2.1c.)

In the real world, however, such perfect relationships tend not to exist. That is, when there is some relationship between two variables, it shows up in correlation coefficient values between -1 and $+1$. The closer we are to $+1$, the more a positive relationship exists. In other words, when one variable increases, the other tends to increase as well, as depicted in Figure 2.2a. The closer the correlation coefficient is to -1, the more of an inverse relationship we have. That is, when one variable increases, the other decreases. This is shown in Figure 2.2b.

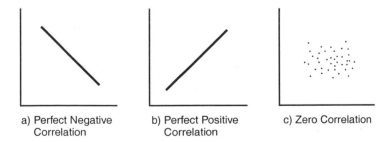

a) Perfect Negative   b) Perfect Positive   c) Zero Correlation
   Correlation   Correlation

Figure 2.1.   Different correlation examples.

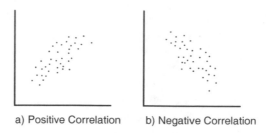

a) Positive Correlation   b) Negative Correlation

Figure 2.2.   Strong positive and negative correlation.

Correlation Scale

The degree of association between two variables can be put into perspective through the use of a *standard correlation scale* (see Figure 2.3). This is a mapping of the range of values that the correlation coefficient can take on where the various values are represented as being indicative of the strength of association—be it positive or negative. This mapping scale is useful because it translates the strength of the association into verbal terms that may be easier to relate to.[7] Correlations greater than 0.5 are considered to be higher than moderate.

In addition to the correlation coefficient, economists also express the strength of the association in terms of the *coefficient of determination,* which is simply the square value of the correlation coefficient. This measure, r^2, shows how much of the variation in one variable can be explained by variation in the associated variables.

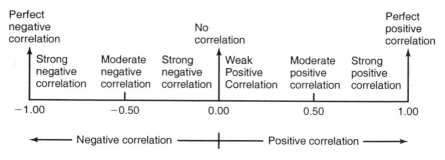

Figure 2.3.   Correlation scale.

---

[7] Robert D. Mason and Douglas A. Lind, *Statistical Techniques in Business and Economics,* 7th Ed. (Homewood, Ill.: Richard D. Irwin & Co.) 1990, 496.

One of the advantages of using the correlation coefficient or the coefficient of determination is that it provides a numerical measure of the degree of association, as opposed to simply saying that there is a good association between the variables in question. For example, the expert may be trying to examine the relationship between the sales of a company and certain deterministic factors, such as various macroeconomic aggregates, like national manufacturing shipments and industrial production. The economist may know that when the economy is expanding, as reflected by upward movements in these macroeconomic aggregates, a company's sales would be expected to increase. The expert may also testify that such a covarying pattern is observable in the data. However, the strength of this testimony may be bolstered by mathematically measuring this association and saying that the correlation coefficient between the company's sales and total U.S. manufacturing shipments is 0.87 while the coefficient of determination is 0.76. The latter measure means that 76% of the variation in the company's sales is explained by variation in manufacturing shipments, which is being used to measure the broad macroeconomic influence of the economy as a whole.

Finding a relatively high correlation coefficient does not *prove* causality. A high positive or negative correlation coefficient tells us there is a high direct or indirect degree of association between two different series of data which, in turn, implies that changes in one of the series *may* cause changes in the other. In our example of the manufacturer, an increase in demand from an expanding economy, as reflected by growth in national manufacturing shipments and increased industrial production, may increase the demand for a company's product which, under normal circumstances, would cause the company's sales to rise. In could be the case, however, that the plaintiff's sales have fallen and the expected increase failed to materialize. If all other factors can be ruled out, this economic analysis may go a long way toward proving that the actions of the defendant may have caused the sales of the plaintiff to decline.

Even a high correlation could simply be *spurious*, without any causality. For example, there is a high correlation between the number of firefighters at fires and the severity of fires. This correlation is normally spurious and one cannot conclude that the number of firefighters is causing the severity of the fire. That notwithstanding, a high correlation coefficient can provide a strong suspicion of causality. Even without establishing causality among the associated variables, it may be useful to show that these variables have tended to move together in the past and that now something has caused this association to cease.

In economic research, economists sometimes employ econometric tools to analyze causality. *Econometrics* is the field of economics that applies statistical analysis to economic issues. Within econometrics a subfield called *time series*

analysis investigates causality.[8] However, although these techniques are sometimes used in econometric research, they are not as often used in commercial
damages analysis and are not an accepted part of the standard methods in this
field. Other more basic methods are usually relied on, including the aforementioned correlation analysis and graphical analysis where plots of relevant
variables are graphically depicted. For example, Figure 2.4 shows a graph of a

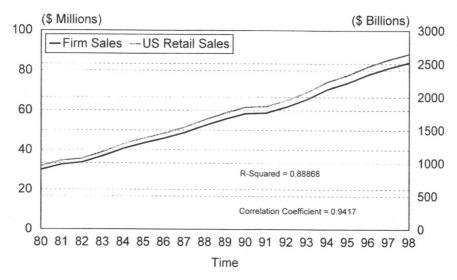

Figure 2.4. Example of correlation between company sales and national retail
sales.
(Source: U.S. Department of Commerce, Bureau of Economic Analysis, Washington, D.C.)

---

[8]The statistical technique in the econometric field of time series analysis called
Granger Causality can be used in a regression of a dependent variable time series $\{y_t\}$
against an independent variable time series $\{x_t\}$. One can conclude that series $\{x_t\}$ fails to
Granger cause $\{y_t\}$ if a regression of y_t on lagged x_i's reveals that the coefficients of the
x_i's are zero. The validity of the Granger test comes from the basic premise that the future
cannot cause the past. "If event A occurs after event B, we know that A cannot cause B. At
the same time, if event A occurs before B, it does not necessarily imply that A causes B."
Granger causality is not causality in the legal sense. For further discussion of this technique see C. W. J. Granger, "Investigating Causal Relations by Econometric Models and
Cross Spectral Models," *Econometrica* 37 (January) 1969, 24–36, and G. S. Maddala, *Introduction to Economatrics* (New York: Macmillan) 1988.

hypothetical national company's sales and U.S. retail sales. Such graphs are sometimes referred to as *scatter diagrams*.

The expert may find that giving the jury the opportunity to visually inspect a plot of the observations over time may reinforce the contention that there is a causal relationship. Based on the belief that a "picture is worth a thousand words," such exhibits of demonstrative evidence in a courtroom can be quite useful and may help win the day.

Figure 2.4 shows a joint plot of the dependent variable (i.e., the plaintiff's sales) and the probable causal variables. In cases of an historical business interruption, the graph can be extended beyond the interruption date at trial to help show what sales of the plaintiff would have been absent the interruption. This extension of the "but for" stream of plaintiff's revenues can be constructed using regression analysis. This statistical technique is further discussed in Chapter 5. However, putting the correlation analysis together with forecasting techniques allows one to see what happens if the historical relationship that was measured using the correlation coefficient is extrapolated over the loss period.

Correlation analysis and graphical demonstration can be most useful but not necessarily conclusive. They can be an important first step in the analytical process. If the results are promising, the analysis may need to be continued.

USING DEMONSTRATIVE EVIDENCE TO HELP THE CLIENT UNDERSTAND ITS LOSSES OR LACK OF LOSSES

Normally we think of preparing graphical and statistical exhibits as part of the pretrial preparatory process. However, such analysis and exhibits can be most helpful early in the expert's work on the case. Often the plaintiff has a biased or emotional view of his losses. For example, the plaintiff may think he has incurred a "seven figure loss." This "feeling" may be inflamed by the animus the plaintiff bears toward the defendant for whatever actions may have precipitated the suit. The plaintiff may attribute a downturn in sales exclusively to the actions of the defendant when other events, such as changes in the degree of competition in the plaintiff's market, may have played a more important causal role. As another example, a plaintiff's sales pattern may have remained essentially unchanged, possibly because of the efforts the plaintiff has exercised to mitigate his damages by substituting other sales for those that were lost. Some fundamental statistical analysis, presented in the form of basic graphical exhibits, can go a long way to demonstrating the impact of these factors. Even when there is a real loss, it may be important for the plaintiff to see how he may have to overcome the appearance that the sales pattern will have in an exhibit prepared by the opposing expert. This may let him know that he and his attorney have an uphill evidentiary battle ahead of them.

The initial statistical and graphical analysis can give the client an advance word on whether they have a convincing liability case and show him the approximate magnitude of his losses. It allows the client to explain what may have caused the trends that may be readily apparent in the graphs. Armed with this information, the client may be able to make a more enlightened decision on how much to invest in the litigation. If the true losses are, for example, less than $100,000, but legal and expert fees through trial will be well in excess of that, the client may decide to withdraw the suit. For this reason it is useful to do some early analysis and allow the client to react to this first step in the analytical process.

One drawback of doing such initial analysis is that it is very preliminary and does not reflect the thorough final analysis that the expert would put forward in a final report. Given that this preliminary analysis may be discoverable at some point, the attorney may have to weigh the possibility of being confronted with the analysis and exhibits at a later date. This is another reason why it is important to have an experienced expert who is aware of the ramifications of putting work in writing that may later be discovered. This does not mean that the expert should try to conceal unfavorable analysis. Rather, the expert should just be mindful of what is written down and how it can be manipulated to mean something other than what was originally intended.

CAUSALITY AND LOSS OF CUSTOMERS

One case where causality may be clear is when there are economic losses that can be attributed to the loss of particular customers. This loss could occur in a variety of ways. An example would be a business interruption in which customers are lost because the ability of the plaintiff to supply products or services to its customers was interrupted. Another potential scenario might be that certain specific customers were stolen through illegal actions of the defendant.

The establishment of causality in the case of the loss of specific customers is more straightforward. Liability may be established through testimony and other means. However, even when liability is established without economic analysis, the economist still must conduct an analysis of the plaintiff's sales, which usually involves a breakdown of sales-by-customer over an historical period. This sales breakdown naturally goes together with the usual steps the attorney would take to legally establish liability.

A model directed at the measurement of sales of lost customers in litigation has recently been developed.[9] This model takes into account an important factor—the historical rate of *customer attrition*. It is normal for firms to lose some of their customers over time. Attrition can occur because of competitive forces, service quality, and a variety of other reasons. Some firms are able to keep a very high percentage of their customers, while others may experience more rapid customer loss rates. If a plaintiff states that he lost certain customers as a result of actions of the defendant, a simple projection of the sales of those lost customers without attempting to factor in an anticipated rate of customer loss may overestimate the true losses.

The analysis of the historical attrition rates may be limited by the availability of data. However, if sufficient data are available, the economist may be able to measure the average length of time that a firm retains its customers or, conversely, the average number of customers that leave in a given year. This is analogous to what is done in employment litigation where the average number of years that a worker would remain in the employ of a particular company is measured using statistics such as tenure with the company, education levels, and other variables.[10]

GRAPHICAL SALES ANALYSIS AND CAUSALITY

In its simplest form, the effects of a business interruption are clearest when there is a dramatic change in the plaintiff's revenues. For example, if the plaintiff's revenues fell dramatically after certain actions by the defendant took place, then the counsel for the plaintiff may find it easier to convince the trier of fact of the plaintiff's loss and the defendant's culpability. Earlier in the chapter, the issue of covariability between certain economic variables and the sales of the plaintiff was defined and examined. If suddenly covariability is interrupted, as would be the case if the economic variables continued to rise while the plaintiff's revenues started declining, the defendant's actions may be a possible explanation.

Another way in which graphical analysis may be used to put forward a statement on causality is by examining the trends in the plaintiff's own historical

---

[9] Laura Bonanomi, Patrick A. Gaughan, and Larry Taylor, "A Statistical Methodology for Measuring Lost Profits Resulting From a Loss of Customers," *Journal of Forensic Economics,* 11(2), 1998, pp. 103–113.

[10] Robert R. Trout, "Duration of Employment In Wrongful Termination Cases," *Journal of Forensic Economics* 8 (2), 1995, 167–177.

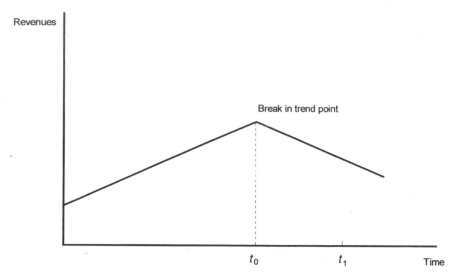

Figure 2.5. Revenues over time with break in trend at t_0.

revenues. If, as in Figure 2.5, there is a significant break in the trend of the plaintiff's revenues that coincides with the actions of the defendant (assumed to have occurred at time t_0), then a causal linkage between the two events may be one explanation. The defendant, of course, may try to put forward alternative explanations for the break in the plaintiff's revenue trend. If it can be shown that another event occurred at time t_0 in Figure 2.5, such as an adverse change in the competitive environment, and the actions of the defendant did not occur until later, at time t_1, with little change in the downward trend in revenues, then the plaintiff may face an uphill liability battle. However, if the actions of the defendant made the plaintiff's revenues decline more rapidly than they would have otherwise, then an argument may be made for some of the plaintiff's losses being attributable to the actions of the defendant.

Simply examining and graphically depicting the plaintiff's revenues may not conclusively establish causality but it may be an integral part of the overall liability portion of a commercial damages case. However, one should be mindful that graphical analysis, while a useful first step, is only one part of a more involved analytical process. Merely noticing that the revenue trend varies consistently with the actions of the defendant does not prove that the defendant caused the plaintiff's losses. However, if the graphical analysis provides promising results, the plaintiff may be one step closer to convincing the trier of fact that the defendant is liable.

ECONOMISTS AND OTHER DAMAGE EXPERTS: ROLE OF CAUSALITY

One of the advantages of using an economist to address causality, as opposed to another type of damages expert, is that the economist normally has training in and regularly uses statistical analysis in his work. Statistical and econometric analysis are normal components of the economist's toolbox. Ignoring causality may be a fatal flaw in the damages presentation. It may be pointless to measure damages if they cannot be linked to the actions of the defendant. This issue, and the selection of the correct expert, was clearly demonstrated in *Graphic Directions, Inc. v. Robert L. Bush* where an accountant testified on damages but did not analyze the causal link between the actions of the defendant and the damages.[11] The Court of Appeals of Colorado rejected the damages argument in this case involving a lost customers analysis as it did not address this important issue.

> Additionally, it is axiomatic that before damages for lost profits may be awarded, one who seeks them must establish that the damages are traceable to and are the direct result of the wrong to be redressed. (citation omitted) GDI's accountant testified that he did not have opinion as to whether the losses were caused by Bush and Dickinson's conduct and stated that he had not related calculation of lost net taxable profits to the lost customers. Nor is there evidence establishing a causal link between all of the lost sales and Bush and Dickinson's solicitation of customers. At least four of the "lost" customers continued to do business with GDI, and GDI presented no evidence that eight other lost customers did any business with Concepts 3.
>
> Based upon our review of the evidence, we conclude that GDI did not present substantial evidence from which the jury could compute its loss of net profits.

CAUSALITY AND THE SPECIAL CASE OF DAMAGES RESULTING FROM ADVERSE PUBLICITY

Another common type of case in which causality is an important issue is one in which damages arise from adverse publicity, whereby a defendant makes defamatory statements about the plaintiff, causing the plaintiff to incur losses. Here the economist can utilize certain basic quantitative techniques that are commonplace

---

[11] *Graphic Directions v. Robert L. Bush*, 862 P. 2d 1020 (Colo. App. 1993).

in the field of public relations to measure the dollar value of the adverse publicity that caused the damages.[12]

Public relations professionals often measure the dollar value of the publicity they generate for their clients by treating it as though it were an advertisement. In order words, if a favorable half-page article touting the positive attributes of a business were placed in a local newspaper, the public relations firm would contend that the market value of that publicity is equivalent to the cost of purchasing that space for an advertisement.

The methodology used by public relations firms to measure the market value of the positive publicity they generate for clients can also be used to measure the market value of adverse publicity. Adverse media publicity can be viewed as an advertisement but one that cited certain negative attributes of an individual or business. When a series of such stories appear in the media, they can be viewed as a negative "advertising campaign." Their market value can be determined using the market value of the print space, or the advertising time if the media is radio or television. The cost of the space or time is readily available from the various media sources who normally provide their rate cards upon request.

It is well accepted that advertising may increase sales. Attempts to quantify the "advertising elasticity of demand" have shown that it can be a difficult exercise.[13] Nonetheless, although the exact measurement of the quantitative impact of advertising on sales is difficult to measure, the positive relationship between the two variables is widely accepted. Quantifying the market value of the adverse publicity can be helpful to a trier of facts by arriving at a measure of its significance. This may be helpful in assessing the causal relationship between the adverse publicity and the alleged losses of the plaintiff.

LENGTH OF LOSS PERIOD: BUSINESS INTERRUPTION CASE

In a business interruption case, losses may be measured until such time as the sales or profits of the plaintiff's business have recovered. In a growing business, this may not necessarily be the time when the plaintiff's revenues reached the preinterruption level. If it can be established that the plaintiff's revenues would

---

[12] Patrick A. Gaughan, "An Application of Exposure Measuring Techniques to Litigation Economics" paper presented at the Eastern Economics Association Annual Meetings.

[13] Leonard Parsons and Randall L. Schultz, *Marketing Models and Econometric Research* (New York: North Holland) 1978, 82–85.

have grown, absent the actions of the defendant, then the recovery period may be when the postinterruption actual revenues reach the forecasted "but for" revenues.

Closed, Open, or Infinite Loss Periods

The loss period can be characterized as either *closed, open,* or *infinite.*[14] In a closed business interruption, the loss period has ended and actual sales, both before and after the interruption, are available. Such a loss period is demonstrated in Figure 2.6. The graph shows that not only has the sales decline ended but also that the postinterruption revenues have increased beyond the preinterruption level of R_1. Indeed, at time t_1, the revenues are consistent with the level that would be forecasted (R_2) if we were to extrapolate a simple linear trend from the downturn point.

The loss period is open when the losses continue into the future. Figure 2.7 shows that the forecasted revenues are continually above the actual postinterruption revenues and that, while the plaintiff surpasses the preinterruption revenue level of R_1, it never returns to its previous growth path. As a result, the revenue

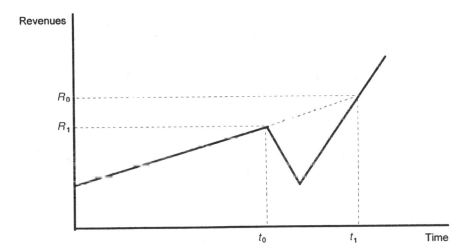

Figure 2.6.   Closed loss period.

---

[14] This categorization of loss periods is derived from Robert R. Trout and Carroll B. Foster, "Business Interruption Losses" in *Litigation Economics,* Patrick A. Gaughan and Robert Thornton, eds. (Greenwich, Conn.: JAI Press) 1993.

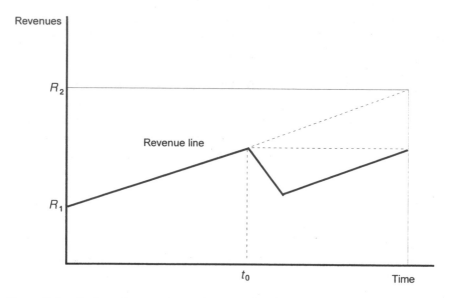

Figure 2.7.   Business interruption with incomplete recovery.

level is continually below where it would have been, had it not been for the interruption. An examination of Figure 2.7 shows that, in this particular example, the firm is growing at the same rate as it did prior to the interruption but that it has lost ground in the amount of $R_2 - R_1$ of revenues during the interruption period. Growing in the postinterruption period at the same rate as preinterruption will never be sufficient to offset the downturn that occurred in the interruption period. Only a higher postinterruption rate of revenue growth would be sufficient to offset the effects of the downturn.

The reader should bear in mind that these examples are somewhat simplistic and feature constant pre- and postinterruption growth, so that convenient conclusions, such as full recovery in Figure 2.6 and inability to ever reach full recovery in Figure 2.7 can be clearly attained. In the real world, however, revenues may not behave so conveniently.

CASE OF POSTINTERRUPTION GROWTH
EXCEEDING PREINTERRUPTION GROWTH

Is it possible for a plaintiff to recover damages if its growth after the business interruption exceeded the preinterruption growth? Just as in the case of a new or unestablished business (see Chapter 5), the analytical and evidentiary burdens of proving such damages beyond a reasonable doubt are greater than in the case where there is dramatic negative growth after the interruption date. However, a plaintiff could indeed be damaged by the fact that it was not able to realize a higher than actual growth due to the actions of a defendant.

An example of how difficult this is to prove occurred in *Bendix Corp. v. Balax, Inc.* In this case, the defendant-counterclaimant argued that its growth was less than what it would have enjoyed had it not had to incur the financial pressures brought on by the plaintiff's patent infringement suit.[15] The defendant's case was made difficult by the fact that its revenues grew from 8% to 26% over this time period. The defendant argued that its growth would have been even higher. Its president testified that their business was only 60% of what it would have been and its sales manager said it was only half as large. However, the defendant-counterclaimant's proofs in the form of testimony from members of its management was unconvincing to the court.

In commenting on the fact that Balax's revenues increased after the actions of the defendant, the U.S. Court of Appeals for the 7th Circuit stated:

> In the ordinary situation of proving damages allegedly caused as a result of certain action of another, the injured person or corporation shows how its sales declined during the pertinent period but even that is not deemed sufficiently probative. . .

> Here, where Balax's revenues increased very substantially, the evidence of damages consists of (1) Val Vleet's testimony that he thinks that "one of the reasons for Balax's Detroit representative discontinuing representing Balax was because a Ford Motor Company plant to which he hoped to sell tapes had learned of the infringement suit"; (2) VanVleet's testimony that "I believe that our business amounted to something like 60% of what it would have amounted to had this action not been brought" and (3) Balax's sales manager's testimony that but for the lawsuit sales would be "I would say at least twice as much as we are currently selling. . . ."

> In other words Balax's business has steadily increased and would have increased more if it had carried cutting tapes, which it does not, though no reason proved to be attributable to the plaintiff.

DISAGGREGATING REVENUES BY PRODUCT LINE TO PROVE CAUSALITY

In cases where the defendant's actions caused a loss in profits for one of a business's product lines or business segments, it is necessary to disaggregate total

---

[15] *Bendix Corp. v. Balax, Inc.*, 471 F. 2d 149 (7th Cir. 1972).

revenues and examine the trends in the revenues of the relevant product line or business segment separately. In cases where total revenues for the entire business have increased after the interruption, the defendant may want to merely examine the trend in total revenues so as to argue that the plaintiff was not hurt. However, on a disaggregated basis, the plaintiff may be able to show that the product line or business segment's revenues fell after the interruption.

An example where the plaintiff was able to make such a convincing demonstration occurred in *Pierce v. Ramsey Winch Co.*[16] In this case, a terminated distributor brought suit against the manufacturer and other distributors. The plaintiff did a standard loss computation where he projected "but for" revenues, deducted revenues from sales of substitute products, and applied a profit factor to the lost incremental revenues. The defendant argued that the plaintiff could not have experienced a loss because its posttermination gross profits were higher than before. The plaintiff responded that these higher gross profits came from other goods it sold, truck beds and trailers, not from the winches that were the subject of this litigation. In this case, the plaintiff was able to segregate its total revenues and profits which, when combined with other segments of the business, masked its true losses. The relevant trend was the trend in the product at issue, winches that would have been sold to the plaintiff by the manufacturer, not in the total revenues and gross profits, which included other products unrelated to this case.

The U.S. Court of Appeals for the Fifth Circuit recognized the problems of proving damages when revenues increase after a business interruption but it also recognized that damages can exist even when revenues and profits have increased.

> Pierce Sales, however, cannot show declining sales. As noted, Pierce Sales's gross profits have risen sharply since termination. For this reason Ramsey's argument that Pierce Sales was not in fact injured by termination indeed has surface appeal.
>
> Improvement in a distributor's business following termination, it seems to us, necessarily flows from (1) a diversion of the resources that were previously devoted to selling products supplied by the defendant; (2) successes in an aspect of the business unrelated to the expenditure of resources freed up by the termination; or (3) a combination of these two sources.
>
> If the distributor's successes flow from the utilization of resources other than those previously devoted to selling the defendant's products, posttermination profits would have no bearing on the fact of damage flowing from termination. If the evidence shows, on the other hand, that posttermination profits exceed pretermination profits and that they are attributable to the use of resources diverted because of termination to other endeavors, it would seem at least possible that posttermination

---

[16] *Pierce v. Ramsey Winch Co.*, 753 F. 2d 416 (5th Cir. 1985).

endeavors are more profitable for plaintiff than operation of the defendant's distributorship. We do not think, however, that a plaintiff is necessarily precluded from showing fact of damage in this latter situation. He may demonstrate fact of damage by showing that (1) he lost sales or revenues during the lag period between termination and completion of his efforts to divert resources to substitute endeavors and (2) although substitute endeavors proved more profitable than distribution of defendant's products did immediately prior to termination, to a level sufficient to earn him greater profits than his substitute endeavors did. He cannot, however, make this showing through speculation or through reliance on unfounded assumptions.

Pierce v. Ramsey Winch Co. is instructive in that it shows that analyzing and graphing total revenues may not capture the relevant trends if only a certain segment of the business is affected by the defendant's actions. If this is the case, then we need to first disaggregate the revenues according to business segment and graph these trends. We may need to do a separate statistical analysis of the relationship between the revenues of the various segments and their causal factors such as those previously discussed.

DISAGGREGATING REVENUES TO SHOW SPILLOVER LOSSES

It may be the case that a defendant's actions directed at one part of the plaintiff's business may have spillover effects onto other parts of the plaintiff's business. In cases like this, it may not be possible to credibly prove damages by merely disaggregating revenues; it may be necessary to disaggregate costs as well. This can sometimes be difficult, particularly when inputs are used for a variety of products. An example where a plaintiff claimed losses on related products resulting from a cut off of supply of beer can be found in *Cooper Liquor v. Adolph Coors Co.* In this case, the plaintiff claimed that beer sales were a loss leader and were used to bring in customers who would buy other products that generated positive profits. The court rejected the plaintiff's loss analysis as it was based upon gross bank deposits with no product-by-product breakdown.[17] The lesson from this case is that if you are claiming interrelated spillover effects, you must be able to demonstrate these effects with a product-by-product revenue analysis, which may mean constructing a table that analyzes not only the trends in historical total revenues, but also in its disaggregated components.

---

[17] *Cooper Liquor Inc. v. Adolph Coors Co.,* 509 F. 2d 758 (5th Cir.), denying petition for rehearing, 506 F 2d 934 (5th Cir. 1975).

LENGTH OF LOSS PERIOD:
PLAINTIFF GOES OUT OF BUSINESS

When a plaintiff has gone out of business, the loss period is "infinite," as shown in Figure 2.8 where a business interruption occurred at time t_0 that caused the plaintiff so much damage that by time t_1 it went out of business. Here again actual sales may only be available for the period when the interruption began until the company went out of business. Although the loss period may have no definite termination date, this does not imply that the losses themselves are infinite. Through the process of *capitalization* it is possible to determine the present value of such losses. The determination of present value places increasingly lower values on amounts that are further into the future. This process is discussed in Chapter 7.[18]

A number of cases involving firms that went out of business due to the actions of the defendant have held that the value of the damages is equal to the market value of the business on the date the operations ceased. In cases where the company operated for a period of time before going out of business, the plaintiff may

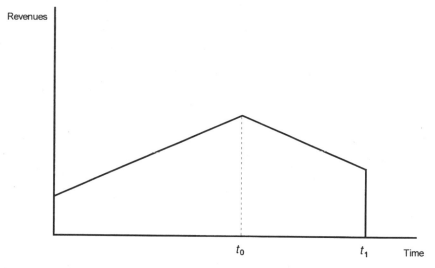

Figure 2.8.   Infinite loss period: Revenues end as business goes out of existence.

---

[18] Although it may be obvious, an unprofitable business, or more importantly, one that does not generate positive operating cash flows, may not be able to show losses even if it goes out of business.

be able to recover lost profits for the interim period between the wrongful acts of the defendant and the date that the plaintiff went out of business, at which time the remaining value of the loss is the value of the business on that date.[19]

LENGTH OF LOSS PERIOD: BREACH OF CONTRACT

In the case of an alleged breach of contract, losses are typically projected until the end of the contract period. Although this may seem fairly straightforward, sometimes it is not, because the actual length of the contract period may also be an issue of dispute. This would be the case when there are early termination clauses or option periods. In the case of an early termination clause, the loss may be shorter than the end of the contract whereas an option period may allow for losses to extend beyond the normal end of the contract. In such cases, the expert may be retained to project losses until an assumed end of the contract period based on his or her client's legal interpretation of the contract. Clearly the expert must look for legal guidance from the attorney who retained her.

For long-term contracts, some courts have displayed reluctance to award damages for the full length of the loss period due to concerns on the degree of certainty associated with long-term projections. The courts have correctly concluded that the further into the future one forecasts, the more is the uncertainty surrounding the forecast. In his review of the case law in this area, Robert Dunn has concluded that while courts have not clearly articulated their reasoning, they have chosen to award damages for periods significantly shorter than the actual remaining years on the contract.[20] In *Palmer v. Connecticut Railway & Lighting Co.,* for example, the court awarded damages for only eight years when 969 years remained of the contract and when the plaintiff itself conceded that it could not project damages beyond 40 years due to the uncertainty of such a projection.[21] In another example of the court simply truncating the remaining years of a contract, the court in *Sandler v. Lawn-a-Mat Chemical & Equipment Corp.* allowed damages for only three years when the contract had a term of 50 years with an option to renew for another 50 years.[22]

---

[19] *Aetna Life and Casualty Co. v. Little,* 384 So. 2d 213 (Fla. App. 1980).

[20] Robert Dunn, *Recovery of Damages for Lost Profits* (Westport, Conn.: Lawpress Corp.) 1992, 402–404.

[21] *Palmer v. Connecticut Railway & Lighting Co.,* 311 U.S. 544 (1941).

[22] *Sandler v. Lawn-a-Mat Chemical & Equipment Corp.,* 141 N.J. Super. 437, 358 A. 2d 805 (1976).

One issue that the court has not addressed is the implicit estimate of no losses that this truncation places on the remaining years of contract. By terminating the losses at a certain date, the court is substituting its own estimate of $0 for losses after the truncation period. The court's position that only damages that can be projected with reasonable certainty are allowed is affirmed in these and other decisions. The courts are simply saying that there may be losses but that at some point in the future such losses may not be measurable with reasonable certainty. In addition, after some passage of time, it becomes more reasonable that the plaintiff would be able to pursue other mitigating activities.

METHODOLOGICAL FRAMEWORK

The methodological framework is a step-by-step process that combines various components that should be part of the overall damages analysis. Although each case may present its own unique aspects, it is common that the following outlined components be integral parts of the overall loss measurement process.

    A. Macroeconomic Analysis
        1. Regional Economic Analysis (if relevant)
    B. Industry Analysis
    C. Firm-Specific Analysis
        1. Revenue Forecasting
        2. Cost Analysis
        3. Financial Analysis
    D. Measurement of Lost Profits
    E. Adjustment for the Time Value of Money

A. Macroeconomic Analysis

Using a top-down due diligence process, this methodology first examines the overall macroeconomic environment within which the alleged loss took place. This examination considers the condition of the overall economy, as measured by a variety of relevant macroeconomic aggregates. The performance of the macroeconomy is then related to the performance of the plaintiff before and after the event/events in question.

1. Regional Economic Analysis

In some instances, the macroeconomy may be less relevant than a more narrow economic environment. This can be the case for firms who are exclusively regional. Here a more narrowly focused group of economic aggregates, such as state economic data as opposed to national data, are used to measure the performance of a relevant regional economic environment.

B. Industry Analysis

An analysis of the plaintiff's industry can provide valuable information about the performance and profitability of the business area within which the plaintiff operates. This, in turn, can give clues as to how the plaintiff should have performed and what level of profits the business should have derived, absent the alleged wrongdoing. It allows the expert to see if the trends at issue in the litigation, such as the plaintiff's losses, are specific to it or are part of a wider industry phenomenon that has nothing to do with the actions of the defendant. A variety of data sources are used to measure this industry performance.

C. Firm-Specific Analysis

Having established the macroeconomic, regional, and industrial environment within which the firm operates, the next step in the top-down process is to analyze the performance of the firm itself. This analysis includes the firm's historical and current performance as measured by a variety of variables, including revenue growth and profitability measures. Depending on the type of case, this firm-specific analysis may include an analysis of the firm's financial statements, which may involve using such standard tools of corporate finance as financial ratio analysis.

D. Measurement of Lost Profits

Having analyzed the performance of the plaintiff in relation to the macroeconomic, regional, and industry economic environments, the expert can begin the actual loss measurement process, typically a two-part process whereby revenues are first forecasted and a relevant profit margin is then applied to the forecasted revenues. In order to derive the appropriate profit margin, a cost analysis needs to be conducted to determine the incremental costs associated with the lost incremental revenues. This loss measurement combines the forecasting skills of an economist with the costs measurement skills of either an economist or an accountant to derive lost profits.

E. Adjustment for the Time Value of Money

The estimated loss measures have to be converted to present value terms so that both historical and future loss amounts are brought to terms that are consistent with the date of the analysis or the trial date. A prejudgment return may be applied to pretrial amounts to bring them current. Similarly, the projected future losses need to be brought to present value by using a relevant discount rate.

SUMMARY

Two broad methods for measuring damages are continually cited in the case law: the before and after method and the yardstick approach. The before and after method involves comparing the plaintiff's performance before the actions of the defendant with its performance after these actions. The plaintiff may attribute differences, such as lower revenues and profits, to the actions of the defendant. The yardstick approach involves finding comparable businesses and attributing the performance of these similar businesses to the plaintiff. Both methods are merely general outlines of an approach to measuring damages. This book provides a broad methodological framework consistent with both methods but is more intricate and yet more flexible.

The economic loss analysis may include an analytical component that helps establish the allegation of causality linking the actions of the defendant to the alleged losses of the plaintiff. The determination of causality may involve some basic statistical analysis to assess the statistical linkage between relevant economic time series and certain performance measures of the plaintiff. Such an analysis may establish, for example, that prior to the business interruption there was a close statistical relationship between the growth in the plaintiff's revenues and the growth in economic activity in the overall economy and in the plaintiff's industry, in particular. The deviation from the normal and expected relationship between these variables in the postinterruption period may be one component, along with other fact-based evidence, of a demonstration of causality.

The loss period varies by type of case. Loss periods can be closed if a business has fully recovered. Open loss periods exist when a business continues to experience losses. Loss periods are infinite when the business goes out of existence. An infinite loss period, however, does not imply that the losses themselves are infinite.

The methodological framework for economic loss analysis is a top-down framework that begins with a macroeconomic analysis of the overall economic to establish the macroeconomic environment in which the damages are alleged to have occurred. In most circumstances, the weaker the macroeconomic environment, the more conservative the projection of damages.

Following the macroeconomic analysis, the focus narrows to the regional level, which occurs only if the alleged damages are confined to a specific region or geographical sector. Many of the same economic time series used at the national level are employed in this analysis but they are narrowed to be confined to a specific region.

The next step in the process is to conduct an analysis of the industry in which the losses are alleged to have occurred. This usually involves collecting industry data, which are then compared to the macroeconomic and regional data as well as to firm specific data. As part of this process, the growth, level of competition, pricing, and other industry factors are analyzed.

The next step in the commercial damages loss framework is to conduct a firm-specific analysis, which involves analyzing trends in the firm's historical revenues and various performance measures such as gross and net profits and cash flows. Preloss trends are contrasted with postloss trends as part of a loss projection process.

The next step typically involves a "but for" revenue projection from which actual revenues are then deducted to derive lost revenues. Having established lost revenues, a cost analysis is conducted to measure the incremental costs associated with the lost incremental revenues. The lost profits are then measured as the difference between the incremental lost revenues and their associated costs.

REFERENCES

Aetna Life and Casualty Co. v. Little, 384 So. 2d 213 (Fla. App. 1980).

Bendix Corp. v. Balax, Inc., 471 F. 2d 149 (7th Cir. 1972).

Bonanomi, Laura, Patrick A. Gaughan, and Larry Taylor, "A Statistical Methodology for Measuring Lost Profits Resulting From a Loss of Customers," *Journal of Forensic Economics,* 11 (2), 1998, 103–113.

Conway, Dolores A., and Harry V. Roberts, "Regression Analysis in Employment Discrimination Cases," in *Statistics and the Law,* Morris H. DeGroot, Stephen E. Feinberg, and Joseph B. Kahane, ed. (New York: Wiley, 1986).

Cooper Liquor Inc. v. Adolph Coors Co., 509 F. 2d 758 (5th Cir.)

Dunn, Robert, *Expert Testimony: Law and Practice,* Vol. I (Westport, Conn.: Lawpress Corp., 1997).

Dunn, Robert, *Recovery of Damages for Lost Profits* (Westport, Conn.: Lawpress Corp., 1992).

Gaughan, Patrick A., "An Application of Exposure Measuring Techniques to Litigation Economics," paper presented at the Eastern Economics Association Annual Meetings.

Granger, C. W. J., "Investigating Causal Relations by Econometric Models and Cross Spectral Models," *Econometrica* 37 (January) 1969.

Graphic Directions v. Robert L. Bush, 862 P. 2d 1020 (Colo. App. 1993).

Katskee v. Nevada Bob's Golf, 472 N.W. 2d 372 (Nov. 1991).

Maddala, G. S., *Introduction to Econometrics* (New York: Macmillan, 1988).

Mason, Robert D. and Douglas A. Lind, *Statistical Techniques in Business and Economics* (Homewood, Ill.: Richard D. Irwin & Co., 1990).

Palmer v. Connecticut Railway & Lighting Co., 311 U.S. 544 (1941).

Parsons, Leonard and Randall L. Schultz, *Marketing Models and Econometric Research* (New York: North Holland, 1978), pp. 82 – 85.

Pierce et al. v. Ramsey Winch Co., 753 F. 2d 416 (5th Cir. 1985).

PRN of Denver v. A.J. Gallagher & Co., 521 So. 2d 1001 (Fla. Dist. Ct. App. 1988).

Sandler v. Lawn-a-Mat Chemical & Equipment Corp., 141 N.J. Super. 437, 358 A. 2d 805 (1976).

Trout, Robert R., "Duration of Employment In Wrongful Termination Cases," *Journal of Forensic Economics* 8 (2), 1995.

Trout, Robert R., and Carroll B. Foster, "Business Interruption Losses," in *Litigation Economics,* Patrick A. Gaughan and Robert Thornton, eds. (Greenwich, Conn.: JAI Press, 1993).

Vuyanich v. Republic National Bank of Dallas, (D.C. Tex. 1980).

3

MACROECONOMIC ANALYSIS FOR MEASURING COMMERCIAL DAMAGES

As noted in Chapter 2, several different forms of economic analysis can enter into a commercial damages analysis. In the top-down framework presented in that chapter, a broad-based macroeconomic analysis is used to assess the overall economic environment. Following that, the focus is narrowed to the regional level if the business at issue is regional in its orientation. The focus then gets progressively narrowed to the firm level where the firm-specific analysis is conducted. This chapter, however, starts the process by developing the macroeconomic and regional economic tools necessary for a thorough commercial damages analysis. The analytical process for macroeconomic and regional analysis is similar although some of the data used is different. The macroeconomic and regional economic analysis then sets the stage for industry analysis, which is discussed in Chapter 4.

MACROECONOMICS

Macroeconomics is the study of the overall economy, as opposed to microeconomics, which focuses on specific subunits of the overall economy, such as specific industries or firms. Within the field of macroeconomics, there is a subfield called business fluctuations, which analyzes the various factors in the economy that cause it to grow and contract. These fluctuations are referred to as *business cycles*. The term "cycles" is unfortunate because it implies a regular periodicity such as that is exhibited by a sine curve. However, the economy does not behave so predictably. Moreover, the economics profession has not been very successful in predicting the turning points of business cycles.

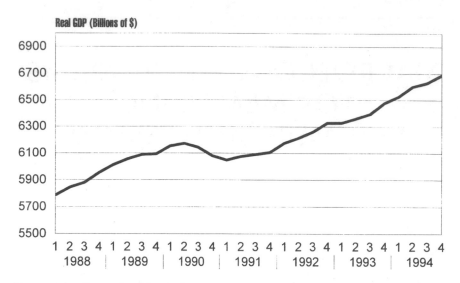

Figure 3.1. Example of the 1990–91 recession.
(Source: U.S. Department of Commerce, Bureau of Economic Analysis, Washington, D.C.)

When the economy turns down and exhibits negative growth, this is termed a *recession.* An example of a recent recession is shown in Figure 3.1. Recessions are generally defined as periods when the economy has two consecutive quarters of negative growth while the strict definition of a recession by the economics profession is made on a case-by-case basis by the Business Cycle Dating Committee of the National Bureau of Economic Research (NBER) using a variety of economic data. Figure 3.2 shows the recessions that occurred in the U.S. economy from 1960 to 1998. The average duration of a recession is 10.4 months, with the severity of recessions historically becoming less in the U.S. economy of the twentieth century.

MEASURING ECONOMIC GROWTH AND PERFORMANCE

Many different economic statistics are used to measure the performance of the overall economy as well as particular subunits of the economy. The broadest measure of economic performance is gross domestic product or GDP. The GDP is the market value of all newly produced goods and services in a country over a period of time such as one year. When this value is not adjusted for inflation it is called *nominal GDP.* When it is adjusted for the effects of inflation, which causes the value to increase due to price inflation, as opposed to greater production, it is

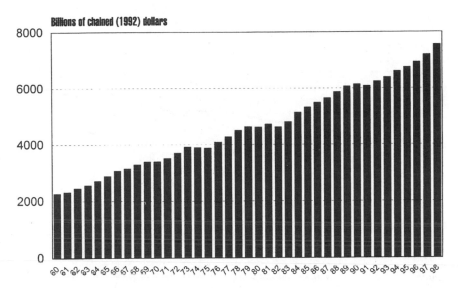

Figure 3.2. Real gross domestic product, 1960–98.
(Source: U.S. Department of Commerce, Bureau of Economic Analysis, Washington, D.C.)

called *real GDP.* Real GDP grows at a lower rate than nominal GDP. This rate is reflected in the flatter slope of the real versus the nominal GDP curve shown in Figure 3.3. Recently the way of computing real GDP was changed to compute what is known as *chained real GDP.*[1] The Bureau of Economic Analysis of the U.S. Department of Commerce publishes this measure to account for variations in the quantities of goods consumed over time. It is believed to be a more accurate measure than prior versions of GDP, which were fixed-weight indices thereby assuming that the quantity of goods consumed each year was the same.

GDP is subdivided into four broad components: personal consumption expenditures, investment, government expenditures, and net exports. Net exports is the difference between exports and imports. The relative contribution of each component is shown in Table 3.1. Table 3.2 shows the real, inflation-adjusted components. However, within each broad component there are still more narrowly defined subcomponents. For example, within total personal consumption expenditures we have expenditures on durables, nondurables, and services. Depending on the business of the plaintiff, we may want to know the overall economic performance as reflected by GDP and personal consumption expenditures; however,

---

[1] See Karl E. Case and Ray C. Fair, *Principles of Economics,* 4th ed. (Upper Saddle River, N.J.: Prentice Hall) 1996, 586–590.

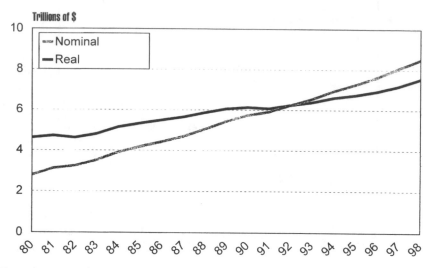

Figure 3.3.   Real versus nominal GDP.
(Source: U.S. Department of Commerce, Bureau of Economic Analysis, Washington, D.C.)

if the plaintiff is a marketer of durables, the durable component of personal consumption expenditures may be more relevant. In addition, if the plaintiff is a retailer, we also may want to review the trend in retail sales in addition to these consumer expenditure data.

Releases of GDP Data

The GDP is the most often cited measure of economic performance. Near the end of every month articles appear in the media about the latest release of GDP data. Given that this measure is so regularly relied on to measure the performance of the overall economy, it is useful to know more about it.[2] GDP statistics are released on a quarterly basis. Each quarterly value released is subsequently revised twice. These revisions can sometimes change the value significantly. Although the GDP numbers are released quarterly and apply to production in the relevant quarter, they are quoted in terms of an annual rate. This allows the values to be comparable to other periods. In addition, the GDP values are seasonally adjusted so that seasonal influences like the increased production that occurs in the fourth quarter in preparation for the holiday season are removed.

---

[2] See John Taylor, *Economics,* 2nd ed., (New York: Houghton Mifflin) 1998, 550–551.

Table 3.1. Nominal GDP and Its Components (billions of dollars)

Year	GDP	Percent Change (%)	Personal Consumption Expenditures	Percent Change (%)	Gross Private Domestic Investment	Percent Change (%)	Net Exports of Goods and Services	Percent Change (%)	Government Expenditures	Percent Change (%)
1980	2,784.2		1,760.4		465.9		−14.9		572.8	
1981	3,115.9	11.91	1,941.3	10.28	556.2	19.38	−15.0	−0.67	633.4	10.58
1982	3,242.1	4.05	2,076.8	6.99	501.1	−9.91	−20.5	−36.67	684.8	8.12
1983	3,514.5	8.40	2,283.4	9.95	547.1	9.18	−51.7	−152.20	735.7	7.43
1984	3,902.4	11.04	2,492.3	9.15	715.6	30.71	−102.0	−97.29	796.6	8.28
1985	4,180.7	7.13	2,704.8	8.51	715.1	−0.07	−114.2	−11.96	875.0	9.84
1986	4,422.2	5.78	2,892.7	6.95	722.5	1.04	−131.5	−15.15	938.5	7.26
1987	4,692.3	6.11	3,094.5	6.98	747.2	3.42	−142.1	−8.06	992.8	5.79
1988	5,049.6	7.61	3,349.7	8.25	773.9	3.57	−106.1	25.33	1,032.0	3.95
1989	5,438.7	7.71	3,594.8	7.32	829.2	7.15	−80.4	25.22	1,095.1	6.11
1990	5,743.8	5.61	3,839.3	6.80	799.7	−3.56	−71.3	11.32	1,176.1	7.40
1991	5,916.7	3.01	3,975.1	3.54	736.2	−7.94	−20.5	71.25	1,225.9	4.23
1992	6,244.4	5.54	4,219.8	6.16	790.4	7.36	−29.5	−43.90	1,263.8	3.09
1993	6,558.1	5.02	4,459.2	5.67	876.2	10.86	−60.7	−105.76	1,283.4	1.55
1994	6,947.0	5.93	4,717.0	5.78	1,007.9	15.03	−90.9	−49.75	1,313.0	2.31
1995	7,265.4	4.58	4,957.7	5.10	1,038.2	3.01	−86.0	5.39	1,355.5	3.24
1996	7,636.0	5.10	5,207.6	5.04	1,116.5	7.54	−94.8	−10.23	1,406.7	3.78
1997	8,083.4	5.86	5,488.6	5.40	1,237.6	10.35	−96.7	−2.00	1,453.9	3.36
1998	8,511.0	5.29	5,807.9	5.82	1,367.1	10.46	−151.2	−56.36	1,487.1	2.28

Source: U.S. Department of Commerce, Bureau of Economic Analysis, Washington, D.C.

Table 3.2. Real GDP and its Components [billions of chained (1992) dollars]

Year	GDP	Percent Change (%)	Personal Consumption Expenditures	Percent Change (%)	Gross Private Domestic Investment	Percent Change (%)	Net Exports of Goods and Services	Percent Change (%)	Government Expenditures	Percent Change (%)
1980	4,615.0		3,009.7		628.3		10.1		941.4	
1981	4,720.7	2.29	3,046.	1.22	686.0	9.18	5.6	−44.55	947.7	0.67
1982	4,620.3	−2.13	3,081.5	1.15	587.2	−14.40	−14.1	−351.79	960.1	1.31
1983	4,803.7	3.97	3,240.6	5.16	642.1	9.35	−63.3	−348.94	987.3	2.83
1984	5,140.1	7.00	3,407.6	5.15	833.4	29.80	−127.3	−101.11	1,018.4	3.15
1985	5,323.5	3.57	3,566.5	4.66	823.8	−1.15	−147.9	−16.18	1,080.1	6.06
1986	5,487.7	3.08	3,708.7	3.99	811.8	−1.46	−163.9	−10.82	1,135.0	5.08
1987	5,649.5	2.95	3,822.3	3.06	821.5	1.20	−156.2	4.70	1,165.9	2.72
1988	5,865.2	3.82	3,972.7	3.93	828.2	0.82	−114.4	36.54	1,180.9	1.29
1989	6,062.0	3.36	4,064.6	2.31	863.5	4.26	−82.7	27.71	1,213.9	2.79
1990	6,136.3	1.23	4,132.2	1.66	815.0	−5.62	−61.9	25.15	1,250.4	3.01
1991	6,079.4	−0.93	4,105.8	−0.64	738.1	−9.44	−22.3	63.97	1,258.0	0.61
1992	6,244.4	2.71	4,219.8	2.78	790.4	7.09	−29.5	−32.29	1,263.8	0.46
1993	6,389.6	2.33	4,343.6	2.93	863.6	9.26	−70.2	−137.97	1,252.1	−0.93
1994	6,610.7	3.46	4,486.0	3.28	975.7	12.98	−104.6	−49.00	1,252.3	0.02
1995	6,742.1	1.99	4,595.3	2.44	991.5	1.62	−98.8	5.55	1,251.9	−0.03
1996	6,928.4	2.76	4,714.1	2.59	1,069.1	7.83	−114.4	−15.79	1,257.9	0.48
1997	7,191.4	3.80	4,869.7	3.30	1,192.2	11.51	−142.1	−24.21	1,270.6	1.01
1998	7,551.9	5.01	5,153.3	5.82	1,330.1	11.57	−238.2	−67.63	1,296.9	2.07

Source: U.S. Department of Commerce, Bureau of Economic Analysis, Washington, D.C.

Business Cycles and Economic Damages

One factor that can cause a firm to experience losses is an overall slowdown in the economy. When the economy is in recession many companies slow down and can generate losses. Such economy-induced declines need to be differentiated from ones caused by the actions of another party. The analysis can become more complicated when both events occur at the same time. That is, it may be more challenging for the economist to filter out the losses caused by an economic downturn that was coincident with the damaging actions of the economy. In some cases, the economy may be solely responsible for the losses of the plaintiff. When the economy-wide influences are not factored into the loss analysis, the defendant may be wrongly blamed for the losses of the plaintiff. In order to understand this we need to learn more about business cycles.

There are varying theories or explanations for the causes of business cycles. For example, one theory currently popular among the economics profession is the Real Business Cycle Theory.[3] This theory sees the causes of the employment and output variations that occur in business cycles in terms of variations in technology and supply shocks.[4] An example of an adverse supply shock was the increase in oil prices in the 1970s, which slowed the economy and helped cause the recessions of 1974–75 and 1980.

Although the role that supply shocks can play in causing a recession is well established, no one accepted theory can convincingly explain all business cycles. Most economists agree that there is no single cause of all economic downturns and that the cause of such recessionary declines in the performance of the economy can vary depending on the particular circumstances that come into play during the specific economic downturn. The forensic economist, however, is not as much concerned about the cause of recessions as about the reality of recessions and their recurring yet unpredictable pattern. One way to assess this pattern is to consider certain trends that are common to the cyclical variation of the national economy. These are the frequency of recessions and the average duration of recession and recoveries. (See Table 3.3.)

During the period 1945–99, there were six recessions in the U.S. economy. The average duration of these recessions was 10.4 months while the average duration of the recoveries that followed was 52.7 months. Recoveries are defined as

---

[3] Finn E. Kydland and E. C. Prescott, "Time to Build and Aggregate Fluctuations," *Econometrica* 50 (Nov. 1982), 1345–1370.

[4] Robert Gordon, *Macroeconomics,* 6th ed., (New York: Harper Collins) 1993, 189–196.

Table 3.3. Recession Comparisons

Recession	Duration[a] (Months)	Real Output[b] (Percent Change)	Payroll Employment (Percent Change)	Unemployment Rate Percentage Points (Change)	Unemployment Rate Percent Change (High)	Unemployment Rate Months after Trough (High)
1948–49	11	−1.4	−5.2	4.5	7.9	0
1953–54	10	−3.7	−3.5	3.6	6.1	4
1957–58	8	−3.9	−4.3	3.8	7.5	3
1960–61	10	−1.6	−2.2	2.3	7.1	3
1969–70	11	−1.0	−1.5	2.7	6.1	9
1973–75	16	−4.9	−2.9	4.4	9.0	2
1980	6	−2.3	−1.4	2.2	7.8	0
1981–82	16	−3.3	−3.1	3.6	10.8	1
Recession Average	11	−2.8	−3.0	3.4	7.8	3
1990–91	8	−2.2	−2.0	2.7	7.7	15

Sources: U.S. Department of Commerce, U.S. Department of Labor, National Bureau of Economic Research, and Economic Report of the President, Jan. 1993.

[a] Duration based on National Bureau of Economic Research dating of business cycle peaks and troughs.

[b] Real output changes are determined from historical GNP or GDP series with base year near the recession period: for 1948–49 and 1953–54, GNP measured in 1954 dollars was used; for 1957–58 and 1960–61, GNP in 1958 dollars; for 1969–70 and 1973–75, GNP in 1972 dollars; for 1980 and 1981–82, GNP in 1982 dollars; for 1990–91, GDP in 1987 dollars. A fixed-weight measure of real output based on the prices of a more recent year (for example, GDP in 1987 dollars) generally changes less than one based on prices of an earlier year. This property creates problems in long-term comparisons of real output. See Allen Young, "Alternative Measures of Change in Real Output and Prices," *Survey of Current Business,* April 1992. Caution should be used in interpreting these data because of definitional changes made to the output measures over time.

Note: Changes determined from series-specific peaks and troughs. Upcoming data revisions may affect the values reported in this table.

the number of months between the trough of the downturn to the peak of the following upturn.

Firms' Reactions to Business Cycles

Cyclical fluctuations need to be explicitly taken into account in a commercial damages analysis. That is, the loss analysis and its associated revenue projection needs to be placed in an overall macroeconomic context. Most firms are procyclical, meaning they do better when the economy is expanding. When the economy is growing, demand for many goods and services increases. In a recession, however, demand may be stagnant or even declining. For companies that face a very cyclical demand, such as automobile or steel manufacturers, the overall cyclical variation of the economy can have great influence on company sales. This factor is important if the plaintiff faces a very cyclical demand and is claiming lost profits for a time period that included a recession, such as in the recent 1990–91 recession. A declining sales level could possibly be explained, in part or even in total, by the declining level of demand in the economy. In order to assess the relationship between the overall economy and the plaintiff's sales, the economist needs to analyze the historical pattern of sales in this industry relative to the overall economy. In effect, the expert needs to filter out the influence of the economy's fluctuations so as to isolate the variation in the plaintiff's sales specifically attributable to the actions of the defendant.

Generally, the greater the rate of growth in GDP, the better the economic conditions.[5] The better the economic conditions, the more likely firms will enjoy an increase in sales. However, this statement is very general and even when the GDP is growing, many companies are declining or going bankrupt. The converse is also true. That is, even when the economy is in recession, many companies could be growing rapidly. Therefore, an examination of the trends in the overall economy, as measured by GDP, is merely a starting point in the macroeconomic analysis

USING MORE NARROWLY DEFINED ECONOMIC AGGREGATES

The expert should be able to select more specific economic aggregates more closely related to the performance of the plaintiff's business. For example, if the plaintiff is a retailer, the expert could look at the variation in consumption expenditures and retail sales (see Figures 3.4, 3.5, 3.6, and 3.7). If the retailer sells only consumer durables such as appliances, then more defined aggregates, such as the consumer durable component of consumption expenditures, can be selected (see Figures 3.6 and 3.7). Depending on the nature of the plaintiff's business, various

---

[5] Recent Federal Reserve policy might suggest some reservations about this statement. The Federal Reserve in the Alan Greenspan era has been concerned when GDP growth appears to be robust, because it sees such growth as potentially inflationary. To the Fed, some growth is good but too rapid a growth is bad. This monetary policy issue notwithstanding, the statement that the more rapidly GDP is growing implies better economic conditions (which often means higher sales for companies) is usually reasonable.

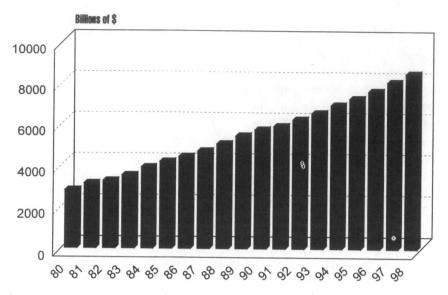

Figure 3.4. Gross domestic product.
(Source: U.S. Department of Commerce, Bureau of Economic Analysis, Washington, D.C.)

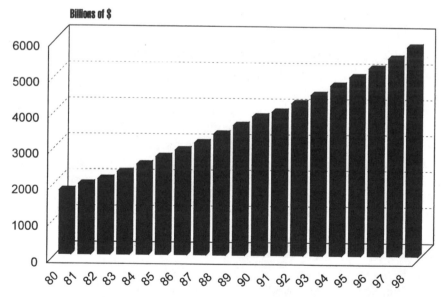

Figure 3.5. Consumption expenditures.
(Source: U.S. Department of Commerce, Bureau of Economic Analysis, Washington, D.C.)

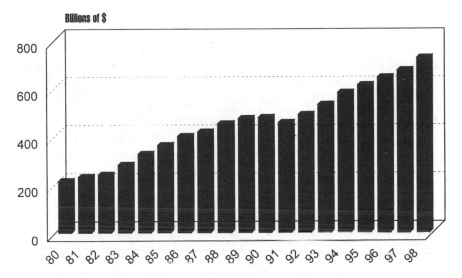

Figure 3.6. Durable goods.
(Source: U.S. Department of Commerce, Bureau of Economic Analysis, Washington, D.C.)

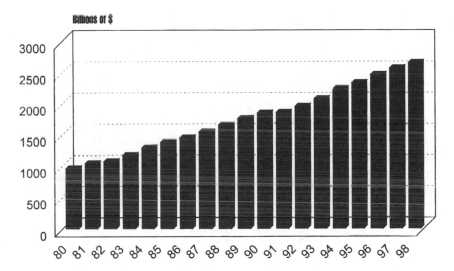

Figure 3.7. U.S. retail sales.
(Source: U.S. Department of Commerce, Bureau of Economic Analysis, Washington, D.C.)

economic aggregates can be selected to determine overall macroeconomic environment. The economist must examine the historical trends of the selected aggregates and the company's sales to make sure that the hypothesized relationship between the overall level of economic activity, as reflected in the trends in the selected aggregates, is consistent with the variation in the plaintiff's sales. That is, the economist needs to verify that when the economy was expanding, as reflected in the variation of the selected aggregates, the plaintiff's business was also expanding. If that covariation is not apparent, then a further investigation must be conducted to make sure that there is a satisfactory explanation for what caused the differences.

Sources of Economic Aggregates

There are numerous sources of economic data. The most often used data are published by the U.S. government, the two most prolific sources being the Bureau of Economic Analysis (BEA) of the U.S. Department of Commerce, and the U.S. Department of Labor. The BEA gathers data on GDP and its various components. The U.S. Department of Labor publishes a variety of labor market data, such as total employment and the unemployment rate, as well as various measures of inflation including the consumer price index (CPI) and the producer price index (PPI). Among the government websites that can be used as data sources are: http://www.federalreserve.gov (Federal Reserve Bank), http://www.dallasfed.org (Federal Reserve Bank of Dallas), http://www.doc.gov (Commerce Department), and http://www.dol.gov (Labor Department). The labor market data can be a useful complement to the data published by the BEA. It allows us to see the impact on economic activity of the number of workers in a given area. The labor market data are often available in narrowly defined regional segments, which is helpful when narrowing the analysis to the regional level. In addition, labor market data are released monthly and are often some of the most current data available.

Quantifying the Strength of the Relationship between Selected Economic Aggregates and Firm Performance

The closeness of the association among these economic aggregates and the revenues of the plaintiff can be quantitatively measured using the correlation analysis that was discussed in Chapter 2. This analysis can be important to consider because it bolsters the economic theory that the economist presents. For example, the expert can say that a retail firm's revenues for the years 1986–87 should

have risen because the economy was expanding as reflected by the fact that national income, consumer expenditures, and retail sales were all rising (See
Table 3.4). The economist can go on to elaborate that the economy was in the
longest postwar expansion in U.S. economic history. It may be even more compelling, for example, to state that 48% of the variation in the sales of the plaintiff
could be explained by variation in national retail sales. A correlation analysis allows such percentages to be derived through the computation of what is known
as the *coefficient of determination,* which is the square of the correlation coefficient. It represents the proportion of the total variation in the dependent variable,
such as the plaintiff's sales, that is explained by, or is accounted for by, variations in selected independent variables such as the national retail sales depicted
in Figures 3.8 and 3.9. This further establishes the importance of considering
these specific economic aggregates.

Nominal versus Real Values

Economists are typically more concerned about variations in real values as opposed to nominal values. When the inflationary component of an increase in an
economic variable, such as GDP, is filtered out, the resulting value is called a
real value. While real values are the appropriate measures to focus on when try-

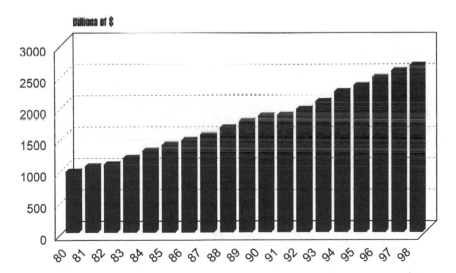

Figure 3.8.   National retail sales.
(Source: U.S. Department of Commerce, Bureau of Economic Analysis, Washington, D.C.)

Table 3.4. Nominal GDP, Retail Sales, and Personal Income

Year	Gross Domestic Product (Billions of $) Nominal	Percent Change (%)	Real (Chained 1992 $)	Percent Change (%)	Retail Sales (Billions of $) Nominal	Percent Change (%)	Real (Chained 1992 $)	Percent Change (%)	Personal Income (Billions of $) Nominal	Percent Change (%)	Real (Chained 1992 $)	Percent Change (%)
1980	2,784.2		4,615.0		9,56.9		1,458.0		2,293.0		3,919.9	
1981	3,115.9	11.91	4,720.7	2.29	1,038.2	8.47	1,463.8	0.40	2,568.5	12.01	4,030.1	2.81
1982	3,242.1	4.05	4,620.3	-2.13	1,068.8	2.95	1,449.4	-0.98	2,727.2	6.18	4,046.7	0.41
1983	3,514.5	8.40	4,803.7	3.97	1,170.2	9.49	1,557.5	7.46	2,900.8	6.37	4,116.9	1.74
1984	3,902.4	11.04	5,140.1	7.00	1,286.9	9.97	1,668.7	7.14	3,215.3	10.84	4,396.2	6.78
1985	4,180.7	7.13	5,323.5	3.57	1,375.0	6.85	1,741.9	4.39	3,449.8	7.29	4,549.2	3.48
1986	4,422.2	5.78	5,487.7	3.08	1,449.6	5.43	1,838.7	5.56	3,658.4	6.05	4,690.7	3.11
1987	4,692.3	6.11	5,649.5	2.95	1,541.3	6.33	1,890.7	2.83	3,888.7	6.30	4,803.2	2.40
1988	5,049.6	7.61	5,865.2	3.82	1,656.2	7.46	1,969.0	4.14	4,184.6	7.61	4,963.1	3.33
1989	5,438.7	7.71	6,062.0	3.36	1,759.0	6.21	2,012.3	2.20	4,501.0	7.56	5,089.5	2.55
1990	5,743.8	5.61	6,136.3	1.23	1,844.6	4.87	2,024.4	0.60	4,804.2	6.74	5,170.7	1.60
1991	5,916.7	3.01	6,079.4	-0.93	1,855.9	0.61	1,974.4	-2.47	4,981.6	3.69	5,145.3	-0.49
1992	6,244.4	5.54	6,244.4	2.71	1,951.6	5.16	2,037.4	3.19	5,277.2	5.93	5,277.2	2.56
1993	6,558.1	5.02	6,389.6	2.33	2,073.8	6.26	2,129.5	4.52	5,519.2	4.59	5,376.0	1.87
1994	6,947.0	5.93	6,610.7	3.46	2,229.9	7.53	2,250.4	5.68	5,791.8	4.94	5,508.0	2.46
1995	7,265.4	4.58	6,742.1	1.99	2,329.3	4.46	2,309.4	2.62	6,150.8	6.20	5,701.2	3.51
1996	7,636.0	5.10	6,928.4	2.76	2,461.2	5.66	2,395.6	3.73	6,495.2	5.60	5,879.8	3.13
1997	8,083.4	5.86	7,191.4	3.80	2,566.2	4.27	2,491.4	4.00	6,784.0	4.45	6,099.2	3.73
1998	8,511.0	5.29	7,551.9	5.01					7,126.1	5.04		
Average		6.43		2.79		6.00		3.24		6.52		2.65

Source: U.S. Department of Commerce, Bureau of Economic Analysis, Washington, D.C.

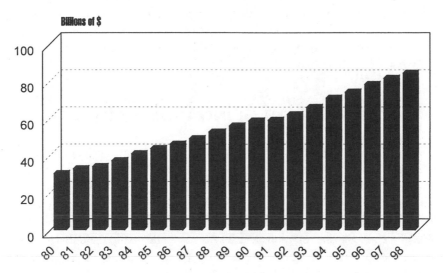

Figure 3.9.   Firm retail sales.
(Source: U.S. Department of Commerce, Bureau of Economic Analysis, Washington, D.C.)

ing to assess the economic progress of an economy, they may not always be the appropriate measures to use when conducting a commercial damages analysis. The plaintiff may have lost the actual unadjusted values and the real values may be less relevant to the loss measurement process. If a comparison is being made to the growth of the plaintiff's revenues relative to selected economic variables, then the nominal macroeconomic aggregates are more relevant to compare with revenues. In an inflationary environment, the growth rates derived from an analysis of the variation in these nominal values also reveal higher growth rates than what would be derived from an analysis of a real time series.

If the expert, however, is merely trying to assess the level of economic activity, then an analysis of real values, such as real GDP, is more relevant because the National Bureau of Economic Research uses such real variables to determine business cycle dating. Merely looking at unadjusted nominal values may obfuscate the real decline in the economic time series. Both real and nominal values have a place in an economic loss analysis. The real values are used to isolate the time periods when demand is slowing. In such time periods, even though a firm may experience an increase in sales, costs may rise even more so that the company is losing ground or experiencing an erosion in its margins.

When constructing a projection of revenues during an affected loss period, greater weight is placed on the rates of growth in the nominal values of the selected macroeconomic aggregates. When one considers that the plaintiff has lost nominal profits and is attempting to be compensated in nominal terms, it becomes obvious that growth rates in nominal series must be used in forecasting whereas real values need to be considered in conducting an analysis of economic fluctuations (See Table 3.4).

OVERSTATEMENT OF INFLATION STATISTICS

Economists have known for some time that the inflation statistics put forward by the Bureau of Labor Statistics overstate the true rate of inflation. These statistics are constructed using what is known as a *Laspeyres Index*. This type of index compares the value of a variable in a specific year with that of a preselected base year. In the case of the CPI, the most often cited inflation measure, the dollar value of a market basket of goods and services is compared to the dollar value in the selected base year. As of the date of this publication, the year 1992 is used as the base year to convert nominal amounts into real terms.

The consumer price index is only one of several different price indices used by economists. Another index is the PPI, which is designed to deflate goods that producers, as opposed to consumers, buy. In addition, various different CPIs are used to deflate a more narrow group of products and services such as the CPI for wages. Many categories of goods and services have their own specific deflators that are available from the Bureau of Labor Statistics.

One of the drawbacks of the CPI is that it does not take into account the substitution effect whereby consumers would switch to less expensive substitutes when prices of certain goods rise. The CPI keeps the market basket the same in both years, so the true market basket, after some substitution to less expensive products, costs less than what the CPI would report. Other flaws of the CPI include not taking into account qualitative differences in products over time. Products such as computers improve substantially over time so that a computer bought for $3,000 may be of significantly greater quality than one sold five or six years earlier for the same price. Other factors ignored in the traditional CPI are discount buying trends that result in lower prices for certain products.

The report of the Advisory Commission to Study the Consumer Price Index headed by Dr. Michael Boskin, chairman of the Council of Economic Advisors, concluded that the Consumer Price Index, which was approximately 3% in 1996, the year of the report, may be overstated by as much as 1.1% per year.[6] This im-

---

[6] Michael Boskin, Ellen R. Dulberger, Robert J. Gordon, Zvi Griliches, and Dale Jorgenson, "Toward a More Accurate Measure of the Cost of Living," Final Report of the

plies that the inflation rate in that year might be below 2%. The authors of the Boskin report have admitted that many of the adjustments they have made were subjective judgments on factors such as qualitative improvements. In making such judgments they have, in effect, created more of a cost of living index than a true price index.

The overstatement of the CPI is important because once the correction to the true rate of inflation is made, the difference between nominal and real values becomes less significant. This, combined with the anti-inflation policy begun by the Federal Reserve in 1980, has kept the inflation rate to around 3% as of the mid-1990s, prior to the adjustment for the overstatement (See Table 3.5).

While the Boskin Commission has quantitatively measured the overstatement of the CPI, a fact that has been widely discussed for many years prior to the Commission's report, the Bureau of Labor Statistics, the publishers of the price index, has not accepted the conclusions of the Commission. Therefore, as of the date of this publication, there is no agreement on the exact amount of the overstatement. This fact is important because the price index is responsible for the exact size of the gap between real and nominal values. Fortunately, inflation has

Table 3.5. Inflation Using the Unadjusted CPI: 1970–98

Year	Inflation Rate (%)	Year	Inflation Rate (%)	Year	Inflation Rate (%)
1970	5.72	1980	13.50	1990	5.40
1971	4.38	1981	10.32	1991	4.21
1972	3.21	1982	6.16	1992	3.01
1973	6.22	1983	3.21	1993	2.99
1974	11.04	1984	4.32	1994	2.56
1975	9.13	1985	3.56	1995	2.83
1976	5.76	1986	1.86	1996	2.95
1977	6.50	1987	3.65	1997	2.29
1978	7.59	1988	4.14	1998	1.56
1979	11.34	1989	4.02		

Averages

1970–80	7.67
1980–90	5.54
1990–98	3.09
1970–98	5.32

Source: U.S. Department of Commerce, Bureau of Economic Analysis, Washington, D.C.

Advisory Commission to Study the Consumer Price Index to the Senate Finance Committee, December 4, 1996.

been maintaining itself at lower levels in recent years, making the size of any overstatement less significant.

OTHER MEASURES OF INFLATION

Although it is the most often cited, the consumer price index is not the only measure of inflation. Two other often cited measures are the producer price index and the *GDP deflator.*[7] The producer price index shows the average level of prices for goods sold by producers. It is sometimes used as an indicator of what is going to happen to consumer prices based on the idea that increases in producer prices may, to varying degrees, be passed on to consumers.

Regional Economic Trends

The fact that there are unique regional differences within a national economy is a well-established proposition within the field of regional economics or what is sometimes also called urban economics.[8] However, although there are many practitioners in the field of regional economics, the published literature contains few textbooks.[9] Nonetheless, the field is an established one with many practitioners and reliable data sources.

When the economy expands, not all regions of the country participate equally in this expansion. For example, California entered the 1990–91 national recession after many other parts of the country. However, the recession in California and the Northeast lasted longer than other regions of the country, such as the Midwest. For companies whose markets are mainly regional, where firms derive most or all of their sales from a particular region, this factor can be important. The macroeconomic analysis then needs to be narrowed to focus on the overall level of economic activity within a particular region.

Many of the data sources available on the national level are also available on a regional level. State governmental agencies, as well as private sources, supply

---

[7] For a good introductory explanation of the use of various price indices see Joseph Stiglitz, *Economics,* 2nd ed., (New York: W.W. Norton & Company) 1997, 580–586.

[8] Edwin S. Mills and Bruce W. Hamilton, *Urban Economics* 5th ed., (New York: Harper Collins College Publishers) 1994.

[9] One such book which seeks to apply a Keynesian approach to regional economic modeling is George Trcyz, *Regional Economic Modeling: Economic Forecasting and Analysis* (Norwell, Mass.: Kluwer Academic Publishers), 1993.

a variety of regional data. Using such data, the economist can observe the trends in regional economic aggregates and investigate the relationship between the plaintiff's sales and the variation in the regional aggregates. Regional aggregates, such as state retail sales (see Figures 3.10, 3.11, 3.12, and 3.13) can be included with the overall macroeconomic framework to put the variation in the plaintiff's sales during the alleged loss period in the proper macroeconomic context. For example, if all of the national and regional aggregates were expanding during the loss period and the plaintiff's sales, which normally move with the variation in these aggregates, moved sharply in the opposite direction, then an explanation other than the level of economic demand needs to be explored. Conversely, when dealing with more of a regional business, and when there is a significant difference between the performance of the regional versus the national economy, there may be a basis for placing more weight on the regional economic data and less on the national data.

Quality and Timeliness of Regional Economic Data

As the geographic region narrows, however, the availability and quality of the economic data may decline. Some data, such as gross state product, are not available from the Commerce Department on a timely basis and may be several years

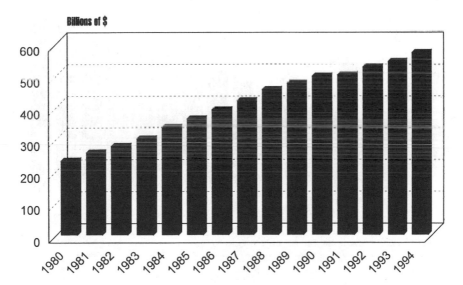

Figure 3.10. New York gross state product.
(Source: U.S. Deparatment of Commerce, Beureau of Economic Analysis, Washington, D.C.)

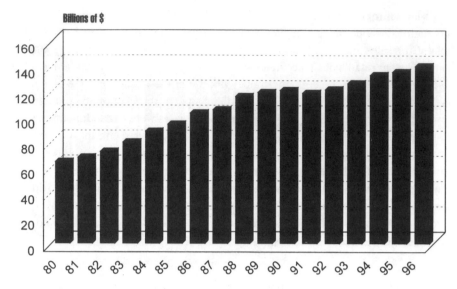

Figure 3.11. New York retail sales.
(Source: U.S. Department of Commerce, Bureau of Economic Analysis, Washington, D.C.)

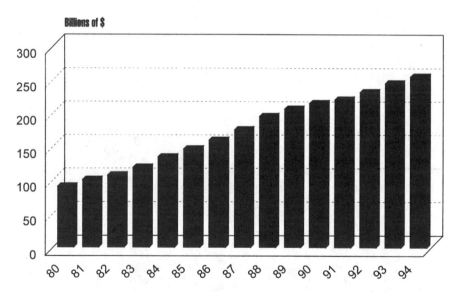

Figure 3.12. New Jersey gross state product.
(Source: U.S. Department of Commerce, Bureau of Economic Analysis, Washington, D.C.)

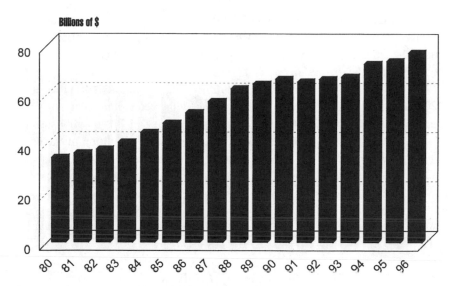

Figure 3.13. New Jersey retail sales.
(Source: U.S. Department of Commerce, Bureau of Economic Analysis, Washington, D.C.)

behind their national counterparts. Lacking access to aggregates such as consumption expenditures, the economist may substitute other closely varying time series such as retail sales, which are available on a more timely basis. This substitution process must be handled on a case-by-case basis and is often influenced by factors such as the nature of the product at issue.

Certain regional economic data are generally available on a timely basis, including employment data produced by the U.S. Department of Labor. Typically, employment data are the most timely and are even available for certain industry subcategories. They also can be used as a guide to the performance of certain sectors for which timely data may not be available. For example, construction employment data are available on a fairly timely basis for specific regions such as states. These data can be used as a guide to the performance of that industry. Although this may not be exactly what the economist would like to have, it is an additional piece of information that may be helpful.

Regional Data Sources

Certain governmental agencies publish some regional economic data. For example, the New Jersey Department of Labor issues a publication called *Economic Indicators* which includes a variety of economic data for the State of New Jersey and its various counties. These data include labor market data as well as other economic data that the New Jersey Department of Labor gathers from other vendors. Other state departments of labor publish data related to this region although most are not as detailed as this publication.

The various Federal Reserve banks publish monthly reports and newsletters on the condition of the regional economy and other economic issues such as monetary policy. For example the Federal Reserve Bank of Boston publishes the *New England Economic Indicators,* which focuses on the condition of the economy in New England. The Federal Reserve Bank of Kansas City publishes a similar report called *Regional Economic Digest.* The various Federal Reserve banks also have websites that can be useful sources of timely data. However, the multiple sources of data notwithstanding, the quantity of timely data is significantly less at the regional level than it is on the national level.

Subregional Analysis

Regional economic analysis is usually done for a broad economic region, such as a geographic area like the Northeast, or multistate areas such as the Tri-State region that includes New York, New Jersey and Connecticut, or for specific states. However, economic data are also often analyzed according to standard metropolitan statistical areas (SMSAs).

In the case of losses of small businesses, regional analysis can be further narrowed within the state economy to focus on cities, counties, towns, or even neighborhoods. It is often possible to get some economic data, such as retail sales and employment data, on the county level (see Table 3.6 and Figures 3.14, 3.15, 3.16 and 3.17). This is important because a national and state economy could be booming while a town's economy could be depressed due, for example, to the exit of key businesses. In this case, using state data, as opposed to more narrowly focused economic data, could present a misleading picture.

The problems of quality and timeliness tend to increase as the region under study narrows. This is ironic because much of the aggregate data are compilations of the various disaggregated components. Nonetheless, the more disaggregated the data are, the more problems might arise.

CAUTION ON USING ECONOMIC
GROWTH RATE DATA TOO DIRECTLY

It is important to know what the growth of the economy, and the more narrowly defined segments of it, was during the loss period. These growth rates should be

Table 3.6.   Economic Data for Morris County, New Jersey

| | Morris County 1980–1997 | | |
Year	Unemployment Rate (%)	Personal Income (Per Capita)	Retail Sales ("000 $")	Population ("000")
1980	4.8	13,672	1,929,218	409.2
1981	5.0	15,390	2,184,363	411.1
1982	6.6	16,606	2,223,881	414.2
1983	5.3	18,141	2,650,685	417.7
1984	3.7	20,170	2,765,050	421.9
1985	3.6	21,854	3,025,438	426.0
1986	3.2	23,617	3,297,566	426.0
1987	2.5	25,769	3,428,230	427.1
1988	2.3	28,391	3,580,754	428.6
1989	2.7	30,323	4,100,308	424.0
1990	3.2	31,747	4,248,388	422.2
1991	4.9	32,240	4,289,744	423.7
1992	6.3	34,549	4,693,086	423.8
1993	5.7	36,489	4,777,070	431.0
1994	5.0	37,182	5,034,782	441.5
1995	4.3	39,179	4,964,416	445.8
1996	4.0	NA	4,994,502	451.8
1997	3.5	NA	NA	NA

Source: N.J. Department of Labor; U.S. Department of Commerce; Bureau of the Census

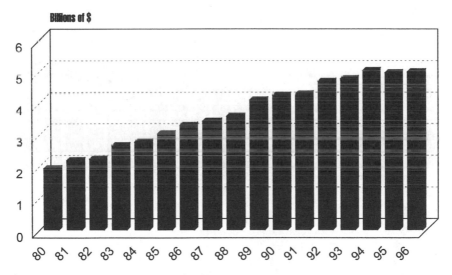

Figure 3.14.   Morris County retail sales.
(Source: N.J. Department of Labor)

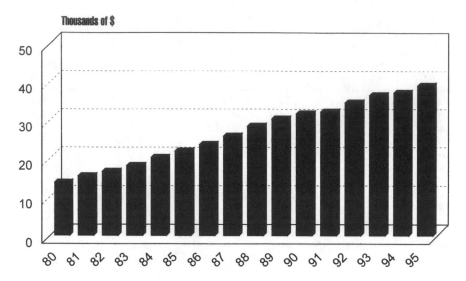

Figure 3.15. Morris County per capita personal income.
(Source: N.J. Department of Labor)

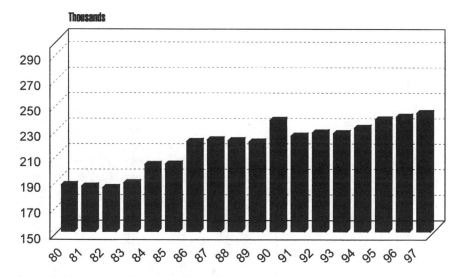

Figure 3.16. Morris County total employment.
(Source: N.J. Department of Labor)

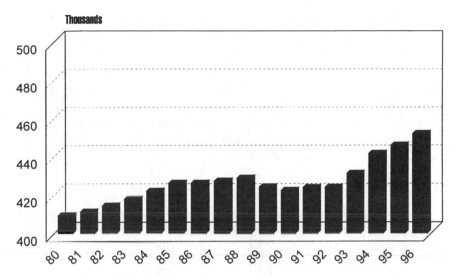

Figure 3.17. Morris County population.
(Source: N.J. Department of Labor)

measured and compared to the historical growth of the revenues or profits of the plaintiff. One must be careful, however, not to blindly attribute the growth of the relevant segment of the economy to the growth of the plaintiff. That is, it does not necessarily follow that if the segment of the national or regional economy was growing at 3% per year during the loss period, then the plaintiff's revenues should also have grown at a 3% annual rate during the loss period. One may want to prepare a table showing the relevant variables, and the changes in their absolute values as well as the percentage changes. These percentage changes can then be averaged over different time periods. Only when the expert has quantitatively established that the association between the plaintiff's business and the economy is so close that the economic growth rates can be used to estimate the growth of the plaintiff, can they be used in this manner. However, it may be easier to simply say that when the economy was growing, the plaintiff's revenues, for example, also grew. Then if during the loss period the economy continued to grow but the plaintiff's business fell significantly, the plaintiff may be one step further along to proving its damages.

INTERNATIONAL ECONOMIC ANALYSIS

For some type of commercial damages analysis, the focus of the economic analysis may need to be widened, rather than narrowed, even beyond the national level. If the plaintiff derived its demand from an international source, that area may have to be focused on. For example, if a U.S. plaintiff derives its sales from a specific country or group of countries outside the United States, the performance of those economies may need to be analyzed. A review of the performance of different national economies can quickly reveal that not all countries grow at the same rate. For example, when the United States economy started to recover and grow after its recession during 1990–91, the Japanese economy, the international economic star of the 1980s, was stagnant and experienced the pains of a recession as shown in Figure 3.18.

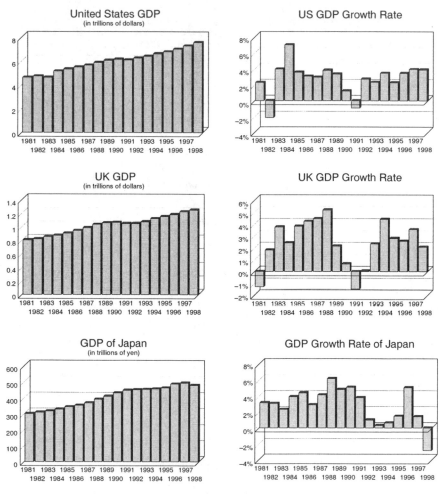

Figure 3.18. U.S. and Japan GDP and their respective growth rates.

For companies that have lost sales that would have been generated in a currency other than U.S. dollars, a currency conversion may need to be made. For historical losses, the historical conversion rates may need to be used to convert the foreign currency into dollars. These statistics are readily available from a variety of sources. For projection of future losses, the value of the respective currencies may need to be taken into account.

The field of international economics is a separate subfield within economics. Economists who work in the field of international economics and who publish in the field's specific journals may not work in other areas. It is common for economists in the field of international economics to focus or specialize on the economies of a specific country or group of countries. In cases that involve international economics, it may be useful to bring in a specialist in international economics who specializes in the economies of the countries in question. However, given that the field of litigation economics and the measurement of commercial damages are also separate subfields of economics, it is likely that the international economist may lack experience in litigation and the techniques of measuring damages. Therefore, such a specialist would be an expert who is brought on to the litigation support team and who works at the direction of the economist who is conducting the loss analysis. That economist will stipulate the method of measuring damages and the damages loss model. As part of that process, certain tasks may be delegated to the international economist who will hand off his or her output to the primary litigation economist. Depending on the issues involved it may also be useful to have both an economist and an accountant, using the interdisciplinary approach advocated in this book, as well as international counterparts for each to deal with relevant international economic and accounting issues. Obviously, the size of the case as well as the international orientation of the issues has to justify having such a group of experts involved

MACROECONOMIC AND REGIONAL ECONOMIC ANALYSIS AND THE BEFORE AND AFTER METHOD

A macroeconomic and regional economic analysis can be an invaluable ingredient to an application of the before and after method. The macroeconomic and regional analysis (when relevant) establishes the economic environment during the before period and compares it to the after period. Differences in the economic environment may explain why the before period should be different from the after period. For example, if the economy was booming during the before period and the plaintiff's revenues also grew rapidly during this period but during the loss period the economy fell into a recession, then the declining performance of the economy may explain some or all of the losses of the plaintiff. The expert should have done some statistical analysis to assess the historical comovement of the plaintiff's revenues and profits relative to the economy. If there was a good amount of cyclical covariation between the economy and the plaintiff, then one might expect declining performance when the economy falters.

When there is reason to believe that the plaintiff's losses are jointly attributable to both the economic decline as well as the actions of the defendant, the analysis can become more complicated. The expert has to filter out the influence of the economy and find out what portion of the losses is attributable to the economy and what portion to the defendant. The defendant may want to argue that all of the plaintiff's losses are attributable to the economy. In such cases, the joint application of the before and after method along with the yardstick approach may be helpful. The yardstick approach may enable the expert to see how similar businesses have declined during the economic downturn. If similar businesses only experienced a mild decline while the plaintiff experienced a precipitous falloff, then there may be a basis for determining what part of the total falloff in the plaintiff's business was attributable to the actions of the plaintiff. The average decline of similar firms *may* serve as a guide to what component is attributable to the economy.

SUMMARY

This chapter introduced the first step in the methodological due diligence process of measuring commercial damages, the analysis of the macroeconomy. In doing this analysis the expert assembles a variety of macroeconomic aggregates starting with gross domestic product and then narrows the focus more directly on the part of the macroeconomy that most directly relates to the business of the plaintiff. In doing this analysis, the expert analyzes the strength of the relationship between changes in the selected macroeconomic aggregates and the plaintiff's revenues and profits. Statistical measures such as the correlation coefficient can be used to measure the closeness or association between the performance of the macroeconomy and the performance of the plaintiff.

Among the uses for the macroeconomic analysis is to determine the extent to which the performance of the economy may have been responsible for the losses of the plaintiff. Conversely, if the economy was doing well, past experience, as assessed by the aforementioned statistical analysis, may create an expectation that the plaintiff would have realized a certain level of revenue and profit growth, while instead it incurred losses. In this case macroeconomic analysis may be an important first step in the economic damages analysis.

After having done the broad-based macroeconomic analysis, the focus may be narrowed to the regional level if the plaintiff was mainly a regional business or if the losses at issue are restricted to a specific region of the country. In this part of the analysis regional economic aggregates are used in a similar manner as they were used for the macroeconomic analysis. Unfortunately, the quantity and timeliness of regional economic data is not as good as it is on the macro level.

The macroeconomic framework sets forth the overall economic environment that the plaintiff and defendant were operating within at the time of the alleged losses. It can be used to find other possible causes of the plaintiff's losses such as an economic downturn. It can also be used to create an expectation of gains instead of losses that are the focus of the litigation, when the economy was doing well in the loss period and when the macroeconomic analysis has shown that the plaintiff has done well in such economic conditions. The macroeconomic analysis is an important first step in the overall damages process. Once it has been done, the next step is to analyze the industry within which the plaintiff was operating.

REFERENCES

Boskin, Michael, Ellen R. Dulberger, Robert J. Gordon, Zvi Griliches, and Dale Jorgenson, "Toward a More Accurate Measure of the Cost of Living," *Final Report of the Advisory Commission to Study the Consumer Price Index to the Senate Finance Committee,* December 4, 1996.

Case, Karl E., and Ray C. Fair, *Principles of Economics,* 5th ed., (Englewood Cliffs, N.J.: Prentice Hall, 1999).

Gordon, Robert, *Macroeconomics,* 6th ed. (New York: Harper Collins, 1993).

Kydland, Finn and Edward C. Prescott, "Time to Build and Aggregate Fluctuations," *Econometrica* 50 (November) 1982.

Mills, Edwin, S and Bruce W. Hamilton, *Urban Economics,* 5th ed. (New York: Harper Collins, 1994).

Stiglitz, Joseph, *Economics,* 2nd ed. (New York: W.W. Norton & Company, 1997).

Taylor, John, *Economics,* 2nd ed. (New York: Houghton Mifflin Company, 1998).

Treyz, George, *Regional Economic Modeling: Economic Forecasting and Analysis,* (Norwell, Mass.: Kluwer Academic Publishers, 1993).

4

INDUSTRY ANALYSIS

An industry analysis is often an integral part of the overall commercial damages analysis. As part of the due diligence process in measuring commercial damages, the expert must research and analyze the economics of the plaintiff's industry. Typically, the economic expert does not specialize in the plaintiff's industry. Depending on the facts and nature of the case, the expert may have to do research on industry trends as well as other factors relevant to the litigation at hand. This process may involve gathering industry data and statistics. Standards tools of economic analysis may be employed to conduct this industry analysis.

Industry analysis draws on the subfield within microeconomics known as *industrial organization,* the study of the structure of an industry and the interaction of companies within that industry. Among the topics covered in this field are the level of competition and the determination of prices and quantities in a given industry. Although industrial organization is a broad field covering many issues that would not be relevant to a litigation-oriented industry analysis, the field does provide some useful tools of analysis that may be appropriate to the case.

There are two main sources of industry data: government and private. Depending on the industry being studied, these data sources can vary significantly in terms of their quality and availability. It is important for the expert to research the specific source and determine how the data was gathered and whether they are reliable. The reliability of industry data sources can vary greatly.

GOVERNMENT SOURCES OF INDUSTRY DATA

The main government data source is the U.S. Department of Commerce. Much of the Commerce Department's data is gathered by the U.S. Bureau of the Census (http://www.census.gov). Unfortunately, there have been significant expenditure cutbacks at the Commerce Department, as a result of which data are not as readily available, and some data sources have been discontinued. One often-cited data source is the *U.S. Industrial Outlook*. This useful publication was temporarily discontinued by the Commerce Department after the 1994 edition. However, it is now being published by DRI/McGraw-Hill and Standard and Poor's and U.S. Department of Commerce/International Trade Administration.[1] The *U.S. Industrial Outlook* is an annual publication that contains detailed data on shipments, revenues, and employment by industry category along with a narrative discussion on recent trends in the industry. Where relevant, a breakdown by subindustry categories is also available. Most industries covered contain the names and telephone numbers of staff at the Commerce Department who regularly studied that particular industry. These individuals can be most valuable to the expert because they can provide the expert with useful information beyond what appears in the *U.S. Industrial Outlook*. In addition, each industry section ends with a bibliography that usually indicates the names of industry associations or other industry publications where one could go for further information. Figure 4.1 is a sample of some of the data that appears in the *U.S. Industrial Outlook*.

Alternatives to the *U.S. Industrial Outlook* are two other Commerce Department publications: the *Statistical Abstract of the United States* and *Business Statistics of the United States*.[2] Unlike the *U.S. Industrial Outlook*, the *Statistical Abstract of the United States* only includes data and does not have any discussion. The experienced analyst, however, can use these data along with other available data sources to conduct a thorough industry analysis. The *Statistical Abstract of the United States* contains much valuable statistical data on a wide variety of topics beyond just industry data, such as demographic and economic data that may be used in other parts of a commercial damages analysis. A sample of how the data included in the *Statistical Abstract of the United States* appear is shown in Figure 4.2.

Business Statistics of the United States is actually a private data source that features government data. It has some limited narrative and does not have the industry-by-industry description of recent trends that the *U.S. Industrial Outlook* had. Much of the data in *Business Statistics of the United States* is general eco

---

[1] *U.S. Industrial Outlook,* annual, U.S. Department of Commerce/International Trade Administration, Washington D.C., and *U.S. Industry and Trade Outlook '98,* DRI/McGraw-Hill and Standard and Poor's and U.S. Department of Commerce/International Trade Administration.

[2] *Statistical Abstract of the United States,* annual, U.S. Department of Commerce, Washington D.C. and *Business Statistics of the United States,* annual, Courtenay M. Slater, ed. Lanham, Md.: Bernan Press. The latter is based on another Commerce Department publication, *Business Statistics,* which is also no longer available.

Figure 4.1. Sample of data in *U.S. Industrial Outlook.*

Paper and Allied Products (SIC 26) Trends and Forecasts (millions of dollars, except as noted)

	1989	1992	1993	1994	1995	1996[1]	1997[1]	1998[2]	Percent Change			
									95–96	96–97	97–98	89–96[3]
Industry Data												
Value of Shipments[4]	131,895	133,201	133,262	143,649	172,638	164,869	168,331	176,917	−4.5	2.1	5.1	3.2
Value of Shipments ($92)	128,783	133,201	135,076	141,329	141,416	138,305	140,795	144,456	−2.2	1.8	2.6	1.0
Total Employment (000)	633	627	626	622	630							
Production Workers (000)	486	479	479	480	486							
Average Hourly Earnings ($)	12.66	13.81	14.09	14.52	14.74							
Capital Expenditures	9,579	7,963	7,370	7,731	8,219							
Product Data												
Value of Shipments[4]	127,266	128,941	128,695	138,540	166,827	159,320	162,978	171,290	−4.5	2.3	5.1	3.3
Value of Shipments ($92)	123,886	128,941	130,568	136,386	136,292	133,296	135,421	138,943	−2.2	1.6	2.6	1.1
Trade Data												
Exports	8,154	10,042	9,457	11,000	14,943	14,002	14,772	15,880	−6.3	5.5	7.5	8.0
Imports	11,935	10,461	10,891	11,772	16,757	14,784	14,193	14,974	−11.8	24.0	5.5	3.1

[1] Estimate
[2] Forecast
[3] Compound annual rate
[4] For definition of industry versus product values, see "Getting the Most Out of Outlook '98"
Source: U.S. Department of Commerce: Bureau of the Census, International Trade Administration

Figure 4.2. Sample of *Statistical Abstract of the United States* Data.

Average Hourly Earnings of Production Workers in Manufacturing Industries, by State: 1980 to 1996 (in dollars)

State	1980	1990	1994	1995	1996
United States	7.27	10.83	12.07	12.37	12.78
Alabama	6.49	9.39	10.75	11.14	11.53
Alaska	10.22	12.46	10.96	11.00	11.14
Arizona	7.29	10.21	11.17	11.16	11.49
Arkansas	5.71	8.51	9.65	10.05	10.41
California	7.70	11.48	12.44	12.55	12.83
Colorado	7.63	10.94	12.26	12.51	12.82
Connecticut	7.08	11.53	13.53	13.71	14.01
Delaware	7.58	12.39	13.92	14.20	14.00
District of Columbia	8.46	12.51	13.46	13.66	13.68
Florida	5.98	8.98	9.97	10.18	10.54
Georgia	5.77	9.77	10.34	10.71	11.17
Hawaii	6.83	10.99	12.22	12.82	12.79
Idaho	7.55	10.60	11.88	11.46	12.15
Illinois	8.02	11.44	12.25	12.64	13.03
Indiana	8.49	12.03	13.55	13.91	14.33
Iowa	8.67	11.27	12.45	12.73	13.13
Kansas	7.37	10.94	12.15	12.39	12.88
Kentucky	7.34	10.70	11.81	12.22	12.70
Louisiana	7.74	11.61	13.11	13.43	13.66
Maine	6.00	10.59	11.91	12.39	12.71
Maryland	7.61	11.57	13.15	13.49	13.71
Massachusetts	6.51	11.39	12.59	12.79	13.04
Michigan	9.52	13.36	16.13	16.31	16.67
Minnesota	7.61	11.23	12.58	12.79	13.18
Mississippi	5.44	8.37	9.41	9.76	10.19

State	1980	1990	1994	1995	1996
Missouri	7.26	10.74	11.77	12.16	12.54
Montana	8.78	11.51	12.49	12.94	13.00
Nebraska	7.38	9.66	10.94	11.19	11.51
Nevada	7.72	11.05	11.83	12.62	13.59
New Hampshire	5.87	10.83	11.74	11.94	12.24
New Jersey	7.31	11.76	13.36	13.56	13.86
New Mexico	5.79	9.04	10.13	10.68	10.97
New York	7.18	11.11	12.19	12.50	12.78
North Carolina	5.37	8.79	10.19	10.56	10.96
North Dakota	6.56	9.27	10.19	10.75	10.94
Ohio	8.57	12.64	14.40	14.42	14.69
Oklahoma	7.36	10.73	11.42	11.52	11.77
Oregon	8.65	11.15	12.31	12.75	13.01
Pennsylvania	7.59	11.04	12.49	12.81	13.39
Rhode Island	5.59	9.45	10.35	10.62	10.94
South Carolina	5.59	8.84	10.00	10.16	10.26
South Dakota	6.50	8.48	9.19	9.36	9.59
Tennessee	6.08	9.55	10.50	10.78	11.28
Texas	7.15	10.47	11.13	11.47	11.82
Utah	7.02	10.32	11.28	11.62	12.22
Vermont	6.14	10.52	11.96	12.21	12.42
Virginia	6.22	10.07	11.24	11.72	12.19
Washington	(NA)	12.61	14.86	14.73	14.70
West Virginia	8.08	11.53	12.60	12.64	12.96
Wisconsin	8.03	11.11	12.41	12.76	13.14
Wyoming	7.01	10.83	11.79	11.96	13.16

NA: Not available.
Source: U.S. Bureau of Labor Statistics, *Employment and Earnings*, monthly.

nomic data although there is some broad categorized industry data such as that shown in Figure 4.3.

The government data sources are good starting points from which to begin an industry analysis. However, the detail needed to complete a thorough analysis may not be sufficient for the litigation expert to put forward a reliable and non-speculative opinion on damages. The expert may then have to gather more detailed data, which can often be done by contacting the U.S. Department of Commerce directly. Often the expert will want to get copies of the relevant sections of the *Annual Survey of Manufactures,* which is gathered by the U.S. Bureau of the Census.[3] The *Annual Survey of Manufactures* provides industry data for those intercensal periods that occur between the various census surveys that the Bureau of the Census takes every five years. Data are gathered from a representative sample of approximately 55,000 manufacturing establishments. These data include statistics on employment, hours, payroll, value added by the manufacturer, capital expenditures, materials costs, end-of-year inventories, and value of industry shipments. The last variable, value of industry shipments, is usually the most useful of the data included in the survey. A sample of how the data are displayed in the *Annual Survey of Manufactures* is shown in Figure 4.4.

Industry data in the *Annual Survey of Manufactures* are organized using Standard Industrial Classification (SIC) codes. This is often the case for both government and private data sources. Knowing a business's SIC code can enable the expert to more quickly locate industry data. Therefore, it is useful to understand this classification system.

STANDARD INDUSTRIAL CLASSIFICATION CODES

The SIC codes are assigned to specific industry and product lines according to a classification system that was designed by the federal government's Office of Management and Budget.[4] The system was first developed in the 1930s and has been periodically revised, with the last revision taking place in 1987. Industries are classified broadly using two-digit groups or more narrowly using three- or four-digit groups. The four-digit numbers range from 0000 to 9999 with the range 2000 to 3999 reserved for the manufacturing sector. The digit 9 that may appear in the third or fourth position of the classification code usually designates

---

[3] *Annual Survey of Manufactures,* U.S. Bureau of the Census, Washington, D.C.

[4] *SIC Code Manual,* U.S. Government Printing Office, 1987, Washington, D.C.

Figure 4.3. Sample of *Business Statistics of the United States.*

Manufacturers' Shipments, Inventories, and Orders: 1950 to 1996 (in billions of dollars, except ratio)

Year	Shipments	Inventories (Dec. 31)[1]	Ratio of inventories to shipments[2]	New orders	Unfilled orders (Dec. 31)
1950	224	32	1.4?	242	41
1951	261	39	1.78	287	67
1952	270	42	1.7?	279	76
1953	298	44	1.90	283	60
1954	280	42	1.71	268	48
1955	318	45	1.63	330	60
1956	333	51	1.74	340	68
1957	345	52	1.90	331	53
1958	327	50	1.75	324	47
1959	363	53	1.63	369	52
1960	371	54	1.79	363	45
1961	371	55	1.67	373	47
1962	400	58	1.75	401	48
1963	421	60	1.65	426	53
1964	448	63	1.62	460	65
1965	492	68	1.58	505	79
1966	538	78	1.70	557	97
1967	558	84	1.71	565	104
1968	603	90	1.76	608	110
1969	642	98	1.81	647	115
1970	634	101	1.91	625	106
1971	671	102	1.76	672	107
1972	756	108	1.58	770	120
1973	875	124	1.63	913	158
1974	1,018	158	1.86	1,047	187
1975	1,039	160	1.77	1,023	171
1976	1,186	175	1.66	1,194	180
1977	1,358	188	1.58	1,381	202
1978	1,523	209	1.55	1,580	259
1979	1,727	239	1.61	1,771	303
1980	1,853	262	1.61	1,876	326
1981	2,018	280	1.74	2,015	323
1982	1,960	307	1.97	1,946	309
1983	2,071	308	1.67	2,105	343
1984	2,288	334	1.75	2,315	370
1985	2,334	330	1.72	2,348	384
1986	2,336	318	1.63	2,342	390
1987	2,476	333	1.58	2,513	427
1988	2,695	363	1.56	2,739	471
1989	2,840	385	1.65	2,875	505
1990	2,912	398	1.70	2,934	527
1991	2,878	384	1.65	2,866	515
1992	3,005	375	1.47	2,979	489
1993	3,128	376	1.44	3,092	453
1994	3,348	396	1.38	3,357	462
1995	3,589	419	1.41	3,604	477
1996	3,735	425	1.37	3,770	512

[1] Beginning in 1982, inventories are stated at current cost and are not comparable to the book value estimates for prior years.
[2] Ratio based on December seasonally adjusted data.
Source: U.S. Bureau of the Census. Current Industrial Reports, *Manufacturers' Shipments, Inventories, and Orders: 1987–1996,* series M3; and monthly press releases.

Figure 4.4. Sample of *Annual Survey of Manufactures.*

Manufacturer's New Orders (Net, millions of dollars)

Year and month	Not seasonally adjusted			Seasonally adjusted										
					Durable goods industries								Transportation equipment	
							Primary metals							
	Total	Durable goods industries	Nondurable goods industries	Total	Total¹	Total	Blast furnaces, steel mills	Non-ferrous and other primary metals	Fabricated metal products	Industrial machinery and equipment	Electronic and electric equipment	Total	Aircraft missiles and parts
1968	607 881	336 614	271 267	607 881	336 614	48 089	24 416	19 182	45 158	52 286	39 182	85 893	28 195
1969	647 874	358 509	289 365	647 874	358 509	54 880	27 247	22 496	47 446	60 226	42 438	83 945	24 704
1970	624 263	328 079	296 184	624 263	328 079	51 793	25 521	21 883	43 990	55 322	41 117	67 380	17 417
1971	671 051	358 856	312 195	671 051	358 856	51 284	25 571	20 704	44 305	55 886	42 639	89 900	22 459
1972	770 181	420 455	349 726	770 181	420 455	61 447	30 996	24 607	52 879	70 941	48 702	96 501	20 963
1973	912 039	511 525	400 514	912 039	511 525	78 395	39 413	31 417	64 733	89 162	58 275	118 194	26 669
1974	1 047 924	562 339	485 585	1 047 924	562 339	98 831	51 047	38 394	74 281	106 101	58 884	114 081	29 934
1975	1 021 662	503 485	518 177	1 021 662	503 485	75 034	38 611	27 864	64 349	92 863	54 610	109 050	26 869
1976	1 194 151	615 680	578 471	1 194 151	615 680	94 491	47 212	37 378	76 372	107 595	66 864	143 502	31 851
1977	1 381 302	732 422	648 880	1 381 302	732 422	105 689	52 103	42 400	92 028	126 235	80 010	175 446	40 625
1978	1 579 542	867 335	712 207	1 579 542	867 335	124 741	62 648	48 319	105 182	154 051	92 781	213 539	54 600
1979	1 771 243	953 796	817 447	1 771 243	953 796	139 783	66 968	58 420	117 428	174 660	107 314	223 226	67 818
1980	1 876 304	952 701	923 603	1 876 304	952 701	134 416	62 473	60 399	116 195	179 750	115 335	202 584	72 514
1981	2 016 298	1 003 845	1 012 453	2 016 298	1 003 845	137 266	67 457	57 545	123 245	201 576	123 053	203 482	63 530
1982	1 945 684	936 764	1 008 920	1 945 684	936 764	98 445	43 013	46 942	113 399	169 274	127 630	209 325	73 365
1983	2 105 410	1 057 677	1 047 733	2 105 410	1 057 677	113 884	49 123	55 566	122 760	178 879	142 131	261 359	86 952
1984	2 314 549	1 201 964	1 112 585	2 314 549	1 201 964	118 354	50 719	56 030	141 650	212 109	165 541	295 202	91 620
1985	2 348 477	1 228 268	1 120 209	2 348 477	1 228 268	112 276	49 079	52 275	142 300	218 395	163 352	311 482	100 889
1986	2 342 444	1 243 761	1 098 683	2 342 444	1 243 761	108 218	46 408	51 294	143 541	208 567	164 282	327 541	107 993
1987	2 512 663	1 329 712	1 182 951	2 512 663	1 329 712	125 989	54 763	60 302	150 716	221 171	173 210	348 224	114 835
1988	2 739 240	1 464 916	1 274 324	2 739 240	1 464 916	152 578	64 002	75 997	158 170	250 055	189 211	389 635	137 443
1989	2 874 861	1 512 664	1 362 197	2 874 861	1 512 664	152 814	62 752	77 249	160 037	257 051	192 482	411 434	153 430
1990	2 934 086	1 507 001	1 427 085	2 934 086	1 507 001	149 338	63 369	72 944	163 285	258 894	195 748	395 737	150 329

Figure 4.4. Continued.

Manufacturer's New Orders (Net millions of dollars)

Year and month	Not seasonally adjusted			Seasonally adjusted — Durable goods industries									
	Total	Durable goods industries	Nondurable goods industries	Total	Total[1]	Primary metals — Total	Blast furnaces, steel mills	Non-ferrous and other primary metals	Fabricated metal products	Industrial machinery and equipment	Electronic and electric equipment	Transportation equipment — Total	Aircraft missiles and parts
1991	2 865 665	1 438 187	1 427 478	2 865 655	1 438 187	134 657	56 366	66 778	158 401	243 450	197 659	363 366	132 645
1992	2 978 548	1 515 694	1 462 854	2 978 548	1 515 694	136 849	58 002	67 337	165 793	258 608	217 966	377 147	110 830
1993	3 092 381	1 596 974	1 495 407	3 092 381	1 596 974	144 018	63 604	57 112	172 121	277 416	233 991	386 643	88 070
1994	3 356 797	1 794 508	1 562 289	3 356 797	1 794 508	167 685	70 960	31 963	191 099	325 788	266 386	440 817	90 217
1995	3 604 239	1 937 624	1 566 615	3 604 239	1 937 624	178 681	75 372	38 273	205 894	356 282	305 736	472 332	114 099
1996	3 770 368	2 039 558	1 730 810	3 770 368	2 039 558	174 865	72 295	35 221	217 468	379 817	321 390	502 861	134 097
1993:													
January	234 245	118 979	115 265	255 593	130 444	12 753	5 808	5 810	14 189	22 503	18 438	31 426	6 293
February	258 421	135 345	123 075	250 024	134 637	12 574	5 794	5 737	14 197	22 474	18 525	34 637	10 042
March	269 549	140 736	128 813	255 935	130 256	12 078	5 404	5 676	14 124	22 364	18 193	31 896	7 047
April	255 804	132 183	123 621	256 829	131 828	11 722	4 999	5 600	14 050	22 160	18 623	32 178	8 110
May	252 941	129 282	123 659	252 132	128 690	11 420	5 033	5 285	14 126	22 410	18 579	31 270	7 931
June	275 107	142 979	132 128	258 492	132 870	11 758	5 196	5 567	14 093	21 930	19 889	34 419	9 883
July	231 267	111 983	119 284	254 196	130 082	11 463	5 021	5 390	14 011	22 885	20 005	30 342	6 469
August	253 474	127 527	125 947	254 050	130 933	11 588	5 076	5 468	14 191	22 973	19 846	30 701	7 793
September	271 193	139 292	131 901	257 220	132 585	11 957	5 278	5 447	14 793	23 467	20 766	29 604	4 715
October	267 903	140 434	127 469	258 908	135 066	12 136	5 414	5 463	14 536	23 448	20 465	32 486	6 385
November	262 412	137 712	124 700	263 344	138 719	12 233	5 325	5 676	14 518	24 920	20 092	33 973	8 023
December	260 065	140 522	119 543	264 303	140 010	12 487	5 444	5 956	15 275	25 430	19 996	33 959	5 824
1994:													
January	249 092	134 295	114 797	270 317	145 722	12 459	5 308	5 936	15 071	24 829	21 282	39 835	12 308
February	267 917	144 202	123 715	268 586	142 567	12 653	5 685	5 853	15 208	25 667	21 254	34 809	7 149
March	288 612	156 639	131 973	273 825	145 201	14 658	5 831	6 876	16 294	26 299	21 169	34 714	5 599

103

Figure 4.4. Continued.

Manufacturer's New Orders (Net, millions of dollars)

| Year and month | Not seasonally adjusted | | | Seasonally adjusted | | | | | | | | | |
| | Total | Durable goods industries | Nondurable goods industries | Total | Durable goods industries | Primary metals | | | Fabricated metal products | Industrial machinery and equipment | Electronic and electric equipment | Transportation equipment | |
					Total[1]	Total	Blast furnaces, steel mills	Non-ferrous and other primary metals				Total	Aircraft missiles and parts
1994: *(cont.)*													
April	270 669	144 819	125 850	271 819	144 844	13 053	5 840	6 115	15 552	26 835	22 552	34 271	6 298
May	276 057	147 431	128 626	274 927	146 618	13 974	5 761	6 953	15 797	26 662	21 660	35 458	7 849
June	296 673	160 888	135 785	279 454	150 118	13 816	5 868	6 684	15 668	27 310	21 804	36 829	8 250
July	248 301	124 836	123 465	275 565	146 869	13 503	5 643	6 707	15 932	27 455	21 186	34 727	5 780
August	284 142	148 091	136 051	283 747	150 992	13 788	5 912	6 788	16 330	28 362	21 993	35 906	6 869
September	299 030	159 553	139 477	284 880	152 658	14 789	6 360	7 212	16 046	27 852	22 924	37 452	7 400
October	292 790	156 859	135 931	283 893	151 307	14 998	6 105	7 676	15 959	28 385	21 816	35 839	6 731
November	290 512	156 012	134 500	291 450	156 885	14 935	6 171	7 519	16 739	28 667	24 255	38 230	8 815
December	293 002	160 883	132 119	298 208	160 805	15 951	6 659	7 728	16 551	26 984	24 287	42 213	7 245
1995													
January	276 929	149 877	127 052	299 495	161 929	15 847	6 462	8 106	17 435	29 270	24 529	38 850	7 446
February	299 264	163 293	135 971	299 555	161 044	15 107	6 298	7 430	17 272	29 513	24 025	40 204	9 975
March	315 301	174 072	141 229	299 157	161 385	15 301	6 800	7 258	17 002	30 041	25 673	39 194	7 966
April	291 331	154 447	136 884	292 785	154 969	14 748	6 170	7 264	16 919	29 048	24 725	35 824	7 287
May	298 191	158 977	139 214	297 451	158 883	14 368	6 186	7 041	17 187	29 627	25 604	37 989	9 698
June	314 020	167 945	146 075	296 429	156 939	14 361	6 003	7 228	16 866	30 108	24 943	36 013	6 357
July	265 281	132 252	133 029	294 040	155 362	14 115	5 772	7 147	16 985	28 290	26 369	35 454	8 054
August	302 190	159 084	143 106	301 449	161 945	15 227	6 366	7 575	17 194	29 667	25 615	38 623	9 221
September	320 200	174 209	145 991	305 828	166 946	14 909	6 071	7 534	17 295	29 851	26 345	43 877	12 736
October	312 976	170 002	142 974	302 899	163 442	14 988	6 450	7 203	17 247	29 698	26 656	43 877	9 537
November	303 396	163 012	140 384	304 567	164 232	14 900	6 479	7 136	17 385	31 208	24 922	40 318	10 498
December	305 160	170 454	134 706	309 948	170 076	14 729	6 275	7 304	17 233	30 181	25 949	46 101	15 213

Figure 4.4. Continued.

Manufacturer's New Orders (Net, millions of dollars)

Year and month	Not seasonally adjusted			Seasonally adjusted			Durable goods industries								
								Primary metals						Transportation equipment	
	Total	Durable goods industries	Nondurable goods industries	Total	Total[1]	Total	Blast furnaces, steel mills	Non-ferrous and other primary metals	Fabricated metal products	Industrial machinery and equipment	Electronic and electric equipment	Total	Aircraft missiles and parts
1996:														
January	286 915	156 859	130 056	308 852	168 420	14 362	6 033	6 905	17 444	30 961	26 058	44 307	13 592
February	303 501	165 811	137 690	303 957	163 553	14 510	5 921	7 099	17 449	32 526	25 019	38 387	8 785
March	322 813	179 595	143 218	306 561	166 267	13 782	5 596	6 860	17 134	30 428	26 706	42 684	15 658
April	307 060	163 620	143 440	308 467	164 329	14 649	5 934	7 295	18 062	30 995	26 031	37 999	7 644
May	316 493	171 243	145 250	315 764	171 209	14 977	6 382	7 212	18 598	31 599	25 853	43 213	12 251
June	331 043	182 129	148 914	313 081	170 382	14 869	6 120	7 188	18 190	31 346	26 567	42 598	9 931
July	287 081	147 034	140 047	318 488	173 087	15 135	6 357	7 223	18 190	32 424	27 930	42 196	10 293
August	312 787	164 086	148 701	311 958	167 204	14 954	6 058	7 378	18 379	32 098	26 712	38 272	7 269
September	335 124	183 300	151 824	319 894	175 113	14 468	6 125	6 886	18 716	32 115	26 556	45 692	13 296
October	333 193	181 955	151 238	322 392	175 015	14 264	5 959	7 051	18 548	31 424	30 901	41 936	11 871
November	321 484	172 506	148 978	322 400	173 636	14 338	5 758	7 102	18 597	31 487	28 307	43 049	11 671
December	312 874	171 420	141 454	316 898	170 016	14 590	6 032	7 033	18 198	31 979	24 086	42 701	11 357

[1]Includes categories not shown separately.

Source: *Annual Survey of Manufactures*, gathered by the U.S. Bureau of the Census, Washington, D.C.

Table 4.1.   Standard Industrial Classification Codes

Numerical Range	Industry Category
0000–0299	Agriculture
0300–0699	Not Assigned
0700–0999	Agricultural Services, Forestry & Fishing
1000–1499	Mining
1500–1799	Construction
1800–1999	Not Assigned
2000–3999	Manufacturing
4000–4999	Transportation, Communications & Utilities
5000–5199	Wholesale Trade
5200–5999	Retail Trade
6000–6699	Finance, Insurance & Real Estate (FIRE)
6700–6999	Not Assigned
7000–8999	Service Sector
9000–9099	Not Assigned
9100–9799	Public Administration
9800–9899	Not Assigned
9900–9999	Nonclassifiable Establishments

miscellaneous industry groups that are not otherwise classified. Table 4.1 provides a breakdown of the various SIC categories.

NEW NORTH AMERICAN
INDUSTRY CLASSIFICATION SYSTEM

Given the many structural changes that have taken place in the U.S. economy, including the growth of the service sector relative to the manufacturing sector, a new industry classification has been developed. This system, called the North American Industry Classification System (NAICS), features 350 new industries and 9 service industry sectors.[5] The system will be implemented by federal government agencies starting in 1999 using data from the 1997 economic census. It uses a six-digit system to categorize specific industries with the first two digits designating the sector, the third the subsector, the fourth the industry group, and the fifth and the sixth designating the NAICS and the national industries. It focuses on the economies of the United States, Canada, and Mexico. The sectors in the NAICS system are shown in Table 4.2.

---

[5] *North American Industry Classification System,* Executive Office of the President, Office of Management and Budget, Washington, D.C., 1997.

Table 4.2. North American Industry Classification System

Numerical Range	Industry Category
11	Agriculture, Forestry, Fishing & Hunting
21	Mining
22	Utilities
23	Construction
31–33	Manufacturing
41–43	Wholesale Trade
44–46	Retail Trade
48–49	Transportation & Warehousing
51	Information
52	Finance and Insurance
53	Real Estate and Rental & Leasing
54	Professional, Scientific & Technical Services
55	Management of Companies and Enterprises
56	Administrative and Support and Waste Management and Remediation Services
61	Educational Services
62	Health Care and Social Assistance
71	Arts, Entertainment and Recreation
72	Accommodation and Food Services
81	Other Services (except Public Administration)
91–93	Public Administration

PRIVATE SOURCES OF INDUSTRY DATA

Government industry data are available through the Commerce Department (such as through the Census of Manufacturers) and also through private vendors, such as through the *Predicasts Basebook.*[6] These data are also organized according to SIC codes. Figure 4.5 shows a sample page from the *Basebook.* As can be seen, detailed subcategories are available which can be used to fit the industry data more precisely to the industry being analyzed. Both unit and dollar volumes, as well as other relevant data, such as employment, are available. The data contained in the *Predicasts Basebook* are available on-line through subscriptions so that users can get more timely access to updated data rather than waiting for the annual hard copy of the book. In fact, given the lag in access to the annual version of the hard copy of the *Basebook,* the expert can quickly access these data on-line and get the benefit of more regular updates. For this reason the hard copy *Basebook* is no longer being published. However, given that many cases focus

[6] For example, *Predicasts Basebook,* annual, Information Access Company, Foster City, California.

Figure 4.5. Sample of *Basebook*.

Sig No	Item Description	1981	1982	1983	1984	1985	1986	1987	1988	1989	1990	1991	1992	1993	1994	Unit of measure	Source	Annual growth
2330	**WOMEN'S OUTERWEAR**																	
23300 00	Women's Outerwear																	
	expend for new plant and equipment	220.3	213.2	154.9	210.9	162.7	148.2	161.0	171.3	227.5	176.8	126.1	—	—	—	MIL $	ASM-1	−1.3b%
	expend for materials	7.47	9.58	9.60	9.34	9.18	9.49	9.78	9.94	9.23	9.15	9.52	—	—	—	BIL mil $	ASM-1	1.7b%
	payroll	3921.	4110.	4455.	4060.	3885.	3799.	4297.	4330.	4197.	4318.	4244.	—	—	—	MIL $	ASM-1	0.9b%
	employment	411.3	386.1	387.9	383.8	361.9	353.6	351.9	344.7	342.4	327.7	319.9	316.5	300.6	—	000 worker	Empl HE US	−2.3b%
	employment	443.8	418.9	417.2	387.8	354.7	329.9	348.5	337.7	317.3	318.2	307.3	—	—	—	000 worker	ASM-1	−3.7b%
	female employment	349.6	326.4	326.2	319.0	298.5	292.6	289.9	284.2	284.7	271.1	262.0	257.0	241.7	—	000 worker	Empl HE US	−2.7b%
	prod workers	353.0	326.9	327.9	323.0	301.7	295.1	293.5	267.3	286.7	273.9	267.4	265.2	251.1	—	000 worker	Empl HE US	−2.6b%
	prod workers	382.7	355.8	353.9	328.1	302.8	276.7	290.2	277.7	267.7	271.5	261.5	—	—	—	000 worker	ASM-1	−1.8b%
	prod wkr wkly hr	33.7	33.0	34.4	34.6	34.9	35.1	35.5	35.7	35.4	35.0	35.7	36.4	36.2	36.1	hrs/wk	Employment	0.7b%
	hours worked	671.3	640.5	646.7	561.6	492.9	483.9	484.8	459.8	467.5	487.6	461.4	—	—	—	MIL hours	ASM-1	3.8b%
	prod wage rate	4.95	5.13	5.31	5.46	5.56	5.60	5.70	5.88	6.09	6.26	6.47	6.58	6.71	—	$/hr	Empl HE US	2.7b%
	prod payroll	2882.	2928.	3150.	2816.	2662.	2544.	2844.	2791.	2841.	2953.	2888.	—	—	—	MIL $	ASM-1	0.1b%
	end inventory	1823.	1805.	1967.	2069.	1983.	2038.	2380.	2399.	2269.	2186.	2346.	—	—	—	MIL $	ASM-1	3.1b%
	value added	8.56	8.58	8.67	8.85	8.28	8.71	9.69	9.78	9.50	10.19	9.95	—	—	—	BIL $	ASM-1	2.1b%
	shipments—industry	16.09	16.22	18.21	18.05	17.49	18.11	19.39	19.75	18.68	19.34	19.43	—	—	—	BIL $	ASM-1	1.9b%
	Women's Shirts and Blouses																	
23310 00	Women's Shirts and Blouses																	
	expend for new plant and equipment	36.8	29.4	40.2	72.5	33.8	35.0	40.1	46.0	22.2	35.6	25.2	—	—	—	MIL $	ASM-1	−2.1b%
	consump of apparel fibers (cotton eqv)	499.	573.	551.	480.	482.	514.	519.	474.	455.	504.	498.	509.	532.	—	000 bales	Cotton Cts	−0.3b%
	consump of apparel fibers	195.0	205.7	216.6	190.3	190.8	204.3	206.9	188.6	182.1	179.2	197.9	201.4	211.9	—	MIL lbs	Cotton Cts	0.2b%
	consump of cotton	132.	154	155.	147.	188.	245.	286.	276.	278.	326.	339.	356.	378.	—	000 Bales	Cotton Cts	8.6b%
	expend for materials	1500.	2032	2031.	1875.	1876.	1907.	1943.	1828.	1700.	1802.	1855.	—	—	—	MIL $	ASM-1	1.2b%
	payroll	761.9	874.7	921.2	897.4	845.6	835.6	856.6	832.1	817.4	865.8	814.0	—	—	—	MIL $	ASM-1	0.7b%
	employment	63.1	60.8	60.3	58.6	52.7	48.9	46.5	44.7	43.0	38.8	36.8	35.7	32.0	—	000 worker	Empl HE US	−5.1b%
	employment	81.9	92.2	93.1	91.5	82.1	78.2	73.4	67.0	64.6	64.4	59.5	—	—	—	000 worker	ASM-1	−3.4b%
	female employment	56.1	53.9	53.3	51.8	46.4	43.2	41.4	39.4	38.1	34.0	32.3	31.3	27.9	—	000 worker	Empl HE US	−5.2b%
	prod workers	55.0	52.2	51.3	49.9	44.1	40.7	38.7	36.8	35.6	31.7	30.2	29.3	26.0	—	000 worker	Empl HE US	−5.6b%
	prod workers	70.6	79.3	79.3	76.5	70.0	66.2	63.2	58.7	55.2	54.3	49.4	—	—	—	000 worker	ASM-1	−3.7b%
	prod wkr wkly hr	34.0	34.1	34.7	34.6	34.8	35.3	35.7	35.8	35.5	35.3	35.9	35.8	35.9	35.7	hrs/wk	Employment	0.4b%
	hours worked	127.7	140.9	141.8	137.3	126.3	119.3	109.0	100.7	98.6	97.8	88.5	—	—	—	MIL hours	ASM-1	−3.6b%
	prod wage rate	4.65	4.77	4.91	5.06	5.13	5.05	5.05	5.13	5.31	5.56	5.80	5.93	6.19	—	$/hr	Empl HE US	2.5b%
	prod payroll	566.1	523.2	655.1	639.1	583.5	555.9	586.6	588.8	561.8	572.5	525.1	—	—	—	MIL $	ASM-1	−0.6b%
	end inventory	319.5	354.5	363.6	392.6	384.3	376.3	437.9	409.9	396.1	423.3	411.4	—	—	—	MIL $	ASM-1	3.1b%
	value added	1557.	1838.	1774.	1738.	1729.	1808.	1918.	1741.	1713.	1955.	1943.	—	—	—	MIL $	ASM-1	1.7b%
	shipments—industry	3027.	3884.	3804.	3579.	3643.	3694.	3831.	3573.	3402.	3733.	3801.	—	—	—	MIL $	ASM-1	1.4b%

Figure 4.5. Continued.

Sig No	Item Description	1981	1982	1983	1984	1985	1986	1987	1988	1989	1990	1991	1992	1993	1994	Unit of measure	Source	Annual growth
	Women's Knit Fabric Shirts																	
23312 00	Women's Knit Fabric Shirts																	
	production	17.07	17.01	14.45	15.51	11.05	11.46	11.65	12.59	11.66	12.22	15.47	15.45	16.41	—	Mil dozen	Cotton Cts	-1.16%
	shipments	448.	678.	645	730.	797.	850.	1255.	1167.	1192.	1099.	1247	—	—	—	Mil $	ASM-2	8.9b%
	Women's Woven Shirts																	
23317 00	Women's Woven Shirts																	
	production—incl blouses	18.47	20.60	25.20	21.99	21.31	20.54	19.95	16.26	15.51	15.02	13.34	14.20	14.36	—	Mil dozen	Cotton Cts	-2.86%
	shipments—incl blouses	2263.	2534.	2442	2283.	2153.	2320.	2176.	2121.	1763.	1840.	1830.	—	—	—	Mil $	ASM-2	-2.66%
	whsle price—incl blouses	98.2	93.5	103.7	107.9	122.1	114.2	115.8	118.6	136.9	143.1	146.6	150.4	—	—	BLS Index	BLS PPIA	4.66%

Source: *Predicasts Basebook*, Information Access Company, Foster City, CA

on past events, the historical data in the published *Basebook* can be most useful. Furthermore much of the data that the *Basebook* contains is available online and can be accessed by setting up an account at the website http://www.gale.com. Many universities have such accounts and, therefore, provides another forum where such data can be accessed.

The publisher of the *Predicasts Basebook* also publishes the *Funk and Scott Index*. This index allows the analyst to search under an industry or product category as well as under a company name. References are given for relevant industry and trade publications. The industry data is published on a timely basis so it allows the researcher to access both historical and current information. Once again, however, on-line access provides access to more timely data.

Private sources often include industry associations. One source containing lists of industry associations is the *Encyclopedia of Associations*.[7] Many industries, even some obscure ones, have an industry association that compiles data and may publish such data in a report. Care must be taken in the use of such data. The analyst should contact the association and learn how the data were gathered. It is often the case that data are gathered in a questionnaire from association members with little verification of the accuracy of the data. If many of the members are closely held firms, the association may have limited ability to verify the data.[8] An example of annual industry shipment data provided by the Carpet and Rug Institute in Dalton, Georgia, as shown in Table 4.3.

Associations differ in how they gather their data. Some employ professional survey companies who try to gather and analyze the data in a reliable and scientific manner. Some associations may employ their own professionals in these areas and may be able to competently gather and analyze the data. Other associations may not gather the data in a reliable manner and the use of such data may be more open to challenge. Later in this chapter we provide some examples where courts have rejected the use of industry data because of their questionable reliability.

Certain private vendors prepare industry reports on specific industries. These vendors include Business Data Analysts, Packaged Facts, and the Freedonia Group. The Freedonia Group claims to have published more than 1,000 studies since 1985.[9] *Packaged Facts* is one of three brands of market intelligence and

---

[7] *Encyclopedia of Associations,* annual, Gale Research Inc., Detroit, MI.

[8] See later discussion in this chapter on the court's position on the use of data from industry associations and problems with their reliability.

[9] *Freedonia Industry Study Catalog,* The Freedonia Group, 3570 Warrensville, Suite 201, Cleveland, Ohio, 44122, 216-921-6800.

Table 4.3. Carpet and Rug Shipments 1970–1997

Year	Square Yards (000's)	Percent Change	Mill Value (000's)	Percent Change	Price Per Square Yard	Percent Change
1970	680,479	5.9	2,215,111	1.3	3.26	−4.1
1971	755,159	11.0	2,395,519	8.1	3.17	−2.8
1972	943,006	24.9	2,936,284	22.6	3.11	−1.9
1973	1,025,389	8.7	3,360,521	14.5	3.28	5.5
1974	939,133	−8.4	3,328,844	−0.9	3.54	7.9
1975	834,037	−11.2	3,092,176	−7.1	3.71	4.8
1976	939,334	12.6	3,636,474	17.6	3.87	4.3
1977	1,074,110	14.3	4,298,660	18.2	4.00	3.4
1978	1,162,256	8.2	4,772,550	11.0	4.11	2.8
1979	1,206,030	3.8	5,099,090	6.8	4.23	2.9
1980	1,058,404	−12.2	4,913,844	−3.9	4.64	9.7
1981	990,619	−6.4	5,250,391	6.8	5.30	14.2
1982	885,811	10.6	4,960,753	−5.5	5.60	5.7
1983	1,090,071	23.0	6,045,255	21.9	5.55	−0.9
1984	1,114,920	2.3	6,461,516	6.9	5.80	4.5
1985	1,159,155	4.0	6,605,686	2.2	5.70	−1.7
1986	1,257,906	8.5	7,311,614	10.7	5.81	1.9
1987	1,297,320	3.1	7,929,117	8.4	6.11	5.2
1988	1,324,003	2.1	8,417,316	6.2	6.36	4.1
1989	1,317,799	−0.5	8,431,130	0.2	6.40	0.6
1990	1,360,043	3.2	8,527,153	1.1	6.27	−2.0
1991	1,278,017	−6.0	7,980,411	−6.4	6.24	−0.5
1992	1,405,778	11.0	8,711,750	9.2	6.20	−0.6
1993	1,482,022	4.4	9,282,524	6.1	6.26	1.5
1994	1,574,703	6.3	9,530,598	2.7	6.05	−3.3
1995	1,589,236	0.9	9,769,691	2.5	6.15	1.7
1996	1,658,193	4.3	10,148,225	3.9	6.12	−0.5
1997	1,696,158	2.3	10,261,816	1.1	6.05	−1.1

industry studies disseminated by Find/SVP.[10] Like most of these vendors, Find/SVP publishes a catalog listing its various industries.[11] The benefit of such reports is that they often include a variety of data broken down by relevant sub categories. In addition, such reports, which often are in excess of 10 pages, usually include a narrative discussion of the industry, which can be helpful to an expert who lacks a prior background in the industry. The testifying expert still needs to do his own industry analysis but the use of such reports can be a bene-

---

[10] *Packaged Facts,* Department PMB, 625 Avenue of the Americas, New York, N.Y. 10011, 1-800-265-9836.

[11] *The Information Catalog,* Find/SVP, 625 Avenue of the Americas, New York, N.Y. 10011, 1-800-346-3005.

fit. The costs of such reports vary, with many being in the $1,000 to $3,000 range. While it may appear on the surface to raise the costs of the expert's services, it may actually save money by the expert not having to engage in a "reinventing the wheel" exercise. By using such studies, the expert can draw on the work of others who have devoted considerable time to studying the particular industry.

Another source of private industry data on consumer goods and one that is very often used in the field of marketing is the data made available by A.C. Neilsen on fast-moving consumer goods (FMCG). This data set includes information compiled from scanner data that is, in turn, gathered at supermarkets, drug stores and other outlets.[12] However, most of these data are cross-sectional rather than time series. Being cross-sectional, the data set is more useful for determining market shares and size of markets as of the survey date. Therefore, the data set is not as useful for determining trends. Nonetheless, it may play a role in a commercial damages analysis for certain consumer goods. One way in which such data can be helpful is in analyzing what market shares are implied by various forecasts. The data can be used to determine what percent of total market revenues are implied by a plaintiff's revenue projection. The reasonableness of such market shares can then be considered. Market share analysis may be useful in a basic industry analysis and may be invaluable in doing an antitrust analysis.

Industry Publications

Many industries have their own publications. Some have several that may be directed at various segments of the overall industry. These publications can contain industry data that may be produced by some associations covering the industry. The expert may be able to learn about important developments and trends that could affect the performance of the industry. Published articles on the plaintiff may provide useful information on the company's performance and may yield alternative explanations for a downturn in the plaintiff's performance that it is attributing to the defendant. These publications can often be accessed through online data sources such as *Nexis*. If the expert does not have an account with *Nexis* he may be able to access it through publicly available sources such as the local or college library.

---

[12] Douglas P. Handler, "Business Economist at Work: Linking Economics to Market Research: A.C. Nielsen," *Business Economics,* 31(4), October 1996, 51–52.

On-Line Data Sources

Numerous on-line data sources are available to augment an industry analysis. The volume of data sources available on the Internet is ever-expanding. Several excellent search engines can be used to access these voluminous data sources. Through these databases, specific industry and trade publications, as well as general business publications, such as the *Wall Street Journal Index* and indexes of other newspapers, can be accessed. In addition, specific financial databases can allow securities market analyst reports to be ordered.

Annual Reports

In cases where a significant percent of the industry includes public firms, the analyst can take advantage of the public filing requirements of securities laws by gathering data from the annual reports and other filings such as 10Ks. Annual reports generally have more information than 10Ks because they contain some verbiage that may include management's "spin" on the facts. If the analyst can isolate some major companies that comprise a large percentage of industry sales, then such reports, and the data they contain, such as revenue and total costs data, may be of use to allow for some useful disaggregation of the total industry revenue data. Annual reports may be used to establish some typical margins, such as the gross, operating, and net margins. This information may give some indications as to what average industry profitability is and the magnitude of the major cost areas. These data may be summarized in other publicly available sources such as *Value Line*.[13] Often, however, this avenue does not prove fruitful, because major companies are diversified and are not required to provide significant detail on divisions. Therefore, total reported revenues and costs may include many industries that are not the object of the analysis. In addition, larger segments of the industry may be private or non-U.S. firms, who do not have to abide by the same U.S. securities laws.

Securities Markets Analysts Reports

In cases where a significant component of the industry is comprised of public firms, it is often possible to find industry analysts at brokerage firms that study

---

[13] *Value Line Investment Survey,* Value Line Publishing Inc., 220 East 42nd Street, New York, NY 10017-5891.

the firms and the industry in general. Analyst reports on the plaintiff and the defendant can be a source of useful information. Their reports may include much useful discussion on important recent trends in the industry as well as other valuable data such as market share and industry growth data. The reports may contain a variety of data used by the expert which otherwise the litigation analysts might not know about or have access to. They may provide other information such as a discussion of other problems of the plaintiff which may be unrelated to the defendant's actions but could be the cause of the plaintiff's losses. The expert may be able to follow up on such reports by contacting the market analysts who wrote the report. Such investigations may unearth the true cause of the plaintiff's losses. Once again, how available and useful such reports may be varies widely from case to case.

RETAINING AN INDUSTRY EXPERT

An industry expert can be of great assistance in the analysis of damages. This may be a testifying expert or a consultant who works with the damages expert. The damages expert may be able to rely on the industry expert's knowledge without this expert having to testify. Having an industry expert can be particularly important in technical industries or in industries in which there have been significant changes that may affect the comparability of historical data. One example of both is the telecommunications industry, which has several highly specialized and technical subcomponents while having undergone significant changes in recent years. If the industry expert does testify, it makes sense that her testimony precedes that of the damages expert as the latter would most likely rely on some of the analysis and opinion expressed by the industry expert. In this manner the industry expert would set forth a foundation of the damages expert's testimony.

Attorneys sometimes try to limit monies spent on damages experts and one place they sometimes try to cut is in retaining another expert who basically supports the damages expert. When the industry expert is not expected to testify, attorneys or their clients may be reluctant to pay the fees of such an expert especially when these fees, on a hourly basis, may be similar to those of the damages expert. However, such reasoning has been included in the "The Ten Most Frequent Errors in Litigating Business Damages" list.[14] Having an industry expert

---

[14] James Plummer and Gerald McGowin, "The Ten Most Frequent Errors in Litigating Business Damages," *Association of Business Trial Lawyers Report,* 5 (1) November 1995, 3–5.

relieves the damages expert of bearing the full burden of being an expert. It also eliminates some of the impact of cross-examination directed at the damages expert's knowledge of the industry. When the damages expert works in conjunction with the industry expert, he may be able to respond to such questions by saying that he has done a certain amount of his own industry analysis but has also relied upon the expertise of the industry expert. Having such an expert to rely on can also bring about a savings in the fees of the damages expert who may have to do additional industry research to acquire some of the information that the industry expert has in her head.

CONDUCTING AN INDUSTRY ANALYSIS

One of the first steps in conducting an industry analysis is to determine the industry growth rate. The growth rate is often computed for units, such as shipments, as well as revenues, although revenues may be more useful, because one of the initial steps in a lost profits analysis is to construct a lost revenues projection. The industry revenue growth rate may be more relevant to the lost revenues projection. This growth can also be depicted graphically such as in Figure 4.6.

The growth rate computation is usually done for various historical time periods such as the past five and ten years. The longer the loss projection, the more historical years need to be considered. This is not to imply that all historical years have equal importance. Generally, the more remote the years of data the less weight is placed on them. However, each case brings its own unique factors requiring the expert to address the specifics of each assignment of a case-by-case basis.

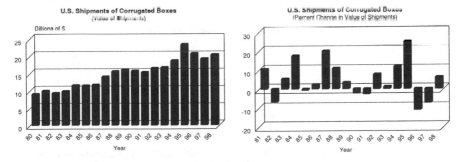

Figure 4.6.   Value of U.S. corrugated box shipments.
(Source: Fibre Box Industry, Annual Report 1998)

Table 4.4. Corrugated Box Industry Shipments and Revenues

Year	Value of Shipments (Billions of $)	Percent Change (%)	Volume of Shipment (Billions of Sq. Feet)	Percent Change (%)	Northeast Volume of Shipments (Billions of Sq. Feet)	Percent Change (%)
1980	9.075		241.377		50.551	
1981	10.020	10.4	246.152	2.0	50.100	−0.9
1982	9.344	−6.7	235.185	−4.5	48.006	−4.2
1983	9.845	5.4	252.539	7.4	50.263	4.7
1984	11.567	17.5	267.547	5.9	51.094	1.7
1985	11.487	−0.7	267.453	0.0	50.078	−2.0
1986	11.753	2.3	283.921	6.2	52.303	4.4
1987	14.097	19.9	297.828	4.9	54.339	3.9
1988	15.627	10.9	308.509	3.6	55.571	2.3
1989	16.157	3.4	313.398	1.6	54.992	−1.0
1990	15.801	−2.2	318.102	1.5	55.098	0.2
1991	15.367	−2.7	320.106	0.6	54.324	−1.4
1992	16.553	7.7	335.696	4.9	56.066	3.2
1993	16.770	1.3	353.755	5.4	58.507	4.4
1994	18.738	11.7	374.808	6.0	59.288	1.3
1995	23.418	25.0	372.501	−0.6	57.192	−3.5
1996	20.819	−11.1	377.778	1.4	59.566	4.2
1997	19.280	−7.4	390.130	3.3	62.294	4.6
1998	20.183	5.4	393.620	1.4	63.049	1.2

Source: Fibre Box Industry Annual Report, 1998.

Table 4.4 shows that over the period 1980–97 these data exhibit an average annual growth rate equal to 4.98% in revenues and 2.99% in units. Over a shorter time period, such as the period 1990–97, the growth rates are 3.50% and 3.17% respectively.

Regional Industry Data

If the plaintiff's is a regional business then the expert may want to try to gather industry data on a regional basis. Obviously, this will depend on the availability of such data. Many industry associations do not publish regional data, but instead merely aggregate all of the data they gather across the nation. If there are significant differences across the nation for the industry, this may be a problem. When such regional data are available, they can be added to the presentation. Figure 4.7 depicts the volume of shipments of corrugated boxes for the Northeast region of the United States. Using the Northeast volume data, a 1.29% growth rate is computed for the period 1980–97 and 1.63% over 1990–97.

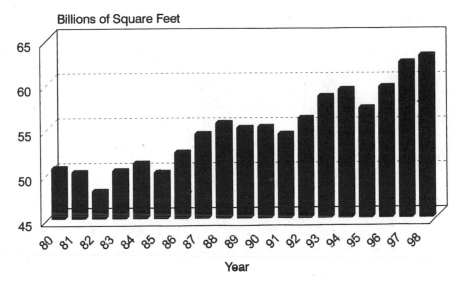

Figure 4.7.   Northeast Shipments of Corrugated Boxes (Volume of Shipments)
Source: Fibre Box Industry, Annual Report 1998.

Industry Growth and Industry Life Cycles

High industry growth implies higher firm sales. However, to simply apply the industry growth rate to a firm's revenue projection would be simplistic and possibly erroneous for a couple of reasons. The industry growth rate cannot be blindly applied to the firm involved in the litigation because the industry might be at a different stage of growth than the injured firm. For example, the industry could be in a mature state while the firm is a new entrant. Such new firms would be expected to experience high rates of growth initially and then experience a lower growth rate as they mature. In addition, various firm-specific factors, in addition to industry factors, may explain the firm's historical sales trends. That is, the firm's growth may follow a life cycle such as that shown in Figure 4.8.

RELATING INDUSTRY GROWTH TO THE PLAINTIFF'S GROWTH

There are several ways that the expert can relate the growth of the industry to that of the plaintiff. Two common ways are to create a firm–industry growth table where the revenues, and possibly shipments, of the industry and the firm are shown side by side. An example is shown in Table 4.5 in which the national and

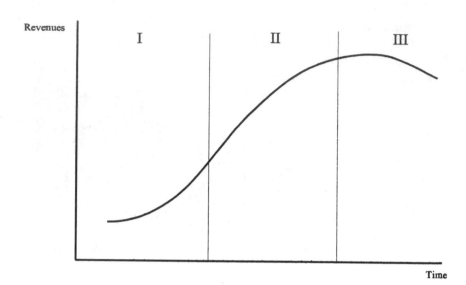

Figure 4.8. Firm's growth life cycle.

Table 4.5. Industry/Firm Corrugated Box Revenues

Year	Industry Revenues (billions)	Percent Change (%)	Firm Revenues (millions)	Percent Change (%)
1980	9.010		10.01	
1981	9.956	10.4	10.95	9.4
1982	9.278	−6.7	10.58	−3.4
1983	9.778	5.4	10.95	3.5
1984	11.491	17.5	11.95	9.1
1985	11.413	−0.7	12.20	2.1
1986	11.673	2.3	12.25	0.4
1987	14.014	19.9	14.65	19.6
1988	15.538	10.9	16.13	10.1
1989	16.066	3.4	17.35	7.6
1990	15.695	−2.2	17.25	0.6
1991	15.264	−2.7	17.00	−1.4
1992	16.447	7.7	17.95	5.6
1993	16.642	1.3	13.64	−24.0
1994	18.609	11.7	17.95	31.6
1995	23.263	25.0	21.25	18.4
1996	20.674	−11.1	22.50	5.9
1997	19.150	−7.4	21.45	−4.7
1998	20.183	5.4	22.48	4.8

regional industry data from the corrugated box industry are compared with the performance of a hypothetical company in that industry. The average growth rates of the industry and the firm are computed for selected historical time periods. It can be seen that the firm experienced similar growth to that of the industry until 1993 when the industry continued to rebound from the 1990–91 recession while the company's revenues fell sharply. The falloff in the company's revenues was short lived and they quickly recovered. These trends are shown in Figure 4.9. An examination of Table 4.4 and Figure 4.9 seems to imply that whatever afflicted the plaintiff in 1993 was not an industrywide phenomenon and that the answer to the plaintiff's declining performance may be found in firm-specific factors.

MEASURING THE STRENGTH OF ASSOCIATION: INDUSTRY VERSUS FIRM

Statistical analysis, such as using correlation analysis, can be used to assess the closeness of association between the historical industry performance and that of the firm. This same type of analysis was used to establish the strength of association between the performance of the national or regional economy and the performance of the firm. In order for such analysis to yield fruitful results, sufficient historical data must be available to allow the results to be statistically reliable.

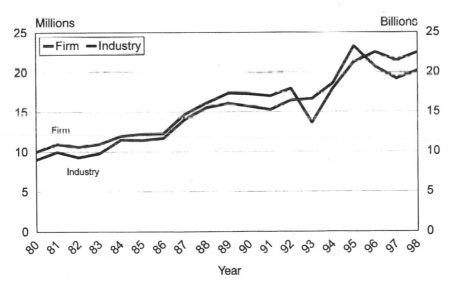

Figure 4.9. Comparative firm–industry trends for corrugated box revenues.

It is important for the expert researching an industry to be aware of important recent trends that might affect the performance of the plaintiff over the loss period. These factors vary by industry and the time when the analysis is being conducted. They also vary from case to case but some of the more common ones are discussed in the following sections.

Changing Level of Competition

Several different market structures in microeconomics (also called *price theory*) vary in terms of the level of industry profitability as well as in how price and output are determined. These structures, which are covered in most introductory textbooks in economics, as well as in all intermediate and advanced microeconomics textbooks, are briefly reviewed in Table 4.6.

If new entrants have increased the level of competition, then profit margins that may be derived from an historical period may no longer apply. In such a case, the new level of competition should be considered when computing the plaintiff's new profitability as greater competition often implies lower profitability.

New Product Innovations

Some industries are very volatile. The computer industry is a case in point. Historical data derived from an environment that was unaffected by important new

Table 4.6.   Alternative Market Structures

Market Structure	Description
Pure Competition	Many small independent companies, each producing a very small percent of total market output, thereby making these firms price takers. Assume no product differentiation and perfect information.
Monopolistic Competition	Many small independent companies that produce a very small percent of total market output. Assume there is some product differentiation.
Oligopoly	A market where there are a few sellers, generally between 3 and 12 sellers. There is product differentiation and usually price is interactively determined by competitors' responses.
Monopoly	Where there is one seller in the market. The monopolist determines either price or output, depending on the structure of the demand curve.

product introductions may not be as relevant to projections made for a period that includes such products. New product introductions in an industry may increase the future sales of the industry. However, new product introductions in other industries could enhance or reduce the sales of the company being analyzed. If more attractive product substitutes have been introduced in another related industry, the future performance of the plaintiff may be adversely affected.

Structural Changes in an Industry

The expert needs to be cognizant of any important structural changes in an industry. If these changes are sufficiently significant they could have an impact on the future of firms in that industry. They may include regulatory change or changes in the channels of distribution in an industry. For example, numerous changes have occurred in the carpet industry over the past several decades that affect all levels of the industry. There has been great horizontal consolidation among the larger carpet manufacturers, with the market shares of many of the surviving companies increasing greatly. In addition, the industry is now a vertically integrated industry with manufacturers selling directly to retailers. This has caused the industry position and profitability of middlemen or distributors to deteriorate. Many such firms have gone out of business as manufacturers went direct as part of their expansion process. If an expert were projecting losses for a carpet distributor, she would have to be aware of this trend, which limited the market and profit potential of such firms. While losing business to manufacturers who are going direct, revenues would fall and retailers, who now have the option of buying direct, would not be willing to pay the same prices for products. Distributors might have to provide better and more costly service to keep revenues from falling while being willing to accept lower margins on the revenues they maintain.

The 1990s witnessed the fifth merger wave in U.S. economic history. Many industries consolidated with companies merging with others. Some of these corporate restructuring transactions resulted in many efficient companies competing more aggressively. Smaller companies that were not able to take such efficiency-enhancing steps could find the competitive environment a more difficult one in which to maintain prior levels of profitability. Such changes could be important when trying to extrapolate future results from historical data.

An example of such restructuring occurred in the banking and telecommunications industries. Partly induced by a changing regulatory environment, these industries are undergoing dramatic changes. Both industries are consolidating as competitors merge to form larger companies. The structural changes in these industries are manifested on both the national and regional level. On the national level, large banks are merging with one another and other related firms, such as Citibank and Travelers Corporation. On the regional level, certain banks, such as NationsBank and First Union Corporation, have acquired competitors to command larger market shares within certain regions. The significance of these structural changes *may* affect the comparability of historical and future financial data. The word "may" has been emphasized as each case has its own unique circumstances and it is difficult to make a broad generalization on the impact of such changes. What is important is to be aware of the potential impact of structural changes in an industry so that, when relevant, they can be specifically analyzed and their impact, if any, is assessed.

YARDSTICK APPROACH AND INDUSTRY ANALYSIS

An industry analysis is a major component of a properly implemented yardstick approach to measuring damages. As described in Chapter 2, the yardstick approach involves finding comparable firms, sometimes called *proxy firms,* which are similar in most relevant respects except that the proxy firms were not affected by the actions of the defendant. As part of the process of finding such firms, one needs to do some analysis of the industry so as to be able to correctly determine which firms are truly comparable. In fact, it is difficult to apply the yardstick approach when doing some industry analysis. In most cases, the industry analysis is a precursor to implementing the yardstick approach.

Court's Position on the Use of Industry Averages

Courts have favorably accepted the use of industry averages when such use was clearly appropriate. For example, in *Bob Willow Motors, Inc. v. General Motors Corp.* the court held that the use of industry sales trends was a useful guide to help project the lost sales of the plaintiff who was an automobile dealer.[15] In this case, the averages served as guides in selecting the appropriate growth rate to use to project "but for" revenues. In commenting on the expert's reliance on industry data to project lost revenues and profits of Bob Willow Motors the court stated:

> Strachota (the plaintiff expert) relied on actual sales by the plaintiff during periods when sufficient vehicles were delivered to the plaintiff's dealership by the defen-

---

[15] *Bob Willow Motors, Inc. v. General Motors Corp.,* 872 F. 2d 788 (7th Cir. 1989).

dant manufacturer. Strachota further relied on national and regional sales to determine sales trends and market conditions in his efforts to determine those sales which the plaintiff should have experienced for the pertinent periods. . . .

To arrive at a lost profits figure, Strachota took a baseline figure (e.g., for Chevrolet he used 1980 when Willow sold 309 cars) and adjusted it by national sales trends. This assumed that Willow would do at least as well as the national sales trends. (This was not without good reason. From 1979 to 1980, sales declined nationally by 18% while Willow's sales increased 83%.). . .

Damages of course may not be speculative or conjectural, but neither are they required to be calculated with scientific precision or mathematical certainty. To calculate damages, Willow had to estimate the number of cars it would have sold— and thus what its profits would have been—had GM not engaged in unconscionable practices.

Court's Rejection of the Applicability of Industry Averages

Courts have rejected the flawed use of averages when the data were not comparable. For example, in *Midland Hotel Corp. v. Reuben H. Donnelly Corp.*,[16] one of many cases involving alleged losses caused by erroneous telephone listings and incorrect or omitted advertisements, the Illinois Supreme Court rejected the use of data on industry hotel occupancy rates due to the fact that the time period being used was not relevant to the loss analysis to which they were being applied. However, in this case it was not the use of industry averages that was the problem. Rather, it was the use of averages from one time period to explain losses in another time period where the court determined other explanatory variables had an impact during the loss period and that the industry averages did not reflect these factors. This is clear from these excerpts from the opinion:

> The plaintiff sought $1,359,857 in lost net profits from July of 1981 to July of 1984. Net profits from July of 1982 to July of 1984 were sought as the consequence of the residual effect of being omitted from the 1981 Guide. John Jaeger, an accountant and plaintiff's expert witness, testified that the damages figure was arrived at by measuring the variance between the plaintiff's occupancy percentage and the average occupancy percentage of other downtown Chicago hotels as derived from a trade publication entitled *Trends in the Hotel Industry* (*Trends*). Jaeger's calcula-

---

[16] *Midland Hotel Corp. v. Reuben H. Donnelly Corp.*, 118 Ill. 2d 306, 515 N.E. 2d 61 (1987).

tion of lost occupancy assumed the plaintiff's occupancy percentage would have equaled the downtown *Trends* average for the three-year period. Jaeger then added the lost revenue from the food and beverage sales as well as lost telephone revenue and deducted from this the plaintiff's variable expenses to arrive at the total lost net profits.

Defendant's expert witness, James Adler, an accountant, testified that Jaeger's calculation of damages was invalid since it incorrectly assumed that plaintiff's occupancy percentage would have otherwise equaled the downtown *Trends* average. Adler noted that for numerous months prior to July of 1981, plaintiff's occupancy percentage was trailing the *Trends* average and that therefore there was no basis for the assumption that the plaintiff would otherwise have equaled the *Trends* average after July of 1981. . . . .

Defendant maintains that as the plaintiff's occupancy rate had been consistently trailing the *Trends* average prior to the issuance of the Guide in July of 1981, there was therefore no basis upon which to conclude that the plaintiff would have otherwise performed as well as the *Trends* average.

The lesson for defendants from *Midland Hotel Corporation v. Reuben H. Donnelly Corp.* is that a key defense to a lost profits analysis based upon industry averages is to challenge the relationship between the industry average and the historical revenue and/or profits (depending on what industry data are being used: revenue or profits). If the defendant can statistically show that there was no historical relationship, then it may be able to challenge the use of the industry data as a predictor of lost revenues. This means that the plaintiff's expert must make sure that such an historical relationship really does exist. If possible, the closeness of association should be measured statistically and demonstrated graphically through the use of exhibits.

Court's Position on the Reliability of Industry Association Data

The courts have also been sensitive to data quality issues, particularly when the data-gathering methods employed by industry associations are suspect. An example of this sensitivity is found in *Polaris Industries v. Plastics, Inc.*, which was a case where a manufacturer of snowmobiles (Polaris) sued a manufacturer of plastic fuel tanks (Plastics). In this case the Supreme Court of Minnesota rejected the use of data culled from a snowmobile industry association due to the fact that there was little assurance that the data reported by the association was accurate.[17] In agreeing with the trial court, the appeals court pointed out that some members did not report data thus making the data a partial sample which contained data with little assurance of reliability.

> Of crucial importance to the plaintiff's proof was the testimony of Joseph Buchan, the director of management services with the accounting firm of Touche, Ross & Co., who had considerable experience with calculating lost profits caused by business interruptions. Mr. Buchan's was excluded almost in its entirety after an extensive offer of proof, in which the witness was examined and cross-examined before the court in the absence of the jury. The trial court found the testimony, exhibits, and conclusions of the witness to lack foundation.
>
> The principal objection made to some exhibits used by Buchan and the conclusions drawn from them was they utilized data from International Snowmobile Industry Association [ISIA] surveys, which were found unreliable after it was determined that it was not known how many snowmobile manufacturers were ISIA members, how many members reported to ISIA, or whether those who did report did so with some degree of accuracy. Since the exclusion of the ISIA reports was proper, the exclusion of the exhibits that graphically displayed the ISIA data was proper.

The foregoing excerpt reveals another opportunity for defendants who face a plaintiff's damages analysis based on the use of industry data. Defendants may want to explore the reliability of the data being used for the projection. In addition to measuring the strength of the association between the historical data and the plaintiff's revenues/profits, the plaintiff's expert must make sure that the data are reliable. It may not be reasonable for the plaintiff to embark on an extensive analysis of the industry association data. However, some research should be done to determine that the data were gathered and analyzed in a reliable manner. If the defendant can find, as it did in *Polaris Industries v. Plastics, Inc.*, that the data were unreliable, then the projection itself may be preempted.

The court's position in *Polaris Industries v. Plastics, Inc.* highlights the problems that can occur in using industry association data. The reliability of such data can vary greatly. As noted earlier, some associations pay greater attention to the quality of the data gathering and analysis than others. Some are better able to enlist the support and compliance of their members than others. Sometimes the associations contract out the surveying process to competent firms that specialize in such work. When specialized firms have conducted the surveying and analysis

---

[17] *Polaris Industries v. Plastics, Inc.*, 299 N.W. 2d 414 (Minn. 1980).

of the data, there *may* be higher comfort level with the data and results. When the association does this work itself, the expert should make sure that it was done competently.

One solution or form of insurance is to have more than one source of industry data. If there is more than one industry association, such as when there are different components of the industry and each has its own data, then these data can be compared. Larger industries, such as the automobile industry, may have several industry subcomponents and some of these have their own data. The trends in these data can be compared for consistency.

SUMMARY

Industry analysis is the second step in the methodological due diligence process. Having assessed the condition of the macroeconomy, the focus is narrowed to the industry in which the plaintiff operates. The analysis considers the performance of the industry, which is compared to that of the macroeconomy as well as to that of the firm. As part of this analysis, the growth of the industry is measured and compared to that of the plaintiff. The historical interrelationship between the two can be assessed using some of the same statistical analysis as was used in the macroeconomic analysis. Once again, if the industry is growing and performing well, the expectation exists that the plaintiff would have also done well. However, this conclusion is very general and simplistic and there may be important factors at play that could cause the plaintiff's experience to differ from the overall industry. This is why industry analysis, like macroeconomic analysis, is but one step in the methodological due diligence process.

In using industry data, the expert needs to make sure that the industry data are reliable. The whole analysis can fall apart if the data themselves are determined to be unreliable. One way this can be done is to do some research into how the data were gathered and analyzed. Another form of assurance is to have more than one source of industry data. In addition, if the trends in the industry data are consistent with trends in other variables, such as the macroeconomic and regional (if relevant) data, then this may provide some limited degree of assurance that the industry data are somewhat reliable.

REFERENCES

Annual Survey of Manufactures, U.S. Bureau of the Census, Washington. D.C.
Bob Willow Motors, Inc. v. General Motors Corp., 872 F. 2d 788 (7th Cir. 1989).

Business Statistics of the United States, Annual, Courtenay M. Slater, ed. (Bernan Press: Lanham, Md.)

Carlton, Dennis, and Jeffrey M. Perloff, *Modern Industrial Organization,* 2nd ed., (New York: Harper Collins College Publishers, 1994).

Douglas P. Handler, "Business Economist at Work: Linking Economics to Market Research: A.C. Nielsen," *Business Economics,* 31 (4) October 1996.

Encyclopedia of Associations, Annual, Gale Research Inc., Detroit, Michigan.

Freedonia Industry Study Catalog, The Freedonia Group, 3570 Warrensville, Suite 201, Cleveland, Ohio, 44122, 216-921-6800.

Midland Hotel Corp. v. Reuben H. Donnelly Corp., 118 Ill. 2d 306, 515 N.E. 2d 61 (1987).

North American Industry Classification System, Executive Office of the President, Office of Management and Budget, Washington D.C., 1997.

Packaged Facts, Department PMB, 625 Avenue of the Americas, New York, NY, 10011, 1-800-265-9836.

Plummer, James, and Gerald McGowin, "The Ten Most Frequent Errors in Litigating Business Damages," *Association of Business Trial Lawyers Report* 5 (1) November, 1995.

Polaris Industries v. Plastics, Inc., 299 N.W. 2d 414 (Minn. 1980).

Predicasts Basebook, Annual, Information Access Company, Foster City, California.

SIC Code Manual, U.S. Government Printing Office, 1987, Washington, D.C.

Statistical Abstract of the United States, Annual, U.S. Department of Commerce, Washington, D.C.

The Information Catalog, Find/SVP, 625 Avenue of the Americas, New York, NY 10011, 1-800-346-3005.

U S Industrial Outlook, Annual, U.S. Department of Commerce/International Trade Administration, Washington, D.C.

U.S. Industry and Trade Outlook '98, DRI/McGraw-Hill and Standard and Poor's and U.S. Department of Commerce/International Trade Administration, 1998.

Value Line Investment Survey, Value Line Publishing Inc., 220 East 42nd Street, New York, NY 10017-5891.

5

PROJECTING LOST REVENUES

In most cases, lost profits can be measured by first projecting lost incremental revenues and then applying a relevant profit margin to the projected lost revenues. This margin should reflect all the incremental costs that would have been incurred in an effort to achieve the forecasted incremental revenues. This chapter focuses on the first step of this process—the revenue projection. It covers the various projection techniques, from basic to more sophisticated ones, that can be used to create a "but for" revenue stream over the relevant loss period. This chapter also discusses the court's position on the use of these methods and related issues such as the data on which the forecast is based. Finally, the chapter focuses on the special cases of forecasting "but for" revenues when data are very limited, as when the plaintiff is a newly established or an unestablished business.

PROJECTIONS VERSUS FORECASTS: ECONOMIC VERSUS ACCOUNTING TERMINOLOGY

Economists tend to use the terms projections and forecasts interchangeably. For example, this was purposely done in the introduction to this chapter. Accountants, however, attach very different meanings to these two terms. When preparing prospective financial statements, accountants consider a financial forecast to be their best judgment of what is going to happen. This forecast can be a range or a point estimate.[1] In projections, however, accountants consider "what if" events and put forward financial data based on hypothetical assumptions.[2] Several possible scenarios can be considered in projections. Only the most likely, however, are included in an accountant's financial forecast.

---

[1] AICPA Guide.

[2] Don Pallais and Stephen D. Holton, *A Guide to Forecasts and Projections* (Fort Worth, TX: Practitioners Publishing Company) 1993, 1-10–1-11.

Clearly, when trying to establish a nonspeculative measure of damages, courts are more interested in what accountants would term forecasts rather than projections. Forecasts carry a greater degree of certainty than the more hypothetical projections. However, in economics, the distinction between the two terms is significantly less meaningful. Economists often use these terms interchangeably. In light of the fact that damages expert witnesses may be either economists or accountants, it is important for attorneys to be mindful of the different use of these terms by these two groups of practitioners.

USING GRAPHICAL ANALYSIS AS AN AIDE IN FORECASTING

Constructing graphs can be quite helpful in detecting the relationship between a business interruption event and the performance of a plaintiff, as reflected in variables such as revenues. Graphical analysis can be particularly useful in the more simplistic business loss scenarios in which an event occurs and revenues fall around the event date. Such graphs can be compelling court exhibits based on the idea that a picture is worth a thousand words. Figure 5.1 is an example of such a graph. It shows that around time t_0 an event took place that caused the company's

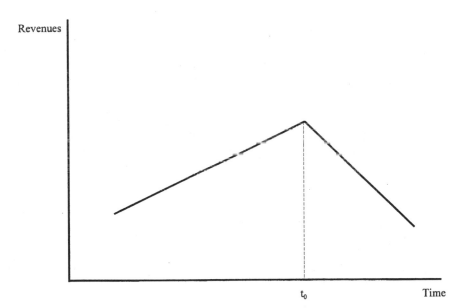

Figure 5.1.   Sharp downward revenue trend caused by a business interruption.

revenues to sharply turn downward. Forecasting comes into play when extending out the revenue curve beyond t_0 to construct a "but for" revenue projection.

The use of graphical analysis can be very helpful early on in the interaction between the damages expert and the attorney who retained the expert, especially when the damages expert has been retained by a plaintiff's counsel who relates a scenario of damages that is very inconsistent with the pattern of revenues. For example, in Figure 5.2, the plaintiff's revenues continue to exhibit a very similar growth pattern after the interruption as they did prior to that date. Often the plaintiff's counsel simply relies on the client's verbal representations without investigating the numbers. If the damages expert is brought in early enough in the litigation, he may be able to advise counsel on the strength of the damages claims. Unless there are compelling reasons to believe that the postinterruption growth should have been significantly higher, Figure 5.2 may be an example of a situation where proving damages could be difficult.

The foregoing discussion is framed in the context of very simplistic business interruptions in which revenues are steadily growing at a nearly constant rate when an interruption causes revenues to sharply turn downward. In the case of growing businesses, however, where an interruption may cause a decline in the growth rate but not in the absolute value of revenues, the impact of the interruption may be somewhat more difficult to discern using graphical analysis. In these cases, one may want to graph the growth rate along with the absolute revenue

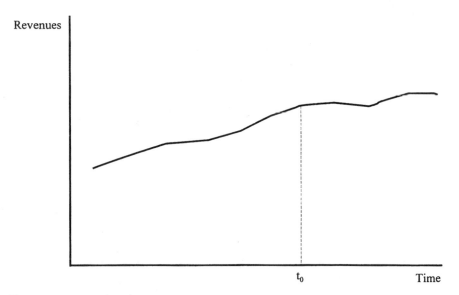

Figure 5.2.   No clear business interruption.

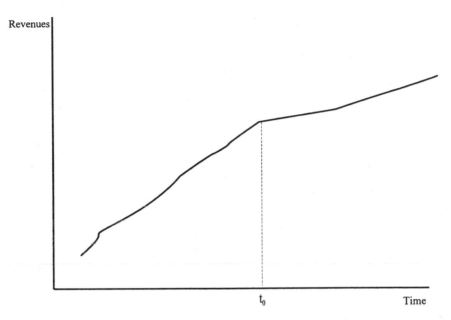

Figure 5.3.   Fall-off in the revenue growth rate.

values. The fall-off in the growth rate may then be clearly seen in graph form as shown in Figure 5.3.

Graphical analysis can also be used to get a quick picture of a possible interrelationship between one series, such as the plaintiff's revenues, and another relevant series, such as the revenues of the industry in which the plaintiff operates or those of a proxy firm. This is shown in Figure 5.4 where the industry continued to grow before and after the plaintiff's business interruption date of t_0 (see 5.4 (b)) while the plaintiff's revenues abruptly declined after that date (see 5.4 (a)).

Graphical analysis is a simple first step that may or may not confirm the impact of a business interruption. However, such analysis may be used throughout the expert's work, from serving as an exhibit in the expert's initial meeting to being an exhibit in a report and possibly at trial.

METHODS OF PROJECTING LOST REVENUES

The revenue forecasting process can vary from basic historical growth rate extrapolation methods to more sophisticated statistical curve-fitting techniques. Several factors enter into the decision of what level of sophistication to employ.

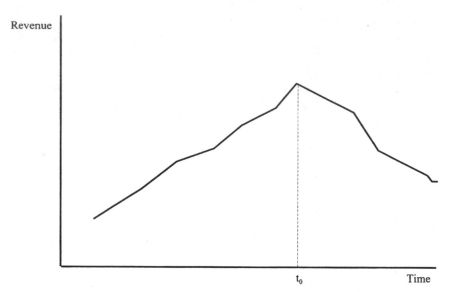

Figure 5.4a. Plaintiff's revenues.

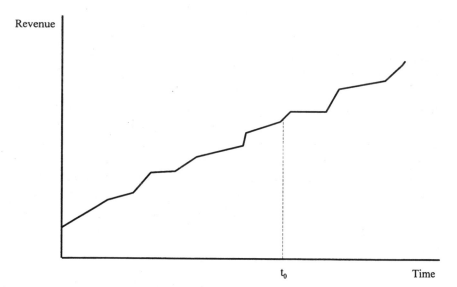

Figure 5.4b. Industry revenues.

The two most important factors are *accuracy* and *simplicity*. Since the methods used must be explained to a judge or jury, who may not have a background in statistical analysis, simpler methods have certain advantages. Only if it can be demonstrated that the more sophisticated methods are significantly more accurate should they be contemplated. The damages expert should bear in mind that sophisticated econometric and statistical analysis is commonly used with success in various types of litigation such as employment litigation. One can argue, however, that the analytical requirements in such litigation are such that simpler methods do not produce the required results and that this is not the case in many commercial damages actions. As with many decisions in commercial damages analysis, the answer will be found on a case-by-case basis.

One limiting factor that determines whether more sophisticated curve-fitting techniques can be pursued is the availability of historical data. These techniques require sufficient historical data to produce accurate forecasts. If such data are not available, then more basic techniques, such as simple growth rate extrapolations, may have to be used.

Basic Growth Rate Extrapolation

Basic growth rate extrapolation is the simplest and most often-used revenue forecasting method. This revenue projection process can be divided into a two-part process that begins with the determination of the appropriate revenue base. A growth rate is then selected and applied to the chosen revenue base to project what are referred to as *but for* revenues. These are the revenues that the plaintiff would have realized, had it not been for the events at issue in the litigation.

Selection of the Revenue Base

An analysis of the plaintiff's revenue history must be conducted in order to determine the appropriate revenue base. If the plaintiff has enjoyed a steady stream of positive annual revenue growth, then the appropriate base for the revenue projection may be the last year of preinterruption revenues. When the plaintiff has experienced both positive and negative growth, the expert must apply judgment in selecting the appropriate base. One possible alternative is the use of average revenues computed over prior years, such as the past three years.

Table 5.1 shows the revenue stream of two companies. Company A is a firm that has had a history of uninterrupted and steady growth prior to the interruption year which is 1997. It seems reasonable that, but for the interruption, revenues would have grown beyond the preinterruption level. Therefore, it would be inappropriate to use the average revenues for the last, say, three years. Rather, the

Table 5.1. Selection of Base for Revenues Forecasts

Year	Company A		Company B	
	Revenues	Growth Rate	Revenues	Growth Rate
1989	2,057,000		2,157,650	
1990	2,270,300	10.4%	2,668,700	23.7%
1991	2,320,000	2.2%	2,920,100	9.4%
1992	2,568,000	10.7%	2,757,950	−5.6%
1993	2,720,800	5.9%	3,059,600	10.9%
1994	2,850,300	4.8%	3,268,900	6.8%
1995	3,087,000	8.3%	3,100,900	−5.1%
1996	3,296,900	6.8%	3,585,620	15.6%
1997	3,596,800	9.1%	3,459,420	−3.5%
1998	3,620,500	0.7%	3,590,236	3.8%
Base Revenues	3,620,500		3,578,213	
Average Growth Rate		6.5%		6.2%
Compounded Growth Rate		6.5%		6.1%

revenues associated with the last year prior to the interruption, $3,620,500, should be used as the base for the projection.

Company B, on the other hand, fails to exhibit a clear trend in its revenue history, which is the same length as Company A. Given the lack of any apparent trend in the revenue data, the simple average of the last three years of revenues, $3,578,213, seems an appropriate base for the projection.

In selecting the base for the projection, the expert may have to choose between the last preinterruption year's revenues versus an average of historical revenue data. For example, if the expert were to conclude that the more recent year's revenues contained more relevant forecasting information than the more remote years, then a weighted average, which placed progressively more weight on more recent years, could be used. Weighting schemes may differ depending on how much weight one wants to assign to various years. An example of a weighted average is shown in Table 5.2.

As Table 5.2 shows, the weighted average places more weight on the more recent year's value which, being higher than the others, causes the weighted average to be higher than the simple average. The rationale for placing more weight on more recent years is that the years closer to the interruption date are likely to be more similar to the "but for"years than prior years. Once again, though, each case brings its own set of facts, which may or may not make this judgment appropriate.

The foregoing discussion is framed in the context of companies that have a history of annual revenues. For newer businesses, which have a shorter history,

Table 5.2. An Example of a Weighted Average

Company B Revenues	
1996	3,585,620
1997	3,459,420
1998	3,590,236

1. Simple Average (equal weights)
   R = 3,585,620(1/3) + 3,459,420(1/3) + 3,590,236(1/3)
   = 3,415,547

2. Weighted Average (different weights)
   R = 3,585,620(0.25) + 3,459,420(0.3) + 3,590,236(0.45)
   = 3,549,837

other forecasting methods must be employed. These are discussed in the context of the losses incurred by new businesses.

Selection of the Projected Revenue Growth Rate

One method of projection is to simply extrapolate the historical revenue growth rate. In doing so, it may be useful to select an historical period that is similar in length to that of the forecast period. For example, if one is forecasting six years into the future, it may be useful to determine the historical revenue growth rate using the revenues for the six years preceding the business interruption.

The compounded annual growth rate can be calculated using the following formula:

$$g = \left(\frac{Y_n}{Y_0}\right)^{1/n} - 1 \tag{5.1}$$

where: g = the compounded growth rate
Y_0 = the first period's sales level
Y_n = the last period's sales level
n = the number of periods

Although it is legitimate to use the compounded sales growth rate as an alternative to the arithmetic mean (average) of the historical annual growth rates, this method can be sensitive to the choice of the beginning and ending points. Note that there is no assurance that a historical period of the same length as the forecast period will be the best predictor of the growth over the forecast period. While this rule of thumb is sometimes used, each case brings its own unique factors that determine if the rule of thumb should apply. Table 5.3 and Figure 5.5

Table 5.3.   Revenues Forecast Using Average Growth Rate

Year	Annual Forecasted Revenues
1998	3,855,833
1999	4,106,462
2000	4,373,382
2001	4,657,651
2002	4,960,399

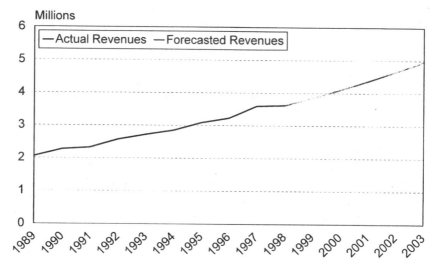

Figure 5.5.   Actual versus forecasted revenues: forecast using average historical growth rate.

show the revenue projection for Company A, using the average growth rate for the historical period available, that is 6.5%.

Curve Fitting Methods and Econometric Models

The curve-fitting method requires the expert to define an equation for a line or a polynomial curve which *"best fits"* the historical data. This line of best fit is placed within the plot of points representing the historical data. The statistical technique known as regression analysis allows the line to be placed in the "middle" of these points. Using the two parameters derived from such a line, the intercept and the slope, the relationship can be used to project values beyond the available historical data. Regression analysis needs a minimum number of data points to produce a reliable estimate of the slope coefficient. Sometimes such data are not available. Therefore, because of lack of data, as well as the higher level of complexity, the expert may simply decide to use a historical growth rate extrapolation. However, if sufficient data are available, the regression method may either be exclusively employed or used in conjunction with simpler methods. Table 5.4 and Figure 5.6 show the revenue projection for Company A, using a simple regression model that postulates that revenues are a function of time. This form of regression analysis, which uses time as the independent variable, is called *time series analysis.*

The forecasted values are derived using the estimated regression equation as follows:

$$Y = 1,841,313 + 181,365(\text{Time})$$

When the historical revenue data do not fit a clear pattern, simple time series curve-fitting methods do not work as well. A statistical alternative is to construct an econometric model that uses selected independent variables to explain the variation in a dependent variable, which in this case is revenue.[3] However, using a more expansive model may increase the data requirements. Table 5.5 and Figure 5.7 show the revenue projection for Company A, using a more sophisticated model that postulates that revenues are not only a function of time, but also of the industry shipments in the previous year.

Table 5.4. Revenue Forecast Using Two-Variable Model

Year	Annual Forecasted Revenues	
1997	3,836,327	
1998	4,017,692	
1999	4,199,056	
2000	4,380,421	
2001	4,561,786	

Variable	Coefficient	T-Statistic
Constant Term	1,841,313	41.49
Time	181,364.8	25.36
R-squared	0.9877	
Durbin-Watson	2.0401	
F-Statistic	643.03	

[3] Foster, Carroll B., Robert R. Trout, and Patrick Gaughan, "Losses in Commercial Litigation," *Journal of Forensic Economics,* VI, (3) Fall, 1993.

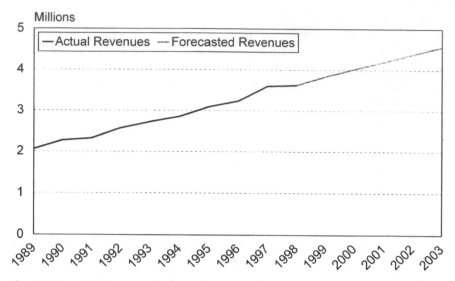

Figure 5.6. Actual versus forecasted revenues: forecast using regression analysis—Model I.

Table 5.5. Revenues Forecast Using A Multivariable Model

Year	Annual Forecasted Revenues
1997	3,873,537
1998	4,065,415
1999	4,258,929
2000	4,454,123
2001	4,651,039

Variable	Coefficient	T-Statistic
Constant Term	51,197,70	5.16
Time	151,526.50	12.76
Indshp (−1)[a]	43,064.38	2.8

R-squared	0.9942	
Durbin-Watson Statistic	2.4630	
F-Statistic	600.87	

[a] In this example, Company A is in the retail appliance business.

UNDERSTANDING REGRESSION OUTPUT AND DIAGNOSTICS

A complete explanation of regression analysis and of the diagnostic statistics produced therein is clearly beyond the scope of this book. However, a brief re-

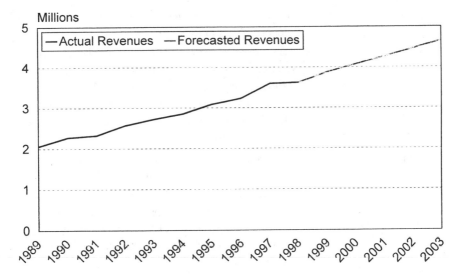

Figure 5.7. Actual versus forecasted revenues: forecast using regression analysis—Model II.

view of some of the more often-cited statistics generated by the major regression computer programs is provided in the following list:

R^2 This statistic measures the degree to which two variables move together. The adjusted R^2 is more often cited. This version makes an adjustment for the number of independent or explanatory variables included in the model or equation. This adjustment is made because adding even irrelevant variables causes the unadjusted R^2 to increase.

Although higher R^2s are certainly a good sign, a high R^2 from sample data does not necessarily mean that the model will generate accurate forecasts out-of-sample. The high R^2 may simply reflect that within the sample, the regression line fits the data well.

t scores   When a regression output is produced, such as the one reproduced in Table 5.5, the reliability of the coefficients' values is judged by their t scores. Scores greater than or equal to 2 are considered good—meaning that there is a relationship between this particular explanatory variable and the dependent variable.

F score

This score measures the overall significance of the complete model including all the explanatory variables. If the value computed is above a certain critical value, then we reject the hypothesis that all the explanatory variables have coefficients of zero and that the model has no explanatory power.

Durbin-Watson Statistic

This score tells us whether the data are inflicted with serial correlation. This statistic can vary between 0 and 4 with values close to two being considered good. Values close to 4 indicate the presence of negative serial correlation while values close to 0 indicate the presence of positive serial correlation

COMMON PROBLEMS AFFECTING REGRESSION MODELS

It is not unusual to see a practitioner blindly use the regression analysis functions of spreadsheet programs to generate forecasts without knowing the reliability of the model and of the resulting forecasts. A brief review of some of the more common problems occurring in regression analysis is provided in the following list:

Serial correlation:

Also referred to as autocorrelation, serial correlation sometimes occurs in time series analysis when there is some systematic relationship between the error terms or residuals of a regression model. The presence of serial correlation can cause the *t* scores to be higher than what they would be without serial correlation. This can cause the user to believe that the relationship that he has measured is better than what it really is.

The presence of simple serial correlation can be detected by the Durbin-Watson statistic. Once detected, various techniques, such as generalized least squares, can be used to correct the problem.

Heteroskedasticity

This problem occurs when the variance of the data changes over the range of the data being considered. The consequences of heteroskedasticity are the same as for serial correlation, in that the t statistics may be higher than what they might be if this phenomenon were not present. Several tests exist, such as the Park test and the Goldfeld test, to detect this phenomenon. Heteroskedasticity can be corrected by redefining the variables.

Multicollinearity   This problem occurs when some explanatory variables in the model are correlated. Regression analysis assumes that the variables are not correlated. The presence of multicollinearity creates a problem in the interpretation of the coefficients, as the magnitude of a coefficient could be a reflection of not just the variable to which it refers but of some other variables as well. Sometimes the solution is the elimination of the redundant variables. In other cases, however, econometricians simply leave the model untouched as the coefficients are still "unbiased" estimators of the "true" coefficients.

Omitted variables   This problem occurs when the model leaves out an important variable. The estimates of the coefficients are not as reliable as they are biased. An estimator is inconsistent if, as the sample used for developing an estimate gets larger, the mean of the sample does not approach the population mean.

Lack of Stationarity

Many of the series that we discussed in Chapter 3 were nonstationary time series. Examples included gross domestic product (GDP), personal consumption expenditures, and retail sales. A *stationary* time series is one that has a constant mean and variance and a covariance between any two values in the series, which only depends on the distance or lag between the values. A nonstationary time series could occur when there is a shift in the average value of the series over time, such as in the case when dealing with variables that increase over time due to the overall growth of the economy. Clearly this is the case with GDP and the aggregates that represent its components.

This discussion sounds technical and in order to make it relevant to a litigation audience it can be useful to consider applications that might arise in litigation. One of the problems that can occur in regression when you have a nonstationary time series is that one may get some impressive regression results when in fact the regression was *spurious*. Consider the following example. Assume that an expert is interested in measuring the losses associated with a group of employees who left an employer. Further assume that the expert is trying to estimate lost sales using the sales of employees who have stayed. The expert may attempt to estimate the relationship between the two groups of employees using their historical sales. The estimated mathematical relationship between the two might then be used to forecast the sales of the employees who left. Unfortunately, if, as may be the case in a growing economy and industry, that causes the sales of both groups to grow, we may be regressing one nonstationary time series on another. The problem is somewhat insidious in that, at first glance, one might get some impressive regression diagnostics, such as a high R^2 and a high t statistic for the explanatory variable. However, one of the test statistics, the Durbin-Watson test statistic may be quite low.[4]

The problems with the example and the reason why we get a spurious regression result is that the two time series are really independent, but the high R^2s falsely imply that there is a relationship between the two series. A full discussion of the problems of nonstationary time series and spurious regressions is well beyond the bounds of this litigation-oriented book. However, a condition known as spurious regression exists and it can render a seemingly impressive regression result seriously flawed. Various tests can be employed to detect nonstationarity and spurious regressions. One such test is the *unit root test,* which examines the relationship between successive values in a given series.[5] A related test is the *tau test* or *Dickey Fuller test,* which compares the value of a test statistic, τ, to some critical value in order to determine if the series is stationary.[6] Those who might encounter nonstationary time series that result in spurious regressions should at least be aware that solutions to the problem exist. These solutions often involve

---

[4] One rule of thumb that has been put forward by Granger and Newbold is that when R^2 is greater than the Durbin-Watson statistic, then there is a decent chance that you have a spurious regression. See C. W. J. Granger and P. Newbold, "Spurious Regressions in Econometrics," *Journal of Econometrics,* 2, 1974, 111–120.

[5] Damodar Gujarati, *Basic Econometrics,* 3rd ed. (New York: McGraw Hill) 1995, 718–719.

[6] D. A. Dickey and W. A. Fuller, "Distribution of the Estimators for Autoregressive Time Series with a Unit Root," *Journal of the American Statistical Association,* 74, 1979, 427–431.

converting the series into one that is stationary, such as by a process known as *first differencing*. The converted series may be stationary and a nonspurious regression can then be conducted.

Once again, a detailed discussion of these topics requires more space than this section permits. However, this is not the goal of this section. Rather, the goal is to make attorneys and users of these techniques aware that the potential problems discussed thus far can make a damages forecast based on regression analysis invalid. Experts who want to use time series analysis should make sure they consult a skilled econometrician. Attorneys who have retained an expert who uses econometric techniques should inquire as to whether the proper testing was done and whether a consulting econometrician was used (assuming the expert is not an econometrician). Cross-examining attorneys should retain a firm that has a good econometrician on staff. Chances are, the expert may not even be aware of the potential flaws inherent in his analysis. When these flaws are exposed on cross-examination, the analysis put forward by the plaintiff's expert may fall apart.

Example of Other Problems Encountered in the Use of Regression Analysis to Measure Damages in Litigation

Several problems can occur when regression analysis and other econometric techniques are used to project lost revenues by an expert who lacks specialized expertise in econometrics. Naive users of regression analysis may be unaware of the presence of large forecast errors resulting from limited data or data that are so variable that they do not lend themselves to accurate forecasting. This is sometimes the case when the users rely on the regression functions of basic spreadsheet software packages that may not even contain the diagnostic test results that would reveal the presence of a problem, if one existed. Even if the user employed the more sophisticated software package, she would have to have the expertise to properly interpret the diagnostic statistics and implement a statistical solution to any potential problem.

The lack of specialized expertise on the part of the user of the econometric techniques creates an opportunity for opposing counsel to challenge both the expertise and the analysis of the expert. Econometrics is a very specialized and challenging field. It has a rich body of literature and requires a strong background in the field to be properly understood and used. A well-coached opposing counsel can use the rigor of this field against the naive user. The opposing counsel may also use his own expert to explain to the court the flaws of the opposing expert's analysis.

This was successfully done in *Worldcom, Inc. v. Automated Communications, Inc. et al.* In this case, *Worldcom* presented a damages analysis that created a lost revenues projection using basic regression analysis produced by a spreadsheet package. The plaintiff's expert was not an econometrician and his analysis was simplistic and unreliable, in the opinion of the defense's expert, Dr. Larry Taylor, of Economatrix Research Associates, Inc. and Lehigh University. The case involved the projection of lost revenues resulting from an alleged breach of a non-compete agreement and claim of employees' pirating. Excerpts from Dr. Taylor's testimony, which are included in the appendix of this chapter, are quite instructive in that they describe a situation in which the plaintiff's analysis was done using a simplistic spreadsheet regression program. This analysis was fraught with some of the econometric problems discussed previously, including heteroskedasticity and spurious regression result.

CONFIDENCE IN FORECASTED VALUES

Statistical tools exist that may allow the economist to introduce evidence on the level of confidence of a forecast. This may help establish that damages are projected within a *reasonable degree of economic certainty.* One method that may be used is to construct *confidence intervals,* statistical bands that are placed around forecasted values. The bands allow the economist to show a range around the forecasted values that contain a predetermined percentage, such as 95%, of the "true values" line. Within the context of a simple two-variable regression model, the use of confidence intervals can be demonstrated as follows:

Let Y = the explained variable
$\hat{Y}$ = the forecasted values of the explained variable
X = the explanatory variable
α = intercept term
β = slope coefficient

$$Y = \hat{\alpha} + \hat{\beta}X_t + \varepsilon_t \qquad (5.2)$$

This relationship can be used to forecast future values of Y. Specifically:

$$\hat{Y}_{t+1} = \hat{\alpha} + \hat{\beta}X_{t+1} \qquad (5.3)$$

The forecast error is then

$$\hat{\varepsilon}_{t+1} = \hat{Y}_{t+1} - Y_{t+1}$$
$$= (\hat{\alpha} - \alpha) + (\hat{\beta} - \beta)X_{t+1} - \varepsilon_{t+1}. \qquad (5.4)$$

There are several sources of error in a regression forecast. The first comes from the random nature of the error process, which will make the forecast deviate from the actual values even when the model is correctly specified and when the parameters are known. The second source of error comes from the fact that we do not know the true parameter values but use instead sample estimates that differ from the true values. When we start forecasting, we add new error elements. We now have to forecast the explanatory variable in addition to the dependent variable. Last, if we relax the assumption that the model is correctly specified, we add still another potential error—misspecification.[7]

The economist in litigation can show that the errors in the forecast are a function of the sample size and the variance of X. The confidence band constructed around the regression line (see Figure 5.8) will have a smaller prediction interval when X is closer to its mean (average) value. A 95% prediction interval can be constructed from the following expression:

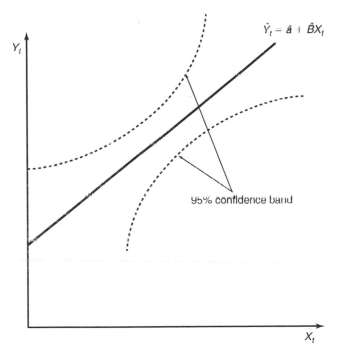

Figure 5.8. Confidence band around a regression line.

---

[7] Robert Pindyck and Daniel Rubinfeld, *Econometric Models and Economic Forecasts,* 5th ed. (New York: McGraw Hill) 1998, 204–206.

$$\hat{Y}_{t+1} - t_{0.05}s_f \le Y_{t+1} \le \hat{Y}_{t+1} + t_{0.05}s_f \tag{5.5}$$

(Note: s_f is the estimated standard deviation of the forecast error)

The estimated standard deviation of the forecast error is the square root of the estimated variance of the forecast error, which is defined by the following equation:

$$s_f^2 = s^2 \left[1 + \frac{1}{t} + \frac{(x_{t+1} - \overline{X})^2}{\sum (X_t - \overline{X})^2} \right] \tag{5.6}$$

Equation (5.5) shows that the distance between the regression line and either confidence band is approximately twice the standard error (given that $t_{0.05}$ is approximately equal to 2). Thus the standard errors of the forecast can serve as a guide to the confidence the economist has in the forecast. It is also clear that the further in the future the economist forecasts, the lower the reliability of the forecast. The benefit of this type of presentation is that the reduction in reliability is now quantified for each time interval into the future. It is important to note, however, that the confidence band approach is applicable only when the economist has decided to utilize regression analysis to measure lost profits.

Two econometric measures exist that allow the analyst to assess the accuracy of a forecast more carefully than the simple application of a confidence band around the forecasted values would. These measures are the *Akaike information criterion* (AIC) and the *Schwartz information criterion* (SIC).

Akaike Information Criterion

The Akaike information criterion measures the out-of-sample error variance. However, this measure applies a penalty for the degrees of freedom, which are the number of parameters to be estimated.

$$AIC = \exp^{[(2k)/T]} \frac{\sum_{t=1}^{T} e^2}{T} \tag{5.7}$$

Schwartz Information Criterion

The Schwartz information criterion is a similar measure to the Akaike information criterion, except that it assesses an even harsher penalty for the degrees of freedom.

$$SIC = T\left(\frac{k}{T}\right)\frac{\sum_{t=1}^{T} e^2}{T} \tag{5.8}$$

FREQUENCY OF THE USE OF ECONOMETRICS TECHNIQUES IN COMMERCIAL LITIGATION

While sophisticated measures of forecast accuracy, such as confidence bands, AIC and SIC, are mentioned here, it is important to note that they are *not* normally a standard part of commercial damages projections. Part of the reason for this is that regression analysis itself is not used all that often. Rather, simple projections using historical growth rates are more commonly used. One of the reasons regression analysis is not used very frequently is the fact that this type of statistical analysis tends to need many historical data points to construct forecasts that have statistical reliability. Such data are often not available. These data related constraints limit the confidence in the regression coefficients and produce very wide confidence bands that would indicate a less reliable forecasting process. Another reason, however, for regression analysis not being used is the lack of expertise of the user who is then relegated to only less sophisticated methods.

Court's Position on the Use of Econometric Analysis in Commercial Damages

Regression analysis and other econometric techniques are mainstays in employment litigation involving claims of bias. For example, in *Vuyanich v. Republic National Bank of Dallas*, the court includes an extensive discussion of statistical and regression models, along with several of the problems that can occur in applying these techniques, such as misspecification and multicollinearity.[8] While relied upon less frequently, econometric techniques in general and regression analysis in particular have been determined by a number of courts to be an acceptable method to project revenues. Such was the case in *White v. Southwestern Bell Telephone Co.* where an accountant used regression analysis to project what the revenues would have been in 1978, the only year in which the plaintiff suffered a loss, based on the revenue history presented to the court, which covered

---

[8] *Vuyanich v. Republic National Bank of Dallas* (D.C. Tex. 1980).

the years 1974 through 1980.[9] The plaintiff claimed a loss due to an incorrect Yellow Pages advertisement. The plaintiff's presentation was buttressed by the fact that he showed that sales through wire services, which should not be affected by Yellow Pages advertising, increased in 1978. The defense tried to show that the purported functional relationship underlying the regression analysis did not exist.

The acceptability of regression analysis in commercial litigation has not been universal. For example, in *ABC Trans National Transport Inc. v. Aeronautics Forwarders, Inc.* the court rejected the use of regression analysis. In particular, this court found that the results of such forecasts were not *conclusive proof of legal damages.*[10] However, in this case, which involved claims that the defendant diverted employees and customers from the plaintiff to itself, the court was troubled by some of the simplistic assumptions of the analysis. Specifically, the analysis, which was performed by a "chartered financial analyst" assumed with a 100% probability that, but for the diversion, the employees and customers would have remained with the plaintiff. Although statistical techniques exist to compute the attrition rates, these were not employed. Therefore, *ABC Trans National Transport Inc. v. Aeronautics* should not be seen as a rejection of econometric techniques, but rather as a rejection of statistical methods based upon flawed and overly simplistic assumptions. More advanced statistical techniques have now been introduced into the field that would directly address the court's concerns regarding attrition rates and customer tenure.[11]

Courts have recognized that the reliability of a regression forecast is a function of the number of historical data points available. In *In re Oil Spill by Amoco Cadiz,* the court stated that the limited number of data points renders the regression analysis unreliable.[12] Other courts have recognized that a misspecified equation or a regression analysis that estimates parameters by relying on data that are not relevant to the plaintiff's business has *little probative value.*[13]

---

[9] *White v. Southwestern Bell Telephone Co.,* 651 S.W. 2d 260 (Tex. 1983).

[10] *ABC Trans National Transport, Inc. v. Aeronautics Forwarders, Inc.,* 90 Ill. App. 3d 817, 413 N.E. 2d 1299 (1980).

[11] Laura Bonanomi, Patrick Gaughan, and Larry Taylor, "A Statistical Methodology for Measuring Lost Profits Resulting From a Loss of Customers," *Journal of Forensic Economics,* 1998.

[12] *In re Oil Spill by the Amoco Cadiz,* 1988 U.S. Dist. Lexis 16832 (N.D. Ill., Jan. 11, 1988).

[13] *Micro Motion, Inc. v. Exac Corp.,* 761 F. Supp. 1420 (N.D. Cal. 1991).

Reasonableness of Econometric Results

Courts try to reconcile the results of an econometric analysis using general reason. Judges may not be trained in statistical analysis, but usually possess a great deal of common sense and experience in evaluating a wide variety of damage claims. The results must make intuitive sense. If not, sound reasons for a counterintuitive result must be put forward. This was the case when the court, in *Polaroid Corporation v. Eastman Kodak Company*, rejected the econometric analysis of the well-known economics professor—Dr. William Baumol. As the excerpt from the following opinion reveals, the court rejected his econometric analysis and found the conclusions he derived from it to be unreasonable.

Professor Baumol freely admits that any model is colored by the assumptions upon which it is based and by influences the model builder chooses to include or omit. Although Professor Baumol chose to include market expansion, I have found with few exceptions, that there was no market mechanism unique to Kodak which the facts show could have expanded the market. Although I cannot paint a perfect picture of the market from the testimony of fact witnesses, contemporaneous documents, and market research, *I find that evidence much more reliable than even the best econometric model* (emphasis added). The direct evidence is, after all, the factual basis of the case, not some approximation built on facts. Besides being contrary to the facts, the extreme results of Professor Baumol's model—that Polaroid would have captured none of Kodak's sales between 1976 and 1978 and only a small percentage from 1979 to 1983—add to my conviction that it is unreliable. I, therefore, reject its conclusions as contrary to other evidence which I find more credible. . . .

While I do not accept these models in this case, I am not critical of the field of econometrics as a whole. I believe that it can provide valuable insight into complicated matters. However, in this case the models contain assumptions contrary to the facts and achieve extreme results which by their very nature are suspect. Perhaps the inner working of the models, which I cannot comprehend, are biased. Perhaps the instant photography market does not lend itself to mathematical interpretation. Whatever the reason, I cannot adopt Professor Baumol's model as evidence of market expansion.

SEASONALITY AND FORECASTING

The issue of seasonality may not be relevant when constructing projections of annual values. However, when there is a need to forecast values within a given year, it may become necessary to make adjustments to take into account the fact that businesses often experience seasonal variation. Some businesses have a very distinct and significant pattern of seasonal variation. For example, in the United States retail sales are typically 24% higher in the month of December than in any other month.[14] This pattern may be even more pronounced in certain types of businesses, such as toy stores, which conduct a very significant percent of their annual sales in the year-end holiday season. It would, therefore, be inaccurate to annualize a toy store's first five months of revenues simply by dividing the revenues by five and multiplying them by 12. Other more sophisticated techniques should be applied.

Seasonal adjustment is regularly done in statistical and econometric analysis for one of three reasons:

1. For comparison of different values that appear at different points in time to be influenced by seasonal variation
2. For better use of regression analysis without being concerned that the results are being influenced by seasonality
3. For more accurate short-term forecasting[15]

One way to handle the seasonal variation is to use a *seasonal decomposition technique.* With this technique, the historical sales pattern is smoothed or averaged out to eliminate the seasonal variation. This process is sometimes referred to as *filtering.* The seasonally adjusted revenue values are then used to construct a smoothed forecast. The economist can then reintroduce the seasonal pattern to obtain revenue values that pertain to each seasonal period.[16]

One of the most basic ways of smoothing out seasonal variation is to use some type of moving average process. For example, assume that we have quarterly revenue data for a plaintiff and that we want to use the preinterruption data to forecast the postinterruption revenues. The greater the quarterly variation, the more concerned we are that the forecasts are going to be biased by the seasonal variation. The expert could try to ignore the quarterly variation by using annual data with the thought that annual revenues associated with the year of the interruption should have some relationship with the prior years, such as a given level

---

[14] Olivier Blanchard, *Macroeconomics* (Upper Saddle River, N.J.: Prentice Hall) 1997, 159.

[15] W. R. Bell and S.C. Hillmer, "Issues With the Seasonal Adjustment of Economic Time Series," *Journal of Business and Economic Statistics* 2, 1984, 291–320.

[16] For a basic discussion of the seasonal adjustment process see William S. Brown, *Introducing Econometrics* (St. Paul, Minn.: West Publishing Co.) 1991, 255–256.

of growth. Unfortunately, an annual analysis may not always be workable. One reason is that there may be only a few annual preinterruption data points and, therefore, the use of quarterly values may add more historical preinterruption data. Another reason could be that the loss period is confined to some short period, such as a quarter. In this case, the focus on quarters instead of years may have an obvious advantage.

A number of different smoothing techniques can be used. We have already mentioned the use of simple moving averages. Data on seasonal weighting factors for a wide variety of industries are available from the U.S. Department of Commerce through their Census II program. Other more sophisticated techniques, such as *exponential smoothing,* are also available.[17] These methods, unlike simple moving average models that weigh all preinterruption values equally, apply more weight to the values that are closer to the interruption date. If the expert believes that more recent values have more information content than more remote values, then an exponential smoothing process may work better than a simple moving average adjustment method. One of the most commonly used exponential smoothing method is the *Holt-Winters exponential smoothing technique.* Basically, all these methods allow the economist to smooth out the seasonal variation and see the underlying pattern in the data more clearly.[18] When doing so, the economist may be better able to discern the underlying trend in the data, having filtered out the component of the total variation in the sales caused by seasonal influences. This pattern can then be used to forecast "but for" revenues.[19]

CAPACITY CONSTRAINTS AND FORECASTS

A common error made in the projection of commercial damages is to project revenues beyond the capacity constraints of the plaintiff's firm. It is not sufficient to merely show that there would have been sufficient demand to support the projected revenue levels. Unless it can be established that the plaintiff had the ability to generate such revenues, perhaps through the use of subcontractors,

---

[17] Spyros Makridakis and Steven C. Wheelwright, *Forecasting Methods for Management,* 5th ed. (New York: Wiley), 1989, 71–76.

[18] See Paul Newbold and Theodore Bos, *Introductory Business Forecasting* (Cincinnati: South Western Publishing), 1990, 158–218.

[19] Applications of these methods are shown in Robert R. Trout and Carroll B. Foster, "Business Interruption Losses," in *Litigation Economics,* Patrick A. Gaughan and Robert Thornton, eds., (Greenwich, Conn.: JAI Press) 1993.

this projection is inappropriate. If the ability of the plaintiff to produce the projected revenues is uncertain, then a capacity analysis needs to be conducted. While such an analysis may be within the expertise of an economist, it requires an understanding of the plaintiff's business in relation to its facilities and their usage levels.

If it can be shown that in the past the plaintiff has manufactured products or services at the projected revenue levels, then capacity may not be an issue. If not, other analytical justifications should be provided. This can be done by analyzing the plaintiff's production function, which is the functional relationship between the inputs that the plaintiff utilizes and the output (goods or services) that he produces. Once this relationship has been established, the maximum production attainable, given the plaintiff's fixed inputs, can be established. This production level represents, at least in the short run, the ceiling for the projected revenues. When a sufficient time period has passed, long enough for the fixed inputs to vary, then the production associated with the projected revenues may exceed this ceiling.

Each case is unique and the presence of capacity constraints may not automatically preclude a forecast beyond the plaintiff's current capacity level. To forecast beyond such constraints, however, the costs and availability of greater capacity needs to be taken into account. In capital intensive industries, capacity constraints may present a formidable barrier that may not be crossed without the investment of significant capital and the passage of the requisite period of time needed to expand capacity.

SENSIBILITY CHECK FOR THE FORECASTED VALUES

It is important that the forecasted values be within a reasonable range, clearly attainable by the plaintiff. The economist may be able to use industry data to test the "reasonability" of the forecast. For example, a standard measure of sales productivity in the retail industry is sales per square foot. The average sales levels for retail establishments are provided by the National Retail Merchants Association's Merchandising Operating Results in what are called MOR reports. When the projected sales are divided by the total square footage or the square footage of the selling space, the projected sales levels can be compared with the industry average. If the projected sales levels are significantly above the levels for even "superior stores," then the projected levels may need to be reconsidered.

Another sensibility check may be to evaluate the *market share* of the plaintiff at the projected sales levels. This evaluation involves making assumptions about the rate of growth in the total market, which may be done through an examination of the industry growth rate. If, for example, the plaintiff had a 2% market share at the time of the business interruption but the projections show the plaintiff would have a 40% market share at the end of the loss period, the reasonableness of the projection needs to be carefully revisited.

Once again, one recurrent caveat in this chapter is that the uniqueness of each case provides varying opportunities to conduct a sensibility test of the forecasted values. Where possible, this test should be done.

PROJECTING LOST SALES FOR A NEW BUSINESS

The losses of a new business may be more difficult to project. However, if the expert responds to this higher level of difficulty by not projecting any loss, he is implicitly assigning a value of zero to the loss. This itself is a projection, and probably one that is substantially less accurate than the best effort's projection that an economist may construct.

The cause of the higher level of difficulty in projecting losses of new or unestablished businesses is the fact that such businesses lack a track record. The courts have been very aware of this difficulty—what one court termed a "paucity of proofs."[20] However, the economist may use *proxy firms*, firms similar in many relevant respects to the plaintiff, such as product line, size, capitalization, and so forth to derive a growth rate and some information about sales volume and profitability. One has to be careful when ascribing the characteristics of a proxy firm to a plaintiff because it must be established that the plaintiff would have truly been like the proxy firms. It is also important to note that the proxy firms are a biased sample of the total population of businesses that were also new at one time. This sample in fact includes only those firms that survived some minimum period, including what may be the more risky years of initial operation. The risk of failure, which may be estimated by using statistics showing the number of similar firms that have failed (if available), needs to be incorporated into the analysis.

Industries that feature many similar firms selling nearly identical products are easier candidates for a failed new business analysis. Franchises, such as fast food chains, can be good examples. Their product lines are designed to be as consistent as possible and they often have a large number of franchisees whose data may be useful in determining the expected sales across different time periods.

---

[20] *Hunters Int'l. Mfg. Co. v. Christiana Metals Corp.,* 561 F. Supp. 614 (E.D. Mich. 1982) aff'd, 725 F. 2d 683 (7th Cir. 1983).

Data available from the franchiser may enable the expert to construct a model that would explicitly factor in regional and demographic factors.

Legal Precedent for Damages for a New Business: Prior New Business Rule

The court's position on new businesses has evolved dramatically over the years. Under the old rule, the courts concluded that damages for a new business were "simply too speculative and incapable of being ascertained with the requisite certainty."[21] The courts had great difficulty getting around the fact that there is too much uncertainty when the cost structure and resulting profitability of new businesses is unknown.[22] In summarizing the prior new business rule this court stated:

> The usual method of proving lost profits is from profit history. It is argued that when a plaintiff is conducting new business with labor, manufacturing, and marketing costs unknown, prospective profits cannot be awarded.

Modern New Business Rule

Under the prior new business rule it was very difficult to prove damages for a newly established business. This situation changed in favor of the plaintiff with the adoption of an easier standard that has become the modern new business rule. This rule allows plaintiffs to establish damages as long as these damages are within a reasonable degree of economic certainty. The plaintiffs still face an uphill battle in proving such damages but under the Modern New Business Rule successful damage claims are achievable.

Franchiser with Limited Track Record

There have been many cases in which a new business with a limited track record has been awarded damages. In *Lightning Lube, Inc. v. Witco Corp.*, a jury awarded the plaintiff, a franchiser of quick-lube businesses, $2.5 million in past damages

---

[21] William Cerillo, *Proving Business Damages* (New York: Wiley), 1997, 46.

[22] *Larsen v. Walton Plywood Co.*, Wash. 2d 1, 16, 390 P.2d 677, 687 (1964), 396 P. 2d 879.

for breach of contract and $7 million in future damages for tortious interference, even though none of the franchisees had been in existence for even one of their 10-year franchise agreements.[23] In reaching its decision, the jury took into account that the plaintiff had entered into 170 franchisee contracts, although less than 40 franchisees had actually opened business. They used the fact that the plaintiff had received a total of more than $330,000 in royalties from these initial franchisees to make a conservative projection of damages over the 10-year contract period. This decision is instructive in light of the fact that the jury used a limited data history to project damages for a significantly longer, contractually determined loss period. Clearly, the standard used by the court was less stringent than what would result if confidence bands, such as those shown earlier in this chapter had been used to determine whether the projection was speculative.

Construction Litigation Involving a Newly Established Business

Litigation is a common occurrence in the construction industry. Projects can remain suspended in a partially completed state for a significant period of time due to a wide variety of conflicts between participants or subcontractors. One example is when finance providers do not provide the financing necessary to continue a project. Courts have been willing to award damages in cases like this even though a project may have only been partially completed. For example, in *South Carolina Federal Savings Bank v. Thornton-Crosby Development Co.*, the South Carolina Supreme Court upheld an award of damages based on testimony of what revenues and profits would have been generated from a developer's eventual sale of condominiums.[24] The court relied on the actual records of precompletion sales (the project was one-half sold) and anticipated sales (the remainder of the project was projected to be completely sold in another nine months) as well as records of various expenses that would have been incurred and testimony that the project would have been fully sold as of a certain date.

Another instructive lost profits case in the construction industry is *S. Jon. Kreedman & Co. v. Meyers Bros. Parking-Western Corp.*, where a California court awarded damages to a lessor due to the failure of a lessee to build a parking garage and lease it to the plaintiff. In this case, the court awarded damages, even though the construction was never completed, after a consideration of the experi-

---

[23] *Lightning Lube, Inc. v. Witco Corp.*, 4 F.3d 1153 (3rd Cir. 1993).

[24] *South Carolina Federal Savings Bank v. Thornton-Crosby Development Co.*, 423 S.E.2d 114 (S.C. 1992).

ence and track record of the plaintiff in this field.[25] In particular, the court relied on the combined testimony of an economist and a long-term employee as well as partial financial histories and the performance records of the parties involved to reach the conclusion that the estimates of damages were not speculative. The employee of Meyers, the cross-complainant and appellant, testified as to the performance and profitability of a similar underground garage operated by Meyers. This is another example of the use of *proxy firms* to fill the void of a financial history when one is not available.

Using Expert Testimony in Newly Established Business Cases

Whereas expert testimony may be invaluable in establishing commercial damages in general, it is particularly useful in cases involving newly established businesses, because of the inherent difficulty in projecting damages when only a limited business history is available. In addition to the normal lost profits methodology, the expert may want to present research on the existence and applicability of data of proxy firms. In articulating its reasoning for a departure from the prior New Business Rule, the court, in *Larsen v. Walton Plywood Company,* used expert testimony to bridge the gap caused by the limited data available for newly established businesses. Specifically, the court stated:

> Experts in the area are competent to pass judgement. So long as their opinions afford a reasonable basis for inference, there is a departure from the realm of uncertainty and speculation. *Expert testimony alone is a sufficient basis for an award for loss of profits.*[26]

In this case, the plaintiff used a combination of damages and industry experts who weaved together a collection of statistical evidence, including various industry statistics to establish lost profits. This inclusion of an industry expert to buttress the analysis of the damages expert can be an effective combination.

PROJECTING LOSSES FOR AN UNESTABLISHED BUSINESS

Measuring losses for an unestablished business can be even more difficult than for a new business. At least with a new business there are some data available on

---

[25] *S. Jon. Kreedman & Co. v. Meyers Bros. Parking-Western Corp.,* 58 Ca. App. 3d 173, 130 Cal. Rptr. 41 (1976).

[26] *See* note 22.

the actual performance of the business. It may be possible to compare this performance to other established businesses with a longer track record to try to determine comparability. These limited data, however, are not available for an unestablished business.

Legal Precedent for an Award of Damages for an Unestablished Business

There are abundant legal precedents for the awarding of damages to a business that was not established as a result of certain acts of a defendant. Once again, an established track record in the field in which the business is operating is beneficial in convincing the court that the estimated profits are not speculative.[27] Such a presentation can be greatly enhanced when there are numerous other proxy businesses that share many of the same characteristics as the plaintiff's and which can be used to reliably approximate how the plaintiff would have performed. Franchisees, such as those in the fast-food industry, can be good examples of the ability to use such proxy firms, as was successfully done in *Smith Development Corp. v. Bilow,* where data on the performance of other McDonald franchisees was used as a guide to show how a McDonald's restaurant that never opened would have performed.[28] In the case of major franchises, such as McDonald's, there are abundant data available on the performance of similar businesses. Moreover, since fast food franchises are designed to be very similar in the products and services that they offer, establishing comparability is not difficult. Finally, in this particular case, the fact that up to the trial date no McDonald's franchisee had ever failed also helped remove an element of speculation that might have otherwise been present with an unestablished business.

Defendants' Successful Challenges To Lost Profits Claims for Unestablished Businesses

While a plaintiff may have to rely on convincing evidence through various sources such as proxy firms to remove the element of speculation surrounding the projection of lost profits involving an unestablished business, a defendant may be able to focus on other factors to show the opposite—that a projection cannot be relied on with a reasonable degree of economic certainty. Just as in

---

[27] *Short v. Riley,* 150 Ariz. 583, 724 P. 2d 1252 (Ariz. Ct. App. 1986).
[28] *Smith Development Corp. v. Bilow,* 308 A. 2d 477 (R.I. 1973).

Smith Development Corp v. Bilow, statistical evidence on the success rate of similar businesses was used to show that the projection was within the realm of economic certainty. In *Rancho Pascado v. Northwestern Mutual Life Insurance Co.*[29] statistical evidence, including data on failure rates as high as 95%, were used to show the level of risk in the plaintiff's business—catfish farming. Other risk factors were explored by the defendant, including problems with the ability of the defendant to distribute the relatively high quantities of the product projected by the plaintiff. In this case, it was shown that only a small minority of firms like the plaintiff actually survive. In such industries, the burdens of proof on the plaintiff may be unsurmountable, particularly when the defendant can supply statistical evidence to support the risk level of the business. If this evidence is not sufficient to void the plaintiff's lost profits projection, it may be still be used to show that the high level of risk should at least be incorporated into a risk premium and added to the discount rate.

CASE STUDY: *LIGHTNING LUBE, INC. V. WITCO*

During the period 1985–89, Lightning Lube, Inc., a New Jersey corporation, was a quick lube franchiser. In this business customers can have the oil in their cars changed, along with other minor services, within a short period of time such as ten minutes. The owner of the business, Ralph Venuto, negotiated with Witco to purchase Kendall motor oil and to have Witco assist Lightning Lube in the purchase of lubrication dispensing equipment. Lightning Lube, Inc. would then sell oil directly to customers while providing them with the equipment it represented to its franchisees that it owned. Venuto testified that he turned down another oil purchase and equipment financing deal with Valvoline in order to go with Witco.

The relationship deteriorated when Witco did not provide Lightning Lube, Inc. with the equipment repayment schedule it requested and when Lightning Lube fell behind by more than 90 days on its payments for oil purchases. Witco placed Lightning Lube, Inc.'s purchases on hold, although it allowed Lightning Lube, Inc.'s franchisees to purchase oil directly from Witco at the same price it sold to Lightning Lube, Inc.

Between 1985 and 1987 Lightning Lube, Inc. sold more than 170 franchises but only 35 to 40 of them actually opened up. The failure of these franchises to open up or to continue with Lightning Lube led to cash flow problems for Light-

---

[29] *Rancho Pescado v. Northwestern Mutual Life Insurance Co.,* 140 Ariz 174, 680 P. 2d 1235 (1984).

ning Lube and to its eventual demise. The reason why the franchises either failed to open up or to continue with Lightning Lube was a major point of debate at the trial. However, in the end the jury was convinced that Witco's actions, such as offering the franchisees free equipment and cheaper oil than what Lightning Lube gave them, constituted tortious interference and helped cause the failure of Lightning Lube.

At trial, Lightning Lube founder and CEO Ralph Venuto was allowed to testify on his revenue and profits projections for the business. Prior to the trial, Witco objected to such lay testimony being admitted but they did not prevail as the court was persuaded of Venuto's knowledge of the business. However, Venuto was not allowed to offer opinion testimony of the kind that an expert might put forward. Venuto's projection was based on 117 contracts that he sold for $17,500 each. He stated that each franchise would generate $28,000 in annual royalties. The record reflects that there were 34 franchisees in the first year and that they averaged $140,000 in annual revenues. Using a 7% royalty rate, this translated to $9,800 in revenues for Lightning Lube for each of these 34 franchisees. Venuto went on to testify that the first year's performance was 40% higher than what he expected. This played an important role in persuading the jury to accept Venuto's projections of the future performance of Lightning Lube.

The defense challenged Venuto's projections stating that he did not account for economic factors, such as the effects of the recession. Venuto responded that the recession might reduce the purchase of new cars but that the declining demand brought on by the economic downturn should not affect car service for existing vehicles. The jury was also impressed by Venuto's testimony that Lightning Lube was one of the fastest growing franchisees in the country.

In the end, Lightning Lube prevailed even though it was a relatively new business with a limited track record. With respect to damages, its success can be attributed to a combination of factors including its performance during the first year period along with the track record and credibility of its CEO.

SUMMARY

A common first step in the damage measurement process is to forecast "but for" revenues. The methods used to forecast revenues range from very basic to somewhat sophisticated techniques. The simple methods, the most frequently used, often involve the selection of a base level to which a growth rate is then applied. The growth rate may come from an analysis of the plaintiff's historical growth. Factors that will often go into the selection of the growth rate may include the growth of the economy, region (if relevant), and the industry. By applying the growth rate to the selected base, a series of "but for" revenues are derived, which are then compared to actual revenues in cases where the business continued at a lower level than in the "but for" revenues projection.

More sophisticated methods of forecasting may involve the use of regression analysis to project "but for" revenues. The statistical projection may be based on a time series analysis, where historical revenues are used to forecast future revenues, or may involve the estimation of an econometric model, whereby future revenues are forecasted based on a functional relationship between historical revenues and certain other selected explanatory variables.

If the forecasting process relies on econometric methods, the users must fully understand the intricacies involved in such analysis. To do so requires having the necessary experience and expertise in using such methods. Attorneys should make sure that their experts either have this expertise or are relying on other experts who have it. When faced with an expert who uses regression analysis, attorneys need to consult an econometrician, as that may result in much useful fodder for cross-examination.

APPENDIX

This appendix contains various excerpts from the testimony of Dr. Larry Taylor of Economatrix Research Associates, Inc. and Lehigh University in *Worldcom v. Automated Communications.*[30]

Q. In the context of Mr. X's written analysis—and I think you referred to his testimony.[31] Were you able to determine from the words of the analysis and the figures that he created and so on whether or not he had done any testing? Did it say so one way or another?

A. It was clear to me that Mr. X was relying solely on the goodness of fit measure—that is, the R^2—from each of the models in order to determine whether or not they are good or bad models. And it is well known in econometrics, especially in the time series literature, that you cannot do that. You are not allowed just simply to look at the goodness of fit measure to determine whether or not a model is valid or invalid. He did not go beyond that.

---

[30] *Worldcom v. Automated Communications,* It should be noted that very minor editing has been applied to this testimony to remove perceived typographical errors by the stenographer and to enhance readability. *LDDS Communications, Inc. v. Automated Communications, Inc.* 35 F. 3d 18 (5th Cir. 1994).

[31] Given the critical nature of the comments, the name of the plaintiff's expert is not revealed.

Q. The goodness of fit measure is a statistic that's generated before any testing is done?

A. It is generated from the estimation stage. And it is intended—as a matter of fact, I have developed goodness of fit measures for more complicated models than the one that is being used here. And in all cases, the goodness of fit measure is simply a first glance.

If your goodness of fit measure is low, then you have to question your model. But if the goodness of fit measure is high, well, that's great, but that's only one of the necessary conditions that must be met in order for the model to be considered valid.

The testimony goes on to explain what more rigorous testing would reveal. One of the problems that more rigorous testing revealed to Dr. Taylor was a condition called nonstationarity that was present in the data. This was not taken into account by the plaintiff's expert and that was one of the reasons why his analysis was flawed.

The Court. Are you saying that you can't make any projections from a nonstationary group?

A. It's very difficult, Your Honor. That's exactly right. There is a big issue in econometrics as to whether or not a series could be estimated or predicted by a strong law like a time trend. So that no matter how far you get off the trend line, there is a law that says you will come back to the trend line. And so no matter, you know, if you work really hard and you network and you, say, increase your account levels to a larger number and are really on a roll, the trend line—the deterministic trend line says that you will automatically—you will just tend to go back to that line.

And the assumption here is that as a group, these 13 individuals will go back toward that line. Now, clearly, you know, in a number of economic situations, including, for example, if we had gross national product and we were trying to estimate gross national product and predict gross national product. We don't think that that is going to be independent of the past.

So with a non-stationary series, what it says is that what you did yesterday and the day before yesterday and the day before that could have a very strong influence on what path you take in the future. And so, therefore, what we are saying is there might be some tendency, for example, to increase your number of accounts by, say, ten or five—just making up these numbers—say five a month. But I cannot actually tell you which direction you're going to be off from that. It could be one month or so that you're up two accounts, another month or so you're down two accounts.

But the whole idea is that I know it's growing, but it's growing in a very unpredictable manner. And that's what we mean by nonstationary. There is no set path. There is no attractor (phonetic) line, say, that this series tends back toward. And that's one of the reasons why with respect to a deterministic trend line like Mr. X has assumed here for the projections from March 1993 onward seems so untenable to me. And it certainly seems to me that in light of what we've learned in the past 20 years in econometrics, that that is something that any serious econometrician would look at.

The Court.   All right.

Q. Thank you. Going back, I think you had just said that you found strong evidence of inertia?

A. That's right.

Q. What did you mean by that?

A. Well, exactly what I was saying with regard to the unpredictability of the line. In other words, past errors tend to accumulate. So if I made an error in forecasting the first month, then chances are I'm going to have an error on the positive side. Say if I have a positive error in the first month I am forecasting, I'm going to have a positive error in the second month. There is strong correlation over time. These series are correlated.

And that's just simply another way of saying that there is strong inertia in the system. This inertia actually is in the errors. But because of that strong inertia in the errors of the model, what that is telling me is that that inertia perhaps could be better brought back into the model. Let's model this inertia in a better way. And so, therefore, I'm saying that it's made me suspect that we had a problem here in the sense that these two series could have been growing independently of each other.

One of the symptoms or one of the clues in this is that, yes, we did see a higher R square for the first model, .94. As Mr. X indicates, that's very close to one. But I know that if there is strong inertia in the errors, that that tends to bias my R square upwards toward one. Not only do I have an R square that's very high, but I have a low Durbin-Watson statistic.

Well, Granger and Newbold in the *Journal of Econometrics* back in 1974 had a very famous paper on spurious regression, which said just this: That if you have strong inertia in the system in the errors, then you had better look to make sure that inertia could not be brought into the model itself. And this high R square, low Durbin-Watson clued me in on that to make me think that maybe this regression was spurious. That, yes, the reason I'm getting this high R square within the estimation period is because both series are growing and it's picking it up. It's picking up the fact they're both growing. But yet are they growing independently?

So I saw this problem. And I investigated it further. And indeed what I found that there is strong evidence that indeed there is a problem here. I think, you know, to best illustrate it, I know based upon these series, I'm getting the sales—the sales of the departing group, and I'm trying to predict that by looking at the control. And what I'm seeing here is that for every account that the control group adds, I should be adding about ten accounts for the departures.

So, therefore, if I just simply look at the growth in accounts and look from period to period to see how many accounts the departing group grows by versus how much the control group grows by—if I just simply regress the growth rates on each other, I should get around ten. For every—for every one unit in the control group, if the control group increases its sales by, the departing group should increase its sales by ten.

However, when I run the regression that I just simply said here on the growth rates in the accounts, what I find is, very interestingly, the coefficient on the control group for this growth model is not anywhere near ten, but rather it's negative .4930, which is extremely close to zero.

Q. Which means what?

A. Which means that it really does not influence the growth rate of sales. Okay?

Q. What doesn't?

A. The growth rate of the control group does not influence the growth rate in the sales group. Even though I would expect that for every one unit increase in the control group, I get ten units over here in the sales group. I'm getting close to zero. There appears as though there is no relationship—no set relationship between the growth in the sales of the control group versus the growth in the sales of the departing sales group. The R square, far from being .94 for this model, which follows logically from the preceding model that Mr. X estimated—

Q. Now, which model are we talking about?

A. Model 1. Okay? Where we've got control group on the right-hand and got departing sales group on the left-hand side. Instead of getting an R square of .94 for this regression, which should have a high R square, if the logic of the first model is correct, I'm getting an R square of .0040072. That's about as close to zero as you're going to find.

Q. And what does that lead you to conclude?

A. That leads me to believe more strongly that these two series are growing independently of each other. And therefore, projecting the sales of the departing group by using the sales of the control group does not make sense. There is also—there are also some other errors.

Q. Are you still in the testing of the Model 1?

A. Just Model 1. There are other issues. There is an issue here with respect to the functional form.

Q. What is that?

A. Functional form just is—let me give you an example. You could have Y is equal to A plus B times X. Or you could have the model, the square root of Y is equal to A plus B times X. Or some other functional form. In other words, you are just simply changing the mathematical relationship between the dependent variable Y and the independent variable X. It entails no new information here. Oh, and by the way, I, want to make it clear that in reading Mr. X's testimony, it is absolutely clear to me that he does not understand this issue.

Q. Why do you say that?

A. Because his statement there is to the effect that the reason we do a misspecification test is to check for omitted variables. That's essentially what he is saying, is there should be other variables in the equation that we do not find. Well, clearly, a functional form test is not a test for omitted variables, not at all.

We're just simply saying whether or not the mathematical relationship between the two variables has been specified properly. The test for inertia in the disturbances is not a test for omitted variables. We just simply have to correct for the inertia in the system. The normality test is the same way. The heteroskedasticity—

The Court.   Not too fast now?

A. I'm sorry.

The Court.   Okay.

A. The heteroskedasticity test suggests that the spread of the disturbances is changing over time, either increasing or decreasing. That involved absolutely no additional information than what you already have at your disposal in order to attempt to correct the problem. The test for normality is similar. We can actually use techniques to correct that particular problem, again without trying to go and search for additional information.

The only thing then that I am pointing out is that conditional upon your information set, conditional upon the variables that you have in your model, there are problems that you can correct without actually trying to access additional data. And Mr. X clearly does not understand this issue from his testimony.

Q. How did you—I am sorry. Were you going to say something else?

Well, I can go on and point out some other tests that Mr. X's models fail, but—in particular a structural change test. But I think I will delay that because the same criticism applies to the second model in the business as usual framework. So I think I will delay.

Q. How did you detect this strong evidence of inertia in Model 1 you mentioned before?

A. There are two tests. First is the low Durbin-Watson test. Durbin-Watson is a very standard test that has been around since about, I would say, in the mid-fifties, maybe the early sixties. And it's a test that we inform all of our undergraduates to look at when they are trying to decide whether or not their model is correctly specified and whether or not they can interpret the regression output correctly.

And that was one of the biggest clues was that this Durbin-Watson value was clearly in the unacceptable region. And for that reason, I thought about looking at the inertia issue. There is also another test which directly tests for serial correlation. And this test rejected at the 10% significance level.

So, again, there was evidence that I should be looking in this particular regression direction in order to determine whether or not the information that Mr. X had had been used in an optimal fashion.

Q. Are you saying that there were some preliminary tests that you performed that generated results that caused you, as an expert econometrician, to know that you needed to look further and perform additional—

A. That's right. This is the same iterative process that we discussed before. That when you get to the testing stage, that regardless of what model you have in the conceptual stage, that if you are in your testing stage and you realize that something is wrong, then you have to iterate back and think through the conceptual stage again as to what might be wrong—how might you correct the model so that it does pass the necessary conditions for it to be a good econometric model.

Q. Based on the testing you performed, did Model 1 pass the necessary tests for it to be a good econometric model?

A. Not at all.

Q. Now, you did some testing with respect to Model 2?

A. Model 2, I had some similar issues. This gets back to the idea of whether or not I could have a deterministic time trend so that I have this law which says that regardless or how far I get away from the trend line, that I will always go back to it eventually versus this idea of a nonstationary process where I have strong inertia and such that I know that if I had done well last month, this might help me to do well this month in term of my sales.

And clearly, it's something worthy of testing. And again, I found that under the business as usual second model, that there is very, very strong evidence of serial correlation in the disturbances even more so than in Model 1. There is strong evidence of a functional form problem. And moreover, there is evidence that there is a structural break in the time series model itself.

In other words, we have a time series line with a variable slope. There is evidence that even within the estimation period, that first period that we see from January 1992 up to February 1993, that the trend line is actually changing its slope. And the way that I did that was I actually estimated the trend line based upon the first 11 observations, the first 11 months. And then I used the last three months in order to construct the test.

Essentially what it's telling me is that there is some sort of structural break; and therefore, the model does not predict well even within the estimation period. So if the model does not predict well even within the estimation period— that is, January 1992 to February 1993—then it's very, very hard to understand how in the world we could rely on these predictions thereafter.

Q. Did you do any other tests with respect Model 2 besides the ones you've described so far?

Just the Chow (phonetic) test, the one—the structural shift, the serial correlation test and functional form test. I did do other tests. The normality and the heteroskedasticity tests actually passed. And so I wasn't particularly concerned about those issues.

Q. Is the fact that Model 2 passed a couple of tests significant?

A. It doesn't work that way. If one of these tests rejects, then you need to investigate further. It's not—it's not one of these issues where it passed three out of four tests or it passed two out of four tests. So, therefore, I'm doing pretty well. You need to at least investigate as to why the test is failing.

And as I said, I think that I discovered—and I do have the supporting evidence to indicate that I do not have a deterministic time trend, but I have more of a nonstationary process. Or at least if not a nonstationary process, at least a process where I can say that my current sales depends upon my previous sales and/or accounts. Okay? And that's important. That is a very important issue because it gets back to the idea of projection and the reliability of my projections.

In its opinion, the court accepted Dr. Taylor's analysis. Specifically, the court's opinion was stated as follows:

Dr. Taylor's testimony persuaded this court that there are problems with Mr. X's models which render the models inadequate for the determination of lost profits argued by the plaintiff. Overall this court is troubled by Mr. X's models being based in part supposedly upon Mr. X's personal experiences. For instance, Mr. X explained that he first calculated lost profits for a period of two years because this was the remaining duration of the noncompete agreements. Then, says Mr. X, the period was changed to three years based upon his personal estimate of the situation.

Furthermore, Mr. X failed to follow econometric principles when setting up his models. On cross-examination, Mr. X admitted that he simply has extended the historic trend of Y's operations as the "business as usual" line without taking any other factors into account such as market saturation, competition, or the ordinary attrition and replacement of Y's sales representatives. The court had difficulty accepting Mr. X's presumption that the approximately six-month period in which it took Worldcom to recover must be translated into a three-year period of damages based on the speculative upward trend of the "business as usual" line in the second and third charts presented.

Finally, Mr. X's models fail econometric tests for consistency, allow for changes in methodology, and ignore market factors crucial to their integrity.

REFERENCES

ABC Trans National Transport, Inc. v. Aeronautics Forwarders, Inc., 90 Ill. App. 3d 817, 413 N.E. 2d 1299 (1980).

AICPA Guide, American Institute of Certified Public Accountants, New York.

Bell, W. R. and S. C. Hillmer, "Issues With the Seasonal Adjustment of Economic Time Series," *Journal of Business and Economic Statistics* 2, 1984, 291–320.

Blanchard, Olivier, *Macroeconomics* (Upper Saddle River, N.J.: Prentice Hall, 1997).

Bonanomi, Laura, Patrick A. Gaughan and Larry Taylor, "A Statistical Methodology for Measuring Lost Profits Resulting From a Loss of Customers," *Journal of Forensic Economics,* 1998.

Brown, William S., *Introducing Econometrics* (St. Paul, Minn.: West Publishing Co., 1991).

Cerillo, William, *Proving Business Damages* (New York: Wiley, 1997).

Dickey, D. A., and W. A. Fuller, "Distribution of the Estimators for Autoregressive Time Series with a Unit Root," *Journal of the American Statistical Association* 74, 1979, 427–431.

Foster, Carroll B., Robert R. Trout, and Patrick A. Gaughan, "Losses in Commercial Litigation," *Journal of Forensic Economics* 6(3) Fall 1993.

Granger, C. W. J. and P. Newbold, "Spurious Regressions in Econometrics, *Journal of Econometrics* 2, 1974, 111–120.

Gujarati, Damodar, *Basic Econometrics,* 3rd ed., (New York: McGraw Hill, 1995).

Hunters Int'l. Mfg. Co. v. Christiana Metals Corp., 561 F. Supp. 614 (E.D. Mich. 1982) aff'd, 725 F. 2d 683 (7th Cir. 1983).

Larsen v. Walton Plywood Co., Wash. 2d 1, 16, 390 P.2d 677, 687 (1964), 396 P. 2d 879

LDDS Communications, Inc. v. Automated Communications, Inc. 35 F. 3d 18 (5th Cir. 1994).

Lightning Lube, Inc. v. Witco Corp., 4 F.3d 1153 (3rd Cir. 1993).

Makridakis, Spyros, and Steven C. Wheelwright, *Forecasting Methods for Management,* 5th ed., (New York: Wiley, 1989).

Micro Motion, Inc. v. Exac Corp., 761 F. Supp. 1420 (N.D. Cal. 1991).

Oil Spill by the Amoco Cadiz, 1988 U.S. Dist. Lexis 16832 (N.D. Ill., Jan. 11, 1988).

Newbold, Paul, and Theodore Bos, *Introductory Business Forecasting* (Cincinnati, Oh.: South Western Publishing, 1990).

Pallais, Donald, and Stephen D. Holton, *A Guide to Forecasts and Projections,* (Fort Worth, Tex.: Practitioners Publishing Company, 1993).

Pindyck, Robert and Daniel Rubinfeld, *Econometric Models and Economic Forecasts,* 5th ed., (New York: McGraw Hill, 1990).

Ramanathan, Ramu, *Introductory Econometrics* (Fort Worth, Tex.: Dryden Press, 1995).

Rancho Pescado v. Northwestern Mutual Life Insurance Co., 140 Ariz 174, 680 P. 2d 1235 (1984).

Short v. Riley, 150 Ariz. 583, 724 P. 2d 1252 (Ariz. Ct. App. 1986).

S. Jon. Kreedman & Co. v. Meyers Bros. Parking-Western Corp., 58 Ca. App. 3d 173, 130 Cal. Rptr. 41 (1976).

Smith Development Corp. v. Bilow, 308 A. 2d 477 (R.I. 1973).

South Carolina Federal Savings Bank v. Thornton-Crosby Development Co., 423 S.E.2d 114 (S.C. 1992).

Studenmund, A. H., *Using Econometrics: A Practical Guide* (New York: Harper Collins, 1997).

Trout, Robert R., and Carroll B. Foster, "Business Interruption Losses," *Litigation Economics,* Patrick A. Gaughan and Robert Thornton eds. (Greenwich, Conn.: JAI Press, 1993).

Vuyanich v. Republic National Bank of Dallas (D.C. Tex. 1980).

White v. Southewstern Bell Telephone Co., 651 S.W. 2d 260 (Tex. 1983).

6

COST ANALYSIS AND PROFITABILITY

In the typical lost profits analysis, certain costs are deducted from projected revenues. This analysis often employs a combination of skills and may involve the interaction of economists and accountants. A common area of analysis for economists working in microeconomics is the relationship between revenues and costs. Much economic research has been directed to various types of costs analysis, including the separation of variable and fixed costs, how costs vary over time, and the relationship between average and marginal costs. For most economists, this analysis is more of a theoretical exercise, although practicing litigation economists working on commercial damages necessarily deal with these issues on a regular basis.

Accountants, particularly cost accountants, are regularly involved in the pragmatic measurement of costs and how they vary with the operations of the firm. Accountants who report on financial statements for public use must understand issues involving consolidation of financial entities, relationship of cost elements of financial statements, and various costing methods, all of which have a significant influence on the reported profitability of the firm.[1] Therefore, the services of accountants can be invaluable in computing the costs associated with lost incremental revenues.

---

[1] For a discussion on the role of accountants in commercial damage analysis which emphasizes the strengths of accountants see Elizabeth Evans, "Interaction Between Accountants and Economists," in *Litigation Services Handbook,* 2nd ed. Roman Weil, Michael Wagner and Peter B. Frank, eds. (New York: Wiley, 1995) 3.1–3.20.

PRESENTATION OF COSTS ON THE COMPANY'S FINANCIAL STATEMENTS

An examination of the appropriate expenses to be deducted from projected revenues begins with a review of the company's financial statements—especially the income statements, which set forth gross revenues and the various cost deductions necessary to arrive at net income. Table 6.1 is an example of a typical consolidated income statement showing the total revenues and costs of Merck Corporation during the calender year 1996. In the right-hand column of Table 6.1, the costs components of the income statement are expressed as a percentage of revenues. Such an expression is often used in financial analysis for what is known as *percentage of sales forecasting.*[2] The expression of costs as a percent of revenues can be very helpful for quickly discerning the average relationship between a company's revenues and specific costs. This, in turn, can be useful when attempting to apply a cost percentage to projected revenues. However, considerable care needs to be used when employing such percentages as they imply

Table 6.1.   Consolidated Statement of Income of Merck

For Year ended December 31, 1996 ($ in millions except per share amounts)		Percentage of Sales
Sales	$19,828.70	100
Costs, expenses, and other		
Materials and production	9,319.20	47
Marketing and administrative	3,841.30	19
Research and development	1,487.30	8
Equity income from affiliates	(600.70)	−3
Gain on joint venture formation Chemical businesses	—	
Provision for joint venture Obligation	—	
Other (income) expense, net	240.80	1
	14,287.90	72
Income before taxes	5,540.80	28
Taxes on income	1,659.50	8
Net income	$3,881.30	20
Earnings per common share	$3.20	

---

[2] Eugene Brigham and Louis C. Gapinski, *Intermediate Financial Management,* 3rd ed., (Hinsdale, Ill.: Dryden Press), 1990, 813–815.

that all costs are variable when in reality some are and some are not. A percentage of sales representation merely shows all costs as a percent of revenues regardless of whether they are fixed or variable. As discussed later in this chapter, the distinction between fixed and variable costs depends on the time interval being considered.

MEASURES OF COSTS

A preliminary step in understanding cost analysis is defining some basic terms. Often these terms are used interchangeably although they can have different meanings in different contexts. In the interest of clarity, these basic terms are defined in Table 6.2.

Table 6.2. Cost Definitions

Fixed Costs	Costs that do not vary with output. As the time interval under consideration varies, as when moving from the market to the short run and to the long run, costs that were once considered fixed become variable.[3] An example is plant and equipment that may be fixed in the short run but can be variable in the long run.
Variable Costs	Costs that vary with output. Examples include labor or materials.
Total Costs	The sum of fixed and variable costs.
Average Costs	Total costs divided by output. This value varies depending on how total costs change as output changes.
Marginal Costs	The added costs of producing an additional unit of output. This concept is used more by economists than by accountants. Marginal cost is a key concept in microeconomic theory where it is used in conjunction with marginal revenue to derive the profit maximizing output level of a firm.
Incremental Costs	Costs incurred over a certain range of output caused by a change in business activity.
Out-of-Pocket Costs	Costs for which there has been a cash outlay.
Sunk Costs	Costs that have already been expended. This concept has particular significance in economics in that sunk costs should not affect decision making, as such decisions should be made at the margin. An example could be research and development expenditures.

---

[3] The market period is an economic concept. It is a time period so short that there can be no change in output. The length of the various time periods, such as the market period, the short run and the long run vary by industry.

PROFIT MARGINS AND PROFITABILITY

Several different profit margins are regularly used in financial analysis. Among the most often cited are the *gross margin,* which is sales minus costs of sales divided by sales; the *operating margin,* which is earnings before interest and taxes (EBIT), divided by sales; and the *net margin,* which is earnings after taxes divided by sales. These margins differ from each other in that they incorporate different cost components. The gross margin includes the fewest costs (costs of goods sold only) while the net margin incorporates all costs including taxes. Although these margins are the ones most often cited in financial analysis, none exactly coincides with the precise margin that may be used in a lost profits analysis.

The true economic losses of a firm are its *lost incremental revenues minus the incremental costs associated with these revenues.* The margin associated with these lost incremental revenues is usually less than, or equal to, the *gross margin* but is greater than, or equal to, the *net margin.* In effect, the lost incremental revenues minus the associated incremental costs becomes the definition of "net profits" that is appropriate to commercial damages litigation.[4] There are abundant legal precedents to support the proposition that gross incremental revenues without a deduction for the costs that would have been incurred to achieve these revenues are an invalid measure of damages.[5] Other cases show that even gross profits, which do not include all the relevant costs associated with the lost incremental revenues, are also an inaccurate measure of damages.[6] The court's wording in *Lee v. Durango Music* is instructive.

> . . . the word profits has a definite meaning. It means the net earnings, or the excess of returns over expenditures, and relates to any excess which remains after deducting from the returns the operating expenses and depreciation of capital, and also, in the proper case, interest on the capital employed. "Profit" in the ordinary acceptation of the law, is the benefit or advantage remaining after all costs, charges, and expenses have been deducted from the income, because, until then, and while anything remains uncertain, it is impossible to say whether or not there has been a profit.[7]

---

[4] See Robert Dunn, *Recovery of Damages for Lost Profits,* 4th ed., Vol. II (Westport, Conn.: LawPress, Inc.) 1992, 354–383; and William A. Cerillo, *Proving Business Damages* (Santa Ana, Calif: James Publishing Co.) 1989, 1-18–1.19.

[5] *Clayton v. Howard Johnson Franchise Systems, Inc.,* 954 F.2d 645, 652 (11th Cir. 1992) and *General Devices v. Bacon,* 888 S.W. 2d 497 (Tex. App. 1994).

[6] *Graphics Directions, Inc. v. Bush,* 862 P.2d. 1020 (Colo. Ct. App. 1993).

[7] *Lee v. Durango Music,* 355 P. 2d, 1083, 1088 (Colo. 1960).

In cases involving a breach of contract, lost profits are the lost revenues from the contract minus the costs of performance. These costs may in general be considered as "savings" to the plaintiff in that the plaintiff did not have to expend them. This, however, is not always the case. If the plaintiff incurred certain costs for items that could not be utilized for other revenue-generating activities, then this may be another element of loss.

BURDEN OF PROOF FOR DEMONSTRATING COSTS

As part of its lost profits presentation, the plaintiff must prove its lost revenues as well as the costs associated with these revenues. That is, the plaintiff bears the burden of proving what expenses it would have incurred while generating the lost revenues. Plaintiffs may try to argue that proving expenses is similar to a mitigation of damages, which may be considered the responsibility of the defendant to prove. However, courts have rejected this reasoning. The plaintiff must focus on the costs associated with the projected lost revenues as closely as the projected revenues themselves.

FIXED VERSUS VARIABLE COSTS

Fixed costs are those costs that do not vary with output. Variable costs, on the other hand, do vary as output changes. Courts have recognized this simple definition, which is standard in economics. For example, in *Autotrol Corp. v. Continental Water Systems Corp.*, the court adopted this definition when providing the distinction between fixed costs and variable costs.

> Economists distinguish between a firm's fixed and variable costs. The former, as the name implies, are the same whether or not the firm does anything; a good example is the fee that a state charges for a corporation charter. The fee is paid before the firm begins operations and is utterly invariant to the firm's fortunes. It would be an improper item of damages for the breach of contract because [they] could not have caused the expense to be incurred. . .
>
> Variable costs are those that vary with the firm's activity—more precisely they are caused by fluctuations in that activity.[8]

In many cases, the distinction between fixed and variable costs is straightforward. For example, rent, lease payments, and other overhead are often treated

---

[8] *Autotrol Corp. v. Continental Water Systems Corp.*, 918 F. 2d 689 (7th Cir. 1990).

as fixed costs. Other costs, such as costs of materials or commissions on sales, are categorized as variable costs because they vary with output. The expert may go beyond the data contained in the financial statements with other information gathered directly from the company to determine which costs vary with output. After the fixed inputs are separated from the variable ones, the percentage relationship between the variable costs and the revenues is used to compute a *variable costs percentage.*

In economics, the typical cost function expresses various categories of costs as a function of output.[9] Our initial presentation of the method used to differentiate between fixed and variable costs also uses such a functional relationship. Regression analysis can again be used to separate those costs that vary with sales from those that do not. A regression of costs against revenues produces a fitted relationship and an equation describing this relationship as depicted in Figure 6.1.

The regression analysis allows the estimation of a fitted regression line based on the following equation:

$$C_t = F + vQ_t + u_t \tag{6.1}$$

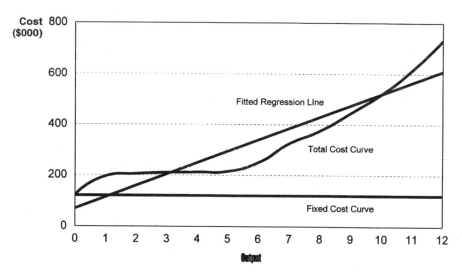

Figure 6.1. Fitting a regression line to cost data.

[9] Donald N. McCloskey, *The Applied Theory of Price* (New York: Macmillan) 1982, 260–287.

where C_t = total cost
 F = fixed cost
 v = variable cost percentage
 Q_t = quantity of output
 u_t = error term

It would be expected that v varies between 0 and 1. That is:

$$0 < v < 1$$

v captures the relationship between costs and revenues.[10] Given that there are usually few observations where output is close to zero, however, the expert may want to be cautious in interpreting the estimate of fixed costs—caution should also be applied when forecasting damages for output levels for which few if any data points are available in the historical data set.

USING REGRESSION ANALYSIS TO ESTIMATE COSTS

While regression analysis can be used to measure the relationship between fixed and variable costs, in a litigation context, it is more common for the expert to present such costs as a percent of revenues. In corporate finance, one of the more often used financial forecasting techniques, *percentage of sales forecasting*, forecasts costs and the resulting profits as a percent of a separately forecasted sales level.[11] However, if the expert can use both approaches and arrive at similar results, the analysis can be even more impressive.

When the damages analysis is conducted by a combination of an economist and an accounting expert, the work may be subdivided according to the respective expertise of the team's members. Typically, the economist conducts an analysis of the economy and of the firm's relevant industry and constructs a projection of "but for" revenues. This projection is then handed off to the accountant who computes the costs associated with the incremental lost revenues. This latter exercise can fall within the domain of cost accounting. When the analysis is done this way, the accountant typically does not use regression analysis to measure costs but rather relies on more traditional accounting methods.

---

[10] Robert R. Trout and Carroll B. Foster, "Economic Analysis of Business Interruption Losses," in *Litigation Economics*, Patrick A. Gaughan and Robert Thornton, eds. (Greenwich, Conn.: JAI Press) 1993. 151–174.

[11] Eugene F. Brigham and Louis C. Gipenski, *Intermediate Financial Management*, 3rd ed. (Chicago: Dryden Press) 1990, 813–819.

Pitfalls of Using Regression Analysis
to Measure Incremental Costs

Regression analysis can be a powerful tool in estimating relationships among variables and in creating projections. However, it has certain limitations and its usefulness will vary from case to case. It is very important that the user of this tool understands both its potential complexity and limitations. As we noted in Chapter 5, too often, experts with little training in statistical analysis and econometrics sometimes blindly use the regression analysis features built into spreadsheet software packages without any appreciation of the complexity or the limitations of the techniques employed. Experts and attorneys should at least be aware of some issues that may arise when using regression analysis to estimate costs and cost functions and make sure that, where relevant, they are at least discussed in advance of the submission of the report.

Possible Nonlinear Nature of Total Costs

If a company's production function is characterized by economies of scale over a certain range of output, then the per-unit costs of production decline over that range. Certain industries, particularly capital intensive industries like public utilities, may have significant ranges of output over which per-unit costs decline. This condition occurs when a company leverages its fixed costs. In financial analysis, this is referred to as *operating leverage*. In other industries, the range over which economies of scale are realized may be small. At some point, however, per-unit costs stop declining and may even increase resulting in diseconomies of scale. The relationship between total costs and per-unit costs is shown in Figure 6.2. For output levels up to $x = 7$, per-unit costs decline. This implies that total costs increase at a decreasing rate. However, beyond the output level of 7, the firm begins to experience diseconomies of scale with a resulting increase in per-unit costs, which causes total costs to increase at an increasing rate.

If the cost function exhibits declining and then increasing per-unit costs, the relationship between total costs and output is nonlinear. Figure 6.3 depicts two costs functions. The cost function depicted in 6(a) shows a linear relationship between costs and output whereas the cost function depicted in 6(b) shows a nonlinear relationship.

Over a range of output where per unit costs are either declining or increasing, the cost function may be better estimated using nonlinear regression analysis as opposed to the more standard linear regression. An example of an equation

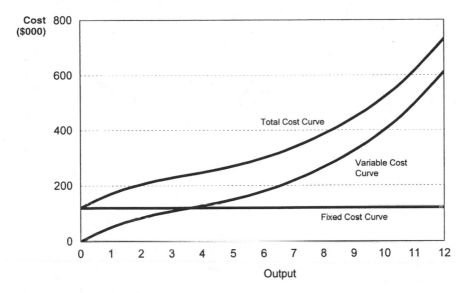

Figure 6.2a. Total and average costs.

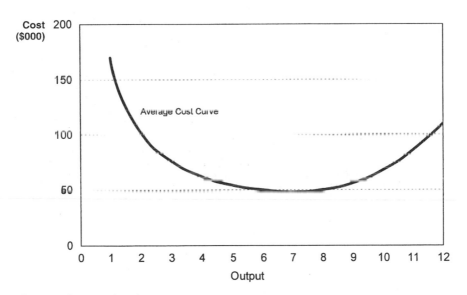

Figure 6.2b. Total and average costs.

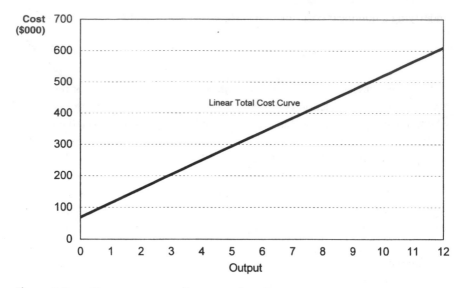

Figure 6.3a.   Linear versus nonlinear cost functions.

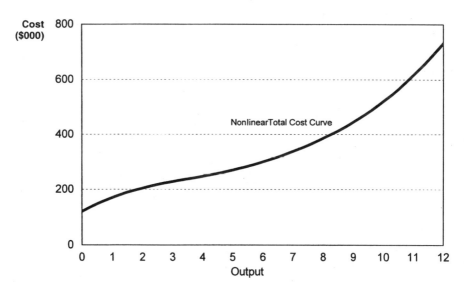

Figure 6.3b.   Linear versus nonlinear cost functions.

underlying a nonlinear cost function is shown in Equation (6.2).

$$C = \delta_0 + \delta_1 X_t + \delta_2 X_t^2 + \delta_3 X_t^3 \tag{6.2}$$

Costs will be inaccurately estimated if the expert were to use linear regression when the true cost function is nonlinear. This condition is shown in Figure 6.4 where linear regression analysis is used to estimate the cost function, thereby implicitly assuming that costs increase at a constant rate as output increases. In this example, however, the true cost function exhibits first economies and then diseconomies of scale. Because of the misspecification of the relationship between output and costs, the true costs will be higher than the estimated ones for low and high levels of output, whereas they will be lower than the estimated ones for intermediate levels of output. The solution would be to use nonlinear regression analysis to estimate costs.

Care must be exercised in reviewing the regression analysis that is included in many reports of economic damages. Some "experts" have had very little expo sure to regression analysis and may not even be aware of nonlinear regression models. Indeed, it is not uncommon for users to simply utilize the linear regression functions included in most spreadsheet packages without even being aware of the existence of other more sophisticated methods that could result in more

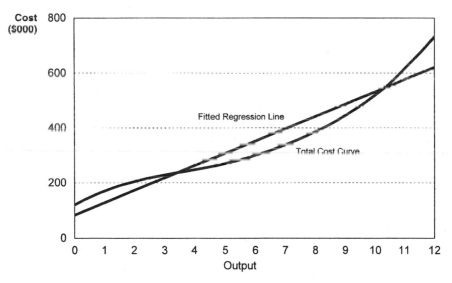

Figure 6.4. Linear regression forecast versus nonlinear actual cost function.

accurate costs estimates. Therefore it is useful to have either an economist with a background in econometrics or an econometrician review any regression analysis included in an opposing expert's report.

Further Complications Involving Nonlinear Costs

If a plaintiff is prevented from generating sufficient sales to enjoy a reduction in per-unit costs, then it is possible that the costs associated with the projected lost revenues may be lower than the level inherent in the historical relationship between costs and units produced. To a certain extent, this situation was explored previously where a solution involving the use of nonlinear costs estimation was recommended. The situation becomes somewhat more complicated if the cost reduction is such that it applies to not only the projected lost revenues but also to actual revenues. This situation could occur in the case of volume discounts. Here the measure of loss would be not only the lost profits on the lost revenues, but also the difference in costs in the units affected by the volume discount.

Other Concerns About Using Regression Analysis to Measure Costs

While there are many instances where courts have endorsed regression analysis and have found it to be of great probative value, courts have been quick to reject a regression analysis based on flawed assumptions. It is important to bear in mind that regression analysis simply measures the relationship between the variables in question that are inherent to the historical data used for the estimation process. If, however, there is reason to believe that the relationship would be different over the loss period, then the estimated coefficients from the regression analysis may not be useful. Such was the case in *Micro Motion, Inc. v. Exac Corp.* where the court stated as follows:

> The Court finds Mr. Holdren's historical and regression analyses to be of little probative value. An historical or regression analysis may be quite useful in a case involving a well-established firm with relatively constant costs and sales. But it is less useful where, as here, the firm can incur substantial nonrecurring costs, which because they can vary from year to year may appear to be, but are not, incremental costs. Moreover, the database Mr. Holdren used for his historical and regression analyses included data not at issue in this case, such as costs and rev-

enues associated with international sales, and sales of meters not affected by Exac's infringement.[12]

CAPACITY CONSTRAINTS
AND FIXED VERSUS VARIABLE COSTS

Although economists are well acquainted with the separation of costs into fixed and variable categories, the simple separation between fixed and variable costs may not suffice for all projections of lost profits.[13] For projections of sales that go beyond the firm's capacity constraints, additional fixed costs may have to be considered, as shown in Figure 6.5. Here fixed costs increase to a higher level in order for the company to be able to go beyond its initial capacity constraints. The form of this relationship is known in mathematics as a *step function.*

The traditional economic treatment divides costs into short-run and long-run cost functions. A more appropriate treatment of this issue for litigation analysis is

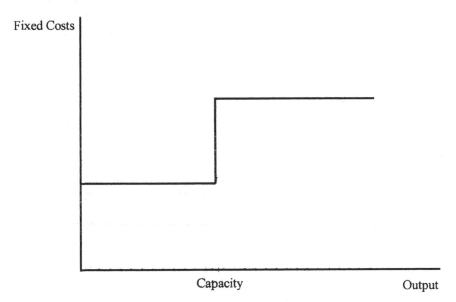

Figure 6.5.   Fixed costs and capacity constraints.

---

[12]*Micro Motion, Inc. v. Exac Corp.,* 761 F. Supp. 1420 (N.D. Ca.).

[13]Roger Leroy Miller, *Intermediate Microeconomics,* 3rd ed. (New York: McGraw Hill) 1986.

to simply divide costs into three categories: *fixed, semivariable, and variable.* Such a division allows the economist to reliably forecast revenues beyond the company's current constraints.

LIMITATIONS OF USING UNADJUSTED ACCOUNTING DATA FOR MEASURING INCREMENTAL COSTS

It may not be accurate to include all of the costs shown on the company's financial records when measuring incremental costs. Certain costs, such as depreciation, may be important for the computation of taxable income but may not be an accurate measure of costs of the depreciable assets in the period for which the depreciation is measured. For example, the Delaware Supreme Court confirmed this idea when it reversed a lower court finding that depreciation was an appropriate costs measure to include in a lost profits computation.[14] The court stated:

> In this loss-of-profits case, we conclude that Barcroft is entitled to recover for any actual loss caused by Cannon's breach, including any actual decline in value or "depreciation" of the plant while it was out of production. But Barcroft's obligation is to establish that loss by showing what, in fact, the decline was. In our judgment, decline (measured by before and after values) cannot be established entirely by reference to an accounting technique, no matter how reliable it is for other purposes.

> We recognize that the straight-line method is commonly used in financial statements, tax returns, and other similar documents, but it is an improper basis for computing damages in this case, which is not concerned with the recovery of costs over useful life, nor with an equitable allocation of use costs over their shutdown period. In short, proof by reference to an arbitrary accounting rule is not an acceptable way of establishing actual loss resulting from depreciation in this litigation which seeks to compensate for lost profits.

This "inaccuracy" of using depreciation as a cost measure may be even more pronounced in cases where the depreciation charge is unusual, such as when there is accelerated depreciation. This situation highlights the artificial nature of depreciation as a measure of actual costs.

Other examples of deficiencies of accounting data include the case when one is trying to measure losses over a period less than a year but the data on em-

---

[14] *Oliver B. Cannon & Son v. Dorr-Oliver, Inc.,* 394 A. 2d 1160 (Del. 1978).

ployee compensation do not vary evenly with output or revenues.[15] This situation can occur when the firm pays year-end bonuses that may reflect work performed over a much longer period, possibly an entire year. In this case, the compensation data should be adjusted to more accurately reflect the time period under consideration.

TREATMENT OF OVERHEAD COSTS

There is a certain amount of confusion in commercial damages analysis regarding the treatment of overhead costs as evident when reviewing the case law and attempting to reconcile certain decisions with basic economic principles. Although confusion may exist, the economic theory is clear on the issue. For example, in the case of contract litigation, the costs of performance should be deducted from the incremental revenues to be derived from such performance. If overhead costs, in the form of fixed costs, such as rent and administrative expenses, were incurred anyway by the ongoing business, it would make little sense to deduct even a portion of these expenses that were already paid. However, if the business closed due to the acts of the defendant, then some or all of the overhead costs may not have been incurred. In this case, the net margin, which includes all expenses including overhead, may be a more appropriate measure of cost to apply to projected lost revenues.

If a deduction for overhead is deemed appropriate, then it can be measured in a number of ways. One of the simplest is to compute overhead costs as a ratio to some output measure, such as production as shown in Equations (6.3) and (6.4).

$$\text{Overhead Ratio (Revenues)} = \text{Total Overhead Costs/Revenues} \qquad (6.3)$$

$$\text{Overhead Ratio (Output)} = \text{Total Overhead Costs/Output} \qquad (6.4)$$

The ratio form is convenient in that it can be mathematically applied to various performance measures, such as revenues, that are projected to occur dependent on events that are the subject of the litigation. One danger in using such ratios is that they make overhead costs look like variable costs when in fact over a large range of output they are usually fixed. As output increases, overhead may be fixed until some relevant capacity constraint is reached and then some or all

---

[15] William Wecker and Roman L. Weil, "Statistical Estimation of Incremental Cost Data from Accounting Data," in *Litigation Services Handbook,* 2nd ed., Roman L. Weil, Michael J. Wagner, and Peter Frank, eds. (New York: Wiley) 1995.

the components of overhead may increase. If the expert is seeking to measure the increase in overhead, the ratios expressed in Equations (6.3) and (6.4) may not be that relevant as they reflect total overhead, including those portions that are fixed over the range being considered.

It may be helpful to compute the overhead ratios over various ranges of output to see how they vary as output varies.[16] This plotting allows us to see how the ratio changes as output increases. A plot of the trend in these ratios reveals how stable they are over various output ranges. The more stable these ratios are, the easier it is to use them over various projected output ranges.

Legal Authority on Deduction of Overhead

Ample legal authority supports the economic reasoning that in business interruption loss analysis, overhead should not be included in the measurement of costs to apply to lost incremental revenues. In his review of the case law in this area, as well as in the debate on this issue in Speidel and Clay and in Childres and Burgess, Robert L. Dunn concludes that "the few cases that analyze the one place in the Uniform Commercial Code, Section 2-708, which addresses overhead "tends to support their (Childres and Burgess) conclusion that overhead costs are not to be deducted from damages under the code."[17] Indeed, in *Universal Power Systems, Inc. v. Godfather's Pizza, Inc.* the court concluded that "variable overhead costs" should be deducted while "fixed overhead costs" should not be deducted.[18] Given that overhead is often considered fixed, this decision seems a contradiction. The association of overhead as a fixed as opposed to a variable cost was also confirmed in *Scullin Steel Co. v. PACCAR, Inc.*[19] Here the court defined reasonable overhead as:

---

[16] Jeffrey H. Kinich, "Cost Estimation" in *Litigation Services Handbook*, 2nd ed., Roman Weil, Michael Wagner, and Peter Frank, eds. (New York: Wiley) 1995, 42.7.

[17] Robert Dunn, *Recovery of Damages for Lost Profits*, vol. 2, (Westport, Conn.: Lawpress Corp.) 1992, 6.6, Richard E. Speidel and Kendall O. Clay, "Sellers Recovery of Overhead Under UCC Section 2-708 (2): Economic Costs Theory and Contractual Remedial Policy," 57 *Cornell Law Review*, 681 (1972); Robert Childres and Robert Burgess, "Sellers Remedies: The Primacy of UCC 2-708 (2) 48" *N.Y.U.L.* Rev. 831 (November, 1973).

[18] *Universal Power Systems, Inc. v. Godfather's Pizza, Inc.*, 818 F. 2d 667 (8th Cir. 1987).

[19] *Scullin Steel Co. v. PACCAR*, 748 S.W. 2d 910 (Mo. App. 1988).

Fixed costs, which dominate "reasonable overhead", commonly include property taxes, salaries, rent, utilities, depreciation, insurance, and other costs not directly affected by fluctuations in productivity.

As discussed later in this chapter, however, some costs are fixed over a certain range of output but become variable as output expands. Such costs are semifixed or semivariable depending on the vantage point. In *Universal Power Systems, Inc. v. Godfather's Pizza, Inc.,* the defense objected that the plaintiff's expert who computed lost profits failed to make any deduction for overhead including depreciation and warehouse expenses. The court, however, failed to accept this argument and concluded that expenses such as depreciation should not be deducted as they did not vary with output.

Overhead could be a legitimate cost element to include in a loss computation where the plaintiff went out of business due to the action of the defendant. When the business did not continue to operate and pay certain overhead expenses while experiencing lower revenues, then the totality of the revenues and all costs should be included in the loss computation.

Overhead as a Recoverable Component of Damages: Cost-Plus Contracts

Some contracts are cost-plus contracts—they allow for the addition of some profit component onto some definition of costs "The cost-plus contract concept in which the contract price is the contractor's estimated costs plus 6% of cost for his overhead and profit is legitimate."[20] The inclusion of overhead costs as an element of damages may depend on whether the agreement provided for recouping of overhead costs. In such contracts, the measure of profits is usually a straightforward function of the level of overhead expenses and can be readily computed. In *Juengel Construction Co., Inc. v. Mt. Etna Inc.* the court computed the lost profits as follows:

> In its cost-plus contract with Mt. Etna, Juengel's profit was to equal 6% of costs. By totaling the low subcontractor bids, Juengel rationally estimated costs to equal $759,442.00, 6% of which is $45,566.52. The latter amount is clearly Juengel's lost profits.

---

[20] *Juengel Construction Co., Inc. v. Mt. Etna, Inc.,* 622 S.W. 2d 510 (1981).

Unabsorbed Overhead as an Element of Damages

Unabsorbed overhead is often an issue in litigation arising out of government contracts. It is defined as the loss derived from an underrecovery of fixed overhead costs due to less work being performed by a contractor. The reduced amount of work can result from a variety of reasons including suspension of the work or some form of delay or interruption. In analyzing damages from unabsorbed overhead, one may need to focus on a period longer than what the plaintiff indicates to be the period where work was insufficient to absorb the required overhead. Such may be the case when work is shifted to another period so that it is overabsorbed in another time period.[21]

Uncertainty about when work may continue during a delay that is not the fault of the plaintiff may cause the plaintiff to restrain from taking on alternative work to mitigate his damages. The principles governing how such overhead may be a compensable element of damages is sometimes referred to as the *Eichleay* formula.[22] When a company can shift resources to other revenue-generating activities, there may not be a valid claim for damages. However, when the company is inhibited from doing so due to either uncertainty about when work will continue or other constraints, such as limited additional binding capacity, then the plaintiff may have a more valid claim.[23]

UNPROFITABLE BUSINESSES AND RECOVERY OF DAMAGES

At first glance it does not seem reasonable that a previously unprofitable business can recover damages. However, it could be the case that a business would have been profitable had it not been for the actions of the defendant. Although actual revenues were insufficient to cover all fixed and variable costs, it is possible that if the business had reached the projected "but for" levels, total costs would have been surpassed and the company would have enjoyed positive profits. The situation becomes somewhat more complicated when it can be shown

---

[21] David G. Anderson, "Practitioner's Viewpoint: Federal Circuit Creates an Invalid Test for Determining Entitlement to Unabsorbed Overhead," *Public Contract Law Review* 26 (3), Spring 1997, 353–372.

[22] *C.B.C. Enterprises v. United States,* 978, F. 2d 669 (Fed. Cir. 1992).

[23] Mech-Con Corp., ASBCA No. 45105, 94-3 BCA ¶ 27,252, at 135,784.

that even if the plaintiff reached the projected revenue levels it would still show a loss. The defendant may then try to argue that its improper actions saved the defendant from incurring losses. It is difficult to put forward one catch-all rule that applies to a virtually infinite number of circumstances. However, the plaintiff's burden in a case such as this is clearly significant. One way the plaintiff may be able to recoup damages is if it can show that its loss was even greater because the defendant's actions prevented it from generating the projected levels. For example, the plaintiff may owe monies to various parties as a result of losses incurred. The plaintiff may use the proceeds of an award to meet part of these obligations.

MITIGATION OF DAMAGES

In computing losses, any cost savings that the plaintiff enjoyed by not having to undertake whatever activities it would have normally undertaken in order to realize the "but for" revenue stream, needs to be deducted as an offset. For example, if the plaintiff does not have to incur all of the costs needed to achieve the projected revenue stream, such as a larger workforce and facilities, this cost saving should be taken into account. The *mitigation of damages* should also include alternative opportunities to earn other profits. Using a contract litigation example, if the plaintiff could mitigate its damages by substituting other business, then the profits from the alternative activities need to be considered. However, if it was possible for the plaintiff to complete performance of both contracts, profits from the alternative contracts should not be deducted from the lost profits.

Although the plaintiff may be required to show that it has pursued other profitable opportunities, the area is somewhat gray when the plaintiff chooses to pursue far riskier opportunities than the business that was lost. The plaintiff's argument may be less persuasive if it can be shown that the plaintiff could have replaced the defendant's lost business without incurring significant search costs with other lower risk business opportunities.

Burden of Proof of Mitigation

The proof of a failure to mitigate damages is the responsibility of the defendant. However, this may be an issue of dispute as the plaintiff may argue that it actually did take reasonable steps to mitigate its damages, while the defendant may argue that the plaintiff had the ability to mitigate its damages beyond the meas-

ures actually taken. The plaintiff only needs to show that it took reasonable steps
to mitigate its damages. It does not need to show that it took all of the steps that
the defendant may assert should have been taken.[24] In the face of such a presentation by the plaintiff, it is up to the court to decide if the mitigation efforts of the
plaintiff were reasonable and sufficient. In *Brandon & Tibbs v. George Kevorkian Accountancy Corporation,* a case involving claims of damages of an accounting practice that was not purchased as agreed by the defendant, the court
explained the law on mitigation of damages as follows:

> A party injured by a breach of contract is required to do everything reasonably pos-
> sible to negate his own loss and thus reduce the damages for which the other party
> has become liable. (cite omitted) The plaintiff cannot recover for harm he could
> have foreseen and avoided by such reasonable efforts and without undue expense.
> However, the injured party is not precluded from recovery to the extent that he has
> made reasonable but unsuccessful efforts to avoid loss.
>
> The burden of proving that losses could have been avoided by reasonable effort and
> expense must always be borne by the party who has broken the contract.(cite omit-
> ted) Inasmuch as the law denied recovery for losses that can be avoided by reason-
> able effort and expense, justice requires that the risks incident to such an effort
> should be carried by the party whose wrongful conduct makes them necessary.(cite
> omitted) Therefore, special losses that a party incurs in a reasonable effort to avoid
> losses resulting from a breach are recoverable as damages.

Other Offsetting Profits Not Treated as Damages Mitigation

It is possible that the plaintiff lost certain revenues due to the actions of the defendant but failed to incur a loss because it was able to substitute other business
so that it was not left in a less advantageous position than the one it would have
been in. Under these circumstances, in order to claim a loss, the plaintiff needs to
prove that it had the capacity to handle *both* the substitute business as well as the
lost business. For example, in *Sierra Wine & Liquor Co. v. Heublein, Inc.,* the
court found that a plaintiff who was a franchisee was only able to recover damages until he secured a replacement franchise based on the reasoning that the
plaintiff could not hold two franchises in the same industry at the same time.[25]

---

[24] *Brandon & Tibbs v. George Kevorkian Accountancy Corp.,* 226 Cal. App. 3d 442,
227 Cal. Rptr. 40 (1990).

[25] *Sierra Wine & Liquor v. Heublein, Inc.,* 626 F. 2d 129 (9th Cir. 1980).

Tax-Related Mitigation

An expert's computation of damages is typically on a pretax basis, because the plaintiff will be taxed on the award. As the court stated in *Polaroid Corporation v. Eastman Kodak Corporation:*

> An award based upon after-tax amounts could result in double taxation. Any award will certainly be scrutinized by tax officials at both the state and federal levels who will determine the correctness and applicability of any rate employed.[26]

In some instances, the plaintiff may receive certain *tax benefits* from the losses he may have incurred as a result of the defendant's actions. These benefits could be in the form of tax losses, which can be used to offset positive income in future periods. Robert L. Dunn reports that in most recent cases the tax benefits a plaintiff may enjoy are not considered in computing damages.[27] Among the reasons that the courts cite are the fact that the awarded profits are themselves taxable and the difficulty in knowing what the relevant rates are going to be in the year that the award is made. The relevant rates may not be known because the full income and other tax-related factors that enter into the determination of the firm's average tax rate for the year of the award may not be known until after the year is over.

The courts even indicate that the plaintiff should receive the benefit of any lower rates it may enjoy after possibly including these offsetting tax benefits, as opposed to the defendant being given the benefit of these offsetting gains the plaintiff enjoyed in the year that the plaintiff incurred the loss that was caused by the defendant. Courts seemed to want to ignore the whole issue of differential tax effects. Indeed, in cases where the plaintiff contended that its tax rates in the year it would receive the award of damages were higher, the court stated that this was not a valid area of damages.

It seems that the court's theory is that when an award is made, the tax effects of that award will more or less offset any tax benefits that may have been incurred since the interruption and that this is a nonissue. The fact that the amount in question may be different or that the time value of the respective amounts may exacerbate these differences does not seem to be an issue that the courts want to incorporate into their consideration of the appropriate amount to award in a lost profits case.

---

[26] *Polaroid Corporation v. Eastman Kodak Company,* 16 U.S.P.Q., 2d, 1481 (1990).

[27] Robert Dunn, *Recovery of Damages For Lost Profits,* 5th ed., (Westport, Conn.: Lawpress), 1998, 465–471.

One can challenge the court's reasoning in the various cases that advocate ignoring tax issues. The argument that taxes cannot be computed due to the inherent complexity of such a computation makes little sense. Courts allow testimony on revenue estimation using complicated models so it would only be reasonable that testimony be allowed on the projection of taxes. Usually, the tax rates involved are the maximum as the incremental lost income in larger commercial cases is most often taxed at the highest corporate marginal rate. The expert can then compute the incremental taxes associated with the lost incremental profits as follows:

$$IT = LITI \times t \tag{6.5}$$

where   IT = Incremental taxes
          LITI = Lost incremental taxable income
          t = Relevant marginal tax rate

Some argue that unless there is a basis for assuming a change in tax rates, future taxes can be computed using current tax rates.[28] In computing historical losses when tax rates have changed and the rates in the year of the award are different than the period of the loss, the goal of the expert is to compute an award that leaves the plaintiff whole. This involves computing the incremental taxes using t_l, the tax rate from the loss period, and determining what the net income of the plaintiff would have been if she received the projected lost profits during the loss period. The award on the trial date, which will be taxed at current rates, t_c, may have to be adjusted to equal what the plaintiff would have received but for the action of the defendant:

$$NLI = LITI - IT \tag{6.6}$$

where NLI equals Net Lost Income.

CASH FLOWS VERSUS NET INCOME: EFFECTS ON THE DISCOUNTING PROCESS

It can be the case that, in order to achieve the forecasted revenues levels, the plaintiff would need to invest certain monies in capital items. These monies may

---

[28] John Jarocz, "Considering Taxes in the Computation of Lost Business Profits," *Creighton Law Review* 25, 1991, 41–72.

Table 6.3. Computing Damages Using Cash Flows versus Net Income

		Cash Basis Damages		
Year	Incremental Operating Cash Flow	Capital Expenditure	Cash Basis Damages	Cumulative Cash Basis Damages
1	50,000	60,000	(10,000)	(10,000)
2	70,000	0	70,000	60,000
3	80,000	0	80,000	140,000
4	90,000	0	90,000	230,000

		Income Basis Damages		
Year	Incremental Net Income	Capital Expenditure	Income Basis Damages	Cumulative Cash Basis Damages
1	50,000	15,000	35,000	35,000
2	70,000	15,000	55,000	90,000
3	80,000	15,000	65,000	155,000
4	90,000	15,000	75,000	230,000

be treated differently depending on whether cash flows or net income is measured. Consider the example shown in Table 6.3. Damages are computed using incremental operating cash flows and incremental net income. The damages computations are equal over the four-year loss period. The difference is a one-time capital expenditure in year one of $60,000. This expenditure is assumed to be necessary in order to achieve the projected cash flows/net income.

When damages are computed on a cash basis, there is no loss in year one, while when computed on an income basis, there is a loss of $35,000. The cumulative amounts are the same—$230,000. This simple example does not address the balance sheet effects of the differences in the cash versus income basis analysis. These effects can be quite complex and, fortunately, are often not necessary for the damages analysis.[29]

One major difference between the cash basis and income basis analysis is in the timing of the damages, which can significantly affect the present value computation. Consider the extension of the foregoing example in Table 6.4 where a 15% risk-adjusted discount rate is used to convert the projected damages amounts to present value terms in year 0. Whereas in Table 6.3 the cumulative

---

[29] Michael Wagner, "How Do You Measure Damages: Lost Income or Lost Cash Flow," *Journal of Accountancy*, February 1990, 28–33.

Table 6.4. Discounted Cash Basis Damages

	Discounted Cash Basis Damages			
Year	Cash Basis Damages	Discount Factor	Discounted Damages	Cumulative Discounted Damages
1	(10,000)	0.8696	(8,696)	(8,696)
2	70,000	0.7561	52,930	44,234
3	80,000	0.6575	52,601	96,836
4	90,000	0.5718	51,458	148,293
	Discounted Income Basis Damages			
Year	Income Basis Damages	Discount Factor	Discounted Damages	Cumulative Discounted Damages
1	35,000	0.8696	30,435	30,435
2	55,000	0.7561	41,588	72,023
3	65,000	0.6575	42,739	114,761
4	75,000	0.5718	42,881	157,643

amounts were equal over the four-year loss period, the differences in the timing of the damage amounts leads to a difference in the cumulative discounted amounts. Because the full impact of the capital expenditure is felt in year one under the cash basis treatment, lower damages are projected in the early years for the cash basis treatment, resulting in lower cumulative discounted damages. The opposite is true for the projection under the income basis treatment. The higher damages in the early years result in higher discounted damages for the income basis damage computation.

Clearly, on a discounted basis, the damages may be different depending on which accounting approach one uses. These differences will be greater the higher the discount rate, the longer the loss period, and the greater the differences in the timing of the damages.

RECASTED PROFITS

In closely held corporations, the net income may not reflect the true compensation to the owners of the company. For example, the company may be controlled by a small number of key shareholders, perhaps even one, who extract a significant component of the profits of the business so that taxable income and tax are minimized. These monies can be extracted in a variety of ways, including officer's compensation, fringe benefits, and other perks. The after-tax net income or bottom line may show limited profitability while the company generates very different positive returns for the owners. Unfortunately, this tax avoidance process, one that may be quite consistent with prevailing tax laws, may present problems for the plaintiff in a lost profits case.

Public versus Private Corporations[30]

When it comes to declaring income, there are significant differences in the objectives of private versus public corporations. Public corporations are much more limited in the actions they can take to minimize taxable income. These limitations come partly through dividend payment constraints that require that income be reported and taxes paid before dividends can be paid. Companies generally pursue a policy of dividend stability where they try to manage the company in such a manner that the payment of dividends is at least stable if not growing.[31] Companies that announce declining or zero dividends can risk various market corrective actions, such as an ouster of management or a takeover by an outside raider who takes advantage of the decline in the company's stock price that often accompanies such announcements.[32] For these reasons, pubic companies are somewhat constrained in how they can manage taxable income. Private companies are more free to control taxable income through the use of expenses that are truly a form of compensation for the shareholders. The controlling shareholders in a private company can choose to take some of their return in the form of officer's compensation as opposed to a distribution of posttax income. These shareholders may also choose to incur costs that provide indirect benefits but that also reduce taxable income. A problem arises when the managed income plaintiff enters into litigation and claims lost profits. The firm's net income history may show only limited profits in a business that is actually generating sizable returns for the shareholders/plaintiffs.

Reconstructing the true profitability of the business is well known to practitioners in finance. The process, called *recasting* of profitability, involves defining

---

[30] This section draws heavily on the following article: Patrick A. Gaughan and Henry Fuentes, "The Minimization of Taxable Income and Lost Profits Litigation," *Journal of Forensic Economics* 4 (1), Winter 1990, 55 – 64.

[31] Lawence D. Schall and Charles W. Haley, *Introduction to Financial Management*, 6th ed. (New York: McGraw Hill) 1991, 478 – 486.

[32] An example was the takeover attempt of ITT Corporation by the Pritzger Group after ITT announced a reduction in its quarterly dividend.

a series of addbacks which, as the term implies, are added back to the bottom line to reconstruct the true profitability of the business. The tax effects of these add-backs must be considered when reconstructing the recasted income. This process is common in a number of circumstances in corporate finance including acquisitions planning and business valuations. In acquisition planning, the cost structure of a target company is evaluated from the viewpoint of the bidder who only considers the costs that the bidder would incur if the acquisition were completed. The elimination of redundant costs, such as duplicate facilities, can form the basis for the synergistic gains that are often cited in a priori acquisition planning.[33]

In the valuation of closely held businesses for nonacquisition purposes, recasting the income statement is also commonplace.[34] Here the true value to an owner is measured for a variety of other reasons, such as in shareholder derivative lawsuits as well as matrimonial litigation. The process is well accepted, but whether it is legally appropriate to utilize the recasted income of shareholders in a corporation as opposed to the reported income of the corporate plaintiff itself is a separate issue. It seems that this issue is still open to debate. The logic of not using the income individuals who are not named parties to a lawsuit seems to be compelling. However, the legal position of the court is not one that the expert will be deciding. Rather, the expert must be presented with an assumed legal position that sets forth the basis for the loss analysis. It is for the legal representatives of the litigants themselves to argue which legal theory applies.

Professional Corporations

In cases involving a professional corporation, the issue of using recasted profits may be even clearer. In a professional corporation, the shareholders and the principals are the same. In order to avoid the double taxation associated with the corporate business structure, the professional corporation may distribute earnings in the form of officer's compensation so as to have a lower taxable income. Courts have treated this officer's compensation as relevant to the computation of the lost profits of the corporation.[35] They have correctly realized that, otherwise, very profitable entities that paid out these profits in the form of compensation could never claim lost profits.

---

[33] Patrick A. Gaughan, *Mergers, Acquisitions and Corporate Restructuring* (New York: Wiley), 1996, 104–112.

[34] Shannon Pratt, *Valuing a Business* (New York: Dow Jones Irwin).

[35] *Bettius & Sanderson, P.C. v. National Union Fire Insurance Co.*, 839 F. 2d 1009 (4th Cir. 1988).

CASE STUDY: PROFITS THAT ARE NOT REALLY PROFITS

This case study involves a distributor of manufactured products that had been in existence for approximately 25 years. One of the points that plaintiff's counsel repeatedly emphasized was the long history of steady revenue growth over the life of the company. This revenue growth was also associated with a steady, albeit weak, profitability. The plaintiff claimed that the purchase and implementation of a computer system caused such severe disruption to the company's business that it resulted in the closure of the company.

A closer examination of the company's finances revealed many long-brewing problems that were coming to a head at the same time that the computer system was being installed. These problems included insufficient write-offs of uncollectable receivables, inappropriate accounting for certain costs, and the failure to write off obsolete inventory. During the company's life, certain reserve for receivables that may not be paid had always been set aside. Inventory purchases were financed through an asset-based lending facility at a major local bank. As Table 6.5 and Figure 6.6 show, operating cash flow was particularly poor. When operating cash flow was no longer sufficient to finance the company's activities, notably additional borrowing, presumably no lending officer at the bank wanted to admit that the prior loans were uncollectable, and the bank continued to lend good money after bad, exceeding its credit limits. The company continued to extend credit to customers who were not current because the only way it could access the additional financing was through generating sales and extending credit, even when the receivables generated from those sales might not be collectable (see Figure 6.7 and Table 6.6). It becomes clear that the seemingly impressive sales growth shown in Table 6.5 was based on profits that did not translate into positive operating cash flows.

This case clearly shows how, if proper accounting adjustments are not made, the resulting net income may not be a reliable amount upon which to base a damage computation. In such a situation, the expert may have to focus on other variables, such as cash flows.

FIRM-SPECIFIC FINANCIAL ANALYSIS

One issue that maybe relevant to a commercial damages analysis is the financial condition of the plaintiff or the defendant. There is a standard set of financial tools that are mainstays of most corporate finance textbooks. Paramount among these is financial ratio analysis, that is, the computation of financial ratios from data contained in the company's financial statements. A financial ratio analysis

Table 6.5. Company X: Summary of Financial Statement Information, 1966–88 (in thousands)

Year	Sales	Net Income	Cash Flows (used) in Opts	Increase (Decrease) in Debt	Interest Expense
1966	5,800	40	45	(20)	1
1967	6,000	50	170	(90)	0
1968	6,900	75	90	(40)	0
1969	9,100	90	(60)	70	6
1970	11,000	120	(140)	240	6
1971	12,100	130	(300)	370	10
1972	14,300	160	(250)	200	13
1973	17,600	190	(150)	120	25
1974	19,000	300	300	(250)	25
1975	18,000	125	(130)	200	22
1976	19,000	100	(1,300)	1,450	100
1977	21,800	100	200	(275)	200
1978	25,400	155	(10)	190	270
1979	27,700	115	(1,000)	1,600	450
1980	32,000	170	300	(400)	670
1981	37,000	170	(800)	1,000	1,000
1982	34,400	90	(60)	100	900
1983	41,800	500	350	(170)	700
1984	47,700	550	(900)	930	800
1985	49,700	300	(500)	1,100	900
1986	56,600	250	(350)	1,050	750
1987	60,400	150	(600)	1,020	890
1988	57,500	(185)	(4,500)	4,450	1,460
Totals 1966–88		3,745	(9,595)	12,845	

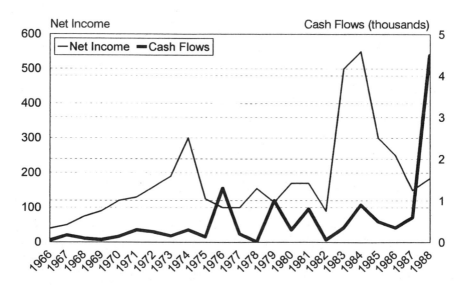

Figure 6.6. Cash flow vs. net income.

Table 6.6. Company X: Historical Sales, Accounts Receivable, and Reserves for Doubtful Accounts (in thousands)

Year	Sales	Accounts Notes Receivable	Reserve Doubtful Accounts	Ratio Reserve to Accounts Receivable(%)	A/R − N/R over 120 Days
1966	5,812	1,719	30	1.7	N/A
1967	5,978	1,748	36	2.1	N/A
1968	6,896	1,833	45	2.5	N/A
1969	9,100	2,534	58	2.3	N/A
1970	11,051	2,494	83	3.3	N/A
1971	12,106	2,623	113	4.3	N.A
1972	N/A	N/A	N/A	N/A	N/A
1973	17,726	4,021	177	4.4	N/A
1974	19,244	3,753	249	6.6	N/A
1975	17,571	3,903	243	6.2	N/A
1976	18,960	4,362	198	4.5	N/A
1977	21,848	5,342	216	4.0	N/A
1978	25,394	6,362	216	3.4	N/A
1979	27,749	7,287	226	3.1	N/A
1980	32,024	7,409	231	3.1	N/A
1981	37,162	7,472	231	3.1	N/A
1982	34,437	7,227	230	3.2	N/A
1983	41,791	8,732	231	2.6	N/A
1984	47,683	9,272	230	2.5	N/A
1985	49,715	9,304	232	2.5	N/A
1986	56,641	11,143	243	2.2	1,512
1987	60,440	11,941	0	0.0	1,603
1988	57,549	14,451	0	0.0	3,001

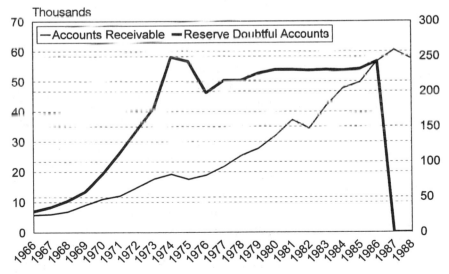

Figure 6.7. Accounts receivable and reserve for doubtful accounts.

can be used to assess the financial well-being of a company. This analysis can be important in cases where it is asserted that a company would have failed anyway, even if the defendant had not taken the actions the plaintiff asserts it did. Conversely, this type of financial analysis may be unnecessary when there is a lawsuit between two companies that continue to be viable with the plaintiff alleging that it is simply less profitable due to the actions of the defendant. Each set of ratios examines a specific aspect of the company's financial well-being. The four categories of these ratios follow:

1. *Liquidity Ratios:* These ratios, which include the *current ratio* and the *quick ratio* look at the relationship between a company's liquid, short-term assets, such as cash, marketable securities, and inventories, and its short term liabilities, to see how liquid the company is. The more liquid a business is, the lower the probability that it could be forced into receivership by not being able to pay its obligations as they come due. A more stringent version of this ratio is the quick ratio which leaves out inventories from the computation.

2. *Activity Ratios:* These ratios measure the ability of the company to use its assets to generate sales. Certain ones, such as *inventory turnover,* examine how quickly a company turns its inventories into sales. Others, such as *fixed asset turnover* and *total asset turnover* measure the business' ability to use its fixed assets or all of its assets to generate sales. Generally, the higher the values of these ratios, the healthier the company but there are exceptions to this generalization.

3. *Leverage Ratios:* These ratios can be used to assess the level of debt, or what is called *financial leverage,* in the company's capital structure. The *debt ratio* or the *debt-to-equity ratio* are two measures that capture the amount of debt the firm has used to finance its operations. The higher the degree of financial leverage, the greater the risk of the firm because it has more fixed obligations in the form of debt to service. Other ratios such as times interest earned, examine the magnitude of operating income (earn-

ings before interest and taxes) relative to interest payments to see how much *interest coverage* the firm has.

4. *Performance Ratios:*   Ratios such as the gross, operating, and net margins are alternative profitability measures that reflect how profitable the company is. They may also be used at other times in a commercial damages analysis when computing profits associated with projected lost revenues.

These ratios are usually compared to readily available industry norms.[36] They may be supplemented by other ratios that the analyst uses to address specific issues.[37]

CROSS-SECTIONAL VERSUS TIME SERIES ANALYSIS

In addition to comparing the firm's financial with industry averages with what is called a *cross-sectional analysis,* it may also be useful to examine the trend in these ratios over time in a *time series analysis* of financial ratios. Such a review may enable one to determine if certain components of a firm's financial condition are deteriorating or improving over time, which may lead to an indication of the start of problems that may be independent of alleged actions of the defendant.

SUMMARY

This chapter explored the steps involved in measuring lost profits that commence after the "but for" revenues have been forecasted. Incremental costs associated with lost incremental revenues have to be measured. These costs are usually only those that vary with output. That is, usually fixed costs are not included. The cost analysis is often done using the services of an accountant trained in measuring such costs. Typically, this expert puts forward either a schedule of specific costs

---

[36] A review of financial ratio analysis can be found in most corporate finance textbooks. For a clear, elementary discussion see R. Charles Moyer, James R. McGuigan, and William J. Kretlow, *Contemporary Financial Management,* 5th ed. (St. Paul, Minn.: West Publishing Company), 1992, 259–280.

[37] *Annual Statement Studies,* Robert Morris Associates.

or a simple percentage that embodies such a cost schedule. Costs can also be measured using a regression analysis, which seeks to compute the variable component of costs by determining the coefficient in a estimated equation that relates sales to costs. The coefficient of the cost variable in such an estimated equation then reflects how much costs would increase for a given increase in revenues. Although regression analysis can be helpful in measuring variable costs, a number of factors have to be kept in mind to be assured that the analysis is reliable and one that truly quantifies what the expert is trying to measure.

In most lost profits analyses, fixed costs, such as overhead, may not be relevant, because much of what is covered by overhead, such as rent or equipment lease payments, may have been already incurred by the plaintiff. If that is the case, then it would not make sense to deduct such costs from incremental revenues. However, if additional fixed costs or higher overhead would have to be incurred to reached the forecasted revenue levels, then such costs may enter into the loss computation.

In computing lost profits, net profits are the appropriate measure of the loss but the definition of net profits that is used may not correspond to the net profits that appear at the bottom of an income statement. It may be equal to or lower than the gross margin but often is higher than the net margin. However, when such net profits do not eventually equate to cash flows, then the focus of the damage measurement process may shift to cash flows and away from net income.

REFERENCES

Anderson, David G., "Practitioner's Viewpoint: Federal Circuit Creates an Invalid Test for Determining Entitlement to Unabsorbed Overhead." *Public Contract Law Review* 26 (3), Spring 1997, 353–372.

Annual Statement Studies, Robert Morris Associates, Philadelphia, PA.

Autotrol Corp. v. Continental Water Systems Corp., 918 F. 2d 689 (7th Cir. 1990).

Bettius & Sanderson, P.C. v. National Union Fire Insurance Co., 839 F. 2d 1009 (4th Cir. 1988).

Brandon & Tibbs v. George Kevorkian Accountancy Corp., 226 Cal. App. 3d 442, 227 Cal. Rptr. 40 (1990).

Brigham, Eugene F., and Louis C. Gipenski, *Intermediate Financial Management,* 3rd ed. (Chicago: Dryden Press, 1990).

C.B.C. Enterprises v. United States, 978, F. 2d 669 (Fed. Cir. 1992).

Cerillo, William A., *Proving Business Damages* (Santa Ana: Calif.: James Publishing Co., 1989), 1-18–1.19.

Childres, Robert and Robert Burgess, "Sellers Remedies: The Primacy of UCC 2-708 (2) 48 *N.Y.U.L.*, Rev. 831 (November, 1973).

Clayton v. Howard Johnson Franchise Systems, Inc., 954 F.2d 645, 652 (11th Cir. 1992).

Copeland, Thomas, Tim Koller, and Jack Murrin, *Valuation: Measuring and Managing the Value of Companies,* 2nd ed. (New York: Wiley, 1995).

Dunn, Robert L., *Recovery of Damages for Lost Profits,* Vol. II, 4th ed. (Westport, Conn.: LawPress, Inc.,1992) 354–383.

Evans, Elizabeth, "Interaction Between Accountants and Economists," in *Litigation Services Handbook,* 2nd ed., Roman Weil, Michael Wagner, and Peter B. Frank, eds. (New York: Wiley, 1995), 3.1–3.20.

Foster, Carroll B., and Robert R. Trout, "Computing Losses in Business Interruption Cases," *Journal of Forensic Economics* (December 1989) 9–22.

Gaughan, Patrick A., *Mergers and Acquisitions* (New York: Harper Collins, 1991)

Gaughan, Patrick A., *Mergers, Acquisitions and Corporate Restructuring* (New York: Wiley, 1999).

Gaughan, Patrick A., and Henry Fuentes, "The Minimization of Taxable Income and Lost Profits Litigation," *Journal of Forensic Economics* 4 (1), Winter 1990, 55–64.

Gaughan, Patrick A., Henry Fuentes, and Laura Bonanomi, "Cash Flows versus Net Income: Issue in Commercial Damages Litigation," *Litigation Economics Digest* (1) Fall 1995.

General Devices v. Bacon, 888 S.W. 2d 497 (Tex. App. 1994).

Graphics Directions, Inc. v. Bush, 862 P.2d 1020 (Colo. Ct. App. 1993).

Jarocz, John, "Considering Taxes in the Computation of Lost Business Profits," *Creighton Law Review* 25, 1991, 41–72.

Juengel Construction Co., Inc. v. Mt. Etna, Inc., 622 S.W. 2d 510 (1981).

Kinich, Jeffrey H., "Cost Estimation" in *Litigation Services Handbook,* 2nd ed., Roman Weil, Michael Wagner, and Peter Frank eds. (New York: Wiley, 1995) 42.7.

Lee v. Durango Music, 355 P. 2d, 1083, 1088, (Colo. 1960.)

McCloskey, Donald N., *The Applied Theory of Price* (New York: Macmillan, 1982).

Mech-Con Corp., ASBCA No. 45105, 94-3 BCA ¶ 27,252, at 135,784.

Micro Motion, Inc. v. Exac Corp., 761 F. Supp. 1420 (N.D. Ca).

Miller, Roger Leroy, *Intermediate Microeconomics,* 3rd ed. (New York: McGraw Hill, 1986).

Moyer, Charles R., James R. McGuigan, and William J. Kretlow, *Contemporary Financial Management,* 5th ed. (St. Paul, Minn.: West Publishing Company), 1992.

Oliver B. Cannon & Son v. Dorr-Oliver, Inc., 394 A. 2d 1160 (Del 1978).

Polaroid Corporation v. Eastman Kodak Company, 16 U.S.P.Q. 2d, 1481, 1990.

Pratt, Shannon, *Valuing a Business* (Homewood Ill.: Dow Jones Irwin, 1996).

Ross, Archibald T., "Stock Market Reaction to the Depreciation Switch-Back," *Accounting Review* 47 (1) January, 1972.

Schall, Lawrence D., and Charles W. Haley, *Introduction to Financial Management,* 6th ed. (New York: McGraw Hill, 1991), 478–486.

Scullin Steel Co. v. PACCAR, 748 S.W. 2d 910 (Mo. App. 1988).

Sierra Wine & Liquor v. Heublein, Inc., 626 F. 2d 129 (9th Cir. 1980).

Speidel, Richard E., and Kendall O. Clay, "Seller's Recovery of Overhead Under UCC Section 2-708 (2): Economic Costs Theory and Contractual Remidial Policy", 57 *Cornell Law Review,* 681 (1972).

Sunder, S., "The Relationship Between Accounting Changes and Stock Prices: Problems of Measurement and some Empirical Evidence," *Empirical Research in Accounting: Selected Studies,* 1973.

Trout, Robert R., and Carrol B. Foster, "Economic Analysis of Business Interruption Losses," in *Litigation Economics,* Patrick A. Gaughan and Robert Thornton, eds. (Greenwich, Conn.: JAI Press, 1993) 151–174.

Universal Power Systems, Inc. v. Godfather's Pizza, Inc., 818 F. 2d 667 (8th Cir. 1987).

Wagner, Michael, "How Do You Measure Damages: Lost Income or Lost Cash Flow," *Journal of Accountancy,* February 1990, 28–33.

Wecker, William, and Roman L. Weil, "Statistical Estimation of Incremental Cost Data from Accounting Data," in *Litigation Services Handbook,* 2nd ed. Roman L. Weil, Michael J. Wagner, and Peter Frank, eds. (New York: Wiley, 1995).

7

TIME VALUE OF MONEY CONSIDERATIONS

Given that the plaintiff may incur a loss prior to and after a judgment date, a potential award needs to take into account the opportunity costs of past losses while also computing a present value of losses that may be expected to occur in the future.[1] If it were established that a plaintiff has lost a certain historical sum, to award the plaintiff that exact sum would be undercompensating him. Had those monies been available at the time of the loss, they could have been invested and equal a greater amount on the trial date. Therefore, a rate of return needs to be applied to convert the monies that are being awarded "late" to trial date terms. Similarly, the reasoning for discounting future losses is that if it is established that the plaintiff will lose certain sums in the future, awarding the projected future amounts on the judgment date will overcompensate the plaintiff. This overcompensation comes from the fact that the plaintiff is getting access to the sums earlier than what would occur in the normal course of business. The monies that are received early can then be invested and equal an even greater amount in the future. To prevent overcompensation, a rate of return must be incorporated into the award computation process to determine the *present value* of the projected future losses.[2]

The computation of the present value of a loss can be broken down into two separate parts: the selection of the appropriate discount (prejudgment) rate and the computation of the present value using the selected rate of return. Prior to

---

[1] John C. Kier and Robin C. Kier, "Opportunity Cost: A Measure of Prejudgment Interest," *Business Lawyer* 39, November 1983, 129–152.

[2] In corporate finance literature the term "present value" is used when referring to discounting future losses. In this book, the term is used more broadly to refer to the conversion of both past and future values to preset or trial date terms.

discussing the application of a prejudgment return and the process of discounting, some background on interest rates and securities markets is provided.

INTEREST RATES AND SECURITIES MARKETS

Determining Interest Rates

Interest rates reflect the rate of return that an investor may earn by forgoing consumption until a future time. The lender loans capital to investors who use it to try to earn a rate of return that is sufficient to compensate the lender for the foregone consumption. For a compounded rate of return this relationship is summarized by the following formula:

$$Y = X(1 + r)^n \tag{7.1}$$

where X = amount lent
r = annual rate of return
Y = amount that must be paid back
n = investment period

When the capital is invested for more than one period, that is when n in Equation (7.1) is greater than 1, investors enjoy a compounded rate of return where interest is earned on interest. This contrasts with *simple interest* where interest is computed only on the original principal not including any accrued interest (see Equation (7.2)).

$$Y = Xrn \tag{7.2}$$

Comparison of Simple versus Compound Interest

Table 7.1 shows a comparison between an investment of $100 that earns only simple interest at a 6% rate versus a compounded 6% return. The compounded value column shows that interest is earned on interest with compounding so investors will have a higher value at the end of the five year period that is used in this example.

Types of Interest Rates

When interest rates are discussed in the media, one can get the impression that there is just one or a few interest rates. In fact, there are many rates. Fortunately,

Table 7.1. Example of Simple versus Compound Interest[a]

Year	Simple Interest		Compound Interest	
	Value	Interest	Value	Interest
1	100.00	6.00	100.00	6.00
2	100.00	6.00	106.00	6.36
3	100.00	6.00	112.36	6.74
4	100.00	6.00	119.10	7.15
5	100.00	6.00	126.25	7.57
Total	130.00		133.82	

[a] Initial Investment = $100.00

they tend to move together so when some rates rise, most others rise also. This comovement has to do with the risk–return relationship between the different interest rate instruments. Some of the more common interest rates cited and used in commercial damages analysis are discussed in the following sections.

Financial Markets: Money Market vs. Capital Market

There are two broad categories of financial markets. the money market and the capital market. These are not specific physical markets such as the New York Stock Exchange. Rather, they are defined by the term and the risk level of the securities included in the various market categories.

Money Market Interest Rates

The money market consists of short term low risk financial instruments.[3] These securities have a maturity of 270 days or less except for one-year Treasuries, which are also included in this market. They differ from their long-term counterparts in that they do not have to be registered pursuant to federal securities laws. Table 7.2 describes some of the major money market securities.

One can learn what the relevant money market rates are in a variety of ways but one of the most common sources is the Credit Markets column that appears in the *Wall Street Journal, New York Times,* and other major newspapers. Figure 7.1 shows a sample from a daily listing in the *Wall Street Journal.* Table 7.3 describes some of the more often-cited interest rates.

Capital Market

Securities with a longer maturity than 270 days are categorized within the capital market. Upon crossing this threshold, insurers of securities, with the exception of

---

[3] See Marcia Stigum, *The Money Market,* (Homewood, Ill.: Dow Jones Irwin) 1983.

Table 7.2. Major Money Market Securities

Treasury Bills	Short-term obligations of the federal government. They vary in maturity, which can be as long as one year. T-bills are sold at a discount from their face value with the difference, as a percent of the purchase price, being the interest return.
Federal Funds	Short-term loans of reserves by banks to other banks. Such loans earn a rate called the federal funds rate. The Federal Reserve Bank focuses on this rate when it is attempting to implement monetary policy.
Commercial Paper	Short-term promissory notes of corporations. They have maturities that vary between 5 and 270 days and are in denominations of $100,000 or more. The issuing companies are generally very credit worthy and the obligations include other guarantees, such as a line of credit sufficient to repay the obligations, thus making them a low-risk investment.
Negotiable Certificates of Deposit	Deposits made by federally insured commercial banks, which can be sold in the money market. These deposits are made for a specific time period or maturity date.
Bankers Acceptances	Bank obligations that often arise in international trade. For example, an importer may want a bank to accept its debt obligation and pay an exporter's bank. The importer's bank may then want to trade this IOU prior to the due date in this active submarket within the money market.

MONEY RATES

Monday, June 28, 1999

The key U. S. and foreign annual interest rates below are a guide to general levels but don't always represent actual transactions.

PRIME RATE: 7.75% (effective 11/18/98). The base rate on corporate loans posted by at least 75% of the nation's 30 largest banks.

DISCOUNT RATE: 4.50% (effective 11/18/98). The charge on loans to depository institutions by the Federal Reserve Banks.

FEDERAL FUNDS: 5 1/4% high, 4 7/8% low, 4 3/4% near closing bid, 4 7/8% offered. Reserves traded among commercial banks for overnight use in amounts of $1 million or more. Source: Prebon Yamane(U.S.A)Inc.

CALL MONEY: 6.50% (effective 11/17/98). The charge on loans to brokers on stock exchange collateral. Source: Telerate.

COMMERCIAL PAPER: placed directly by General Electric Capital Corp.: 5.12% 30 to 35 days; 5.13% 36 to 100 days; 5.20% 101 to 164 days; 5.36% 208 to 270 days.

EURO COMMERCIAL PAPER: placed directly by General Electric Capital Corp.: 2.57% 30 days; 2.58% two months; 2.60% three months; 2.61% four months; 2.62% five months.

DEALER COMMERCIAL PAPER: High-grade unsecured notes sold through dealers by major corporations: 5.20% 30 days; 5.23% 60 days; 527.00% 90 days.

CERTIFICATES OF DEPOSIT: 4.69% one month; 4.75% two months; 4.83% three months; 4.98% six months; 5.30% one year. Average of top rates paid by major New York banks on primary new issues of negotiable C.D.s, usually on amounts of $1 million and more. The minimum unit is $100,000. Typical rates in the secondary maket 5.21% one month; 5.32% three months; 5.45% six months.

BANKERS ACCEPTANCES: 5.12% 30 days; 5.15% 60 days; 5.18% 90 days; 5.23% 120 days; 5.25% 150 days; 5.30% 180 days. Offered rates of negotiable, bank-backed business credit instruments typically financing an import order.

LONDON LATE EURODOLLARS: 5 3/16% - 5 1/16% one month; 5 1/4% - 5 1/8% two months; 5 5/16% - 5 3/16% three months; 5 11/32% - 5 7/32% four months; 5 13/32% - 5 9/32% five months; 5 15/32% - 5 11/32% six months.

LONDON INTERBANK OFFERED RATES (LIBOR): 5.2100% one month; 5.3275% three months; 5.46375% six months; 5.78875% one year. British Banker's Association average of interbank offered rates for dollar deposits in the London market based on quotations at 16 major banks. Effective rate for contracts entered into two days from date appearing at top of this column.

EURO LIBOR: 2.63813% one month; 2.66425% three months; 2.71975% six months; 2.93163% one year. British Banker's Association average of interbank offered rates for euro deposits in the London market based on quotations at 16 major banks. Effective rate for contracts entered into two days from date appearing at top of this column.

EURO INTERBANK OFFERED RATES (EURIBOR): 2.636% one month; 2.664% three months; 2.718% six months; 2.928% one year. European Banking Federation-sponsored rate among 57 Euro zone banks.

FOREIGN PRIME RATES: Canada 6.25%; Germany 2.50%; Japan 1.375%; Switerland 3.125% (eff. 6/28/99); Britain 5.00%. These rate indications aren't directly comparable; lending practices vary widely by location.

TREASURY BILLS: Results of the Monday, June 28, 1999, auction of short-term U.S. government bills, sold at a discount from face value in units of $10,000 to $1 million: 4.750% 13 weeks; 4.960% 26 weeks.

OVERNIGHT REPURCHASE RATE: 4.98%. Dealer financing rate for overnight sale and repurchase of Treasury securities. Source: Telerate.

FEDERAL HOME LOAN MORTGAGE CORP. (Freddie Mac): Posted yields on 30-year mortgage commitments. Delivery within 30 days 7.76%, 60 days 7.82%, standard conventional fixed-rate mortgages: 5.625%, 2% rate capped one-year adjustable rate mortgages. Source: Telerate.

FEDERAL NATIONAL MORTGAGE ASSOCIATION (Fannie Mae): Posted yields on 30 year mortgage commitments (priced at par) for delivery within 30 days 7.72%, 60 days 7.78%, standard conventional fixed-rate mortgages; 6.45%,6/2 rate capped one-year adjustable rate mortgages. Source: Telerate.

MERRILL LYNCH READY ASSETS TRUST: 4.39%. Annualized average rate of return after expenses for the past 30 days; not a forecast of future returns.

CONSUMER PRICE INDEX: May, 166.2, up 2.1% from a year ago. Bureau of Labor Statistics.

Figure 7.1. Sample of the money markets table in the *Wall Street Journal*.

Table 7.3. Often-Cited Interest Rates

Prime Rate	The rate that banks charge their most credit-worthy customers. Interest rates are often quoted as some increment above the prime rate (see Figure 7.2).
Federal Funds Rate	The rate that banks charge each other in the trading of federal funds, which may take place through the efforts of intermediaries. This rate is often used by the Federal Reserve Bank as a guide to the tightness of short-term credit markets which, in turn, is used to guide monetary policy.
Treasury Bill Rate	T-bill rates are the rates on the lowest risk, money market investments. They are at the bottom of the yield curve, which slopes upward with higher rates being associated with longer term Treasuries (see Figure 7.2).
Discount Rate	The rate charged on loans by the Federal Reserve Bank to member banks. The banks must present collateral, such as Treasury securities, and, in return, they receive an amount less than the face value of the securities. This difference as a percent of the loan amount is the discount rate.

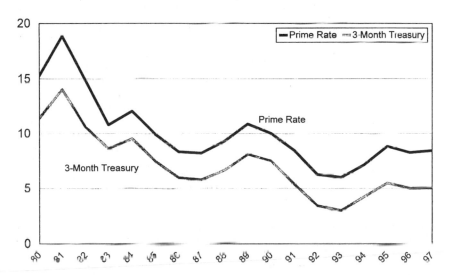

Figure 7.2. Prime rate and the three-month Treasury rate: 1980–97.

the U.S. Treasury, are required by the Securities Act of 1933 to register the securities with the Securities and Exchange Commission, which was formed in 1934 as part of the Securities Exchange Act of 1934. Insurers of these securities use the proceeds of these offerings for long-term capital needs. With the additional length of term, purchasers of these securities must assume a greater risk and, therefore, they expect a higher rate of return.

Table 7.4. Capital Market Security Categories

Treasury Bonds	Both intermediate-term and long-term Treasuries are considered capital market securities. Intermediate term Treasuries have a maturity of 1–10 years while long term Treasuries have a maturity of 10 years or more. With the longer term, and the greater risk that this entails, they offer a higher rate of return. Unlike other capital market securities, this risk does not come from additional default risk, since the insurer is the U.S. Treasury. Given the creditworthiness of the U.S. Treasury, any additional default risk is considered negligible. The increased risk comes in the form of greater *reinvestment risk,* which is the risk that payments derived from these securities over the life of the investment, such interest and principal payments will be reinvested at a lower rate than the original investment.
Corporate Bonds	The long-term debt obligations of corporations. They are a more risky investment than Treasury securities and, therefore, offer a higher rate of return.[4] Investors can assess the degree of risk of these bonds through a rating system offered by firms such as Standard and Poor's and Moody's. For example, Standard and Poor's rates the highest quality bonds as AAA while the lowest quality, those in default, are rated D. The lower the quality of the corporate bonds, the higher the rate needed to compensate investors for assuming the increased risk.
Common Stock	These securities constitute the equity interest of the owners of corporations. They are the first securities to be issued by a corporation and the last to be retired. Stockholders are compensated through dividend payments and capital gains (losses). These securities bear a higher degree of risk than corporate bonds as the latter category of securities enjoys a preference in the bankruptcy liquidation process, whereby monies derived from the sale of liquidated corporate assets cannot be paid to equity holders until the claims of bondholders are satisfied. Given that stockholders often get little or nothing in liquidation and often do poorly in corporate reorganizations, stock is considered more risky than bonds. However, stockholders may participate in the prosperity of a company that enjoys increased profitability while bondholders, who hold fixed income obligations, maintain the same return. Therefore, the return of stockholders is expected to be higher than bondholders, reflecting the greater risk and return of these securities.

Table 7.4 describes some of the more important categories of securities that trade in the capital market. Table 7.5 and Figure 7.3 show the historical rates of return for these securities.

---

[4] This discussion implies that the higher the level of risk, the greater the rate of return. Strictly speaking, however, this is not accurate. It has been demonstrated that the market does not compensate investors for all types of risk but only for those risks that cannot easily be avoided through diversification. This risk is called *systematic risk* and there is a good relationship between rates of return and the level of systematic risk.

Table 7.5. Government Yields and S&P 500 Return

	Yields on Government Securities			
Year	3-month Treasury Bills (%)	10-year Treasuries (%)	30-year Treasuries (%)	S&P 500 Total Return (%)
1980	11.51	11.43	11.27	32.54
1981	14.03	13.92	13.45	−4.91
1982	10.69	13.01	12.76	21.53
1983	8.63	11.10	11.18	22.57
1984	9.35	12.46	12.41	6.28
1985	7.47	10.62	10.79	31.72
1986	5.98	7.67	7.78	18.64
1987	5.82	8.39	8.59	5.26
1988	6.69	8.85	8.96	16.61
1989	8.12	8.49	8.45	31.68
1990	7.51	8.55	8.61	−3.09
1991	5.42	7.86	8.14	30.46
1992	3.45	7.01	7.67	7.62
1993	3.02	5.87	6.59	10.07
1994	4.29	7.09	7.37	1.33
1995	5.51	6.57	6.88	37.57
1996	5.02	6.44	6.71	22.96
1997	5.07	6.35	6.61	33.37
1998	4.81	5.26	5.58	28.58

Source: Board of Governors of the Federal Reserve System, Washington, D.C. The Federal Reserve Bank of St. Louis, St. Louis, MO

Real versus Nominal Interest Rates

When lenders establish interest rates, they want to ensure that they will be repaid by dollars that have at least the same buying power as the ones they lent. That is, they want to make sure that they earn a specific rate return in excess of the rate of inflation. The return in excess of the inflation rate is known as the *real* rate of return. If, for example, a loan is made during a period of inflation, and the inflation was unanticipated, the dollars that are repaid may have less buying power than the dollars that were lent. Consider a loan of $100,000 that is made at a time when inflation was anticipated to be 3%. Based on this belief, the lender loaned

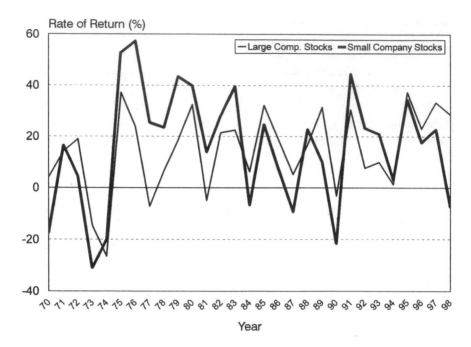

Figure 7.3. Historical rates of return for selected capital market securities.

money at a 9% rate, seeking a 6% real rate of return. However, over the term of the loan, if inflation unexpectedly rose to 5%, it would erode the real rate of return to 4% from the anticipated 6%.

In inflationary periods, if the inflation is unanticipated, borrowers gain because they pay back dollars that have a lower buying power than the dollars they lent. This gain comes at the expense of lenders who incorrectly anticipate the inflation. This loss and gain is known as the *redistribution effect* of inflation.[5] To avoid the adverse consequences of inflation, market participants must ensure that they correctly anticipate inflation. If inflation is stable, it is easier to anticipate inflation correctly. An unstable inflationary environment makes financial markets more difficult for participants and results in higher interest rates.

One of the first great American economists, Irving Fisher, clearly delineated the relationship between nominal and real interest rates in what is called the *Fisher Equation*.[6] This equation, Equation (7.3), shows that the nominal rate of interest is equal to the real rate of return and the expected rate of inflation.

---

[5] Milton Friedman, *Dollars and Deficits* (Englewood Cliffs, N.J.: Prentice Hall) 1968.
[6] Irving Fisher, *Theory of Interest,* (New York: A.M. Kelley Publishers) 1965. This book was originally published in 1930.

$$r_n = r_r + P_e \qquad (7.3)$$

where r_n = nominal rate of interest
       r_r = real rate of interest
       P_e = inflation rate

When lenders quote a loan rate, they anticipate the rate of inflation over the course of the loan, P_e, and add this inflation premium to the real rate of return that are seeking (r_r).

Historical Relationship Between Inflation and Interest Rates

Based on the desire of capital providers to select an interest rate that more than keeps pace with inflation, we would expect interest rates to be higher than the inflation rate. Depending on their risk characteristics, securities offer a higher rate of return than the inflation rate. Therefore, for each security, there is a nominal return and a real return, which is the nominal return less the rate of inflation. This difference can be computed as the basic arithmetic difference between these two rates or as a geometric difference, which is expressed as follows:

$$(1 + r_r) = \frac{(1 + r_n)}{(1 + P_e)} \qquad (7.4)$$

Interest Rates and The Supply and Demand for Loanable Funds

In each market, interest rates are determined by the supply and demand of capital. The interaction of providers of capital and those who want to borrow results in an equilibrium rate such as that shown in Figure 7.4. An increase in demand causes rates to rise, whereas a decline in demand causes rates to fall, as shown in Figure 7.5. An increase in the supply of loanable funds causes rates to decline, whereas a decrease in the supply of loanable funds causes rates to rise as shown in Figure 7.6.

Relationship between Risk and Return

Generally, the higher the level of risk of a security, the higher its rates of return. To understand this, consider two securities that are the same in all respects in-

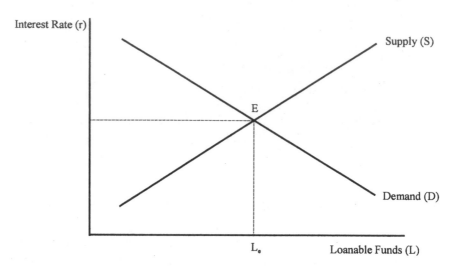

Figure 7.4. Demand and supply of loanable funds.

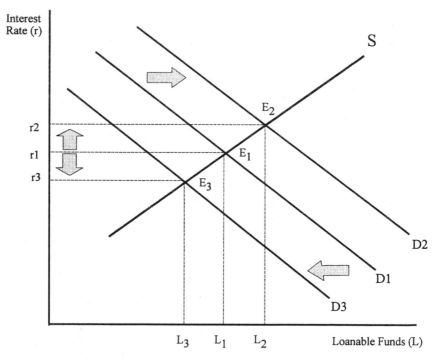

Figure 7.5. Changes in demand for loanable funds.

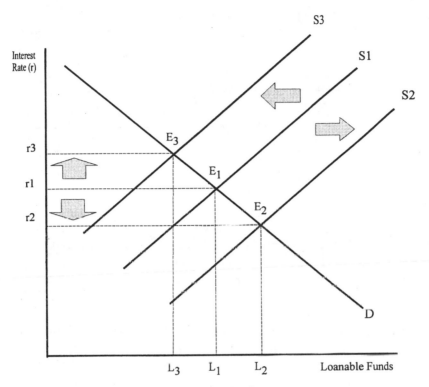

Figure 7.6. Changes in supply of loanable funds.

cluding their rates of return but which differ in the their risk. Security Y has more risk than security X. Sellers seeking to sell both security X and Y will find that buyers are unwilling to buy Y as it offers only the same return as X but requires buyer to assume more risk than X. The only way that sellers will be able to sell Y, which faces competition with X, is to offer a higher rate of return than X. How much higher depends on the risk that buyers perceive in Y. The result of this risk–return tradeoff is a ranking of securities in the marketplace, where securities with higher risk have to offer higher rates of return in order to compete for the available funds of investors.

This risk–return relationship can be seen in Table 7.6, which shows various average rates of return for securities that vary in their risk levels with common stocks having higher risk than corporate bonds which, in turn have higher risk than Treasuries. Table 7.5 shows how these securities offer higher rates of return according to the risk that the market perceives in these securities.

Table 7.6.   Average Yields and Rates of Return (in percent)

Period	Yields			
	3-month Treasury Bills	10-year Treasuries	30-year Treasuries	S&P 500 Total Return
1990-98	4.90	6.78	7.13	18.76
1980-98	6.97	8.79	8.94	18.46

Source: Board of Governors of the Federal Reserve System, Washington, D.C. The Federal Reserve Bank of St. Louis, St. Souis, MO

Sources of Yield and Rate of Return Data

Various sources of data on yields and rates of return exist. Rates of return on different mutual funds that are tied to equity indexes, such as the S&P 500 Index and Russell 2000 Index, can be found on the websites of most companies such as T. Rowe Price Associates, Inc., The Vanguard Group, etc. These sites present a wealth of information on the fund's performance, usually since the date of inception, and normally compare it to the benchmark. Yield data on U.S. Treasury securities are also accessible on the Internet. One of the most commonly used sites is that of the Board of Governors of the Federal Reserve System, at http://www.federalreserve.gov. This site presents daily, monthly, and annual statistics on issues such as 3- and 6-month Treasury Bills, and 10-, 20-, and 30-year Treasuries.[7] These data can also be found in the *Economic Report of the President,* in the table on "Bond Yields and Interest Rates." Another important website is that of the Federal Reserve Bank of St. Louis.[8] This site contains a historical database of economic and financial statistics, among them being the total return on the S&P 500 Composite Index.

PREJUDGMENT LOSSES

There are several reasons why a prejudgment rate of return may need to be applied to pre-trial losses. The first is to place the parties in the same position they would have been in had the wrongful acts not occurred. Providing the plaintiff with a damage award of monies it would had access to years earlier clearly under compensates the plaintiff. Therefore, some rate of return needs to be applied to the award so as to make the plaintiff whole. There are also efficiency-related reasons why a prejudgment return should be applied. Adding prejudgment interest helps ensure full compensation thereby requiring the parties to take into account

---

[7] Much of these data are also available in *The Federal Reserve Bulletin* which is published by the Board of Governors of the Federal Reserve System.

[8] The web address is http://www.stls.frb.org.

the full consequences of their actions when engaging in the activities that were the case of the lawsuit. Without prejudgment interest the defendant may be able to avoid complete compensation and thus may be insufficiently deterred from engaging in actions that are the cause of the trial. Another efficiency-related reason for prejudgment interest is that if there is no provision for prejudgment interest, the defendant may have an incentive to prolong the litigation. By extending the litigation, a guilty defendant may be forcing the plaintiff to extend an interest free loan. Awarding prejudgment interest helps eliminate this incentive.[9] In cases where the defendant's rate of return on capital exceeds the prejudgment rate, this incentive may still persist although only at a diminished rate.

An example of the reasoning applied by the courts in awarding prejudgment interest was clearly articulated in the 1992 *Amoco Cadiz* case in which the court awarded the French plaintiffs $65 million in damages and $148 million in prejudgment interest. The Seventh Circuit's reasoning in awarding prejudgment interest on cleanup costs of the Brittany coast following an oil spill is set forth as follows:

[C]onsider what would have happened if the French parties had borrowed $60 million to finance the cleanup in April 1978, and Amoco had put that sum in trust to fund an award of damages. . . . The victims would have to pay the market rate of interest . . . If they arranged to repay the debt in a single balloon payment at the end (when they recouped from Amoco), and if the rate of interest averaged 12%, then by April 1991 the victims would owe their creditors $262 million. Meanwhile the trust fund, lending out its assets at the market rate of 12%, would have grown to $262 million. Scores would be fully settled if Amoco tendered its interest in the fund: It would thus "pay" $60 million as of 1978, and the victims would receive $60 million as of 1978; the lenders who financed the cleanup would receive full payment for the use of their money. (We use these dates and rates only as illustrations; the periods and rates actually used in this case differ. We also disregard taxes.)

Victims who finance their own cleanup lend to themselves; forced to devote money to a project not of their own choosing (money they otherwise could have lent out at the market rate of interest), they are entitled to compensation for the "hire" of this capital. Tortfeasors who choose to reinvest their money in the business (as Amoco had done) rather than create a trust fund. . . are in no position to complain when called on to pay prejudgment interest. An injurer allowed to keep the return on this money has profited by wrong.[10]

---

[9]Michael S. Knoll, "A Primer on Prejudgment Interest," *Texas Law Review*, (75), 1996, 293–374.

[10]*In Re Oil Spill by the Amoco Cadiz Off the Coast of France*, 954 F. 2nd 1279, 1330 (7th Cir. 1992).

Selection of Appropriate Prejudgment Rate

There are differing views within economics and finance as to the appropriate rate of return to apply to historical damages to bring them to trial date terms. It is clear that, at a minimum, past losses should be converted to present value terms using a risk-free rate such as the rate on U.S. Treasury bills.[11] Some believe that the defendant's debt rate should be used as the prejudgement rate of return based on the theory that once the defendant engaged in its wrongful actions, it was, in effect, in debt to the plaintiff as it "owed" the plaintiff its lost profits.[12] The use of the defendant's debt rate, which is higher than the risk-free rate, results in a higher present value of losses. This choice of prejudgment rates of return, however, is not generally accepted within this field. The use of the risk-free rate, or the defendant's debt rate, may not fully compensate the plaintiff for its opportunity costs. If the plaintiff had received the lost profits at the time it would have earned them but for the actions of the defendant, it may have either reinvested them back into the business and/or distributed a component to shareholders. The use of the lower rates described may not compensate the plaintiff for the lost investment opportunities that it could have enjoyed. An alternative guide to the determination of the prejudgment rate may be the plaintiff's cost of capital, which is the expected rate of return that the market requires in order to attract funds to a particular usage or investment.[13] This figure is the weighted average of each of the individual costs of capital for each of the components in the company's capital structure. For example, if the firm derived half its capital from borrowing and half from equity investments, each weight is 0.50. The rate of return on equity would be higher than the debt rate due to the increased risk associated with equity investments. Let us assume that the debt rate is 10% and the equity rate is 15%. The weighted cost of capital would be as follows:

$$\text{Cost of capital} = w_d r_d + w_e r_e \qquad (7.5)$$

---

[11] R. F. Lanzillotti and A. K. Esquibel, "Measuring Damages in Commercial Litigation: Present Value of Lost Opportunities," *Journal of Accounting, Auditing and Finance,* 1989, 125–142 and Franklin M. Fisher and R. Craig Romaine, "Janis Joplin's Yearbook and the Theory of Damages," *Journal of Accounting, Auditing and Finance,* 1989, 145–157.

[12] James M. Patell, Roman L. Weil, and Mark A. Wolfson, "Accumulating Damages in Litigation: The Role of Uncertainty and Interest Rates," *Journal of Legal Studies* 11 (2), June 1982, 341–364.

[13] Shannon P. Pratt, *Cost of Capital: Estimation and Applications* (New York: Wiley) 1998, p. 3.

where w_d = percent of debt in the capital structure
w_e = percent of equity in the capital structure
r_d = rate paid on debt
r_e = rate of return on equity

Based on the parameters of the foregoing example, the cost of capital would be $0.50(10\%) + 0.50(15\%) = 12.5\%$.

When the firm has a more varied capital structure, with different layers of debt and other forms of capital, such as preferred stock, the cost of capital can be expressed in the following weighted average form:

$$\text{Cost of capital} = \sum_{i=1}^{n} w_i r_i \qquad (7.6)$$

where w_i = percent of total capital the ith type of capital in the firm's total capital structure
r_i = rate of return on the ith capital source

Equation (7.6) simply means that the cost of capital is the weighted average of the costs of the components of the firm's capital mix. Equation (7.5) shows an example of how the weighted average cost of capital can be computed.

For a profitable firm, the return provided by the cost of capital may be lower than the actual rate of return the firm might earn in a given year (depending on how you define this rate of return). The cost of capital, however, is a rate of return sufficient for a company to meet its interest obligations and repay its debt principal, while also allowing for an equity return that is consistent with this type of business. It is important to note that the payment of a rate of return equal to the cost of capital is not a break-even return. It is a return that is equal to the return contracted for by new nonequity capital providers, while enabling new equity holders to receive the return they probably expected at the time they made their investment.

In computing damages for a division of a diversified firm that operates in many lines of business, and which has several divisions, it may be more appropriate to use the divisional cost of capital. When that is not as easily defined, the economist might look at the costs of capital for companies that are similar to the division in question. The individual components of the capital mix of a firm and their respective costs are discussed next.

Plaintiff's versus Defendant's Typical Positions on Using the Cost of Captial as the Prejudgment Rate

Using the cost of capital may yield a higher prejudgment rate compared to other alternatives such as the defendant's debt rate or a Treasury rate. Therefore, it may be preferred by plaintiffs and opposed by defendants. While plaintiffs may assert that using a lower rate will under compensate them, defendants may claim that the plaintiff did not incur any opportunity costs as it did not necessarily lose out on any investment opportunities. This defense argument assumes that the plaintiff could access capital markets to borrow and attract equity capital to fund the business activities. This "perfect capital markets" assumption, however, *may* not be relevant to the actual circumstances in which the plaintiff does business. Particularly in cases where the plaintiff incurred significant financial damage due to the actions of the defendant, its access to capital markets may have become limited.

COST OF CAPITAL

Components

Cost of Debt

The rate of return on debt is more straightforward than the equity rate. The debt rate is stipulated when the firm enters into borrowing agreements. For example, if the firm always borrows at the prime rate, this may be a good estimate of the debt rate. The situation becomes only slightly more complicated when the firm has more than one debt source.

If the company has borrowed from banks at varying rates, a weighted average can be taken for a historical period, such as five years. The weights used are the amounts borrowed. When the company has borrowed in securities markets by issuing corporate bonds, however, the rate on these securities needs to be added to the debt rate calculation in the same weighted manner as before.

It is the norm in corporate finance to express the debt rate on an after-tax cost basis,[14] which reflects the tax benefits derived through the tax deductibility of interest payments. On an after-tax basis, the cost of debt can be expressed as:

---

[14] Eugene Brigham and Louis Gapinski, *Intermediate Financial Management,* 3rd ed., (Chicago: Dryden Press) 1990, and R. Charles Moyer, James R. McGuigan, and William J. Kretlow, *Contemporary Financial Management,* 5th ed. (St. Paul: West Publishing Company) 1992.

$$r_d^t = r_d(1 - t) \tag{7.7}$$

where t = firm's tax rate
   r_d = before-tax debt rate
   r_d^t = after-tax debt rate

For public debt in the form of corporate bonds, these rates can be further adjusted to reflect the flotation costs.

Preferred Stock

Preferred stock typically pays a constant dividend and is more similar to debt than common stock. The cost of preferred stock can be expressed in the following way:

$$r_p = \frac{d_p}{P_{net}} \tag{7.8}$$

where d_p = preferred stock dividend
   P_{net} = net proceeds of the preferred stock offering after deducting flotation costs

Rate on Equity

The determination of the appropriate rate of return on equity is less straightforward. This rate of return is expected by the firm's equity investors. For publicly held companies, the historical return on equity is a readily available statistic. It tends to be higher for riskier firms. For newer firms, however, the rate of return on equity provided by securities markets may not be as useful. In such instances, it is valuable to consider the equity rates of *proxy companies*. These companies are in the same industry, are of similar size, and have similar risk characteristics as the injured company. The rate of return on equity for such companies can be used as a proxy for the injured company's equity rate.

Using another approach, the appropriate risk-adjusted return relationship can be approximated using the *capital asset pricing model*. This model generates *betas* to weight the difference between the market rate of return and the risk-free rate. Betas are derived from a regression analysis of the historical movements of the individual firm's stock return (r_i) and the excess market return $(r_m - r_f)$. Betas reflect the variability of the stock's return, which can be explained by market movements and is referred to as *systematic risk*. Systematic risk is that component of total risk that cannot be reduced through diversification. Each firm has its own beta that is used to adjust the excess return $(r_m - r_f)$ to reflect the firm's unique risk characteristics. Using this model, the following equity rate can be derived:

$$r_i = r_j + \beta_i(r_m - r_f) \tag{7.9}$$

where r_i = rate of return for security i
r_f = risk-free rate
r_m = market rate of return
β_i = beta for company i.

The capital asset pricing model and betas in particular, have been the subject of recent criticism.[15] The strength of the hypothesized positive, linear relationship between betas and security returns was challenged when Fama and French showed that the inclusion of other variables, such as size, significantly reduces the explanatory power of betas. They have expanded the usual capital asset pricing model (CAPM) model into a *three-factor model,* which includes other explanatory variables, such as firm size. Their results follow some other challenges to the capital asset pricing model. However, the model has certainly not been discarded and continues to be a valuable tool in corporate finance.

Betas for many companies can be found in a variety of places. Many investment publications, such as *Value Line Investment Survey,* include betas in the collection of financial statistics they publish on the companies covered in their publication.[16] Another source is the *Beta Book* published by Ibbotson Associates.[17]

For privately held companies, the rate of return on equity is more difficult to establish. These statistics are not as readily available as they are for publicly held firms. The problem is even greater for the smaller private companies, which, since they are not encumbered by the requirement to meet expected returns for stockholders, tend to have higher "costs" than they otherwise would. The rates of return on equity for these businesses, therefore, are not comparable to those provided by securities markets. The rates for similar public firms can be used after the addition of a risk premium in order to account for the increased risk and illiquidity associated with many private firms. The expert needs to determine the appropriateness of this approach on a case-by-case basis.

---

[15] Eugene F. Fama and Kenneth French, "The Cross Section of Expected Stock Returns," *Journal of Finance* (June 1992), 427–465.

[16] *Value Line Investment Survey* (New York: Value Line Publishing Inc.).

[17] *Beta Book* (Chicago, Ill.: Ibbotson Associates).

Sources of Cost of Capital Data

The cost of capital for a company can be measured directly by determining the various components in the company's capital mix and the relevant rate that the company pays for each of them. Using these data, weights for each component can be computed and applied to the relevant rates to arrive at a weighted average costs of capital. These data may be acquired directly from the company or from public filings that the company may have generated.

Another source of cost of capital data is the *Cost of Capital Quarterly* yearbook.[18] This data source includes capital costs, such as the cost of equity, and is organized by Standard Industrial Classification (SIC) code. Capital costs are available for approximately 300 different SIC codes. The data is available by industry category rather than for particular companies.

Ibbotson Associates culls these data from the Compustat data files, a data source published by Standard & Poor's that has financial data, including financial statements, for a larger number of public companies.

Cost of Capital as an Element of Damages

In one District of Columbia case, a plaintiff appealed a district court's award of the costs of capital, which was applied to damages resulting from a breach of contract.[19] In its ruling, the Court of Appeals indicated that such an award is appropriate in a breach of contract claim but not in a negligence claim. It its ruling, the court stated as follows:

> It remains unclear whether pre-judgment interest (interest from the time of the tort to the date of court judgment) is available in a negligence action. Nonetheless, . . . in addition to finding Williams negligent, the District Court had found that Straight has breached its contract with Smoot. Further, because Williams agreed to indemnify Straight in full, the court did not error by including the costs of capital in the damage award assessed against Williams—whether or not the court allows a cost of capital award in a negligence action.

---

[18] *Cost of Capital Quarterly* (Chicago, Ill.: Ibbotson Associates).

[19] *Williams Enterprises, Inc. v. The Sherman R. Smoot Company,* 938 F. 2d 230, 290 U.S. App. D.C. 411 (October 8, 1991).

Cost of Capital in Public Utility Environment

Cost of capital is a fundamental concept in public utility rate making. Many hearings in which economic experts have testified on the costs of capital have been held before various rate-making commissions.[20] The commissions typically meet to decide whether a given utility may receive an increase in its rates to reflect their higher costs as well as a return on invested capital. Courts ruling on related issues have endorsed the use of a sufficient rate of return to allow a company to *maintain its credit and attract capital.*[21] This rate has been found to be one that affords a rate of return similar to other investments having comparable risk levels.

Time Period of Which Rate of Return Is Derived

There are several alternatives that can be considered when selecting the time period over which the prejudgment rate is to be derived. One alternative would be to select the relevant rate as of the judgment date. In light of the fact that rates can fluctuate, picking a rate that prevailed on a specific date can lead to a biased result. In *Amoco Cadiz* the court articulated its reasoning as follows:

> It should be plain that the market rate in question is the one during the litigation—when the defendant had use of the money that the court has decided belongs to the plaintiff—not the going rate at the end of the case (cite omitted). Market rates have been above 23% and below 10% for different portions of the period. As it would be inappropriate to award prejudgment interest at a 20% rate if it happened to prevail in the last week of a case (and the rate had been 5% in the preceding decade), so it is inappropriate to use a lower rate such as 7% for which money may be rented at the conclusion, when higher rates presisted during the bulk of the case. The district court's remark (when denying the French parties motion for reconsideration) that inflation is irrelevant to the choice of a rate of interest reflects a misunderstanding of the relation between inflation and interest rates. The market rate includes a prediction of inflation—which is why it is necessary to use the rates in force during the case and not whatever prevails at the end.[22]

---

[20] Keith Howe and Eugene F. Rasmussen, *Public Utility Economics and Finance* (Englewood Cliffs: Prentice Hall), 1982.

[21] *FPC v. Hope Natural Gas Co.,* 320 U.S. 591, 64 S. Ct. 281, 88, L. Ed. 333 (1944).

[22] In *Re Oil Spill by the Amoco Cadiz Off the Coast of France,* 794 F. Supp. 261; 1992 June 15, 1992 decided.

Sample Prejudgment Computation

An example of the actual simple interest computation method used by the court in *Amoco Cadiz* is set forth below in a later decision in the same case where the new principal was $21,748,577. Here the court applied the same simple interest formula introduced earlier in this chapter:

$$\text{Interest} = \text{Principal} \times \text{Rate} \times \text{Time}$$

The year was taken to be a 360-day year which is a common number of days used for such computations in finance. The amount of interest is calculated in Table 7.7.

Losses Due to the Impairment of Capital

A common type of litigation is one caused by the loss of a construction company's *bonding capacity*. Construction contractors are often requested by purchasers of their services, such as other companies or governmental entities, to post a bond, which guarantees their performance and protects the purchasers from a variety of failures on the part of the contractor. Such bonds may be purchased by a surety. In making their assessment of the contractor's bonding capacity, sureties tend to look at a limited number of financial variables and, prime among them, is the liquidity of the contractor as measured by the size of its

Table 7.7. Interest Computation in *Amoco Cadiz* Case

Year	Principal	Rate	Time	Interest
1	$21,748,577	.1231	(360/360)	$2,677,249.83
2	$21,748,577	.1231	(360/360)	$2,677,249.83
3	$21,748,577	.1231	(360/360)	$2,677,249.83
4	$21,748,577	.1231	(360/360)	$2,677,249.83
5	$21,748,577	.1231	(360/360)	$2,677,249.83
6	$21,748,577	.1231	(360/360)	$2,677,249.83
7	$21,748,577	.1231	(360/360)	$2,677,249.83
8	$21,748,577	.1231	(360/360)	$2,677,249.83
9	$21,748,577	.1231	(360/360)	$2,677,249.83
10	$21,748,577	.1231	(360/360)	$2,677,249.83
11	$21,748,577	.1231	(360/360)	$2,677,249.83
12	$21,748,577	.1231	(360/360)	$2,677,249.83
13	$21,748,577	.1231	(130/360)	$966,784.66
Total Prejudgment Interest:				$33,093,782.62

working capital. Working capital is the difference between current assets and current liabilities. This is explained in the various excerpts included below from *S.C. Anderson v. Bank of America:*[23]

> Anderson claimed consequential damages, consisting of lost profits, based upon an alleged impairment of bonding capacity.
>
> A contractor must furnish a performance bond if it is to be awarded a public works construction project. A bid bond is a document issued by a bonding company which is attached by the contractor to its bid. The bond represents to the project owner that the contractor is bondable, and if the contractor is awarded the job, the surety company will issue a performance bond covering the work.
>
> A surety, such as Travelers, calculates a contractors bonding capacity by assessing, among other things, the contractor's working capital. Working capital consists of current assets less allowed current liabilities. By mid-1986, Anderson's financial statements disclosed that the CPII and TAII receivables had not been paid for several months. This impacted Anderson's working capital and, in August, 1986, resulted in a reduction in Anderson's bonding capacity from an aggregate exposure of $10 million to an aggregate exposure of $5 million.

There are several ways to measure the damages that a plaintiff may suffer as a result of a loss of bonding capacity. One is to measure the reduced amount of business the plaintiff experienced due to the lower bonding capacity. The lower capacity may prevent him from taking on jobs beyond a certain combined level. Defendants should explore whether the loss of the bonding capacity is truly due to their actions or is the result of other factors, such a mismanagement by the contractor. Defendants should also be mindful that a lower total business volume does not necessarily imply lower overall profitability. Some companies can generate more total profits on a smaller business volume. Yet, their pursuit of being a larger company may cause them to take on more business and dilute their overall profitability. It can also be the case that the plaintiff is prevented from bidding larger jobs due to a lower bonding capacity but can bid more smaller jobs — some of which may not have the same bonding requirement of larger jobs. The defendant should compute the profitability margin by jobs for the plaintiff in order to assess the relative profit contribution of large versus small jobs.

Another factor that should be explored by defendants in loss of bonding capacity cases is the cost of securing alternative bonding capacity. If alternative

---

[23] *S.C. Anderson v. Bank of America,* 24 Cal. App. 4th 529 (1994).

bonding capacity can be acquired at a higher price, then this difference in price may be one measure of damages instead of a lost profits analysis. If that is the case, then the issue simplifies into a higher costs of capital analysis as opposed to a lost profits exercise.

Computation of Prejudgment Interest in Patent Infringement Cases

The courts have not presented a unified position on how to compute the prejudgment return in patent infringement cases. Various rates have been found acceptable, ranging from money market rates to the prevailing prime rate during the infringement period.[24] However, there have been cases where a plaintiff was able to demonstrate that rates in excess of the prime rate, which were the rates that it had to pay to obtain capital to stay solvent during the infringement period, were appropriate.[25]

In patent cases, prejudgment interest is applied to what is known as *base damages*. Base damages, the amount of damages awarded, usually are a measure of lost profits or a reasonable royalty. Punitive multipliers may also be applied to these base damages.[26]

Risk Adjustment of Past Losses

Past losses usually are not known with certainty but must be estimated. Given this uncertainty, their estimation should reflect some risk adjustment process. It is important to note, however, that the uncertainty associated with past losses is markedly different than that of future losses. A number of important deterministic variables influence the level of sales and profits that a firm can receive, including factors such as the overall level of demand in the economy, the performance characteristics of particular types of products, consumer preferences, and actions of competitors. In making an ex-post projection, some of these factors are already known. Indeed, the methodological framework put forward in earlier chapters of

---

[24] *Uniroyal, Inc. v. Rudkin-Wiley Co.*, F.2d 1540 (Fed. Cir. 1991).

[25] *Lam, Inc. v. Johns Manville Corp.*, 718 F. 2d. 1056, 219 U.S.P.Q. 670 (Fed Cir. 1983).

[26] *Gyromat Corporation v. Champion Spark Plug Company*, 735 F. 2d 549 (Fed. Cir. 1984).

this book attempted to explicitly take into account such factors in the loss estimation process. Given the more complete nature of the information set that applies to past losses compared to future losses, there is a very different level of uncertainty associated with past and future losses. For future losses, many of the deterministic variables are unknown, while for past losses they are known historical values. To the extent that the historical loss estimation process already took the variation in the relevant risk factors into account, the past losses may already be risk adjusted through the use of the information set available as of the date of the analysis. If the expert explicitly attempted to do this in the estimation process, then no further risk adjustment of past estimated losses may be necessary. If not, then some accommodation for such uncertainty needs to be made. The risk adjustment process for past losses can present a fertile area for cross-examination when the expert has ignored this issue while estimating losses.

DISCOUNTING

Discounting Projected Future Profits

Future projected losses must be converted to present value because if an award of damages is made as of a trial date, but the future losses would not be incurred for some period of time in the future, then the early receipt of such an award would overcompensate the plaintiff, since such monies could be invested and would equal an even greater amount in the future. Thus, a lesser amount, the present value of future losses, needs to be computed.

In order to compute the present value of a future amount, a *discount rate* must be selected. This rate may include a premium to account for the riskiness of a projected income stream. Generally speaking, risk is the possibility that the rate of return may deviate from expectations. In investment analysis, risk is the variability of an asset's returns.[27] This risk is quantified using statistical measures such as the variance and standard deviation of returns. In corporate finance, the risk adjustment process is focused on variables such as cash flows and is measured using a variety of statistical techniques.[28] If one were to graph the variability of common stock returns relative to a lower risk security, such as long-term Treasuries, one would see that there is a greater degree of dispersion for stock re-

---

[27] See Edwin J. Elton and Martin J. Gruber, *Modern Portfolio Theory and Investment Analysis* (New York: Wiley) 1995, 128–180.

[28] Aswath Damodaran, *Corporate Finance* (New York: Wiley) 1997, 286–326.

turns compared to the returns on long-term Treasuries. On average, stocks pay a higher return but the variability of this return is greater than for Treasuries. This variability is the risk associated with these different securities. It is why these securities offer different rates of return. Using similar reasoning, the return and risk of corporate bonds are generally less than for common stock but are higher than for Treasuries.

The convention in personal injury economic loss analysis is to select a risk-free rate, or at least a rate that is free of default risk.[29] In effect, this assumes that the projected wage and benefit stream is virtually certain. In this type of analysis, economists make risk adjustments by adjusting the future stream itself. This adjustment is done by applying an unemployment adjustment factor or by curtailing the length of the stream, as with projections to the worklife expectancy only.

In commercial damages analysis, the risk adjustment process is often incorporated in the discount rate.[30] This type of risk adjustment process is standard in corporate finance and is routinely done in capital budgeting analysis. Capital budgeting is the area of corporate finance that deals with the analysis, evaluation, and selection of investment projects. In capital budgeting, projects are evaluated using various techniques, such as discounted cash flows and the internal rate of return. In discounted cash flow analysis, a technique regularly used in the valuation of businesses, a risk-adjusted discount rate is used to convert projected future cash flows to present value terms. The discount rate is adjusted upward in accordance with the perceived variability of riskiness of the projects's projected cash flows.[31]

One possible source of discount rates is the cost of capital of the corporation. Once again, the weighted average cost of capital can be employed but now as the discount rate to bring future projected losses to present value terms. If, however, the expert is measuring losses associated with a particular project, then it may be more appropriate to use the project's costs of capital, if this cost is significantly different than the overall company's cost of capital.[32] Another alternative to using the weighted average cost of capital as the discount rate is to select a risk premium that can be added to the risk-free rate. Treasury securities provide several

---

[29] Michael Brookshire and Frank Slesnick, "A 1996 Study of Prevailing Practice in Forensic Economics," *Journal of Forensic Economics,* 10 (1), Winter 1997, 11.

[30] Jeffrey C. Bodington, "Discount Rates for Lost Profits," *Journal of Forensic Economics* 5 (3), Fall 1992, 209–219.

[31] See James C. VanHorne and John M. Machowiz, *Fundamentals of Financial Management* (Englewood Cliffs; N.J.: Prentice Hall) 1995, 414–416.

[32] Richard A. Brealey, Stewart C. Myers, and Alan J. Marcus, *Fundamentals of Corporate Finance* (New York: McGraw Hill, Inc.) 1995, 262–263.

different risk-free rates (free of default risk) that vary according to the maturity of the security. The risk-free rate that is similar in length to the term of the loss projection should be selected. For example, in a ten-year future loss projection, the rate on ten-year treasury notes will be applicable. To this risk-free rate would be added a risk premium that as closely as possible reflects the anticipated variability in the projected stream of future losses. Once again, the securities market may be used as a guide. For example, higher risk securities, such as junk bonds (bonds with a Dun & Bradstreet rating of BB or lower) can be used as one possible guide among many to reflect the anticipated risk of the loss projection. If the perceived variability of the projected losses exceeds what is accounted for by junk bond returns, then other risk premia can be considered, such as the rates of return required for investments in closely held companies.[33]

This method of adding a risk premium to the risk-free rate, where the premium is derived from various securities traded in the marketplace, is regularly used in the field of business valuations.[34] The method is referred to as the *build-up method.* Here the expert has to make a judgment as to whether the risk premia embodied in the rates of publicly traded securities are assumed to be comparable to the premia associated with the business activity whose income is being brought to present-value terms.

Discounting with Nominal versus Real Rates

There has been much debate in the forensic economics literature regarding whether discounting should be done using nominal or real interest rates.[35] Much of this debate has centered around personal injury litigation. However, many of the same basic principles apply to the measurement of commercial damages. Therefore, it is instructive to explore this debate and the court's position on it.

---

[33] This "build-up" discount rate is discussed in Robert R. Trout, "Introduction to Business Valuation," *Litigation Economics,* Patrick A. Gaughan and Robert Thornton, eds. (Greenwich, Conn.: JAI Press) 1993, 107–150.

[34] Shannon Pratt, Robert F. Rielly, and Robert Schweihs, *Valuing a Business,* 3rd ed. (New York: Irwin Professional Publishing), 1996, 161–165, and Jay Fishman, Shannon Pratt, J. Clifford, and D. Keith Wilson, *Guide to Business Valuations* (Fort Worth: Practitioners Publishing Company) 1995, 5-14–5-23.

[35] See W. Criis Lewis, "On the Relative Stability and Predictability of the Interest Rates and Earnings Growth Rate," *Journal of Forensic Economics,* Winter 1991, 9–26, and Laura Nowak, "Empirical Evidence on the Relationship Between Earnings Growth and Interest Rates," *Journal of Forensic Economics* Spring/Summer 1991, 187–202.

One of the simplest ways of projecting future earnings and then discounting them to the present is to simply assume that the rate of earnings growth will be approximately equal to the interest rate used to discount the future earnings. Discounting then becomes quite simple in that you simply multiply the length of the loss period by the annual loss in the first year of the loss. The result is an inflation-adjusted and discounted loss. This method is referred to as the *total offset method*. Although the courts have acknowledged the mathematical validity of using a net discount rate, one that deducts the inflation rate from the discount rate so that discounting is done using a real or inflation-adjusted rate, the courts have not accepted the simplistic total offset method.[36] Given that it can be shown that interest rates have been generally above the rate of inflation, it is difficult to justify using the total offset method.

The decision of whether to use a nominal versus real discount rate depends on how the inflation adjustment is done in the projection. If revenues and lost profits are projected using an annual inflation adjustment, a nominal interest rate should be used to discount the projected amounts to present value terms. Only when the projection is not adjusted for the effects of inflation would it make sense to use a real rate in the discounting process. Given that the methodology described in this book specifically incorporates inflation and growth into the projection process, nominal as opposed to real rates are used for discounting.

Court's Position on the Appropriate Risk Premium

Discounting to present value has been well received and accepted by the courts and there is abundant legal precedent to confirm this.[37] In fact, the Delaware Chancery Court has characterized the discount cash flow method of valuation, an application of discounting discussed in Chapter 8, as the preferred method of valuation.[38] Furthermore, Robert Dunn has observed that in the few instances where he has found that the courts have refused to recognize that only discounted profits should be allowed, the defendant had failed to introduce proof on this issue as to what such discounted values would be.[39] This implies that at a

---

[36] *Jones and Laughlin v. Pfeifer,* 462 U.S. 523 (1983).

[37] See, for example, *Lee v. Joseph E. Seagram & Sons,* 552 F. 2d 447 (2d Cir. 1977).

[38] *Charles L. Gaines v. Vitalink Communications Corporation,* No. 12334, Del Ch. 1997 WL 538676 (August 28, 1997).

[39] Robert L. Dunn, *Recovery of Damages for Lost Profits* (Westport, Conn.: Lawpress Corp.) 1992, 414.

minimum a defendant should be mindful of the need to prove this issue to the court.

Although we have explored the reasoning behind all of the components that should be incorporated in the risk premium to arrive at a discount rate that fully reflects the risk of the projected future lost profits stream, some courts have been reluctant to accept a discount rate that incorporates all of this risk. For example, in *American List Corp. v. U.S. News and World Report,* the trial court accepted an 18% discount rate based on the perceived risk associated with the plaintiff's ability to perform the contract in the future.[40] However, the New York Appeals Court rejected the 18% discount rate as too high and remanded for a recomputation of this discount rate. This reluctance to accept a higher risk premium by one court should not preclude the expert from applying standard financial principles to construct a risk-adjusted discount rate that fully reflects the risk of the projected lost stream of lost profits.

Process of Capitalization and the Loss of an Indefinite Stream of Future Profitability

Assuming that it is legally established that the plaintiff should be compensated for the loss of a stream of future profitability of indefinite length, it is possible for the expert to value such a stream using *capitalization.* Applied to commercial damages analysis, this process values a continuous stream of projected future profits. This valuation is done by dividing the growth-adjusted capitalization rate into the next period's projected lost profits. The growth adjustment refers to the projected rate of growth of the profit stream. If, for example, the selected discount rate is 15% and the annual profit stream is projected to grow at a 5% rate, then the growth-adjusted capitalization rate equals 10%. Mathematically, dividing by 0.10 is the same as multiplying by 10. Similarly, using a growth-adjusted capitalization rate of 20% is equivalent to multiplying by five. For each rate that is used as a divisor, an equivalent multiplier is implied by the divisor.

The capitalization process is shown in equation (7.10).

$$\text{Capitalized Value} = \frac{\text{Annual Earnings}}{(k_i - g_i)} \qquad (7.10)$$

where k_i = the capitalization rate for firm i prior to growth adjustment
   g_i = the growth rate of future annual earnings

---

[40] *American List Corp. v. U.S. News & World Report,* 75 N.Y. 2d 38, 550 N.Y.S. 2d 590 (1980).

Difference between a Capitalization Rate and a Discount Rate

When we forecast specific future monetary amounts, such as cash flows, and then use a discount rate to convert each of these amounts to present value terms, we refer to this process as *discounting* and the rate that we use to convert the future amounts to present value terms is the *discount rate*. Continuous monetary streams that are a growing at a certain positive rate or not growing at all are called *perpetuities*. When we compute the present value of such a stream, the process is called *capitalization*. The interest rate we use for this present value conversion of a perpetuity is called a *capitalization rate*. Sometimes these terms are used interchangeably but such usage is generally incorrect.

SUMMARY

The time value of money is a fundamental concept in economics and finance and also plays an important role in commercial damages analysis. It is based on the rates of return available in financial markets. The rates are offered by various securities, which vary according to their term to maturity and their risk levels As a rule, the longer the term to maturity, the higher the rate. The greater the level of risk, the higher the rate of return. Securities with greater risk levels have higher risk premia built into their rates of return to compensate security holders for this higher level of risk.

One of the ways in which the time value of money enters into commercial damages analysis is through the use of a prejudgment rate of return. Such a return is designed to compensate a plaintiff for receiving its past damages on the trial date as opposed to when these damages were actually incurred. Several alternative prejudgment rates are available for a court to apply. The selection process may be simplified if a statutory rate exists within the relevant jurisdiction which must be applied to all historical losses. If the law is not clear on this issue, then there may be room for testimony on what rate would fully compensate the plaintiff for receiving these monies late. One option would be to select relatively low money market rates to bring the historical losses to present value terms. Other options would include the debt rates and cost of capital, which may more accurately reflect the plaintiff's opportunity costs.

The other way in which the time value of money enters into commercial damage analysis is when projected future losses are converted to trial date terms. This process involves selecting a discount rate that fully reflects the risk or expected variability of the future loss stream that the expert has projected. The more the perceived risk, the higher the discount rate. The higher the discount rate, the lower the resulting present value. The further into the future the projected amount, the lower its present value. Experts look at the variability in returns of securities traded in public markets as their guide to selecting an appropriate rate to discount the future losses. Courts, however, have not been fully receptive to accepting these high risk-adjusted rates, which are normally accepted in financial markets. This attitude is probably attributable to the presentations made in these cases that dealt with this issue.

REFERENCES

American List Corp. v. U.S. News & World Report, 75 N.Y. 2d 38, 550 N.Y.S. 2d 590 (1980).

Beta Book (Chicago, Ill.: Ibbotson Associates).

Bodington, Jeffrey C., "Discount Rates for Lost Profits," *Journal of Forensic Economics,* 5 (3), Fall 1992.

Brealey, Richard A., Stewart C. Myers, and Alan J. Marcus, *Fundamentals of Corporate Finance* (New York: McGraw Hill, 1995).

Brigham, Eugene, and Louis Gapinski, *Intermediate Financial Management,* 3rd ed., (Chicago: Dryden Press, 1990).

Brookshire, Michael, and Frank Slesnick, "A 1996 Study of Prevailing Practice in Forensic Economics," *Journal of Forensic Economics,* 10 (1), Winter 1997.

Charles L. Gaines v. Vitalink Communications Corporation, No. 12334, Del Ch. 1997 WL 538676 (August 28, 1997).

Cost of Capital Quarterly, (Chicago, Ill.: Ibbotson Associates).

Damodaran, Aswath, *Corporate Finance* (New York: Wiley, 1997).

Dunn, Robert L., *Recovery of Damages for Lost Profits* (Westport, Conn.: Lawpress Corp.) 1992.

Elton, Edwin J., and Martin J. Gruber, *Modern Portfolio Theory and Investment Analysis* (New York: Wiley, 1995).

Fama, Eugene, and Kenneth French, "The Cross Section of Expected Stock Returns," *Journal of Finance* June 1992.

Fisher, Franklin, M., and R. Craig Romaine, "Janis Joplin's Yearbook and The Theory of Damages," *Journal of Accounting, Auditing and Finance,* 1989.

Fisher, Irving, *Theory of Interest* (New York: A.M. Kelley Publishers, 1965).

Fishman, Jay, Shannon Pratt, J. Clifford, and D. Keith Wilson, *Guide to Business Valuations* (Forth Worth: Practitioners Publishing Company, 1995).

FPC v. Hope Natural Gas Co., 320 U.S. 591, 64 S. Ct. 281, 88, L. Ed. 333 (1944).

Friedman, Milton, *Dollars and Deficits* (Englewood Cliffs, N.J.: Prentice Hall, 1968).

Gyromat Corporation v. Champion Spark Plug Company, 735 F. 2d 549 (Fed. Cir. 1984).

Keith Howe and Eugene F. Rasmussen, *Public Utility Economics and Finance* (Englewood Cliffs: Prentice Hall, 1982).

Ibbotson, Roger, and Rex Sinquefeld, "Stocks, Bills, Bonds and Inflation: Year-By-Year Historical Returns (1926–1974)," *Journal of Business* 49 (2), January 1976.

In Re Oil Spill by the Amoco Cadiz Off the Coast of France, 954 F. 2nd 1279, 1330 (7th Cir. 1992).

Jones and Laughlin v. Pfeifer, 462 U.S. 523 (1983).

Kier, John C., and Robin C. Kier, "Opportunity Cost: A Measure of Prejudgment Interest," *Business Lawyer* 39, November 1983.

Knoll, Michael S., "A Primer on Prejudgement Interest," *Texas Law Review,* (75) 1996, 293–374.

Lam, Inc. v. Johns Manville Corp., 718 F. 2d. 1056, 219 U.S.P.Q. 670 (Fed Cir. 1983).

Lanzillotti, R. F., and A. K. Esquibel, "Measuring Damages in Commercial Litigation: Present Value of Lost Opportunities," *Journal of Accounting, Auditing, and Finance,* 1989.

Lee v. Joseph E. Seagram & Sons, 552 F. 2d 447 (2d Cir. 1977) .

Lewis, W. Criis, "On the Relative Stability and Predictability of the Interest Rates and Earnings Growth Rate," *Journal of Forensic Economics,* Winter 1991.

Moyer, Charles R., James R. McGuigan, and William J. Kretlow, *Contemporary Financial Management,* 5th ed. (St. Paul: West Publishing Company, 1992).

Nowak, Laura, "Empirical Evidence on the Relationship Between Earnings Growth and Interest Rates," *Journal of Forensic Economics,* Spring/Summer 1991.

Patell, James, Roman L. Weil, and Mark A. Wolfson, "Accumulating Damages in Litigation: The Role of Uncertainty and Interest Rates," *Journal of Legal Studies,* 11 (2), June 1982.

Pratt, Shannon P., *Cost of Capital: Estimation and Applications* (New York: Wiley, 1998).

Pratt, Shannon P., Robert F. Rielly, and Robert Scheihs, *Valuing a Business,* 3rd ed. (New York: Irwin Professional Publishing, 1996).

S.C. Anderson v. Bank of America, 24 Cal. App. 4th 529, 1994.

Stocks, Bills, Bonds and Inflation, Annual, (Chicago: Ibbotson Associates).

Stigum, Marcia, *The Money Market* (Homewood, Ill.: Dow Jones Irwin, 1983).

Trout, Robert R., "Introduction to Business Valuation," in *Litigation Economics,* Patrick A. Gaughan, and Robert Thornton eds. (Greenwich, Conn.: JAI Press, 1993).

Uniroyal, Inc. v. Rudkin-Wiley Co., F.2d 1540 (Fed. Cir. 1991).

Value Line Investment Survey (New York: Value Line Publishing, Inc.).

VanHorne, James, and John M. Machowiz, *Fundamentals of Financial Management* (Englewood Cliffs, N.J.: Prentice Hall, 1995).

Williams Enterprises, Inc. v. The Sherman R. Smoot Company, 938 F. 2d 230, 290 U.S. App. D.C. 411 (October 8, 1991.

8

BUSINESS VALUATIONS

Robert Trout*

As discussed in Chapter 5, in cases where a business is injured by the actions of another party, the outcomes generally follow one of three paths described by Foster and Trout.[1] First, the business interruption loss can be closed, where the loss period is finished, and the business continues to operate somewhat as before the event. Second, the business interruption can be open, where the loss continues into the future for an unknown length of time. Third, the loss can be complete, where the business has ceased operations resulting from the actions of another party.

In situations where the loss is complete and the business has closed, the loss can be estimated by using traditional business loss methods described in Chapter 2. Alternatively, the loss can be determined by valuing the business just prior to the event that caused the demise of the business and then comparing this value with any residual value of the business after its closure or sale to another party. In certain situations, such as condemnation proceedings, the business loss is uniformly computed in this manner. In these latter cases, the goal of the valuation expert is to measure the loss of business goodwill.

This chapter provides an overall view of how to value a closely held business and related types of financial assets in a business loss situation. Business valuation is basically the process of assigning a value to a financial asset for which there is typically no financial trading market available to determine its value. Businesses whose securities (e.g., common stock, preferred stock, and bond) are traded on exchanges are valued every day by market investors. These are known as publicly held companies, because their ownership is held by "the public." The

*Robert Trout is a member of Lit-Econ in San Diego, California and an associate of Economatrix Research Associates, Inc.
[1] Carroll B. Foster and Robert R. Trout, "Computing Losses in Business Interruption Cases," *Journal of Forensic Economics,* December 1989, 9–22.

ownership is usually widely dispersed, and such companies must normally abide by various rules and regulations created and enforced by the Securities and Exchange Commission (SEC) and various state agencies. Losses incurred by these companies are often determined by observing changes in market prices for the firm's common stock. For example, in securities fraud cases, economic losses are measured by using the market model in what are called *event studies.*

While many businesses have securities regularly traded on national or regional exchanges, even more companies have securities that are traded only occasionally over the counter, or very seldom, if at all. This latter group of companies, which far exceeds the class of exchange-listed securities in number, is the population of companies for which business valuations are often needed. These types of businesses are usually referred to as being "closely held," because a small number of individuals own the common stock. Most of these are nonpublic companies because there is no trading market for their common shares, and their common stock is usually not registered with the SEC. However, some closely held companies are actively traded. These companies have publicly traded stock, but a majority of the stock is likely owned by a single family or a related group of shareholders. Prior to beginning a valuation, the valuation expert must answer three important questions:

1. What is the purpose of the valuation?
2. What specifically is being valued?
3. What is the date of valuation?

The purpose of the valuation in a business loss cases is clear. What was the value of the business prior to the action(s) that injured the business? What is being valued is also important. Is it the total firm, or a single class of securities, such as the common-stockholders, or the preferred-stockholders. The date of valuation is obviously very important. In business loss cases the exact date may be difficult to determine and may be contested by the opposing parties.

It may be useful for a valuation expert to first prepare an outline or flow chart that indicates the analytic process to be followed in valuing a business. An example of such a chart is shown in Figure 8.1, which presents a generic outline of the valuation process for valuing an all-equity firm. If appropriate, the value of preferred stock or debt could be added to the value of the equity in arriving at a total firm value. Note that the value of the firm is reached by considering several possible valuation models, the accounting book value, and any recent prior sales of stock. The process then branches off to measure the economic value to a minority or majority owner, after considering appropriate discounts or premiums. The important components of Figure 8.1 are explained in this chapter.

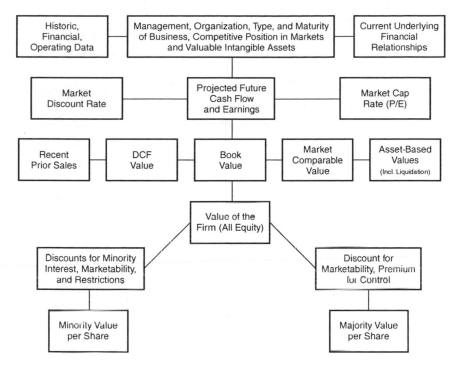

Figure 8.1. Pathway to valuation.

On a larger scale, other factors shown in the following list must be considered before beginning the pathway shown on Figure 8.1.

1. *Macroeconomic Factors.* The economy, gross domestic product growth, interest rates, inflation, foreign factors, regional influences, equity markets
2. *Microeconomic Factors.* Industry analysis, industry valuation ratios, intraindustry competition, typical use of debt in the industry, customers, suppliers
3. *Firm-Specific Factors.* Makret share, historic financial characteristics, debt ratio, diversification, customers, wsuppliers, competitive position in the market
4. *Selection of Comparable Companies.* Similar financial and operating risk characteristics, same or similar industry, similar level of diversification
5. *Determination of Market Comparables for Target Company.* Comparable group valuation ratios, such as price/earnings, market/book value, price/cash flow, or price/sales

All of these factors should at least be considered in preparing a valuation report, even if some of the factors do not play an important part in the analytic process. The macro- and microeconomic effects on business value are explained in Chapter 5.

For most larger companies, the macroeconomic and industry relationships should be considered in the valuation. In valuing smaller companies, the regional or local business environment may be more important in the long run success (and value) of the business. Macroeconomic data are available in a variety of publications produced by the Bureau of Economic Analysis, U.S. Department of Commerce, some of which is reproduced in the *Economic Report of the President,* and in the *Statistical Abstract of the United States,* both published annually. Most states have agencies that produce similar economic and financial data at the regional and state level.

Regional effects can often be important. For example, when basic oil prices declined in the 1980s, there was an economic ripple effect throughout the local economies in Houston, Denver, Calgary, and other cities tied to the energy industry. Changes in government spending can often affect a region. For example, when army, navy or air force bases are expanded or closed, there is usually a ripple effect throughout a local economy.

Industry effects may be more pertinent in many business valuations. At a minimum, the valuation expert should consider how the firm being valued fits into the local economy and its local competitive position. Industry data are discussed in Chapter 4. The industry and local effects are normally included in the overall valuation analysis through a risk-adjusted discount rate, or through a cash flow multiplier. Regional effects on the value of a business are discussed earlier in Chapter 3.

As discussed in Chapter 3, data about the U.S. economy can be found in monthly publications such as the *Monthly Labor Review, Survey of Current Business, Treasury Bulletin,* and the *Federal Reserve Bulletin.* More up-to-date information can be found on the internet at the web sites of the Bureau of Labor Statistics [http://stats.bls.gov], the Bureau of Economic Analysis [www.bea.doc.gov/], the White House [www.whitehouse.gov/], the Federal Reserve Board [www.bog.frb.fed.us/], and various Federal Reserve bank, commercial bank, and investment bank web sites.

The purpose of this chapter is not to present a detailed analysis of how to perform a business valuation or to value a closely held business. Rather, this chapter contains an overall presentation of how generally to conduct a business valuation with numerous references for more specific data and details. This chapter does not present any examples of actual valuations. Detailed examples of business valuations can be found in other reliable sources, such as Pratt,[2] Miles,[3] Zukin,[4] and in Fishman et al.[5] Another good source for an example of a business valuation is Billingsley.[6] In his monograph for the Association for Investment Management Research (AIMR) Billingsley used several different valuation models to determine the intrinsic value of Merck & Company, a publicly traded company listed on the New York Stock Exchange (NYSE).

MEASURES OF BUSINESS VALUE

Three general types of value are assigned to a business. The easiest of these to measure is the firm's accounting book value, which is nothing more than the balance sheet value of the firm's equity, defined by subtracting outstanding liabilities from the net depreciated value of the assets.

Another valuation concept is liquidation value, which is the amount of money that would be received by the owners of a business if it were liquidated. The term can apply to an orderly liquidation of assets at their best available prices, or it can also apply to a forced liquidation situation, such as bankruptcy.

Market value is the price someone would pay to purchase an entire business, or the equity (i.e., the common stock) of the business. Market value is closely related to fair market value. Fair market value is defined as the price at which an asset would be transferred between a willing buyer and a willing seller, where each party is fully appraised and knowledgeable of the relevant facts necessary to determine the value of the asset.[7]

Since the practice of business appraisal deals with valuing the equity of a company, or both the equity and the debt, this chapter focuses primarily on establishing fair market value. This notion of value was recently defined by the *Economist* magazine:

---

[2] Shannon P. Pratt, *Valuing a Business,* 3rd ed. (Homewood, Ill.: Dow-Jones Irwin) 1989.

[3] Raymond C. Miles, *Basic Business Appraisal* (New York: Wiley) 1984.

[4] James H. Zukin, *Financial Valuation: Business and Business Interests* (Boston, MA: Warren, Gorham & Lamont), 1996.

[5] Jay E. Fishman, Shannon P. Pratt, J. Clifford Griffith, and D. Keith Wilson, *Guide to Business Valuations,* 6th ed. (Ft. Worth, TX: Practitioners Publishing Co.) 1996.

[6] Randall S. Billingsley, *Merck & Company: A Comprehensive Equity Valuation Analysis,* (Charlottesville, VA: Association for Investment Management Research) 1996.

[7] See IRS Revenue Ruling 59–60, section 2.

In the end two things determine the price of a share [or any financial asset]: the amount of cash investors expect to receive from the company's earnings, and the difference between that amount and the income investors could earn by choosing instead to place their money in a safe fixed-interest investment.[8]

Although not necessarily a reflection of fair market value, book and liquidation values can often provide a minimum floor value for a fair market valuation. Throughout this chapter distinction is often made between accounting income and economic income, which often appear to be quite similar, but are not (see also Chapter 6). For example, Gallinger and Healey define accounting income as:

Profit is defined as the amount by which realized revenue for a period exceeds the historical cost of the assets used up to obtain the revenue.[9]

The authors point out that this definition is similar to an economist's definition of profit, except that the economist would also consider other types of costs to charge against revenues, such as opportunity costs, and many implicit costs incurred by a business, including charging research and development (R&D) off as a current cash expense, and capital projects as well, while the accountant would depreciate these items. A comparison of the components of accounting value and economic value appears in Figure 8.2.

EQUITY VALUATION MODELS

The value of the firm (V) is the sum of the value of common stock equity (V_e) plus the value of debt (V_d). This relationship is:

$$V = V_e + V_d \qquad (8.1)$$

If the company also has preferred stock outstanding, then the equation can be expanded to include that component (V_p). If the valuation analyst needs to know the value of the equity but has utilized a model that produces a total value for the firm, then it is a simple process to obtain the value of the equity by subtracting the value of the debt from the total value of the firm. The remainder is the value of the equity.

---

[8] *The Economist,* August 9, 1997, p. 13.
[9] George W. Gallinger and Basil P. Healey, *Liquidity Analysis and Management* (Reading, Mass.: Addison-Wesley) 1987.

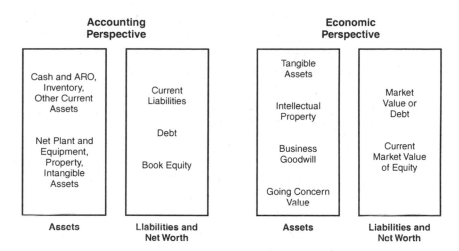

Figure 8.2. Balance sheet: Accounting versus economic.

Conversely, if the value of the firm is desired and the value of equity has been estimated, then the analyst need only add the value of the debt to the value of the equity. The basic difference in valuing the whole firm, and valuing only the equity, is the treatment of interest on the debt.

Because the value of the firm is the sum of the values of debt and equity, one could also value the total firm by capitalizing the net operating income (NOI). NOI is not the gross profit, which is normally defined as revenues less direct operating expenses. Rather, NOI is revenues less all expenses, except interest and taxes. NOI is also referred to as earnings before interest and taxes (EBIT). While net income (NI) is affected by the amount of interest payments the firm must make (i.e., its financial leverage), NOI is unaffected by financial leverage. Thus, a different capitalization rate must be used, since the variability of NOI over time (its economic risk), will be less than the variability of NI over time (its equity risk). A valuable discussion of the differences in the NOI and NI valuation models is presented in VanHorne and Wachowicz.[10]

Modern finance theory posits that the value of the firm, as defined as the sum of the market values of equity and debt, is not changed by altering the mix of equity and debt in the capital structure.[11] However, in many business valuation

---

[10] James C. VanHorne and John M. Wachowicz, *Financial Management and Policy* (Englewood Cliffs, N.J: Prentice Hall) 1996.

[11] See, for example, Thomas E. Copeland and J. Fred Weston, *Financial Theory and Corporate Policy,* 3rd ed. (Reading, Mass.: Addison-Wesley) 1988, Chap. 13.

cases the value of the firm and the value of the equity may be one and the same (because $V_d = 0$), so the two approaches should arrive at the same value.

A variety of valuation methods are available, some more rigorous than others. Valuation models can be classified into three general types:[12]

1. Discounted cash flow
2. Market comparables
3. Asset valuations

The most widely taught of these methods, at least at schools of business, is the DCF model. Most corporate finance textbooks stress discounting future cash flow as the proper method to value any asset. Moreover, recent studies (both academic and those from Wall Street investment firms) indicate that securities investors increasingly look to estimated cash flows in making investment decisions, which in turn affect securities prices.[13]

Cash flows are paid to investors in two forms: dividends and capital gains. The IRS has regulations that differentiate payments to shareholders as being one or the other. Generally, a cash payment to a shareholder from the company is assumed to be a dividend unless it meets certain criteria that allow it to be considered a return of capital, or a repurchase of stock by the company.[14] Earnings consist of dividends and reinvested capital. The payout ratio is the dividend divided by the earnings, while the retention ratio is the amount of earnings not paid out

---

[12] For a further discussion of the taxonomy of valuation models, see Shannon P. Pratt, *Valuing a Business,* 3rd ed. (Homewood, Ill.: Dow-Jones-Irwin) 1996; Raymond C. Miles, *Basic Business Appraisal* (New York: Wiley) 1984; Kent Hickman and Glenn H. Petry, "A Comparison of Stock Price Predictions Using Court Accepted Formulas, Dividend Discount, and P/E Models, *Financial Management,* Summer 1990; and James G. Wolf, "Market Approach to Valuation," in Valuation of Closely Held Companies and Inactively Traded Securities (Charlottesville, Va.: Institute of Chartered Financial Analysts) 1990.

[13] Copeland and Weston explain this idea as follows: "The objective of the firm is *not* to maximize earnings per share. The correct objective is to maximize shareholders' wealth, which is the price per share that in turn is equivalent to the discounted cash flows of the firm." [Copeland, Thomas E., and J. Fred Weston, *Financial Theory and Corporate Policy,* 3rd ed. (Reading, Mass.: Addison-Wesley) 1988, 24.] For further discussion, see Brealey, Richard and Stuart Myers, *Principles of Corporate Finance,* 4th ed. (New York: McGraw-Hill), 1991.

[14] The distinction between dividends and a return of invested capital (i.e., a distribution) is covered in Section 303 of the IRS Code.

in dividends divided by earnings. These ratios can be expressed as a percentage or a fraction, as indicated:

$$\text{Payout Ratio } (b) = \text{Dividends/Earnings}$$

$$\text{Retention Ratio } (1 - b) = \text{Retained Earnings/Earnings}$$

Retained earnings are typically used for investment purposes by the business. Those businesses with significant investment opportunities typically have small (or zero) payout ratios. Investors in those companies are willing to receive deferred dividends in the expectation of future capital gains. Capital gains can be received by an investor if the company buys back the stock, or when the stock is sold to another investor.

Although the DCF model is generally described by financial economists as the preferred model for valuing financial assets, the output of the model is an estimate of the intrinsic value of the asset. More often, the comparables model is used to value a closely held company. The comparables model, described in the next section, compares price to earnings ratios (P/E) or related financial ratios of the company to be valued (i.e., the target company) with similar valuation ratios for a group of comparable risk companies, usually from the same industry.

EARNINGS-BASED MODELS

One method for valuing a company or any financial asset using its expected future earnings is the discounted cash flow model DCF. The DCF model does what its name implies—it discounts future expected cash flows using an appropriate discount rate. As a practical matter, the discounted cash flow category also includes discounted future income, various capitalization models, and the excess earnings method. The difference between discounting the present value and capitalization was discussed in Chapter 7.

DCF Model

The DCF model requires three inputs to determine a financial asset's value:

1. Estimated future cash flows
2. Duration of future cash flows
3. The appropriate risk-adjusted discount rate

Mathematically the DCF model can be expressed as:

$$Value = \sum_{t=1}^{n} \frac{CF_t}{(1+i)^t} \qquad (8.2)$$

where CF_t = the cash flow in each future year (t)
n = the number of years
i = the risk-adjusted discount rate

The discount rate is used to determine the current value of the future cash flows. Basically, this is the amount of money an investor would pay at the present time to receive some estimated level of cash in the future. In this case the estimated future amount to be received is not guaranteed and is not known with any certainty. That is why the discount rate must be risk adjusted. The risk adjustment takes into account these unknown factors. In the case of an investment in U.S. government bonds, the future payment is both known and certain to be paid to the lender on time. Thus, the risk of this investment is relatively lower than the risk associated with owning equity in a business. This higher risk translates into a higher risk-adjusted discount rate, and, relatively speaking, a lower current value. Risk and economic value are therefore inversely related.

The length of time over which future cash flows can reliably be estimated is often an issue. Most practical texts on business valuation suggest limiting future cash flow projections to about five years.[15] If a five-year projection period is used, then the current value is the sum of the present values of the cash flows for the next five years added to the discounted value of the firm at the end of the fifth year. This, of course, means that the asset value in the fifth year must be estimated as well and then discounted back to the present. The terminal value in the fifth year is equal to the estimated sixth year dividend payout divided by the long-run relationship between the cost of capital (k) and estimated future growth rate in dividends (g).

Mathematically, this is expressed as:

$$Current\ Value = \sum_{t=1}^{5} \frac{CF_t}{(1+i)^t} + \frac{V_5}{(1+i)^5} \qquad (8.3)$$

---

[15] This is not the case for start-up companies or new ventures. New venture investors recognize that positive cash flow may not emerge until five to ten years out. Therefore, limiting the cash flow projection to a five-year time frame would not be useful in valuing a new venture. However, most business valuations involve more mature companies that have previously established some historic positive cash flows.

The suggested five-year period is for illustration only, despite the fact that valuation experts often use five years of historical data for purposes of projecting five years into the future.[16] In this case, the current value is the expected cash flow for the first year, divided by the discount rate factor $(1 + i)$, plus the expected cash flow for each of the next four years, divided by the discount factor raised to the power of the number of years in the future. That is, the fifth year's cash flow would be divided by the factor $(1 + i)$ raised to the fifth power. The fifth year residual asset value, V_5 is also divided by the interest factor raised to the fifth power. The residual asset value in the fifth year is the estimated stock price five years in the future.

The most important factor in selecting a projection period is the ability to reliably forecast future cash flows. This factor in turn will be influenced by the financial history of the company and the future prospects for the company and its industry. The value in the fifth year (V_5) can be estimated by using a long run multiplier or a constant growth model such as the Gordon Model. The Gordon Model posits that the current value of a constantly growing dividend stream is equal to the next period's dividend divided by the (growth-adjusted) net discount rate.

Mathematically, this is expressed as:

$$P_0 = \frac{D_1}{(k - g)} \qquad (8.4)$$

where P_0 = current price per share of the firm's equity

D_1 = the next period's dividend per share, or total dividend payment

k = the firm's cost of equity capital (discount rate) and,

g = the expected constant growth rate of future earnings and dividends

The difference between k and g is the net discount rate used to capitalize the expected dividend. Equation (8.4) can be used to estimate the value in the fifth period, which is then discounted to the present and added to the present value of the interim five years of cash flows.

One could also determine V_5 by multiplying E_5 by the future expected P/E ratio. The valuation expert should take into consideration the likelihood that P/E_5

---

[16] See the Internal Revenue Service's *IRS Valuation Guide for Income, Estate and Gift Taxes* (Chicago: CCH) 1994, for a discussion of the IRS's viewpoint on the number of years of past data to forecast future income and the number of years into the future one ought to examine.

may be different from P/E_0. In fact, the future P/E is often lower than the current P/E, since a high current P/E is a reflection of growth potential. When the growth potential is realized, one would expect the P/E in the future to decline somewhat. Again, the five year-time horizon suggested here is somewhat by convention. The analyst should select the terminal year based on factors such as a projected leveling off of revenue growth and profit margins and a decline in annual investment.

When there is no growth in dividends, for example, when all earnings are paid out as dividends and no earnings are retained to create growth, then growth rate $g = 0$, and the valuation model is thereby reduced to:

$$P_0 = \frac{D_1}{k} = \frac{E_1}{k} \qquad (8.5)$$

Equation (8.5) can be rearranged so that $k = D_1/P_0$, which means that in the case of a firm with no growth and a dividend payout of 100%, the cost of capital is equal to the current dividend yield. In this case the dividend yield is also the earnings yield. It also means that the P/E is equal to the reciprocal of the cost of capital, since $D_1 = E_1$. Dividends equal earnings because no part of earnings is retained to finance future growth in sales and earnings. In this case, the firm's cost of capital equals the capitalization rate. This equality of rates is not usually the case.

Equation (8.5) indicates that P/E can be multiplied by E to obtain P. This is called capitalizing an earnings stream. For a mature firm that has no significant prospects for growth, capitalizing earnings may be appropriate if the valuation expert includes in earnings all other amounts paid to owners in nondividend form. Market-based P/E ratios offer the valuation expert the advantage of being objective, if the publicly traded surrogate companies are correctly selected.

Discount rates can be easily converted to capitalization rates (i.e., multipliers) by making some assumption about the expected duration of cash flow. With an infinite cash flow assumption, the multiplier is the inverse of the discount rate $[1/k = P/E]$. If growth is nonzero, then the discount rate equals the capitalization rate minus the growth rate. Or, stated differently, for a firm retaining any part of its earnings, the capitalization rate is equal to $k - g$, the cost of capital less the expected growth rate in earnings.

For other expected cash flow durations (i.e., payback periods), the multiplier can be computed using the standard present value of an annuity formula.[17] Some

---

[17] Multiplier $= [1 - (1 + i)^{-n}]/i$

Table 8.1. Multipliers for Varying Durations and Real Discount Rates Payback Time Horizon

Real Discount Rate (%)	3 Years	5 Years	10 Years	15 Years	More Years
10	2.5	3.8	6.2	7.6	10.0
15	2.3	3.4	5.0	5.8	6.7
20	2.1	3.0	4.2	4.7	5.0
25	2.0	2.7	3.6	3.9	4.0

examples of multipliers converted from discount rates for varying payback periods are shown in Table 8.1. Note that the discount rates are "real" discount rates, meaning expected inflation has been removed. This means that the multiplier can be applied to the current level of cash flow, and the inflation in future cash flows does not need to be considered, since it was removed from the discount rate prior to converting it to a multiplier.

Note that discounting and capitalizing can be separately used in valuing a business. While one can convert a discount rate to a capitalization rate with the help of Table 8.1, it is also possible to obtain a somewhat different valuation using another approach, particularly when the capitalization rates for the target company are obtained from P/E ratios of publicly traded companies and then compared with a discount rate from a build-up method. The build-up method asserts that the discount rate is the sum of the risk-free interest rate, plus expected inflation, plus various risk components (e.g., industry, financial, or specific business risk) associated with the company being valued. The build-up method is described by Ibbotson.[18]

While many valuation assignments provide factual situations where a small firm has reached a steady level of business, with other firms near-term growth may be significant, resulting in both a higher growth rate of earnings and a lower dividend payout ratio (even zero in many cases). For these situations the supernormal growth (or differential growth) valuation model may be appropriate. This valuation model is described in most finance texts.

In using any DCF model where a future value of the firm must be estimated and then discounted to present value, the analyst encounters the problem of knowing what P/E ratio to apply to the future level of earnings to establish the price in the future which would then be discounted to present value. Several possibilities are available. For example, one could use the current P/E or an ex-

---

[18] Ibbotson Associates. *Stocks, Bonds, Bills and Inflation: 1999 Yearbook,* Valuation Edition (Chicago, Ill.: Ibbotson Associates, 1999).

pected steady-state P/E ratio for a more mature firm in the same industry, for example the historic average P/E ratio for the firm's industry. In establishing a future P/E, the analyst should consider the relationship between P/E, firm risk, and expected growth. High P/E ratios generally reflect higher-than-average expected growth and/or lower investment risk. Low P/E ratios, by comparison, reflect lower expected growth and/or higher investment risk. Leibowitz and Kogelman have shown that as earnings increase to expected higher levels, the P/E ratio may fall, resulting in a case where earnings growth exceeds price growth.[19] As a reference point, the Standard & Poor's Composite 500 Index P/E ratio has ranged from 7.4 to 23.7 during the thirty year period from 1967 through 1996. This annual data, along with the S&P dividend yield, U.S. government T-bills, and stock market indexes are shown in Table 8.2. A graph of the Standard & Poor's Composite 500 Index P/E ratio appears in Figure 8.3. Industry and individual company P/E ratios are available from Morningstar and Value Line for listed companies, and from Biz Comps and Pratt's Stats for smaller unlisted companies involved in sales transactions.

Excess Earnings Method

Another model often included in the earnings-based valuation category is the excess earnings model. This model, sometimes called the *formula approach,* was first developed by the U.S. Treasury.[20] The model posits that a firm's value can be divided into two parts: the value of its tangible assets, and the value of its intangible assets (e.g., goodwill, patents, customer lists).[21] That is:

$$\text{Total Value} = \text{Tangible Value} + \text{Intangible Value} \qquad (8.6)$$

Although this model is sometimes used in cases where business goodwill needs to be computed, such as divorce cases and condemnation cases, it is seldom used in business loss cases, because there are better methods of valuing the entire equity part of a business than this model. Even the IRS suggests that other models should be used in preference to the excess earnings model, when other

---

[19] The authors also show that the P/E ratio is really comprised of a base P/E, and a P/E related to new investment, and therefore related to the growth of the firm. Martin L. Leibowitz and Stanley Kogelman, *Franchise Value and the Price/Earnings Ratio* (Charlottesville, VA: Institute of Chartered Financial Analysts, 1994-B).

[20] See U.S. Treasury (A.R.M. 34).

[21] The method is described in IRS Revenue Rulings 65-192 and 68-609.

Table 8.2. Market Indexes & Yields, 1967–1997

Year	Dow Jones	S&P 500	Did Yield (%)	E/P	P/E	T-Bills (%)	10-Yr. Govts (%)
1967	879	92	3.20	5.73	17.5	4.3	5.1
1968	906	99	3.07	5.67	17.6	5.3	5.7
1969	877	98	3.24	6.08	16.4	6.8	6.7
1970	753	83	3.83	6.45	15.5	6.5	7.4
1971	885	98	3.14	5.41	18.5	4.4	6.1
1972	951	109	2.84	5.5	18.2	4.1	6.2
1973	924	107	3.06	7.12	14.0	4.0	6.8
1974	759	83	4.47	11.59	8.6	7.9	7.6
1975	802	86	4.31	9.15	10.9	5.8	8.0
1976	975	102	3.77	8.9	11.2	5.0	7.6
1977	895	98	4.62	10.79	9.3	5.3	7.4
1978	820	96	5.28	12.03	8.3	7.2	8.4
1979	844	103	5.47	13.46	7.4	10.0	9.4
1980	891	119	5.26	12.66	7.9	11 5	11.5
1981	933	128	5.20	11.96	8.4	14.0	13.9
1982	884	120	5.81	11.6	8.6	10.7	13.0
1983	1,190	160	4.40	8.03	12.5	8.6	11.1
1984	1,170	160	4.64	10.02	10.0	9.6	12.4
1985	1,328	187	4.25	8.12	12.3	7.5	10.6
1986	1,793	236	3.49	6.09	16.4	6.0	7.7
1987	2,276	287	3.08	5.48	18.2	5.8	8.4
1988	2,061	266	3.64	8.01	12.5	6.7	8.8
1989	2,509	323	3.45	7.42	13.5	8.1	8.5
1990	2,679	334	3.61	6.47	15.5	7.5	8.6
1991	2,929	376	3.24	4.79	20.9	5.4	7.9
1992	3,284	416	2.99	4.22	23.7	3.5	7.0
1993	3,522	451	2.78	4.46	22.4	3.0	5.9
1994	3,794	460	2.82	5.03	17.2	4.3	7.1
1995	4,494	542	2.56	6.09	16.4	5.5	6.6
1996	5,743	671	2.19	5.24	19.1	5.0	6.4
1997	7,441	873	1.77	NA	NA	5.1	6.4

Source: Economic Report of the President, 1998.

models are available. The IRS has suggested a limited role for this model, as expressed in Revenue Ruling 68-609. In part, this revenue ruling states:

> The formula approach should not be used if there is better evidence available from which the value of intangibles can be determined.
>
> Accordingly, the "formula" approach may be used for determining the fair market value of intangible assets of a business only if there is no better basis therefore available.

An alternative method for finding business goodwill, when it is necessary to know this value, is to value the total firm using a DCF or market comparables

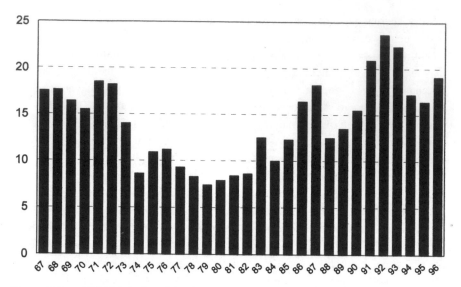

Figure 8.3.   S&P 500 Index: Price/earnings ratios.

model, and then subtract the value of the tangible assets from the value of the total firm.[22] The residual value would be the business goodwill value, plus the
value of other intangible assets, if any.

ESTIMATING CASH FLOWS

General Observations

It is important to distinguish between accounting income and economic cash
flow. But first we should consider the source of data for both of these variables.
The data necessary to perform a business valuation normally comes from the
company's own accounting statements. These may include a balance sheet showing the company's assets, liabilities, and net worth as of a particular point in
time; an income statement showing the company's revenues and expenses for
some period of time (e.g., a year or a quarter); and a statement of cash flows
showing where cash originated and how it was used over some period of time.
Accounting income is a residual when accounting expenses are subtracted from

---

[22] The value of the tangible assets, (e.g., buildings, fixtures, land, or machinery) is usually expressed as the *value in use.*

cash or accrual revenues. Some of the recorded business expenses may be non-cash, such as depreciation, depletion, and amortization, and some expenses may be influenced by changes in inventory policy. For closely held companies, the expenses may also include payments to owner(s) in the form of company-purchased owner benefits. Examples of these benefits are excessive retirement funding; purchase of a car or a house by the company for the use of the owner; bonuses paid to the owner-manager, which would be classified as dividends in a publicly traded company; and rental paid to the owner for property used by the company and owned by the owner or related persons.

An example of the use of accounting data in the valuation process appears in Tables 8.3, 8.4, and 8.5. The data shown in these exhibits is actual accounting data taken from the Hewlett-Packard (HP) Corporation's 1996 Annual Report.

Table 8.3 presents a condensed version of Hewlett-Packard's statement of earnings, also called an income statement or profit and loss statement. At the top are revenues, and below revenues, operating costs are listed and subtracted from revenues to arrive at operating income. The operating income divided by revenues is often referred to as the *gross margin,* or *operating profit margin.* Next, research and development (R&D) costs are subtracted, as are selling, general, and administrative (S, G&A), to arrive at EBIT. After making interest additions and subtractions, the final result is *net income.* When net income is divided by shares of common stock outstanding, the result is *earnings per share.*

Table 8.4 presents HP's abbreviated consolidated balance sheet. Assets are listed first and are separated into current assets—those that should be used within a year—and fixed assets, such as plant, equipment, property, and invest-

Table 8.3. Statement of Earnings, Hewlett-Packard Corp. (Millions of $)

	1996	1995
Net Revenues	38,420	31,519
Cost of Products Sold	22,013	17,069
Cost of Services	3,486	2,945
Operating Profits	12,921	11,505
Profit Margin	33.6%	36.5%
R & D	2,718	2,302
S, G & A	6,477	5,635
EBIT	3,726	3,568
Interest Income	295	270
Interest Expense	327	206
Taxes	1,108	1,199
Net Income	2,586	2,443
EPS	2.46	2.31

Table 8.4. Consolidated Balance Sheet, Hewlett-Packard Corp. (Millions of $)

	1996	1995
Cash & ST Investments	3,327	2,616
Accounts Rec.	7,126	6,735
Inventories	6,401	6,013
Other Current Assets	1,137	875
Total Current Assets	17,991	16,239
Fixed Assets	10,198	8,747
Accumulated Depreciation	(4,662)	(4,036)
LT Investments	7,172	3,477
Total Assets	27,699	24,427
Current Liabilities	10,623	10,944
Long Term Debt	2,579	663
Other Liabilities	1,059	981
Shareholders' Equity	13,438	11,839
Book Value/Share	12.77	11.25
Total Liab & Equity	27,699	24,427

Table 8.5. Statement of Cash Flows, Hewlett-Packard Corp. (Millions of $)

	1996	1995
Cash Flows From Operations:		
Net Earnings	2,586	2,433
Dep & Amortization	1,297	1,139
Deferred Taxes	(284)	(102)
Change (Increase) in AR	(293)	(1,696)
Change (Increase) in Inventory	(356)	(1,740)
Change in Other Current A & L	506	1,579
Net Cash From Operations	3,456	1,613
Cash Flows from Investments:		
Investments in Prop, Plant & Equip	(2,201)	(1,601)
Disposition of Prop, Plant & Equip	316	294
Purch & Sales of ST Invest.	(290)	132
Net Cash Used in Investing	(2,175)	(1,175)
Cash Flows From Financing:		
Changes in Notes Pay	−1137	755
Net Issuance of LT Debt	1948	102
Net Issuance of Common Stock	−726	−325
Dividends Paid	−450	−358
Other, net	−4	4
Net Cash Used in Financing	−369	178
Net Change to Cash Position	912	616
[a]Free Cash Flow (FCF)	1,255	12

[a]FCF = Net Cash Flow from Operations − Investments in Prop. Plant & Equip.

ments in other entities. Liabilities are shown below, separated into current liabilities, those due to be paid within a year, and long-term debt and other obligations. The remainder of the liability side of the balance sheet is shareholders' equity, which includes paid in capital for common and preferred stock, and accumulated earnings.

Table 8.5 presents an abbreviated version of HP's statement of cash flows, which are divided into three categories: cash flows from operations, cash flows from investments, and cash flows from financing. The bottom of this table shows the net change to HP's cash position on a year-to-year basis, after considering all three categories of cash creation and use by the company. The last line shows "free cash flow," which is described in the following pages.

In valuing a closely held company, the valuation expert must first examine historic expense data to determine what expenses should be classified as true expenses, and those that are "in lieu" payments to owner(s). Part of this examination requires that the analyst determine what a nonowner manager ought to be paid for employment in that capacity. Sources for determining what managers ought to be paid, as well as other typical expenses and return ratios for similar companies, are both Leo Troy and Robert Morris Associates.[23] Officer compensation studies are also available to the valuation analyst to use in determining a comparable salary and bonus.[24] The general process for handling these adjustments is described by Gaughan and Fuentes and by Desmond.[25] In addition to direct and indirect compensation, other business expense items need to be examined for comparability with other companies in the same industry. These expenses often include rent, retirement plans, and depreciation and inventory methods.

Next, the historic cash flows must be computed by removing from expenses those items that are noncash, so that cash income to a new owner can be used in valuing the firm. These cash flows available to a new buyer are often referred to in the literature as *free operating cash flows,* or *free cash flow.* The preference for cash flow over earnings has been demonstrated through countless academic and

---

[23] Leo Troy *Almanac of Business and Industrial Financial Ratios* (Englewood Cliffs, N.J.: Prentice Hall) 1996. Robert Morris Associates, RMA Annual Statement Studies, 1998–1999 (Philadelphia, PA: Robert Morris Associates, 1999).

[24] One such source is the *Officer Compensation Report,* produced annually by Panel Publishers in New York City.

[25] Patrick A. Gaughan and Henry Fuentes, "The Minimization of Taxable Income and Lost Profits Litigation," *Journal of Forensic Economics* 4 (1), Winter 1990, 55–64; Glen Desmond, *Handbook of Small Business Valuation Formulas and Rules of Thumb,* 3rd ed. (Camden, Me.: Valuation Press, 1993).

investment company studies of the relationship between common stock prices and cash flow and prices and earnings.[26] Courts have taken a somewhat mixed view of which measure of financial viability is best and appear to have generally accepted either. Bogdanski analyzes some of the different court decisions regarding the use of cash flow and/or earnings in the valuation process.[27]

Free cash flow is the cash available to *all* of the holders of a firm's securities. Therefore, free cash flow is unaffected by the level of a firm's financial leverage. Note that the discount rates for capitalizing these separate cash streams to equity and debt holders could very well be different, reflecting the impact of financial leverage on risk, and therefore the discount rate. Computing free cash flow follows the general format presented in the folloiwing box:[28]

Free Cash Flow Computation Steps

A shortcut method to find cash flow is to take net cash from operations and subtract the capital expenditures for that year. For HP, Table 8.5 indicates the free cash flow for 1996 amounts to $1.255 billion. This definition of cash flow should be used in valuing the whole firm. If the analyst is interested in valuing only the firm's equity, then interest must be subtracted from EBIT, taxes recomputed, and debt repayments subtracted. The end result will be an estimate of free cash flow to use in valuing the firm's equity.

---

[26] See, for example, Thomas E. Copeland and J. Fred Weston, *Financial Theory and Corporate Policy,* 3rd ed. (Reading, Mass.: Addison-Wesley) 1988; Thomas E. Copeland, Tim Koller, and Jack Murrin, *Valuation: Measuring and Managing the Value of Corporations,* 2nd ed. (New York: Wiley) 1994; Steven N. Kaplan and Richard S. Ruback, "The Market Pricing of Cash Flow Forecasts: Discounted Cash Flow vs. The Method of 'Comparables,'" *Journal of Applied Corporate Finance* 8 (4), 1995; Kenneth S. Hackel and Joshua Livnat, *Cash Flow and Security analysis,* 2nd ed. (Chicago: Irwin) 1996; Patrick A. Gaughan, *Mergers, Acquistitions and Corporate Restructurings* (New York: Wiley) 1996.

[27] John A. Bogdanski, *Federal Tax Valuation* (Boston, Mass.: Warren, Gorham & Lamont) 1996.

[28] *Add other noncash expenses or subtract noncash forms of income.* Numerous studies indicate that investors exclude this noncash income in pricing regulated utility common stocks. Kaplan and Ruback include after-tax asset sales in computing free cash flow. (Steven N. Kaplan and Richard S. Ruback, "The Valuation of Cash Flow Forecasts: An Empirical Analysis," *Journal of Finance* 50 (4) September 1995.)

Valuation analysts often use a firm's consolidated statement of cash flow as a quick source to arrive at free cash flow. Generally, to arrive at free cash flow you need only subtract capital expenditures from net operating cash flow. A detailed example of this procedure can be found in Billingsley, particularly Table 3 of his valuation report.[29]

Many smaller firms being valued might have limited growth prospects. Cash flow for these companies may consist solely of net income and depreciation, which thereby reduces the complexity of the valuation. An alternative definition would be net income plus depreciation minus capital expenditures necessary to maintain the business. To maintain a steady-state small business, depreciation (if straight line) might approximate the capital expenditures necessary to continue the business. It should be noted that this is often the primary definition of free cash flow used by some analysts and business writers. However, the term "free cash flow" does not have a universally accepted meaning to all who use the phrase.

When capitalizing or discounting future free cash flow, the valuation expert must be sure to define what is meant by "free cash flow."

Historic Data

Historic accounting/financial data are useful in the valuation process only to the extent that it is helpful in making accurate predictions about future cash flow. Considerable evidence shows that changes in reported accounting data cause changes in securities prices, *if the accounting changes reflect changes in cash flow*, and therefore the value of a firm. This suggests that securities analysts pay attention to historic earnings in their attempt to forecast future earnings. Gaughan summarizes many of the relevant studies and concludes:

> ... the evidence covering decades of research is that the market values cash flows, and where it is possible to discriminate between events that have different accounting earnings and cash flow impacts, the market tends to favor the cash flow effects.[30]

---

[29] Billingsley presents a detailed example of how this definition of cash flow was applied to several valuation models used to value Merck & Company. Randall S. Billingsley, Merck & Company: A Comprehensive Equity Valuation Analysis (Charlottesville, Va.: Association for Investment Management and Research) 1996.

[30] Patrick A. Gaughan, *Mergers, Aquisitions and Corporate Restructurings* (New York: Wiley) 1996.

Forecasts of future earnings are the backbone of predicting current "intrinsic value," which is the value that a security *ought* to sell for if the market only considered specific forecasts of future earnings in determining securities prices. Valuation experts should show that past earnings and financial data have been considered (or why they were not) in forecasting future cash flows.

Forecasting Cash Flows

Typically, the valuation analyst bases future cash flows on the productive capacity of the business. The productive capacity refers to the ability of management to use labor, technology, and capital in an efficient way so that the value of the company is maximized.[31]

Historic relationships among revenues, costs, and assets provide the analyst with a basis for forecasting the future.[32] This is done by preparing a *pro forma* financial picture of the business, based on assumptions about growth in revenues, if any, and the underlying relationships of revenues, costs, and asset utilization. For a mature, nongrowing firm, the process is fairly simple. The analyst must correct the cash flow statement for excessive payments to owners through bonuses, rental agreements, company purchases of goods or services for the owners, and similar items.

Where growth is forecast for the future, the past growth in earnings and cash flow can be useful in forecasting the future cash flows. An example of this forecast is presented in Figure 8.4, where the firm's historic sales pattern is projected for five years into the future. This projection was then used to produce pro forma income and cash flow statements for the business. Business expenses can either be forecasted independently or can be estimated by using historic revenue/expense ratios to determine future expenses based on the estimated level of future revenues.[33]

---

[31] Most economists would agree that the notion of a firm consisting of only labor and capital, organized by management, is no longer correct. For a wide variety of industries, technology may be more important than the other components.

[32] A good explanation of this process may be found in Donald E. Fischer and Ronald J. Jordan, *Security Analysis and Portfolio Management,* 5th ed. (Englewood Cliffs, N.J.: Prentice-Hall) 1991, Ch. 7, and Bradford Cornell, *Corporate Valuation* (New York: Irwin) 1993.

[33] See Carroll B. Foster, Robert R. Trout, and Patrick A. Gaughan, "Losses in Commercial Litigation," *Journal of Forensic Economics,* 6 (3) Fall 1993.

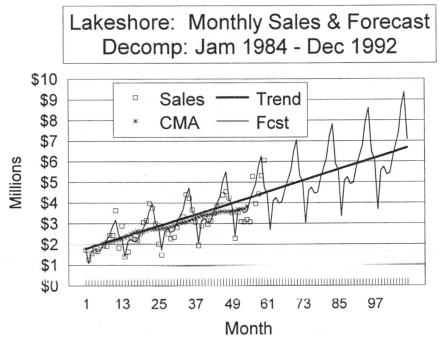

Figure 8.4. Distribution company monthly sales.

ESTIMATING DISCOUNT RATES

One of the most difficult parts of the valuation process is finding an appropriate discount rate to reduce the future cash flows to present value. In analyzing discount rates, the beginning point is the realization that risk and return are positively correlated. That is, for risk-averse (or even risk-neutral) investors to accept more risk, the investor must have the expectation of a higher realized return.

Risk and Return

Risk to an investor is the probability of an outcome with a lower return than the expected (i.e., most likely) return. That is, if an investor expects a 10% annual return, risk is the probability that the annual return will be less than 10%, or at the extreme, the value of the investment will be reduced to zero. To a large extent, earnings per share and changes in earnings per share determine the investor-expected returns and the associated risk. At the company level, risk can be classified as operating risk, related to the ability of the firm to produce a product or service at a profit, and financial risk, related to the use of interest-bearing debt to finance the operations of the company.

The basic risk–return relationship stipulates that required return is a function of several risk–return components, as shown in Equation (8.7).

$$k = r + i + d \qquad (8.7)$$

Equation (8.7) indicates that expected return (k) is the sum of the expected risk-free *real* return (r), plus a component for expected inflation (I), plus a component for specific investment risk (d). In this formula, a single factor (d) captures all risks beyond inflation. This factor includes industry (i.e., microeconomic), economy-wide (i.e., macroeconomic), and specific business risks. Fischer and Jordan[34] develop a similar equation with five risk components added to the risk-free rate of return. Methods for estimating the expected market rate of return are discussed below.

Capital Asset Pricing Model

The Capital Asset Pricing Model (CAPM) asserts that the return required by an investor for a particular asset (R_j) is the sum of the current risk-free rate of return (R_f), plus a component that reflects the relative risk (B_j) of the specific investment compared to the market return (R_m).[35] The CAPM is primarily used by valuation experts to determine the proper discount rate to use in a DCF type model or to explicitly discount future cash flows in a pro forma type financial analysis. Using the CAPM does not directly lead to a value for a business.

This risk–return relationship, shown in Equation (8.8), is consistent with the relationship presented in Equation (8.7). Risk is measured by the relationship of the return on the asset (R_j) to the return on a market index (R_m), such as the Standard & Poor's 500 Index.[36] The relationship is often expressed in terms of excess

---

[34] Donald E. Fischer and Ronald J. Jordan, *Security Analysis and Portfolio Management,* 5th ed. (Englewood Cliffs, N.J.: Prentice Hall) 1991.

[35] For a detailed discussion of the CAPM, see Thomas E. Copeland and J. Fred Weston, *Financial Theory and Corporate Policy,* 3rd ed. (Reading, Mass.: Addison-Wesley) 1988, or any modern textbook about corporate finance or investments.

[36] The Standard & Poor's 500 Composite Index is often used as a market index because (1) It includes most of the major companies in the U.S. economy (with a few no-

returns, as shown in Equation (8.8). The excess return is the level of return that exceeds the risk-free rate of return. The relationship between the overall securities market and individual security returns can be computed by using a statistical regression model. The model, called the market model, produces a statistic (β_j), called beta, which is the slope of the regression line from Equation (8.8).

$$(R_j - R_f) = \alpha_j + \beta_j(R_m - R_f) + e_j \qquad (8.8)$$

Beta indicates the change in R_j as R_m (the return on the market index) changes. Beta measures the systematic risk of the particular investment, that is, the investment risk associated with the overall stock market. A beta of 1.0 indicates the asset is of average risk, while a beta of greater than 1.0 indicates that the company's returns in the past have exceeded the market's returns during periods the market index increased and fallen further than the market index during periods of decline. The alpha statistic (α_j) is the intercept value, which is theoretically the rate of return when the market return is zero.

$$R_j = R_f + B_j[R_m - R_f] \qquad (8.9)$$

Equation (8.9) is the standard CAPM. Several assumptions are necessary for the model's results to be meaningful. A straightforward presentation of the model's assumptions can be found in any current corporate finance or investment analysis textbook. One important assumption in the model is that investors hold diversified portfolios, and thereby eliminate unsystematic (i.e., nondiversifiable) risk from their portfolios of investments. It is unlikely that most owners or purchasers of a small business would have a diversified portfolio, which means that beta would not completely measure the investment risk of the particular business.

The valuation expert can use a beta from a similar company, if one can be found, based on similar operating, financial, and industry characteristics. Any such derived beta is likely to result in an underestimate of the proper discount rate for the closely held company because beta does not measure the individual nondiversifiable risk associated with the closely held firm. Pratt[37] has suggested solutions to this problem by estimating a beta by adding up the separate risk components for a company.

---

table exceptions like Intel and Microsoft); and, (2) It is a value-weighted index giving more influence to larger companies as measured by their equity value.

[37] Shannon P. Pratt, *Valuing Small Businesses and Professional Practices* (Homewood, Ill.: Dow Jones-Irwin) 1996.

Historic Returns

The first large scale study of the returns to investors in common stocks was performed by Fisher and Lorie.[38] Their study investigated returns from investments in common stocks listed on the New York Stock Exchange during the period 1926 – 60. The results of their study indicated that investments in NYSE listed common stocks produced an average return of slightly less than 10% per year over a 35-year period.

Ibbotson and Sinquefield repeated the Fisher-Lorie study a few years later, and included corporate bonds, T-bills, and treasury bonds, as well as changes in the Consumer Price Index (CPI) in their database.[39] They replaced NYSE common stocks with stocks contained in the Standard & Poor's 500 (S&P 500) Composite Index. Using these data, they were able to estimate both long-term nominal returns on common stock investments (as Fisher and Lorie had previously done), and real rates of return (by subtracting out inflationary changes), as well as equity risk premiums. A risk premium is defined as the difference between the annual returns from common stock investments and the annual returns from government bond investments. Risk premiums, also called equity risk premiums or risk premia, indicate the return demanded by investors for risking their investment dollars in financial assets riskier than U.S. government bonds. The comparison is normally made between common stock returns and U.S. government T-bill returns. The equity risk premium (R_p) is defined in Equation (8.10) as:

$$R_p = \left[(1 + R_m)/(1 + R_f)\right] - 1.0 \qquad (8.10)$$

where R_m is the return on the market and
R_f is the total T-bill rate of return.

The Ibbotson data also report the small stock premium, which is the excess returns earned by small capitalization stocks (roughly under $80 million of equity), compared with returns on large capitalization stocks. The small stock premium (R_q) is defined as:

$$R_q = \left[(1 + R_s)/(1 + R_m)\right] - 1.0 \qquad (8.11)$$

---

[38] Lawrence Fisher and James Lorie,"Rates of Return on Investements in Common Stocks," *Journal of Business,* January 1964, 1–24.

[39] The Ibbotson-Sinquefield study was first done in 1982. It is currently updated every year by Ibbotson Associates, located in Chicago, Il.

where R_s is the return for small stocks and

R_m is the market return as before.

This last relationship is very useful for valuation experts, since many times the expert is required to value a small capitalization firm with much different risk characteristics than firms listed on the larger New York Stock Exchange or the NASDAQ National Market (NNM).[40] Ibbotson's review of the average geometric and arithmetic *after-tax* returns for the period 1926–97 is shown in Table 8.6.[41]

The geometric returns are most useful for measuring investment performance over prior periods of time. Arithmetic returns are most useful for estimating equity risk premiums.[42] The CAPM is an additive model (the risk-free rate added to the risk-adjusted rate) where the cost of capital is the sum of two components.

Table 8.6. Selected Average Historical Rates of Return

Description	Geometric Returns (in percent)	Arithmetic Returns (in percent)
Large Company Stocks	10.7	12.7
Small Company Stocks	12.6	17.7
Long Term Government Bonds	5.1	6.0
T-bills Total Returns	3.7	3.8
Inflation	3.1	3.2
Equity Risk Premium	6.8	8.9
Small Stock Premium	1.8	5.0

[40] The NASDAQ National Market is a stock market of several thousand securities that exists in a computer network and is managed by the NASD, rather than a physical building, like the NYSE.

[41] From Ibbotson Associates, 1998 Yearbook, published in 1998. Geometric returns are average compound rates of return, where compounding is done monthly. Arithmetic returns are the average monthly returns over the time period and are always slightly larger than geometric returns. The investment returns are after payment of corporate income taxes, but before payment of any individual income taxes.

[42] The preference of arithmetic returns over geometric returns for estimating risk premiums is explained in Ibbotson Associates, *Stocks, Bonds, Bills and Inflation 1999 Yearbook,* The Valuation Edition (Chicago: Ibbotson Associates) 1999; Stephen A. Ross, Randolph W. Westerfield, and Jeffrey Jaffe, *Corporate Finance,* 4th ed. (St. Louis, Mo.: Times Mirror) 1996; and Mahamood M. Hassan, "Arithmetic Mean and Geometric Mean of Past Returns: What Information Do These Statistical Measures Reveal?" *The Journal of Investing,* 4 (3), Fall 1995.

For the entire time period in the Ibbotson study, the equity risk premium amounted to 6.9%. This is the premium one would add to a government bond rate to obtain a basic cost of equity for a typical S&P 500 firm, without reference to specific factors concerning that firm. Interestingly, Kaplan and Ruback estimated implied equity risk premiums from highly leveraged initial public offerings (IPOs) to be 7.4%.[43]

MARKET COMPARABLE MODELS

General Observations

A common approach to business valuation is the comparable sales method, which is widely used in valuing real estate properties. There are a variety of ways the valuation expert can compare one company with another similar company (whose value is known) to estimate the value for a closely held firm. The IRS and the courts have relied on market comparable models in the past, and financial economists have historically used such models. The estate tax regulations explain the market comparable approach as follows:

> In general, if there is a market for stocks and bonds, on a stock exchange, in an over-the-counter market, or otherwise, the mean between the highest and lowest quoted selling prices on the valuation date is the fair market value per share or bond.[44]

The comparable companies are supposed to be those engaged in the same or a similar line of business that are listed on an exchange.[45] Numerous court cases have expanded on the meaning of "comparability." Both Pratt and Bogdansky[46] describe some of the more important cases that address the issue of what exactly is a group of comparable companies for valuation purposes.

Research by Hickman and Petry found that market comparable models performed somewhat better in estimating values of exchange listed securities than

---

[43] Steven N. Kaplan and Richard S. Ruback, "The Market Pricing of Cash Flow Forecasts: Discounted Cash Flow vs. The Method of Comparables," *Journal of Applied Corporate Finance* 8, (4) 45 – 60.

[44] Reg. Sec. 20.2031-2(b)(1). For gift tax, see Sec. 25.2512-2(b)(1).

[45] Reg. Sec. 2031(b).

[46] Pratt, 1996 and Bogdanski, 1996.

did a variety of discounted cash flow models.[47] The primary comparable ratios used by economists for valuing firms are the price/earnings, market/book, and price/revenue ratios. Other ratios have also been accepted by the court.[48] The primary valuation ratios are described below in the following sections.

Price/Earnings Models

The Gordon Model (Equation (8.5)) postulates that a stock's price is equal to the next year's dividend divided by the difference between the company's cost of capital and its expected growth, for a constant growth company. If dividend growth is zero, then the equation shows that the inverse of the cost of capital is the P/E ratio. Higher P/E ratios are therefore consistent with lower costs of capital, all other things held constant. Several economists have examined how P/E ratios vary across companies within a particular industry and across larger cross-sections of companies.

Basically, in using P/E ratios to value a company, the analyst must first define a similar group of related companies to use as a benchmark. The benchmark companies must be similar to the company being valued in terms of business risk and must have regularly traded common stock. Similarity can be determined by examining a variety of factors, including primary industry, size, historic growth, and by comparing various financial ratios across firms. Ratio analysis is discussed by Brigham[49] and by Desmond and Kelley.[50] Normally the valuation expert gathers 5 to 10 similar companies to use as a benchmark group, then computes a median long-run price-earnings ratio to apply to the earnings of the closely held firm.[51] It is important that the earnings of both the closely held business and the benchmark companies reflect similar accounting treatment.

---

[47] Kent Hickman and Glenn H. Petry, "A Comparison of Stock Price Predictions Using Court Accepted Formulas, Dividend Discount, and P/E Models," *Financial Management,* Summer 1990, 76–87.

[48] In *Estate of Hall v. Commissioner,* 92 TC 312 (1989), the court listed five valuation ratios for valuing stock in a closely held company.

[49] Eugene F. Brigham, *Financial Management: Theory and Practice,* 3rd ed. (Chicago, Ill.: Dryden Press, 1982).

[50] Glenn Desmond and Richard E. Kelley, *Business Valuation Handbook* (Los Angeles, Calif.: Valuation Press, 1980).

[51] Leopold A. Bernstein, *Financial Statement Analysis,* 4th ed. (Homewood, Ill.: Irwin, 1989).

An interesting application of ratio analysis in investment and valuation theory is called the DuPont formula. Basically, the DuPont formula divides the return on equity (ROE) into five components: leverage, asset utilization, profit margin, interest burden, and tax burden.[52] The mathematical relationships contained in the DuPont system are shown in Equation (8.12) and graphically in Figure 8.5.

$$\text{ROE} = \frac{\text{Assets}}{\text{Equity}} \times \frac{\text{Sales}}{\text{Assets}} \times \frac{\text{EBIT}}{\text{Sales}} \times \frac{\text{Pretax Profit}}{\text{EBIT}} \times [1 - \text{Tax Rate}] \quad (8.12)$$

Using historic values for these ratios as well as current values, the valuation expert can separately estimate each of the five components to estimate the firm's ROE. The ROE figures prominently in determining future value of a company, whatever valuation model is used.[53] The DuPont analysis is useful for estimating

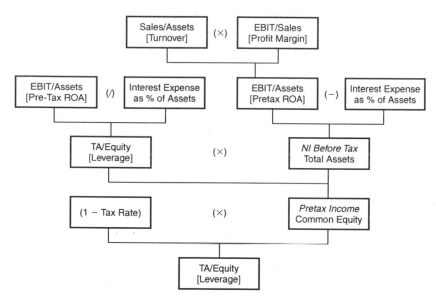

Figure 8.5. The DuPont ROE analysis.

---

[52] Return on equity is an accounting measure of company profitability used by investment analysts. It is computed by dividing the company's net income by its net book value. Net book value is the difference between the accounting value of the assets and liabilities.

[53] The DuPont Formula is explained more fully in Chapter 18 of Zvi Bodie, Alex Kane, and Alan Marcus, *Investments,* 2nd ed. (Homewood, Ill.: Irwin) 1993; and in Russell J. Fuller and Glenn H. Petry, "Inflation, Return on Equity and Stock Prices," *Journal of Portfolio Management,* Summer 1981.

future rates of return on equity, which can be used as future ROE values in a pro forma financial analysis model that estimates future cash flows, which become the basis of a current value.

Table 8.2 shows historic average P/E ratios for the Standard & Poor's Composite Price Index. The range of P/E ratios for the period 1967 to 1996 was about 7.4 to 23. Note that P/E ratios for an index of large, well established firms in the S&P Index will provide a high estimate to use in valuing most closely held firms. It is unlikely that the market would give such a high P/E ratio to most closely held firms.[54]

Market/Book Models

For certain industries characterized by a large proportion of fixed assets to total assets, use of market/book (M/B) ratios in valuing a company may be appropriate. With an all equity firm, gross assets (net of depreciation) will be equal to book value plus current liabilities.

$$M/B = \frac{(1 - b)ROE}{k - (b \times ROE)} \tag{8.13}$$

Beginning with Gordon's constant growth valuation model, one can easily derive an M/B valuation model. Equation (8.5) stipulates that price is equal to expected dividend (D_1), divided by the difference between the cost of capital (k) and the growth rate (g). Using some arithmetic substitution, and the following relationships:

$$ROE = Earnings/BV$$
$$g = b \times ROE$$

then Equation (8.13) expresses the relationship between M/B and ROE, where b = earnings retention ratio, or 1.0 − payout ratio.

In the case where the firm just earns its cost of equity capital, then market price ought to equal book value, and M/B = 1.0. This relationship has been used in regulated utility rate cases to determine the cost of capital for a regulated utility (e.g., an electric power company).

---

[54]California courts have found P/E models inappropriate, when used alone, for use in divorce cases. See *In re Hewitson,* 141 Cal. App. 3d 874 and *In re Lotz,* 120 Cal. App. 3d, 379.

For valuation cases where fixed assets are proportionately large, it makes sense to consider the M/B ratios of publicly traded firms for which M/B ratios can be computed as a basis for pricing the equity of a closely held firm. Service firms, high inventory turnover firms, and those without significant fixed assets are not candidates for this valuation model.

Price/Revenue Models

For a large number of valuation situations, a price/revenue (P/R) model may be appropriate. Many small businesses and professional practices are sold on the basis of their revenues. One reason for this is that a buyer may not fully believe the business expenses reported on the financial statements of the business. The revenues are likely to be an accurate reflection of actual revenues, but the expenses may include many hidden transfers of cash to the current owner. In addition, a new owner may have a different cost structure in mind for the business.

Thus, prices for professional practices and some small businesses, particularly retail trade businesses, are often based on some measure or ratio of sales. Desmond presents rule-of-thumb P/R models that can be useful in valuing a variety of small businesses, particularly when there is insufficient data to use another more detailed valuation method.[55] These references, as well as Pratt [1996], list trade organizations that can provide helpful information on valuing businesses within their trade organization.[56] Gilbert has examined price/sales ratios for publicly traded companies, and found a strong relationship between company prices and revenues for companies in many non-growth industries.[57] More recently Barbee, and Barbee, Mukherji and Raines, found a strong relationship between sales/price ratios and common stock returns. In comparing sales/price ratios with other valuation models they note:

> One reason the S/P (ratio) may have greater explanatory power for stock returns than the P/E (ratio) is that a company's annual sales may be a more reliable indicator of the firm's long-term profit potential than its reported earnings. Earnings are more unstable than sales and can be affected to a greater extent by temporary occurrences.[58]

---

[55] Glen Desmond, *Handbook of Small Business Valuation Formulas and Rules of Thumb,* 3rd ed. (Camden, ME: Valuation Press, 1993).

[56] Pratt, 1996

[57] Gregory A. Gilbert, "Price/Sales Ratios," *Business Valuation News,* June 1986.

[58] William C. Barbee, "Forecasting the Performance of a Company's Common Stock with a Model Based on the Sales/Price Ratio," *Spectrum,* Fall 1989, 45 – 49; William C.

Finally, Leibowitz describes a theoretical model for relating corporate market value to corporate sales. Interestingly, Leibowitz shows that the price/sales ratio of the Dow Jones Industrial Average appears to stay rather constant.[59] For example, from 1992 through 1996, the price/sales ratio remained within a range of about 0.9 to 1.2, despite the fact that the Index ranged from 16 to 24, with little correlation between the ratio and the Index.

ASSET VALUATION MODELS

Previously, book value was described as offering a proxy for determining fair market value under certain situations. The net worth of a firm usually does not measure the economic value of the firm, because it does not indicate the earning power of the firm or the efficiency of utilization of its assets. However, when valuing-holding companies or companies whose primary value is derived from certain specific assets, such as land or buildings, an *adjusted net worth* approach is useful. It is also appropriate when valuing a company whose primary revenues are derived from certain financial contracts, such as loans, leases, or commission agreements. Asset valuation models are usually not appropriate for valuing operating, manufacturing, or service firms.

There is no exact model to follow when valuing a firm using an asset model. Basically, the valuation expert begins with the reported net worth (i.e., book value) of the firm and then adjusts the firm's recorded assets to their respective market values, a process described by Nicholas.[60] The liquidity or marketability of the firm's assets must be considered in determining their economic values. Some assets, such as cash and equivalents are valued at 100% of book value. Other assets, such as accounts receivable and inventories, are valued at reduced amounts based on the prospects of converting them to cash.[61] Fixed assets are often valued at undepreciated book value, while land, resource properties, and buildings are valued at current market values.

Barbee, Sandip Mukherji, and Gary Raines, "Do Sales-Price and Debt-Equity Explain Stock Returns Better than Book-Market and Firm Size?," *Financial Analysts Journal,* March/April 1996, 56–60.

[59] Martin L. Leibowitz, "Sales-Driven Franchise Value," (Charlottesville, VA: Institute of Chartered Financial Analysts) 1997.

[60] David W. Nicholas, "Adjusted-Book Value Approach to Valuation," in *Valuation of Closely Held Companies and Inactively Traded Securities* (Charlottesville, Va.: Institute of Chartered Financial Analysts, 1990).

[61] See Revenue Ruling 77-12 for advice on valuing inventories.

Normally, the liabilities of the firm would be valued at their reported amounts on the balance sheet and then subtracted from the economic value of the assets to arrive at net adjusted book value. However, liabilities that are owed to management or related entities should be closely examined for their economic merit. Deferred taxes are often given no consideration in measuring liabilities.

SUMMARY OF VALUATION MODELS

Business valuations used in business loss cases do not necessarily have to follow the requirements put forth for tax purposes. Nonetheless, it is useful to review the methodology the IRS and the courts follow in valuations for tax purposes since the courts may be familiar with them and more willing to accept a tax-court type method than something else. The most important IRS document on valuation is Revenue Ruling 59-60. Section 2 of Revenue Ruling 59-60 suggests that the valuation expert examine eight factors to arrive at the value of a business:

1. The nature of the business
2. General and industry economic outlook
3. Book value of the stock
4. Earning capacity of the company
5. Dividend-paying capacity
6. Goodwill and intangible values
7. Previous sales of securities
8. Market prices of comparable companies

Earnings (item 4) is considered by the IRS (Rev. Rul. 59-60, Section 5(a)) to be the most important of these eight factors. The general economic climate and the particular industry of the company to be valued are important in determining future revenues and cash flow, which are the basis of current value. The dividend-paying capacity does not necessarily mean actual dividends paid; rather, it is the ability of the firm to pay dividends currently and in the future. The earning capacity of the firm more accurately captures its dividend paying capacity. There is scant evidence that either actual dividends or dividend paying capacity accounts for differences in firm values.

Business goodwill is captured in the present value of future cash flows with the Discounted Cash Flow (DCF) model, but in asset valuation models, goodwill must be valued separately. Previous sales of securities are important; but they should be given only minimal weight in the valuation process if they are not arms-length transactions, do not reflect the current situation of the company, or reflect only small and infrequent trades of stock. The last element in Rev. Rul. 59-60, comparisons with other companies, is taken into account with both P/E and M/B valuation models. These are the models that would most often be applied in a business loss case.

While Rev. Rul. 59-60 has precedence in IRS cases, it is not a required tool in other types of valuation cases. Nonetheless, it is a useful guide in nearly all valuation cases, and state courts often use Rev. Rul. 59-60 as a reference point. A good review of the IRS position on each of the components previously listed can be found in Todd and Hemphill.[62]

Several valuation models have been previously described. Each model produces a somewhat different value for the business than the other models. The valuation expert is left with the decision to select from among them or mix them together. In an important valuation case, *Central Trust Co. v. United States,*[63] the Court determined that the valuation of a company should be based 50% on the value determined by capitalizing earnings, 30% based on capitalizing dividends, and 20% on the market/book value. The decision in that case does not mean that this particular weighting scheme should be applied to all cases. Again, this was a tax case and might not have much weight in a state court handling a business loss case. However, it is instructive to note that the Court relied on a mixing of three models together, rather than rejecting two (or more) in favor of a single model. Other courts have followed the same pattern, although not necessarily reaching the same weighting scheme.[64]

One tax court decision particularly worth reading concerning the overall process of business valuation is *Pabst Brewing Co. v. Commissioner.*[65] In his written opinion, Judge Laro presented four guiding principles for valuing a company. Briefly, they are:

1. Remember that the willing buyer and willing seller in a fair market transaction are hypothetical persons, rather than specific individuals or entities.

2. Fair market value is determined as of the valuation date, and no knowledge of unforeseeable future events that could affect value should affect the

---

[62] See J. F. Todd and C. L. Hemphill, *Valuation of Corporate Stock* (Washington, D.C.: Bureau of National Affairs 831 T.M.) 1992.

[63] 305 F 2nd 393 (1962).

[64] See *Bader v. United States,* 172 F Supp 833 (1959) and *Estate of Tully,* 78-1 USTC Sec 13.228 (1978).

[65] No. 18466-92, 1996, WL655710, TC Memo 1996-506. A brief summary is presented in *Business Valuation Update,* January 1997.

value. An exception to this rule occurs with condemnation cases where loss of business goodwill can be claimed in certain jurisdictions. The actual loss of business goodwill may not be observable and quantifiable until some time after the taking of the property and possible relocation of the business. (See Trout and Wade[66] for more information on this topic.)

3. Fair market value equals the highest and best use to which the property could be put on the date of valuation.

4. *Expert testimony is not useful to the Court when the expert is merely an advocate for the position argued by the party.*

Judge Laro summarized this by stating:

> We do not accept the conclusions of any of the experts in total, but we find parts of each of their opinions to be helpful in understanding the operation of the [beer] industry.

Indeed, there have been several cases where tax court judges have rejected the testimony of appraisal experts for both the taxpayer and the government.

DISCOUNTS AND PREMIUMS

In nearly all valuations of closely held companies for tax situations, minority partner buyouts, and divorce cases, the issue of a minority discount, a liquidity discount, and/or a control premium will arise. This is not generally the case in litigation cases concerning an interruption of a business, which causes its demise. In these cases only the value of the total business and its classes of ownership become an issue. However, for completeness we include a brief discussion of these elements in this chapter.[67]

Courts and the IRS have both recognized the existence of, and necessity to consider, discounts and premiums in valuing closely held companies, both for tax cases and business loss cases. The situations where discounts and premiums

---

[66] Robert R. Trout and William W. Wade, "The Role of Economics in Regulatory Takings Cases," *Litigation Economics Digest* I (1), Fall 1995.

[67] A more complete coverage of these factors can be found in Robert R. Trout, "Module III: Reference Guide for Valuing a Closely Held Business," in *Expert Economic Testimony: Reference Guides for Judges and Attorneys* (Tucson, Az.: Lawyers & Judges Pub. Co.) 1998; or in Shannon P. Prattt, *Valuing a Business,* 3rd ed. (Homewood, Ill.: Dow-Jones-Irwin) 1996.

Table 8.7. Discounts and Premiums Associated with Valuing Stock in a Closely Held Business

Valuation Model	Minority Position		Majority Position	
	Minority Discount	Liquidity	Control Premium	Liquidity
DCF	No	Yes	Yes	Maybe
P/E	No	Yes	Yes	Maybe
Asset-based	Yes	Yes	No	Maybe

are necessary to consider are presented in Table 8.7. This table summarizes discounts and premiums in the sale and purchase of either a minority share in a closely held firm or the majority share of total equity in a closely held firm.

Briefly, a *minority discount* reflects the diminished value of a minority interest in a closely held firm. The IRS Valuation Guide (1994) defines a minority discount as:

> . . . the ownership of an amount of stock which does not enable the holder to exercise control.

It is inappropriate to consider a minority discount for common stock in a publicly held company, because the market prices already reflect the minority status of the financial asset, and in some cases, a minority nonvoting status. Publicly held common stock owners normally have a readily available market in which to dispose of their investment. In fact, the market prices of exchange listed and over-the-counter (OTC) trades reported every day reflect current market-based trades, which in turn measure the minority value of the shares traded.

Table 8.7 indicates that using the DCF or the P/E models to value a closely held firm means that no additional discount should be subtracted for a minority interest. However, if an asset-based approach is used, which measures the value of the entire firm, or a DCF model is used, with a discount rate that reflects purchasing a whole firm (and thereby control over the firm), then a minority discount should be applied when one is valuing a minority interest in such a firm.

A *liquidity discount* is appropriate if there is no readily available market in which an owner of a security can sell the security at a price that reflects its current value. The IRS Valuation Guide (1994) defines a marketability discount as: ". . . the absence of a ready or existing market for the sale or purchase of the securities being valued." This term is also referred to as a discount for *lack of marketability*. However, the lack of marketability may also be related to the fact that the particular stock has legal restrictions concerning its resale.

As noted in Table 8.7, a discount for lack of liquidity or marketability, is always required when valuing a minority interest in a closely held firm, regardless of the method(s) of valuation. It is also the case that a liquidity discount is appropriate in valuing regularly traded common stock, where there are restrictions concerning resale of the stock (e.g., investment letter or Rule 144 stock). The IRS has conceded that such a discount is appropriate, and Revenue Ruling 77-287 explains the rationale for a marketability discount.

Finally, a *control premium* may be appropriate when valuing a majority interest in a closely held firm, because the primary methods of valuing the equity (DCF and P/E models) produce values that reflect the minority value per share and exclude any premium for control. In some states, the value of control belongs to all the shareholders and cannot be assigned solely to the control block. However, in a sale of the entire business, this latter consideration becomes irrelevant.

Estimating Discounts

It is well recognized that a minority block of common stock ought to sell for a lower price per share than the majority block of the same common stock. The IRS has recognized this fact in its Revenue Ruling 81-253 (1981-2, C.B. 187). Determining the proper discount for a minority position in a closely held business is difficult, becasue there is no precise model to use for this purpose. The *Federal Tax Valuation Digest* contains a survey of allowed discounts and premiums in a variety of tax court cases.[68] Table 8.8 shows the range of values for various types of discounts allowed by courts.

Table 8.8. Summary of Discounts, 1970–94

	Type of Discount			
	Minority	Liquidity	Restriction	Blockage
Percent Reduction				
Range	5–50	5–30	22–100	5–35
Mean	24	22	45	21
Median	20	25	40	20

Source: Federal Tax Valuation Digest, 1996–97 Cumulative ed. (Boston: Warren, Gorham & Lamont) 1996.

---

[68] See Idelle A. Howitt, *Federal Tax Valuation Digest,* 1995/1996 Cumulative Edition (Boston: Warren, Gorham & Lamont) 1995.

Liquidity discounts are usually associated with minority stock positions but are the result of different effects on stock ownership. The liquidity effect is associated only with the ability to dispose of a financial asset such as common stock. Holders of common stock or preferred stock in closely held firms have a liquidity problem for two reasons: (1) Because there is no active market in which the stock can be sold, and (2) because the stock itself very often is restricted from resale, even if some market for the resale of the securities exists. Thus, there are two components of a lack-of-liquidity discount: one tied to possible legal restrictions and one tied to the lack of a functioning trading market.

Table 8.8 indicates that the range of liquidity discounts allowed by courts is 10 to 50%, while the median value is 20%. The IRS has recognized that a discount for lack of marketability is appropriate in Revenue Ruling 77-298 (1977-2, C.B. 319).

A more recent study of public offerings of small companies by Emory over several years, based on comparisons of 1985–97 post-IPO prices with pre-IPO prices from trades of minority blocks, indicated the percentage discount for lack of liquidity averages about 43%. A similar study conducted by Willamette Management Associates (WMA) over the period 1975–85 measured liquidity discounts ranging from 42 to 74%.[69]

Another approach to analyzing the lack of marketability is to compare restricted (i.e., unregistered) common stock with unrestricted common stock of the same company. A study of restricted investment letter stock was conducted by Trout and several other researchers.[70] Trout's analysis determined that the average discount associated with restricted common stock of exchange listed companies was 34%. For smaller, nonlisted companies, the average discount was about 45%.[71]

The estimates of discounts from common stock resale restrictions are entirely consistent with those of WMA and Emory, in that the larger Emory-WMA estimates would include discounts for both restrictions on resale and lack of a trading market. All of the methods of determining a discount for lack of marketability are presented in Mercer, including Mercer's own discount model, called the Quantitative Marketability Discount Model.[72]

---

[69] See Shannon P. Pratt, Robert F. Rielly, and Robert P. Schwoihs, *Valuing a Business,* 3rd ed. (New York: McGraw Hill), 1996.

[70] Robert R. Trout, "Estimation of the Discount Associated with the Transfer of Restricted Securities," *Taxes,* June 1977, 381–85.

[71] See J. F. Todd and C. L. Hemphill, *Valuation of Corporate Stock* (Washington, D.C.: Bureau of National Affairs 831 T.M.) 1992, pages A-44 to A-48 for a discussion of stock restrictions. See also, Revenue Ruling 77-287.

[72] Christopher Z. Mercer, *Quantifying Marketability Discounts* (Memphis, Tenn.: Peabody Publishing) 1997.

The discount for lack of marketability results from two related but distinct causes. The empirical studies show discounts of at least 34% for lack of liquidity caused by nonregistration. The additional discount for lack of a trading market is at least an additional 20%. Previous court decisions often tend to mix the two factors together.[73] If we simply add the median values for restrictions (45%) to the median value for lack of liquidity (20%), we would have an estimate of the discount for both types of illiquidity. A 65% discount would fall within the range of the results from the Emory and WMA studies described previously.

In valuing a closely held company, the analyst must be aware of situations where there are differing classes of common stock. The results of the studies just described can be of assistance in adjusting the values of nonvoting common stock from the value of the voting common stock. The case of *Hall v. Commissioner* presents some insight into valuing different classes of stock with different voting rights.[74]

VALUING OTHER FINANCIAL ASSETS

Valuing Debt

In most business loss cases where a business has ceased to exist as a result of the actions of another party, the issue is: What was the business worth? If the equity is valued separately, then the debt (if any) must be valued separately. Alternatively, the business can be valued without reference to the specific financing, in which case the value of the debt is its value on the balance sheet. This debt must be extinguished out of the total payments for the loss of the business. This section on valuing debt is included for the rare situations where it is appropriate to consider. This is also true of the next section concerning preferred stock.

$$P_0 = \sum_{t=1}^{n} \frac{I_t}{(1+i)^t} + \frac{FV}{(1+i)^n} \qquad (8.14)$$

The standard valuation model used for valuing debt is shown in Equation (8.14), where I_t represents periodic interest payments, FV is the face value of the bond, i is the discount rate, and n is the maturity of the bond. The discount rate for debt

---

[73] *Estate of Andrews,* 79 T.C. 738 (1982) indicates that discounts for a minority interest and lack of liquidity are separate and distinguishable types of discounts.

[74] *Hall v. Commissioner,* 92 TC No. 19 (1989).

(*I*) is largely determined by national rating agencies, such as Moody's and Standard & Poor's. These agencies assign a risk class rating to issuers of both private and public debt. The bond rating largely determines the current market-based yield-to-maturity (YTM) required by market investors to hold debt instruments.

Most closely held companies do not have market-traded debt, but may have sizeable bank loans or long-term loans from financial institutions. Such loans may have to be repaid at face value if a company is sold, unless the new buyer can arrange with the lender to continue the loans. In either of these situations, the debt of the company should be valued at its face value. In rare instances where individual investors own the debt and the common stock can be transferred without repaying the debt, then it should be valued using a market value approach with reference to current YTM's for similar companies. In most instances, the valuation (e.g., B or BB rated) is a proxy for the market determined rate that would apply to the company being valued. The analyst should remember that on occasion a specific issuer may have issues with different bond ratings, and these differences must be recognized in determining a proper rating for the company being valued. Bond rating information can be found in Standard & Poor's *Bond Guide,* produced monthly.

Valuing Preferred Stock

Preferred stock is valued using the commonly accepted valuation formula shown in Equation (8.15).

$$P_0 = \frac{D_t}{(1 + i)} \tag{8.15}$$

where D_t is the periodic required dividend, and i is the discount rate. As with bonds, the discount rate must be selected with reference to market-determined discount rates for similar risk investments. Preferred stock is more likely to be a part of the capital structure of a closely held firm than debt. It is often the case with closely held firms that the preferred stock has voting power as well, and in some cases the preferred stock has *all* of the voting power.

In situations where the preferred stockholders have total voting control, the value of the *common* stock could be negligible, because the holder of preferred stock controls the flow of dividends or other cash distributions to all classes of shareholders. In some cases, the preferred stock may not have a stated required dividend, in which case common and preferred shares would normally be merged together as a single class for determination of dividends per share. If the number of preferred shares significantly outweighs the number of common shares, a disproportionate amount of total dividends would flow to the preferred shareholders, thereby diminishing the value of the common stock and enhancing the value of the preferred stock.

Valuing Intangible Assets

A business is comprised of tangible and intangible assets. The tangible assets include plant, equipment, property, inventory, cash and investments, and many other categories as well. Intangible assets include business goodwill, going concern value, and a variety of assets categorized together under the title "intellectual property." The division of assets was previously presented in Figure 8.2. Intellectual property includes a variety of intangibles, such as

- Patents and inventions
- Copyrights and artistic compositions
- Trademarks, trade names, and brand names
- Franchises, licenses or contracts
- Methods of production, systems, programs, customer lists, and technical data

Increasingly, these types of assets produce more value to a business than do tangible assets. A comparison of five large companies in Table 8.9 demonstrates this trend. The first two columns of Table 8.9 indicate the market value of equity and book value of debt. Assuming the market value of debt is approximately equal to its book value, the total market value of each firm is shown in column 3, which is called "Total." Total assets, which roughly correspond to the tangible

Table 8.9. Tangible and Intangible Assets (Billions $)

Company	Market Value of Equity (July 97) (1)	Debt (2)	Total (3) (1)+(2)	Total Assets (4)	Book Equity (5)	Estimated Intangible Value (6) (3)−(5)	Ratio of Intangible to Tangible (7) (6)/(4)
Gen. Elec	197,617	170,770	338,387	272,402	37,125	65,985	0.2
Exxon	147,201	32,848	180,049	95,527	43,542	84,522	0.9
Merck	109,057	7,494	116,551	124,293	11,971	92,258	3.8
Intel	124,078	2,000	126,078	23,735	16,872	102,343	4.3
Microsoft	148,589	760	149,349	10,093	6,908	139,256	13.8

assets of the business, appear in the fourth column. The estimated intangible value of the firm is measured by subtracting the total asset value from the total market value of the firm.

For example, Exxon, which hasn't changed its core business in many years, has intangible assets roughly equal to its total assets, with a ratio of intangible to tangible assets of 0.9, shown in the seventh column. General Electric, has an even smaller ratio of intangible to tangible assets. Merck, a pharmaceutical business with many brand names and patented drugs, has a more robust value of 3.8 to 1 for its intangible to tangible asset ratio. Intel's ratio is slightly larger yet than Merck's ratio. Microsoft, a firm that has a tremendous market value, has only $10 billion in tangible assets but about $140 billion in intangible assets, as valued by investors in mid-1997. For a variety of reasons, the values shown in Table 8.9 may not reflect accurate estimates of tangible and intangible values, but they are generally close in size to the true values and show their importance to modern corporations.

An important asset of any company is its business goodwill, which is related to the willingness of buyers of products and services to return again for new purchases and as referrals to other buyers. For smaller firms, this may be the only intangible asset present. Determining its value is usually done by either valuing the total business and then subtracting the value of tangible assets, or by using the excess earnings model described earlier in this chapter. Other intangible assets cannot be valued so easily.

Valuation experts usually rely on three basic methods to value intangible assets. The three basic models, as described in Smith and Parr are:[75]

1. **Cost Approach.** This approach attempts to measure the value of the intangible asset by examining what it would cost to replace the asset, or provide future services that are equivalent to those provided by the asset being valued.

2. **Income Approach.** The income approach uses the present value concept, which is the basis of the discounted cash flow valuation model. By estimating the present value of the future cash flows that result from the asset, the valuation analyst then knows what someone would pay for the asset, or the rights to use the asset, and therefore its "value."

---

[75] See also Revenue Ruling 74-456 (1974). The Courts have recognized three methods for valuing intangibles *collectively,* which are: (1) Bargain of the Parties; (2) Residual Gap Method; and, (3) Capitalization Method. These methods are not useful for valuing individual intangible assets. For a description of these methods, see *IRS Valuation Guide* (1994, Chapter 13).

3. Comparables Approach. Also called the market approach, this method determines the value of an intangible asset by using market transactions for similar intangible assets as the basis for the value. This is equivalent to using the P/E, M/B, and P/S ratios to value a business.

SUMMARY

The process of business valuation in the context of valuing closely held firms is that of applying accepted financial models to the financial characteristics of a firm in order to estimate a market value for the firm, as though an active market for its shares existed. There are two consistent ways of accomplishing this task. One way is to estimate future cash flows for the business, taking into account the economic risks, relevant industry risks, local factors, management and specific business risks facing the firm, and then to discount the future cash flows to the present with a market interest rate. The second way to accomplish this task is to locate similar publicly traded firms for comparison with the privately held company being valued. Applying average market/book, price/earnings, and price/sales ratios from a group of such companies provides the analyst with an estimate of the value of the nontraded company. These are both forward looking approaches because they focus on what investors require in the future for an investment today.

REFERENCES

Barbee, William C., "Forecasting the Performance of a Company's Common Stock with a Model Based on the Sales/Price Ratio," *Spectrum,* Fall 1989.

Barbee, William C., Sandip Mukherji, and Gary Raines, "Do Sales-Price and Debt-Equity Explain Stock Returns Better than Book-Market and Firm Size?" *Financial Analysts Journal,* March/April 1996.

Bernstein, Leopold A., *Financial Statement Analysis,* 4th ed. (Homewood, Ill.: Irwin, 1989).

Billingsley, Randall S., "Merck & Company: A Comprehensive Equity Valuation Analysis," (Charlottesville, Va.: Association for Investment Management and Research, 1996).

Bodie, Zvi, Alex Kane, and Alan Marcus, *Investments,* 2nd ed. (Homewood, Ill.: Irwin, 1993)

Bogdanski, John A., *Federal Tax Valuation* (Boston, Mass.: Warren Gorham & Lamont, 1996).

Brealey, Richard and Stuart Myers, *Principles of Corporate Finance,* 4th ed. (New York: McGraw-Hill, 1991).

Brigham, Eugene F., *Financial Management: Theory and Practice,* 3rd ed., (Chicago, Ill.: Dryden Press, 1982).

Copeland, Thomas E., Tim Koller, and Jack Murrin, *Valuation: Measuring and Managing the Value of Corporations,* 2nd ed. (New York: Wiley, 1994).

Copeland, Thomas E., and J. Fred Weston, *Financial Theory and Corporate Policy,* 3rd ed. (Reading, Mass.: Addison-Wesley, 1988).

Cornell, Bradford, *Corporate Valuation* (New York: Irwin, 1993).

Desmond, Glenn, and Richard E. Kelley, *Business Valuation Handbook* (Los Angeles, Calif.: Valuation Press, 1980).

Desmond, Glenn, *Handbook of Small Business Valuation Formulas and Rules of Thumb,* 3rd ed. (Camden, Me.: Valuation Press, 1993).

Emory, John D., "The Value of Marketability as Illustrated by Initial Public Offerings of Common Stock: November 1995 through April 1997," *Business Valuation Review,* 16 (3) September 1997.

Fischer, Donald E., and Ronald J. Jordan, *Security Analysis and Portfolio Management,* 5th ed. (Englewood Cliffs, N.J.: Prentice-Hall, 1991).

Fisher, Lawrence, and James Lorie, "Rates of Return on Investments in Common Stocks," *Journal of Business,* January 1964.

Fishman, Jay E., Shannon P. Pratt, J. Clifford Griffith, and D. Keith Wilson, *Guide to Business Valuations,* 6th ed. (Ft. Worth, Tex: Practitioners Publishing Co., 1996).

Foster, Carroll B., and Robert R. Trout, "Computing Losses in Business Interruption Cases," *Journal of Forensic Economics,* December 1989.

Foster, Carroll B., Robert R. Trout, and Patrick A. Gaughan, "Losses in Commercial Litigation," *Journal of Forensic Economics,* 6 (3) Fall 1993.

Fuller, Russell J., and Glenn H. Petry, "Inflation, Return on Equity and Stock Prices," *Journal of Portfolio Management,* Summer 1981.

Gallinger, George W., and P. Basil Healey, *Liquidity Analysis and Management* (Reading, Mass.: Addison-Wesley Publishing Co, 1987).

Gaughan, Patrick A., *Mergers, Acquisitions and Corporate Restructurings* (New York: Wiley, 1996).

Gaughan, Patrick A., and Henry Fuentes, "The Minimization of Taxable Income and Lost Profits Litigation," *Journal of Forensic Economics* 4 (1) Winter 1990.

Gilbert, Gregory A., "Price/Sales Ratios," *Business Valuation News,* June 1986.

Hackel, Kenneth S., and Joshua Livnat, *Cash Flow and Security Analysis,* 2nd ed. (Chicago, Ill.: Irwin, 1996).

Hassan, Mahamood M., "Arithmetic Mean and Geometric Mean of Past Returns: What Information Do These Statistical Measures Reveal?" *The Journal of Investing* 4 (3) Fall 1995.

Hickman, Kent, and Glenn H. Petry, "A Comparison of Stock Price Predictions Using Court Accepted Formulas, Dividend Discount, and P/E Models," *Financial Management,* Summer 1990.

Howitt, Idelle A., *Federal Tax Valuation Digest,* 1995/1996 Cumulative Edition (Boston, Mass.: Warren, Gorham & Lamont, 1995).

Ibbotson Associates, *Stocks, Bonds, Bills and Inflation 1999 Yearbook,* The Valuation Edition (Chicago, Ill.: Ibbotson Associates, Inc, 1999).

Internal Revenue Service, *IRS Valuation Guide for Income, Estate and Gift Taxes* (Chicago, Ill.: CCH, 1994).

Internal Revenue Service, *Valuation Training for Appeals Officers,* Department of the Treasury, October 1993.

Kaplan, Steven N., and Richard S. Ruback, "The Valuation of Cash Flow Forecasts: An Empirical Analysis," *Journal of Finance* 50 (4) September 1995.

Kaplan, Steven N., and Richard S. Ruback, "The Market Pricing of Cash Flow Forecasts: Discounted Cash Flow vs. The Method of 'Comparables,'" *Journal of Applied Corporate Finance* 8 (4), 1995.

Leibowitz, Martin L., "Sales-Driven Franchise Value," (Charlottesville, Va.: Institute of Chartered Financial Analysts, 1997).

Leibowitz, Martin L., and Stanley Kogelman, *Franchise Value and the Price/Earnings Ratio* (Charlottesville, Va.: Institute of Chartered Financial Analysts, 1994-B).

Mercer, Christopher Z., *Quantifying Marketability Discounts* (Memphis, Tenn.: Peabody Publishing Co., 1997).

Mergerstat Review (Los Angeles, Calif.: Houlihan, Lokey, Howard & Zukin), published annually.

Miles, Raymond C., *Basic Business Appraisal* (New York: Wiley, 1984).

Morris, Robert, *RMA Annual Statement Analysis* (Philadelphia, Pa.: Robert Morris Associates, 1996).

Nicholas, David W., "Adjusted-Book Value Approach to Valuation," in *Valuation of Closely Held Companies and Inactively Traded Securities,* (Charlottesville, Va.: Institute of Chartered Financial Analysts, 1990).

Pratt, Shannon P., *Valuing Small Businesses and Professional Practices* (Homewood, Ill.: Dow Jones-Irwin, 1986).

Pratt, Shannon P., *Valuing a Business,* 3rd ed., (Homewood, Ill.: Dow-Jones-Irwin, 1996).

Pratt, Shannon P., Robert F. Rielly, and Robert P. Schweihs, *Valuing a Business,* 3rd ed. (New York: McGraw Hill, 1996).

Pratt, Shannon P., "Discounts and Premia," in *Valuation of Closely Held Companies and Inactively Traded Securities* (Charlottesville, Va.: Institute of Chartered Financial Analysts, 1990).

Reilly, Frank K., and Keith C. Brown, *Investment Analysis and Portfolio Management,* 5th ed. (Ft. Worth, Tex.: Dryden Press, 1997).

Ross, Stephen A., Randolph W. Westerfield, and Jeffrey Jaffe, *Corporate Finance,* 4th ed. (St. Louis, Mo.: Times Mirror, 1996).

Smith, Gordon V., and Russell L. Parr, *Valuation of Intellectual Property and Intangible Assets,* 2nd ed. (New York: Wiley, 1994); and Supplement, 1997.

Todd, J. F., and C. L. Hemphill, *Valuation of Corporate Stock* (Washington, D.C.: Bureau of National Affairs 831 T.M., 1992).

Trout, Robert R., "Estimation of the Discount Associated with the Transfer of Restricted Securities," *Taxes,* June 1977.

Trout, Robert R., and William W. Wade, "The Role of Economics in Regulatory Takings Cases," *Litigation Economics Digest* 1 (1) Fall 1995.

Troy, Leo, *Almanac of Business and Industrial Financial Ratios* (Englewood Cliffs, N.J.: Prentice-Hall, Inc., 1996).

Van Horne, James C., and John M. Wachowicz, *Financial Management and Policy* (Englewood Cliffs, N.J.: Prentice-Hall, Inc. 1996).

Wolf, James G., "Market Approach to Valuation," in *Valuation of Closely Held Companies and Inactively Traded Securities* (Charlottesville, Va.: Institute of Chartered Financial Analysts, 1990).

Zukin, James H., *Financial Valuation: Businesses and Business Interests* (Boston, Mass.: Warren, Gorham & Lamont, 1996).

9

INTELLECTUAL PROPERTY

The field of intellectual property litigation has grown significantly in recent years, which has led to increased demand for the computation of damages for violation of intellectual property claims. Intellectual property issues revolve around four main types of intellectual assets. They are:

- Patents
- Copyrights
- Trademarks
- Trade secrets

PATENTS

A patent is a grant of a property right extended by the Patent and Trademarks Office of the U.S. Department of Commerce. The right bestows upon the owner of the patent the ability to exclude others from using the patent without permission from the holder of the patent. For this reason, a patent is referred to as an exclusionary right. The patent holder has the right to sue those who violate the patent in federal district court. In such a suit, the patent holder may seek two general types of relief—an injunction and damages.

Patent Time Periods

There are two categories of patents: utility and plant patents and design patents. Utility and plant patents extend for 17 years from the approval date. Design patents last for 14 years. Once patents expire, the public may freely use the patented product.

Changing Legal Framework

The first patent act in the United States was written by Thomas Jefferson and passed by Congress in 1790. Although the patent laws have evolved over the years, the legal treatment of patents underwent fundamental change in 1981 when the federal court system created a special Court of Appeals of the Federal Circuit. This court exclusively handles appeals of intellectual property lawsuits and has issued numerous decisions that have further defined the law in this area.

In the case where an infringer claims a patent is invalid, the court places the burden of proof on the infringer who must prove the lack of validity. The standard of proof is demanding, thus raising the costs of violations. If the use is proved invalid, the infringer may demand significant damages. This has been underscored by some large damage awards that have raised the costs of unauthorized use of patents.

The owner of the intellectual property may ask the court for an injunction. However, courts have been somewhat reluctant to grant injunctions. In patent cases they require the owner of the patent to meet certain standards, such as a convincing likelihood of success. They also require a showing of irreparable harm that may outweigh any harm the injunction may inflict upon the defendant. The key requirement is likelihood of success, and if this requirement is met the court may simply presume the existence of other criteria such as irreparable harm.[1] The presumption of irreparable harm is partially based on the fact that a patent is only bestowed for a limited time, and continued use of the patent during that time will erode the value of the patent to its holder.

Direct versus Contributory Infringement

Direct infringement refers to the unauthorized use of a patented product. The owner of the patent then has the right to bring an action seeking damages against the infringer. Contributory infringement results when one party facilitates the infringement by others. The owner of the patent then has the right to bring an action against the party who made it possible for others to infringe on the patent.[2] This creates certain opportunities for the patent owner who may be able to pur-

---

[1] *Smith Int'l. Inc. v. Hughes Tool Co.*, 718 F. 2d 1573, 1581 U.S.P.Q. 686 (Fed Cir. 1983) *cert denied*, 464 U.S. 966 (1983).

[2] Jeffrey Samuels and Linda B. Samuels, "Contributory Infringement: Relief for the Patent Owner," *The Corporation Law Review*, 1981, 332–345.

sue one action against the facilitator as opposed to a more costly process of pur's-ing many separate actions against many infringers.

Defenses Claimed by Alleged Patent Infringers

The users of intellectual property, such as patented products, may either claim that they did not infringe or that the patent is invalid. The lack of validity may be asserted by claiming that the invention was anticipated by a prior art and there-fore was not patentable. The defendant may also claim that the United States Patent and Trademark Office failed in its duty to disclose the best prior art or re-search data that would not have supported the patent.[3]

Computation of Damages for Patent Infringement

There are two categories of damages for owners of intellectual property: lost profits and royalties. Of the two alternatives, courts prefer lost profits. Royalties are used when the plaintiff cannot prove its lost profits.[4] While much of the methodology of lost profits computations discussed elsewhere in this book also applies to lost profits computations for intellectual property violations, certain differences need to be noted.

Legal Requirements Necessary to Prove Lost Profits

As in most commercial damages cases, patent holders must first prove causality followed by a computation of damages. In the context of patent litigation, these requirements are set forth in four factors, called *Panduit factors* from the case *Panduit Corp. v. Stahlin Brothers Fibre Works, Inc.*[5] The four *Panduit* factors are:

---

[3] R. Peyton Gibson, "Infringement of Patents and Related Technology," in *Commercial Damages: A Guide to Remedies in Business Litigation,* Charles L. Knapp ed. (New York: Matthew Bender) 1997, 49-6 – 49-7.

[4] *Hartness International, Inc. v. Simplimatic Engineering Co.,* 819 F.2d 1100, 1112 (Fed. Cir. 1987).

[5] *Panduit Corp. v. Stahlin Brothers Fibre Works, Inc.,* 575 F. 2d 1152, 1156 (6th Cir. 1978).

1. *Market demand.* The sales of the infringer may be used as proof that there was sufficient demand in the market for the product.[6]

2. *Unavailability of noninfringing substitutes.* This factor involves an examination of the characteristics of the product and the claimed substitutes. Court decisions have rendered this requirement less relevant as they have often found that no alternatives were acceptable unless there was a very strong similarity between the infringed product and the substitutes.[7]

3. *Ability to produce and market product.* This factor also may not be that important as the court may bend over backward to give the plaintiff the benefit of the doubt.[8]

4. *Computation of the lost profits.* Because this book is about the computation of damages, this factor is discussed at length.

The *Panduit* factors represent an application of an array of 15 factors that the court set forth in *Georgia Pacific Corp. v. U.S. Plywood Champion Papers, Inc.* when it was establishing factors for determining a proper royalty. In *Panduit*, the court considered those 15 factors and applied them to the determination of lost profits.

Computation of Lost Profits

Patent owners can incur lost profits in a number of ways. The most basic lost profits computation measures *incremental profits*. Incremental profits are defined as follows:

$$\text{Incremental profits} = (\text{Units sold by infringer}) \times (\text{Patentee's incremental profit margin}) \quad (9.1)$$

The patentee's profit margin is defined in a similar manner to other types of commercial damage cases where fixed costs that do not vary with output are not included.[9] In an effort to minimize its damages, an infringer may focus on the

---

[6] *Gyromat Corporation v. Champion Spark Plug,* 735 F.2d 5489, 552 (Fed. Cir. 1984).
[7] *See* note 3.
[8] *Gyromat Corporation v. Champion Spark Plug,* 735 F.2d 549, 554 (Fed. Cir. 1984).
[9] *Paper Converting Machinery Co. v. Magna-Graphics Co.,* 745 F. 2d 11, 22 (Fed. Cir. 1984).

magnitude of its sales of the infringed product as well as the costs being included in the patentee's incremental profit margin.

One major difference between lost profits computations in patent infringement cases and other commercial damages cases is the lower requirements for proving the demand for the product. The norm is to simply assume that the infringer's sales would have been the patentee's. It is usually not necessary to develop a more complete analysis of the demand determinants, as would be normally done in a business interruption analysis. This sidesteps the question of whether the patentee would have been able to sell as many units as the infringer did or whether the patentee would have received the same price.

Measurement of the Infringer's Profit's

The infringer's profits *may* not be that relevant to the computation of the plaintiff's lost profits. The key is what profits the patentee would have realized from the sales the infringer made. The measurement of the infringer's profits may play a more important role when it is difficult to measure the patentee's lost profits. In such cases, the court may look to the infringer's profits when determining a reasonable royalty.

Lost Profits Due to Price Effects

In addition to being deprived of the profits on sales made by the infringer, the profits actually received by the patentee could also be adversely affected by the infringer's actions. Had the infringer not entered the market with its unauthorized products, the owner would have had a monopoly position. As a monopolist, it would have the ability to pick the price-quantity combination on the product's demand curve that maximized its profits. However, when the infringer enters the market, the price may be affected as the owner and the infringer become competitors. This situation can lead to another form of losses—reduced prices received by the owner for the products actually sold as shown in Figure 9.1, where the increased output due to the infringer entrance causes a movement down the product demand curve from q_1 to q_2 resulting in a lower price of p_2 instead of the price associated with output level q_1, which would have been p_1. The lower prices erode the owner's profit margin leading to lower profits on the sales actually made by the owner.

It may be difficult to precisely measure the price effect that results from the *duopolistic* market structure (two sellers) in which the owner and the infringer are competitors. However, the court in *Kaufman Co. v. Lantech, Inc.* eased the burden of proof when measuring lost profits in a duopolistic market structure by

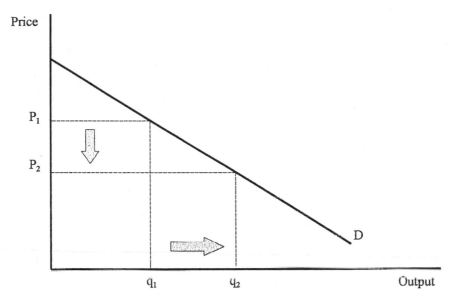

Figure 9.1. Lost profits due to price effects.

concluding that "when the patentee and the infringer are the only suppliers present in the market, it is reasonable to infer that infringement probably caused the loss of profits."[10] The improper competition changes the marketplace and economists have to estimate what the monopolist's price would have been in the absence of the competition. Economists have theoretically tried to trace the competitive effects of duopolists through game theoretic techniques that analyze the interactive effects of competitors.[11]

Lost Profits Due to Changing Cost Conditions
Another less obvious way the owner can incur lost profits is by not realizing some of the economies of scale that he would have enjoyed had it been in a monopoly position as opposed to the duopoly that would result from the owner competing with one infringer. Whether such losses exist depends on the cost function of the owner. If the owner's production process is characterized by

[10] *Kaufman Co. v. Lantech, Inc.,* 926 F. 2d 1136 (Fed Cir. 1991).

[11] M. Shubik, "Information, Duopoly and Competitive Markets: A Sensitivity Analysis," *Kyklos* 26 (1973) and Charles R. Plott, "Industrial Organization Theory and Experimental Economics," *Journal of Economic Literature* 28, December 1982.

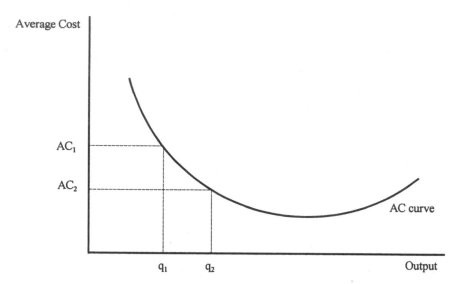

Figure 9.2.   Changing cost conditions.

economies of scale, such as that reflected in the average cost (AC) function depicted in Figure 9.2, then producing an output such as q_1 where per unit costs are
AC_1, as opposed to a higher output q_2 where per unit costs are AC_2, results in
higher costs equal to the $(AC_2 - AC_1)q_1$.

ROYALTY ARRANGEMENTS

The owner of intellectual property may choose to license its use in exchange
for a royalty. In cases where the owner is already doing this, the royalty that
it charges authorized users *may* be used to compute the owner's losses. Royalty fees can also be used to construct the proper compensation for the owner
even in cases where the owner is not authorizing users to use the product in
exchange for a royalty. This method of compensation recognizes that royalties are chosen by owners to obtain compensation from users. Therefore, in
the absence of an explicit a priori arrangement, such a hypothetical royalty
would be one way of compensating the owner. This method may be helpful
when similar products are traded in the marketplace using common royalty
formulas. The existence of such formulas may facilitate the damage computation.

Types of Royalties

There are two types of royalties: running royalties and lump sum royalties.[12] Running royalties are variable costs that are either computed as a percent of revenues or as a simple per-unit cost. An example of a running royalty would be the 8% of infringing sales established in *H. K. Porter Co. v. Goodyear Tire and Rubber Co.* based upon expert testimony.[13] Lump sum royalties are a fixed sum that the user pays the owner, which give certain rights of use to the user in a manner that does not vary with usage volume. An example of a lump sum royalty was the $2,600 annual fee per furnace that was established in *Trio Process Corp. v. L. Goldstein's Sons, Inc.* based on a prior and existing license.[14]

Running royalties have certain efficiency effects on the market. The variable nature of the running royalty is a factor that the user takes into account when determining its optimal profit maximizing output. If this causes the user to put a lower output on the market than what it would in the absence of additional variable costs, then economic theory would indicate that a less than socially optimal output may reach the market. In this sense the lump sum royalty is more economically efficient as it transfers some of the profits that the user enjoys from selling its profit maximizing output from the user to the owner without affecting the price-output combination. This is because the lump sum royalty is a *sunk cost,* which should not affect decisions at the margin.[15]

Reasonable Royalties

The computation of royalties in patent infringement cases is different from the same computation in the normal operation of commerce. In patent cases the stan-

---

[12] Elizabeth A. Evans, Martha S. Samuelson, and Robert A. Sherwin, "Economic Analysis of Intellectual Property Rights," in *Litigation Support Handbook,* 2nd ed. (New York: Wiley), 1995, 17-1–17-20.

[13] *H. K. Porter v. Goodyear Tire & Rubber Co.,* 536 F. 2d 1115, 191 USPQ 486 (6th Cir. 1976).

[14] *Trio Process Corp. v. L. Goldstein's Sons, Inc.,* 612 F. 2d 1353, 204 USPQ 881 (3rd Cir. 1980) cert denied, 449 U.S. 827 (1980).

[15] Jack Hirshleifer and David Hirshleifer, *Price Theory and Its Applications,* 6th ed. (Upper Saddle River, N.J.: Prentice Hall) 1998, pp.174–175.

dard is a *reasonable royalty,* not a commercially acceptable royalty. Courts have recognized that the computation of such an expost royalty is a legal fiction.[16]

In *Panduit Corp. v. Stahlin Brothers Fibre Works, Inc.* the court stated as follows:

> The setting of a reasonable royalty after infringement cannot be treated, as it was here, as the equivalent of ordinary royalty negotiations among truly 'willing' patent owners and licensees. That view would constitute a pretense that the infringement never happened. It would also make an election to infringe a handy means for competitors to impose a "compulsory license" policy upon every patent owner.

A royalty may be computed even when the patent owner expressed no desire to license the product. The goal is to compute a royalty high enough to compensate the plaintiff who suffered as a result of the infringer's actions. However, in searching to find the magnitude sufficient to compensate the plaintiff, courts have gone so far as to accept royalties that not only are greater than the standard royalties that prevail in commercial transaction but which have been as much as 50% of the product's price and more than 100% of the expected profits.[17] It seems that once the court has concluded that the infringement has taken place, the court moves to give the benefit of the doubt to the patentee.

Factors to Consider in Determining Royalties

The *Panduit* court referred to *Georgia Pacific Corp. v. U.S. Plywood-Champion Papers, Inc.* wherein that court delineated 15 factors that should be considered when determining a royalty rate. The court stated that it derived these factors from various leading cases. In *Georgia Pacific* the parties stipulated a reasonable royalty was the proper measure of damages. The *Georgia Pacific* factors are:

Georgia Pacific Royalty Factors

1. The royalties received by the patentee for licensing of the patent in suit, proving or tending to prove an established royalty.
2. The rates paid by the licensee for the use of other patents comparable to the patent in suit.

---

[16] *Georgia Pacific Corporation v. United States Plywood-Champion Papers, Inc.,* 446 F. 2d 295 (2d Cir. 1971).

[17] See note 3, 49-6.

3. The nature and scope of the license, as exclusive or nonexclusive, or as restricted or nonrestricted, in terms of territory or with respect to whom the manufactured product may be sold.

4. The licensor established policy and marketing program to maintain his patent monopoly by not licensing others to use the invention or by granting licenses under special conditions designed to preserve that monopoly.

5. The commercial relationship between the licensor and the licensee, such as, whether they are competitors in the same territory in the same line of business, or whether they are inventor and promoter.

6. The effect of selling the patented speciality in promoting sales of other products of the licensee, the existing value of the invention to the licensor as a generator of sales of his nonpatented items, and the extent of such derivative or conveyed sales.

7. The duration of the patent and the term of the license.

8. The established profitability of the product made under the patent, its commercial success, and its current popularity.

9. The utility and advantages of the patent property over the old modes and devices, if any, that had been used for working out similar results.

10. The nature of the patented invention, the character of the commercial embodiment of it as owned and produced by the licensor, and the benefits to those that have used the invention.

11. The extent to which the infringer has made use of the invention and any evidence probative of the value of that use.

12. The portion of the profit or of the selling price that may be customary in the particular business or in comparable businesses to allow for the use of the invention or analogous inventions.

13. The portion of the realizable profit that should be credited to the invention as distinguished to nonpatented elements, the manufacturing process, business risks, or significant features or improvements added by the infringer.

14. The opinion testimony of qualified experts.

15. The amount that a licensor (such as the patentee) and a licensee (such as the infringer) would have agreed on (at the time the infringement began) if both had been reasonably and voluntarily trying to reach an agreement; that is, the amount that a prudent licensee—who desires, as a business proposition, to obtain a license to manufacture and sell a particular article embodying the patented invention—would have been willing to pay as a royalty and yet be able to make a reasonable profit and which amount

would have been acceptable by a prudent patentee who was willing to grant a license.

Lost Profits versus Royalties

As noted previously, courts view lost profits as the preferential measure of damages in patent infringement cases.[18] As stated in *Hansen v. Alpine Valley Ski Area, Inc.,* "If the record permits the determination of actual damages, namely, the profits the patentee lost from the infringement, that determination accurately measures the patentee's loss. If actual damages cannot be ascertained, then a reasonable royalty must be determined."

Plaintiffs may prefer lost profits as they may exceed a reasonable royalty. Plaintiff's counsel may want to compute the losses both ways in advance of a trial as part of the selection of the best damages strategy to pursue. However, the court in *Hartness International, Inc. v. Simplimatic Engineering Company* endorsed using lost profits as the preferable method with a reasonable royalty being used "when actual lost profits cannot be proven."[19] Other courts have stated that the reasonable royalty should merely be used as the floor for damages.[20] Therefore, damages need to be computed using both approaches. In fact, there are cases where a combination of both lost profits and royalties have been awarded.[21]

Entire Market Value Theory

The entire market theory is the view that damages should be computed based on the market for the entire product, which contained the infringed product. This means that if the infringed product is a component in an overall product, the patent damages should be computed based on the market for the overall product. Courts may look to apply the entire market theory in cases where the infringed product plays a very large role in determining the value of the overall product.[22] Under the entire market value rule, damages are recoverable on the

---

[18] *Hansen v. Alpine Ski Area, Inc.,* 718 F. 2d 1075, 1078 (Fed. Cir. 1983).

[19] *Hartness International, Inc. v. Simplimatic Engineering Company,* 819 F. 2d 1100, 1112 (Fed. Cir. 1987).

[20] *Bandag, Inc. v. Gerrand Tire Co.,* 704 F.2d 1578, 1583 (Fed. Cir. 1983).

[21] *Fonar Co. v. General Electric Co.,* 902 F. Supp. 330, 351 (E.D.N.Y. 1995).

[22] *Julien v. Gomez & Andre Tractor Repairs, Inc.,* 512 F. Supp. 955, 959 (M.D. La. 1981).

value of a patentee's entire apparatus containing several unpatented features where the patent-related feature is the basis for consumer demand.[23] Such an expanded base for damages can significantly increase the damages resulting from infringement.

COMPUTER SOFTWARE

When the laws relating to intellectual property were first written, the computer industry was not near its current size, but since then the computer software industry has exploded. Given the valuable nature of proprietary computer software, companies want to protect and regulate its usage. In 1981 the U.S. Supreme Court removed legal barriers that had kept software from receiving some of the same protection of patent laws that other products enjoy. Since then computer software can be protected by a patent. However, owners of the software may also choose to protect their assets through copyrights or as a trade secret.

COPYRIGHTS

A copyright protects the expression of an idea. It is important to note, however, that it is the *expression* of the idea that can be copyrighted as opposed to the idea itself. A copyright can be registered with the Copyright Office of the Library of Congress. A copyright is typically denoted by the symbol ©.

The Copyright Act of 1976, along with the Berne Convention Implementation Act of 1988, set forth the remedies for copyright infringement. These laws created the legal framework that had been governed by the Copyright Act of 1909.

Section 102 and 103 of the Copyright Act provide copyright protection to the following types of work:

- Literary works
- Musical works and sound recordings
- Pictorial and other artistic works
- Pantomimes and choreographic works
- Motion pictures

---

[23] *Fonar Co. v. General Electric Co.,* 902 F. Supp. 330, 351 (E.D.N.Y. 1995) quoting *Rite Hite Corp. v. Kelly Co.,* 56 F. 3d 1538, 1544 (Fed. Cir. 1995).

Copyright Time Periods

Copyrights are protected for the life of an author plus fifty years. However, in the case of "works for hire," copyright protection lasts 75 years from the date of publication or 100 years from the date of creation. When the copyright expires then it can be freely used by the public.

Remedies for Copyright Infringement

The Copyright Act provides various remedies for copyright violations including injunctions, impoundment, or destruction of the infringing items as well as damages. An injunction may be granted when the copyright owner can demonstrate a realistic likelihood of success in the action along with an expectation that the owner will incur irreparable injury. While irreparable injury normally means damages that cannot be adequately compensated for either due to their magnitude or the uncertainty in measurement, courts often simply presume the existence of irreparable damages leaving the defendant to prove otherwise.

Introduction to the Economics of Copyright Law

An analytical framework for the economics of copyright law has been developed by William Landes and Richard Posner.[24] Following is an overview of this framework.

Let P = price of a copy
   $q(P)$ = market demand for copies of a work
   X = number of copies an author produces
   Y = number of copies copiers produce
   Z = the level of copyright protection

$Z \geq 0$ is a function of

1. The degree of similarity between two works before infringement is determined

---

[24] William E. Landes and Richard A. Posner, "An Economic Analysis of Copyright Law," *Journal of Legal Studies,* 18, June 1989, 325–363.

2. Elements of the work that are protected

3. Period of time work is protected

Assume that copiers supply copies up to point where $P = MC$ (marginal cost) and that MC increases as the number of copies increases level of copyright protection increases

$$Y = Y(P, Z) \qquad Y_p > 0 \quad Y_z < 0 \tag{9.2}$$

Author's profits are

$$\Pi = (P - C)X - e(z) \tag{9.3}$$

where e = author's marginal cost of a copy

Substitute for X:

$$\Pi = (P - C)[q(P) - Y(P, Z)] - e(z) \tag{9.4}$$

where $e(z)$ is the author's cost of expression.

The greater the copyright protection is, the higher the author's cost of expression.

R = author's gross profits
N = number of works created

$$N = N(R, Z) \quad \text{where} \quad N_r > 0 \text{ and } N_z < 0$$

The net effect in N of an increase in copyright protection depends on two effects.

1. As R increases, the number of works increases.
2. As Z increases, the number of works decreases.

At a low Z, there is little incentive to produce works and thus free riders will dominate. Therefore, N increases as Z increases up to some level Z^*. Beyond Z^* there are adverse effects on other potential authors. Some protection is good, but too much protection is bad. The solution is to find the optimal Z^*.

Landes and Posner go on to show the welfare implications in deriving Z^*. Among other conclusions of their framework are:

1. At Z^* the producer and consumer surplus per work exceeds the cost of producing the marginal work.

2. Optimal copyright protection should be set below the level that maximizes the number of works created.

3. The more valuable the work, the greater the optimal amount of copyright protection as the cost of copying relative to the value received from copying will decline.[25]

Measurement of Damages for Copyright Infringement

A copyright owner is entitled to its lost profits in addition to those components of the defendant's profits not included in the copyright owner's lost profits computation. The award of the lost profits is designed to compensate the owner of the copyright while the award of the defendant's profits is designed to eliminate the incentive to infringe.

Copyright Owner's Lost Profits

The plaintiff's lost profits are usually measured by the plaintiff's lost sales less any cost savings from not producing these products. However, the plaintiff must measure these lost sales in a nonspeculative manner. The copyright owner cannot simply assume that the defendant's sales would have been its sales. Courts have held that a variety of factors, such as the sales prices of both companies, need to be considered in the lost revenue projection process.[26] In cases where the defendant sold the infringed product to the plaintiff's own former customers at similar prices, the assumption that the defendant's sales would have been the plaintiff's becomes easier for a court to accept.

In projecting lost sales due to copyright infringement, the forecasting methods discussed in Chapter 5 are useful. Indeed, courts have accepted significantly more basic projection techniques than those explained in Chapter 5. For example, in *Taylor v. Meirick* the court accepted a simple computation of the plaintiff's average sales for the two-year period prior to the infringement, without inflationary adjustment, as a nonspeculative forecast of what the plaintiff's sales would have been for the three-year infringement period.[27] Lost sales were then computed as

---

[25] *Id.*

[26] *Stevens Linen Associates, Inc. v. Mastercraft Corporation*, 656 F 2d. 11 (2d Cir. 1981).

[27] *Taylor v. Meirick*, 712 F.2d 1112 (7th Cir. 1983).

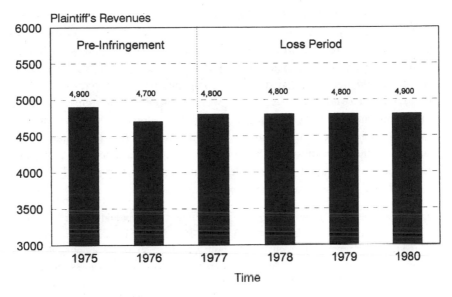

Figure 9.3. Simplistic revenue projection in *Taylor v. Meirick*.

the difference between these projected sales and the owner's actual sales. The simplistic nature of the damage estimation process is depicted in Figure 9.3.

Defendant's Profits

In order to prove the defendant's profits, the copyright owner only has to prove the infringer's gross revenues.[28] Once this is established, the defendant then has to establish what its costs are. Defendants may try to put forward a more full definition of its costs that plaintiffs would prefer. At this point the issue comes down to a cost analysis and the services of a good cost accountant can be invaluable. If, however, the defendant did not enjoy any profits from the infringement, then there are no profits to award and the damages are simply the plaintiff's lost profits.[29]

The analysis of the defendant's profits can be complicated when it is difficult to separate the costs attributable to the infringed product from the defendant's

---

[28] Ira Jay Levy and Paul S. Owen, "Infringement of Copyright and Literary Property," in *Commercial Damages: A Guide to Remedies in Business Litigation* (New York: Matthew Bender & Co.) 1997.

[29] *Deltak v. Advanced Systems, Inc.*, 574 F. Supp. 400 (N.D. Ill. 1983).

other costs unrelated to the infringed product. As with other types of lost profits analysis, the goal is to measure the incremental costs associated with the incremental revenues generated from the infringement. In *Deltak, Inc. v. Advanced Systems, Inc.* the court recognized that fixed costs, such as rent or depreciation, generally should not be included in this computation.[30] However, other courts have found that overhead costs, which were measured by a simple overhead costs/revenue ratio, should be applied to gross profits as an allowable deduction.[31]

An excerpt from the court's opinion in *Deltak, Inc. v. Advanced Systems, Inc.*, a case where the plaintiff sued for the improper use of architectural plans that were used to build an apartment complex, is instructive in that it sets forth what one court found to be reasonable cost deductions:

> In consideration for the construction of the apartment complex and garage located at 1830–32 Knox Street, Empire paid Belmont $512,569 ($511,520 contract price plus $1,309 in reimbursed expenses). Belmont introduced evidence showing that it incurred $451,450.56 in direct deductible expenses, thus realizing a gross profit of $59,709.44 on the project. Belmont contends that it is entitled to deduct from the gross profit a portion of its administrative and general overhead expenses by a formula which would reduce its gross profit to a net profit of $12,878.94.
>
> The rule is that overhead expenses which assist in the production of an infringing work are deductible from the gross profit of the infringer. (cite omitted) The burden is upon the defendant infringer to prove the actual expenditures for ordinary overhead and a fair method of allocating the overhead to the particular infringing activity in question. (cite omitted) The defendant need not, however, prove that each item of overhead was used in connection with the infringing activity. (cite omitted)
>
> The law requires no such minutiae, for it would make trial interminable. When appellant proved the actual expenditures for ordinary overhead, and a fair method of allocation, it carried its burden in the first instance. If, on cross-examination or otherwise, it appears that ordinary overhead is not chargeable, in whole or in part, to the infringing business, then a proper charge only should be made. But all allowance should not be denied because stenographers, bookkeepers, janitors, and presidents were not called to testify that they did perform specific tasks on this specific business. Courts and accountants resort to allocation to obviate this particular difficulty.

Statutory Damages

In cases in which the computation of the plaintiff's lost profits and the defendant's profits cannot be measured in a nonspeculative manner, the courts will

---

[30] *Id.*

[31] *Aiten v. Empire Construction Co.*, 542 F. Supp 252 (D. Neb. 1982).

look to an award of statutory damages. A plaintiff may elect to pursue statutory damages instead of its lost profits and the defendant's profits.[32]

Statutory damages are bounded within the monetary limits of greater than or equal to $500 but less than or equal to $20,000 for each infringement. However, in cases where the courts find that the infringer was not aware of its infringement, they may reduce the statutory damage award.

TRADEMARKS

Companies may devote substantial resources to develop a trademark with which they hope that the market will associate their business and its products and services. In the traditional sense, trademarks are used to certify the authenticity of a product which, in turn, causes consumers to have a certain quality expectation. In the case of trademark for service providers, the trademarks are called *service marks*.

Trademarks provide protection for names such as those associated with major brands. They also can provide protection for a variety of different products including fragrances, packaging, sounds, and designs such as those embodied in clothing. The protection for trademarks is provided by the Lanham Act, which provides a variety of legal remedies including injunctive relief and monetary damages. This law deals with a broader array of business practices beyond just trademark infringement. A variety of improper business practices such as unfair competition, of which trademarks is a form, are made illegal by this law.

A candidate for a trademark applies at the Patent and Trademark Office to register the trademark. The applicant provides certain basic information such as the date of the first use of the trademark and indicates the products or services to which the trademark will apply. Once accepted, trademarks are published in the *Official Gazette*.

Trademark Time Periods

Trademarks have been defined by the Trademark Act of 1946. A trademark is valid for 20 years and may then be renewed for another 20 years. The holder of the trademark, however, must attest to its continued use between the fifth and sixth year of its life, lest the registration be canceled.

---

[32] *See* note 28, 50–52.

The Economics of Trademarks

The main economic benefit of trademarks is that they reduce search costs of consumers. Since the trademark is clearly identified with the marketer of the product, it is in the interest of the trademark owner to invest resources to maintain the quality of the product or services. Landes and Posner express this in the form of a simple economic model as follows:[33]

$$\pi = P + H(T; Y, W) \tag{9.5}$$

where π = the full price of a good
P = the money price
H = search costs incurred by buyers
T = trademark
Y = a vector of factors, including advertising, value of consumer's time, and number of competing products, other than T that affect search costs.
W = availability of word and symbols that can be used to construct a trademark (this is usually not relevant).

Landes and Posner show that firms with stronger trademarks (T) have lower search costs (H) and are able to command higher prices (P) because the lower H is, the higher P can be without causing π to change from its optimal level.

Trade Dress

An area related to trademark infringement is what is known as *trade dress*. Trade dress refers to the physical features of the product that have become known in the marketplace to be associated with a particular marketer of that product. These features signify what the source of the product is. One example is the pink color of Owens Fiberglass insulation.[34] When trade dress protection is afforded to a product, then other companies are barred from duplicating these features. It is possible for a company to qualify for trade dress protection on a product that was once patented but where the patent has expired with the passage of time.

---

[33] William M. Landes and Richard A. Posner, "Trademark Law: An Economic Perspective," *Journal of Law and Economics,* 30 (2), October 1987, 265–309.

[34] *In re Owens-Illinois Fiberglass Corp.,* 774 F. 2d 1116 (Fed Cir. 1985).

Damages for Trademark Infringement

Owners of trademarks can recover their damages, which may be a royalty, as well as the infringer's profits in addition to other possible monetary relief such as treble damages, legal fees, and other litigation costs. As with patent damages, lost profits must be proved in a nonspeculative way. Courts place the burden of proof on the plaintiff when it is trying to establish its damages. However, when the defendant's actions have made it difficult for the plaintiff to measure its damages, the defendant is generally not allowed to profit from this and use this as a defense.

Recovery for damages from trademark infringement requires that the trademark owner demonstrate that it has been damaged and is able to measure these damages as well as to convincingly draw a causal link between the defendant's action and these damages.[35] A trademark owner is allowed to recover both its lost profits and the defendant's profits but not where these derive some of the exact same sales.[36] If the plaintiff contends that the infringement caused confusion in the marketplace resulting in its not being able to make certain sales, it must be able to demonstrate the ability to generate such sales in the marketplace in the absence of such confusion. If it cannot, due to factors such as insufficient resources, then the court may not award the owner those damages.[37]

As with other types of commercial damages cases, in establishing damages for trademark infringement, there is a higher degree of proof required in establishing that damages actually occurred.[38] However, once proof has been established, then the courts are more lenient in the measurement of the actual damages and they may not require exactness. Courts have recognized that economic factors, such as the impact of the competition between the plaintiff and the defendant may distort the market by making it more difficult to measure the plaintiff's lost sales.[39]

---

[35] Ethan Horwitz, "Improper Use of Trademarks and Trade Names," in *Commercial Damages: A Guide to Remedies in Business Litigation*, Charles L. Knapp ed. (New York: Matthew Bender, 1997), p. 51.01–51.08.

[36] *Polo Fashions, Inc. v. Extra Special Products, Inc.*, 208 U.S.P.Q. 421, 428 (S.D.N.Y. 1980).

[37] *Maltina Corporation v. Cawy Bottling Company*, 613 F. 2d 582 (5th Cir. 1980).

[38] *See* note 35.

[39] *Donsco, Inc. v. Casper Corporation*, 205 U.S.P.Q. 246, 248 (E.D. Pa. 1980).

Plaintiff's Damages from Trademark Infringement

A trademark owner can be damaged in a variety of ways when its trademark is violated. Sales can be diverted from the owner to the infringer. In addition, if the goods are produced in an inferior manner and the consumer believes that they are the products of the owner, the reputation of the owner may suffer resulting in diminished future sales. Other damages can occur from the owner using its marketing resources to build up a brand name, which the defendant benefits from without having to incur these costs. Ironically, the owner may then have to invest even more advertising and marketing monies to correct the consumer's perceptions. Such *corrective advertising* may be another area in which the damage expert can be helpful.

Royalties as Measure of the Plaintiff's Damages

When royalties are the selected measure of the plaintiff's damages, their computation can be straightforward when there is an existing agreement between the plaintiff and defendant that sets forth these amounts. When there is no agreement, then royalties may be measured by the standards in that industry. These standards may be established through expert testimony.[40]

Defendant's Profits

When the defendant's infringement is established, the plaintiff is awarded the defendant's profits so the defendant cannot benefit from its illegal behavior. In computing these profits, the plaintiff must measure the value of the infringing revenues and then deduct the incremental costs associated with generating these incremental revenues. This method is used in a variety of business interruption cases.

As with patent infringement discussed previously, all the plaintiff has to do is prove the defendant's revenues. Then the burden shifts to the defendant to prove its costs.[41] Courts have accepted simple measures of costs, such as using the ratio of infringing sales to the defendant's total sales and applying this ratio to the de-

---

[40] *National Bank of Commerce v. Shaklee Corporation,* 503 F. Supp. 533, 207 U.S.P.Q. 1005 (W.D. Tex. 1980).

[41] *Playboy Entertainment, Inc. v. P.K. Sorren Export Company,* 546 F. Supp. 987, 997 (S.D. Fla. 1982).

fendant's total costs.[42] However, courts have also accepted more sophisticated analysis of incremental costs, which seeks to identify only those specific costs incurred in the generation of the infringed sales. When the infringing sales are a more significant component of the defendant's total sales, a portion of fixed costs may have to be included in total costs. When these sales are a small percent of total sales, then the court may disallow this deduction.[43]

TRADE SECRETS

Trade secrets come under the protection of the Uniform Trade Secrets Act. However, a firm and narrow definition of trade secrets is difficult as they can come in a variety of forms that vary with the variability of business in general. A trade secret must, however, be information that allows the business to generate profits and enjoy some competitive advantage in the marketplace. The source of the profitability of the trade secrets may be from enhancing revenues or reducing costs or both. The value of these secrets may be underscored by efforts that the business exercises to keep the knowledge from leaking to competitors.

Some trade secrets may even be patentable but the business may decide not to apply for a patent so as to prevent competitors from using them after the life of the patent. Unfortunately, it may be difficult to maintain such secrecy for such a time period. In addition, the law provides stronger protection for patents than it does for trade secrets.

Following is a list of some of the forms of trade secrets:

- *Compilations of data.* These compilations can include various data that can be used to generate profits. Such data can be compiled in computer databases that may have helpful organizational features that the business has developed over time. A good example are databases of current and potential customers. However, in order for a company to prevent unauthorized use of customer lists, such as by former employees, the firm must maintain the list as a secret. Employees may be able to use remembered information on former customers.
- *Product of experience.* The product of the company's experience may have led to perfecting certain procedures and processes, which may come in a variety of forms including machine settings, drawings, and manuals.

---

[42] *Lawrence of London, Ltd. v. Count Romi, Ltd.,* 159 U.S.P.Q. 383 (N.Y. App. 1968).
[43] *S.C. Johnson & Son, Inc. v. Drop Dead Company,* 144 U.S.P.Q. 257, 260 (S.D.Cal. 1965).

- *Formulas and recipes.* Many manufacturers of food-related products closely guard the formulas for creating a product. A good example is the formula for Coca Cola. Recipes can be jealously guarded by restaurants and chefs.
- *Research findings and test results.* Companies involved in research and development closely guard the results of their research and preliminary tests. These secrets are often collected in research logs or preliminary reports, which are considered proprietary.

In order for a trade secret to be legally protected it must have economic value and the owner must have taken some measure to keep it secret. If one uses improper means to acquire a trade secret, such as engaging in industrial espionage, then a court may find that such users have to compensate the owner of the trade secret. However, it is legal for an individual or business to acquire a trade secret through legitimate means, such as reverse engineering.

Damages for Misappropriation of Trade Secrets

There are two alternative measures of damages for trade secret misappropriation: the plaintiff's lost profits and the defendant's gain. The plaintiff can recover one, but not both. In order for the plaintiff to prove its losses, it may need to prove causality as well as the magnitude of damages.[44] Causality may also involve showing that the sales that were diverted to a competitor would have been the plaintiff's sales but for the misappropriation of the trade secret.[45]

Trade secrets damage analysis can present some interesting economic and accounting issues. For example, if the secret was the product of costly research, the defendant may be able to undercut the plaintiff's prices and take market share from the plaintiff. This action could have an extended impact on the plaintiff if consumers are reluctant to pay the plaintiff's higher prices in the future.

In order to measure the defendant's profits derived from the use of the trade secret, an accounting of the defendant's profits attributable to the use of the secret needs to be compiled. Depending on the nature of the secret, it may or may

---

[44] Michael J. Herbert and William F. Johnson, "Improper Use of Trade Secrets and Customer Lists," in *Commercial Damages: A Guide to Remedies in Business Litigation,* Charles L. Knapp, ed. (New York: Matthew Bender) 1997, p. 52–34.

[45] *Monsanto Chemical, Company v. Perfect Fit Product Manufacturing Company,* 349 F. 2d 389 (2d Cir. 1965) *cert denied,* 383 U.S. 942 (1966).

not be easy to segregate these sales and profits from the other sales and profits of the defendant. Once the defendant's profits are measured, then a court can consider remedies such as restitution. Another remedy is a royalty, however, it is not commonly used.[46] Royalties are used in trade secret cases when the plaintiff cannot prove its losses. In *Carter Products, Inc. v. Colgate Palmolive Company,* the court awarded royalties that were computed as a percent of the defendant's sales in addition to the defendant's profits.[47] Royalties may also be used when the defendant did not make a profit from use of the misappropriated secrets.[48]

Measuring the Plaintiff's Losses in Misappropriation of Customer Lists

The analysis of losses due to the misappropriation of customer lists has to do with the measurement of the plaintiff's losses and the defendant's gains from sales to customers on the misappropriated lists. In *Jet Spray, Inc. v. Crampton,* the court stated that the plaintiff may not recover both his own lost profits and those of the defendant.[49] This makes sense since for any given sale, we may be talking about the same sale and, but for the misappropriation, the sales would not have been made twice (although a given customer could be sold to more than once). The defendant may try to prove that the plaintiff would not have made the particular sales that the defendant made.[50] The burden of proof for this is on the defendant. In *Michel Cosmetics v. Tsirklas,* the court considered the trend in the plaintiff's sales and noted that its revenues and profits did not fall after the misappropriation. The court further noted that the sales were not even made in the plaintiff's territory.

One factor that needs to be considered in lost customer cases is the length of the projection. For longer term projections, the rate of customer attrition should be considered. The attrition rate and average customer duration was discussed in Chapter 5.

---

[46] See note 44, 52-40.

[47] *Carter Products, Inc. v. Colgate Palmolive Company,* 214 F. Supp. 383 (D. Md 1963).

[48] *University Computing Co. v. Lykes-Youngston Corp.* 504 F. 2d 518, 535 (5th Cir. 1974).

[49] *Jet Spray Cooler, Inc. v. Crampton,* 385 N.E. 2d, 1356.

[50] *Michel Cosmetics v. Tsirkas,* 282 N.Y. 195, 26 N.E. 2d (1940).

SUMMARY

Four different categories of intellectual property exist: patents, copyrights, trademarks, and trade secrets.

Patents are a grant of a property right by the Patent and Trademark Office of the U.S. government which give the patent holder the right to exclude others from using the patent for certain specific periods of time. Patents afford protection for 17 years in the case of utility or plant patents whereas design patents last 14 years. A copyright protects the expression of an idea such as a literary or musical work. Copyright protection last for 75 years after the date of publication or 100 years after the date of creation. Trademarks are used to certify the authenticity of a product which, in turn, comes with the expectation on the part of a consumer of the quality of the product or services. A similar concept is trade dress, which refers to the physical features of the product that have become known in the marketplace to be associated with a particular marketer of that product.

Two different types of infringement can exist: direct and contributory infringement. Direct infringement refers to the unauthorized use of a patented item; contributory infringement refers to facilitating others to engage in unauthorized use. Two types of damages can be awarded for patent infringement: lost profits or reasonable royalties. As with other types of commercial damages, lost profits must be measured within a reasonable degree of certainty. Certain factors, called *Panduit* factors, have been set forth by the courts as items that may be taken into account when attempting to measure lost profits. Reasonable royalties are used when lost profits cannot be measured within a reasonable certainty. A series of 15 factors have been set forth by the courts as warranting consideration when determining a reasonable royalty.

Lost profits for copyright infringement must also be measured within a reasonable degree of economic certainty. If the copyright owner is not able to measure such losses, then she may be entitled to statutory damages. A copyright owner may be entitled to receive the infringer's profits. In making this computation the plaintiff need only prove the infringer's revenues and then the burden shifts to the defendant to prove the costs associated with these revenues.

Trademark owners may also be entitled to damages, which may be based upon a royalty or could be focused on the infringer's profits. Other economic issues which the damages expert may have to focus on include possible damage to the reputation caused by the infringer as well as possible corrective advertising.

Trade secrets can come in a variety of forms including data compilations, formulas, recipes or research findings, and test results. Damages can arise from a variety of possible factors such as diverted sales or cost advantages.

Much of the methodology that has been developed in the overall damages framework set forth in chapters 1 through 5 can be applied to measuring damages in intellectual property litigation. However, the area does provide some interesting variants such as measuring the defendant's profits in addition to just focusing on the lost profits of the plaintiff. The expert should review some of the major cases as the case law is different than the body of other commercial damages case law. However, the skills and expertise of the damages expert is not appreciably different except that the expert should be familiar with the area and the relevant issues that the expert will be called on to analyze.

REFERENCES

Aiten v. Empire Construction Co., 542 F. Supp 252 (D. Neb. 1982).

Bandag, Inc. v. Gerrand Tire Co., 704 F.2d 1578, 1583 (Fed. Cir. 1983).

Carter Products, Inc. v. Colgate Palmolive Company, 214 F. Supp. 383 (D. Md 1963).

Deltak v. Advanced Systems, Inc., 574 F. Supp. 400 (N.D. Ill. 1983).

Donsco, Inc. v. Casper Corporation, 205 U.S.P.Q. 246, 248 (E.D. Pa. 1980).

Evans, Elizabeth A., Martha S. Samuelson, and Robert A. Sherwin, "Economic Analysis of Intellectual Property Rights," in *Litigation Support Handbook,* 2nd ed. (New York: Wiley 1995).

Fonar Co. v. General Electric Co., 902 F. Supp. 330, 351 (E.D.N.Y. 1995).

Georgia Pacific Corporation v. United States Plywood-Champion Papers, Inc., 446 F. 2d 295 (2d Cir. 1971).

Gibson, Peyton R., "Infringement of Patents and Related Technology," in *Commercial Damages: A Guide to Remedies in Business Litigation,* Charles L. Knapp ed. (New York: Matthew Bender, 1997).

Gyromat Corporation v. Champion Spark Plug, 735 F.2d 5489, 552 (Fed. Cir. 1984).

Hansen v. Alpine Ski Area, Inc., 718 F. 2d 1075, 1078, (Fed. Cir. 1983).

Hartness International, Inc. v. Simplimatic Engineering Company, 819 F. 2d 1100, 1112 (Fed. Cir. 1987).

Herbert, Michael J., and William F. Johnson, "Improper Use of Trade Secrets and Customer Lists," in *Commercial Damages: A Guide to Remedies in Business Litigation,* Charles L. Knapp ed. (New York: Matthew Bender, 1997).

H. K. Porter v. Goodyear Tire & Rubber Co., 536 F. 2d 1115, 191 USPQ 486 (6th Cir. 1976).

Hirshleifer, Jack, and David Hirshleifer, *Price Theory and Its Applications,* 6th ed. (Upper Saddle River, N.J.: Prentice Hall, 1998).

Horwitz, Ethan, "Improper Use of Trademarks and Trade Names," in *Commercial Damages: A Guide to Remedies in Business Litigation,* Charles L. Knapp ed. (New York: Matthew Bender, 1997).

In re Owens-Illinois Fibreglass Corp., 774 F 2d 1116 (Fed Cir. 1985).

Jet Spray Cooler, Inc. v. Crampton, 385 N.E. 2d, 1356.

Julien v. Gomez & Andre Tractor Repairs, Inc, 512 F. Supp. 955, 959 (M.D. La. 1981).

Kaufman Co. v. Lantech, Inc. 926 F. 2d 1136 (Fed cir. 1991).

Landes, William M., and Richard A. Posner, "An Economic Analysis of Copyright Law," *Journal of Legal Studies,* 18, June 1989.

Landes, William M., and Richard A. Posner, "Trademark Law: An Economic Perspective," *Journal of Law and Economics* 30 (2), October 1987.

Lawrence of London, Ltd v. Count Romi, Ltd, 159 U.S.P.Q. 383 (N.Y. App. 1968).

Levy, Ira Jay, and Paul S. Owen, "Infringement of Copyright and Literary Property," in *Commercial Damages: A Guide to Remedies in Business Litigation,* Charles L. Knapp, ed. (New York: Matthew Bender & Co. 1997).

Maltina Corporation v. Cawy Bottling Company, 613 F. 2d 582 (5th Cir. 1980).

Michel Cosmetics v. Tsirkas, 282 N.Y. 195, 26 N.E. 2d (1940).

Monsanto Chemical Company v. Perfect Fit Product Manufacturing Company, 349 F. 2d 389 (2d Cir. 1965) *cert denied,* 383 U.S. 942 (1966).

National Bank of Commerce v. Shaklee Corporation, 503 F. Supp. 533, 207 U.S.P.Q. 1005 (W.D. Tex. 1980).

Panduit Corp. v. Stahlin Brothers Fibre Works, Inc., 575 F.2d 1152, 1156 (6th Cir. 1978).

Paper Converting Machinery Co. v. Magna-Graphics Co., 745 F. 2d 11, 22 (Fed. Cir. 1984).

Playboy Entertainment, Inc. v. P.K. Sorren Export Company, 546 F. Supp. 987, 997 (S.D. Fla. 1982).

Plott, Charles R.,"Industrial Organization Theory and Experimental Economics," *Journal of Economic Literature* 28, December 1982.

Polo Fashions, Inc. v. Extra Special Products, Inc., 208 U.S.P.Q. 421, 428 (S.D.N.Y. 1980).

Rite Hite Corp. v. Kelly Co., 56 F. 3d 1538, 1544 (Fed. Cir. 1995).

Samuels, Jeffrey and Linda B. Samuels, "Contributory Infringement: Relief for the Patent Owner," *The Corporation Law Review,* 1981.

S. C. Johnson & Son, Inc. v. Drop Dead Company, 144 U.S.P.Q. 257, 260 (S.D.Cal. 1965).

Shubik, M., "Information, Duopoly and Competitive Markets: A Sensitivity Analysis," *Kyklos* 26 (1973).

Smith Int'l. Inc. v. Hughes Tool Co., 718 F. 2d 1573, 1581 U.S.P.Q. 686 (Fed Cir. 1983) *cert denied,* 464 U.S. 966 (1983).

Stevens Linen Associates, Inc. v. Mastercraft Corporation, 656 F 2d. 11 (2d Cir. 1981).

Taylor v. Meirick, 712 F.2d 1112 (7th Cir. 1983).

Trio Process Corp. v. L. Goldstein's Sons, Inc., 612 F. 2d 1353, 204 USPQ 881 (3rd Cir. 1980) *cert denied,* 449 U.S. 827 (1980).

University Computing Co. v. Lykes-Youngston Corp., 504 F. 2d 518, 535 (5th Cir. 1974).

10

SECURITIES DAMAGES

Damages can occur in various different forms in securities litigation. They are:

- Fraud on the market
- Mergers-related damages
- Churning and broker portfolio mismanagement

This chapter discusses some of the major areas in which experts may provide testimony on damage claims in these various forms of securities litigation.

FRAUD ON THE MARKET

Fraud on the market refers to the sale of securities pursuant to some material misrepresentation which investors may or may not have relied upon. It is an example of a violation of Rule 10(b)5 of the Securities Exchange Act of 1934. One of the most common ways that this fraud occurs is when an insurer has released financial information that creates an overly optimistic picture of the company's financial condition. For example, a company may have inflated its profits by releasing inaccurate financial data, perhaps in the form of overstated revenues or understated costs. Other examples of a fraud on the market can come from misleading or inaccurate statements about events that would affect the stock price. An example would be a denial of merger negotiations while such negotiations were actually taking place. This is actually what occurred in one of the most famous securities fraud cases, *Basic, Inc. v. Levinson.*

In *Basic, Inc. v. Levinson,* representatives of Basic, Inc. denied in public statements that merger negotiations were ongoing. However, starting in the fall of 1976, representatives of Basic, Inc. had active discussions with Combustion Engineering, Inc. regarding the possibility of a merger. In December 1978, some in-

vestors were then surprised to learn that Basic, Inc.'s board of directors approved
a merger with Combustion Engineering.

It was argued that had such a disclosure been made, the common stock price
would have traded at a higher level, because in an acquisitions target shareholders received a premium above the stock's price.[1] Shareholders who sold their
shares believing that a takeover premium was not forthcoming may have incurred damages by selling their holdings at a lower price.

In its ruling, the court in *Basic, Inc. v. Levinson* endorsed the *efficient markets
hypothesis.*[2] This theory of financial markets considers the speed or efficiency
with which financial markets internalize new information into the prices that securities trade at.[3] There are three versions of the efficient markets hypothesis:
strong form, semistrong form, and weak form. In the strong form all information,
both public and private, is internalized in securities prices. The semistrong version
assumes that the market is efficient with respect to public information only. The
weak form, focuses on one type of public information—prior trends in security
prices—and assumes that the securities prices internalize this particular type of
information. In *Basic, Inc. v. Levinson,* the court endorsed the semistrong version
of the efficient markets hypothesis. In doing so, it assumed that if information on
merger discussions were made known to investors, the market would have incorporated this public information into the price of Basic's common stock. The extent to which markets are considered to be efficient has been one of the most actively researched topics in finance.[4] Much of the research literature in this area
relies on *event studies,* which look at the market's security price reaction to the
dissemination of a particular type of information. For example, studies have
looked at the market's reaction to annual or quarterly earnings reports and other
types of announcements, such as new products or exchange listings. While there
are many studies that support market efficiency, many others challenge some aspect of market efficiency. Several of these challenging studies show that market
anomalies may exist in which investors may persistently enjoy extranormal prof-

---

[1] Patrick A. Gaughan, *Mergers, Acquisitions and Corporate Restructuring* 2nd ed.
(New York: Wiley) 1999.

[2] For a very readable discussion of the efficient markets hypothesis and the related literature see Burton Malkiel, *Random Walk Down Wall Street,* 5th ed. (New York: Norton &
Co.) 1995.

[3] Eugene F. Fama, *The Theory of Finance* (New York: Holt, Rinehard and Winston,
1972) and Eugene F. Fama, "Efficient Capital Markets II," *Journal of Finance* 46 (5), December 1991, 1575–1617.

[4] Frank K. Rielly, *Investment Analysis and Portfolio Management* (Fort Worth, Tex.:
Dryden Press) 1994, 194–239.

its based on the utilization of public information. One such example is the *turn-of-the-year effect* or *January anomaly* where it has been shown that tax-loss motivated trading can allow investors to realize above-normal profits during the month of January.[5] Other often-cited market anomalies are the *size effect* and *neglected firm effect* in which smaller firms or companies that are not as closely followed by investors and stock analysts can be a source of above-normal gains.[6]

Disgorgement

In Securities and Exchange Commission enforcement actions, if found guilty, the defendant may be required to disgorge the ill gotten gains so that he does not become unjustly enriched by the illegal activities. This precedent was established in the *Texas Gulf Sulphur* cases in which various employees of *Texas Gulf Sulphur* purchased stock and call options in the company prior to an announcement of a major mining discovery.[7] In these cases, the courts required the defendants to disgorge their profits. The amount to be disgorged can be the actual profits that the defendant enjoyed or what is referred to as *paper profits,* which may be defined as the difference between what the defendant paid for the shares and the value that the court may assess. This value may be determined by relevant stock price data around the time of the event. In the case of positive information that a defendant may have been trading on prior to the release of that information to the public, the paper profits may be the difference between the price paid for the shares prior to the public announcement and the *full information price.* The full information price is determined by judgment based on the time that market has finished reacting to the new information. Paper profits can clearly be different from actual profits. If the illegal trader sold at the full information price the two might be the same. However, if the trader held on to the shares and other factors

---

[5] Ben Branch, "A Tax Loss Trading Rule," *Journal of Business* 50 (2) April 1977, 198–207; Donald B. Keim, "Size Related Anamolies and Stock Return Seasonality," *Journal of Financial Economics* 12 (1) June 1983, 13–32.

[6] R.W. Banz, "The Relationship Between Return and Market Value of Common Stocks," *Journal of Financial Economics* 9 (1) March 1981, 3–18; Marc R. Reinganum, "Misspecification of Capital Asset Pricing: Empirical Anomalies Based On Earnings Yield and Market Values," *Journal of Financial Economics* 9 (1) March 1981, 19–46. S. Basu, "The Relationship Between Earnings Yield, Market Value and Return to NYSE Common Stocks," *Journal of Financial Economics* 12 (1) June 1983, 129–156.

[7] *SEC v. Texas Gulf Sulphur Co.,* 401 F. 2d 1301 (2nd Cir.), *cert denied,* 404 U.S. 1005 (1971).

caused the stock price to move to another level, the actual profits will vary and will be determined at time of sale. If the trader holds on to the shares and other factors cause the stock price to fall below the purchase price and he then sells the shares, there could be a situation where he is forced to disgorge positive paper profits when his overall trading in the stock actually resulted in losses.

Measuring Out-of-Pocket Damages

The most common method of measuring damages for fraud on the market is an out-of-pocket measure of damages.[8] This measure draws on the reasoning of Judge Sneed in *Green v. Occidental Petroleum Corp.*[9] Judge Sneed set forth an acceptable way of measuring such damages as the difference between what he called the *price line* and the *value line*. The price line reflects the "corporate defendant's wrongful conduct." In a case involving inflation of corporate profitability, this would be the stock price that was a function of the exaggerated income. The value line would be the stock's price in the absence of exaggerated prices. This difference is depicted in Figure 10.1, where the shaded area shows the magnitude of the damages that may have been incurred by investors. The two curves, called lines by the court, start off at the same point. It is assumed that t_i is the date when the misrepresentation occurred. At this time it is assumed that an overly optimistic picture of the company's performance is portrayed, thus causing the market price, as reflected by the price line, to be above what its true value would have been, absent the misrepresentation.

Establishing the Loss Period
The loss period usually begins with the date when the inaccurate information was released to the market. It usually ends with the date of disclosure.[10] If one assumes that markets are very efficient, then the time period narrowly focuses on these two dates. If, however, markets are not assumed to be very efficient, then the loss period becomes less clearly centered on these dates.

The establishment of the loss period may not be that clear cut. It is often not the case that there is one improper announcement or material misrepresentation.

---

[8] Bradford Cornell and R. Gregory Morgan, "Using Finance Theory to Measure Damages in Fraud on the Market Cases," *UCLA Law Review* 37, June 1990, 883–924.

[9] *Green v. Occidental Petroleum Corp.*, 541 F. 2d 1335.

[10] This statement is very broad. Obviously, the facts of each case determine the true loss period and the measure of damages.

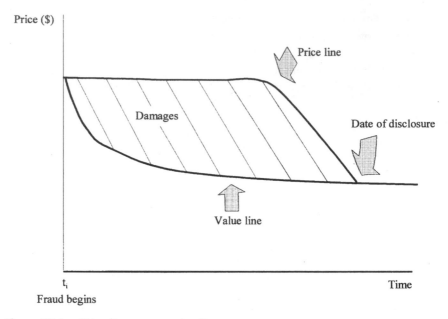

Figure 10.1.   Price line versus value line.

Rather, there is often a series of such false statements. This situation requires the expert to make a judgment as to the correct start of the loss period. This judgment may be made more difficult when there is a series of improper statements or misrepresentation as the expert must make a determination of when the inflating effects on the market began. The end of the loss period may also be unclear. The issuer may make a series of statements that address the initial misrepresentation, which may cause the market to correct in a series of steps. Or, it could cause the market to overreact by thinking that the misrepresentation was greater than what actually was the case.

Measuring Damages

The measurement of out-of-pocket damages is the difference between the price line and the value line times the number of securities in question. The major challenge here is to calculate the value line, which can be computed in different ways. One is to arithmetically reconstruct what the stock price should have been during the loss period. This method examines the percent change in the stock prices of various other comparable companies. This can be done using basic percentages or by employing regression analysis. Another method is the *Compara-*

ble Index Approach, which attempts to predict the security's return using explanatory variables such as the market return and the industry return.

Security and Market Returns

The percentage return of security is defined as the combined effects of the income that is received, such as the dividends from a share of stock, and the price changes of the securities reflected in the form of capital gains or losses. This percentage return has two components: the dividend yield and the capital gains return. The dividend yield is the component of the return that is attributable to the dividend income.[11] This can be expressed as follows:

$$\text{Dividend Yield} = D_{t+1}/P_t \qquad (10.1)$$

where P_t = stock price at time t
   D_{t-1} = dividend paid in time period $t + 1$

The component of the total return attributable to the security's price movements is the capital gains return. This is expressed as follows:

$$\text{Capital Gains Yield} = (P_{t+1} - P_t)/P_t \qquad (10.2)$$

Both components of a security's return can be combined to form the percentage return of the security, as shown in Equation (10.3).

$$R_t = \frac{\begin{array}{c}\text{Dividends paid} \\ \text{during the period}\end{array} + \begin{array}{c}\text{Change in the market} \\ \text{value of the security}\end{array}}{\text{Value of the security at the beginning of the period}} \qquad (10.3)$$

The return on the market can be computed in a similar manner using an accepted market proxy such as the Standard & Poor's 500 composite market index, a market index that uses the market value of 500 securities to measure the performance of the market.

Comparable Index Approach

The Comparable Index method uses econometric methods to estimate the relationship between a security's return and the return on the market and the indus-

---

[11] For a discussion of the computation of returns see Stephen Ross, Randolph Westerfield and Bradford D. Jordan, *Fundamentals of Corporate Finance,* 2nd ed. (Homewood, Ill.: Richard D. Irwin) 1993, 333–365.

try. The relationship is estimated and then used to compute the security's "value," which is then compared to the security's actual price. In order to estimate the relationship, historical return data are gathered for the security, the industry, and the market. This period should exclude the alleged fraud so that the estimated relationship is not tainted by the events in question. The decision of the proper period to use will affect the value of the coefficients $\alpha_0 \ldots \alpha_2$ that are estimated. The estimated function is of the form shown in Equation (10.4).

$$R_{it} = \alpha_0 + \alpha_1 R_{Mt} + \alpha_2 R_{It} \qquad (10.4)$$

where R_{it} = the return on security i at time t
           R_{Mt} = the return on the market at time t
           R_{It} = the return on the industry at time t

The difference between the estimated value and the actual price is sometimes referred to as the damage ribbon or simply inflation. This gap reflects the damages incurred by investors. The relationship between a hypothetical price and value line was depicted graphically in Figure 10.1.

Example of the Comparable Index Approach

Let us assume that historical data have been used to estimate the following equation:

$$R_{it} = .005 + .70R_{mt} + .30R_{It} \qquad (10.5)$$

The relationship is applied to the historical market and industry return data to compute the predicted return shown in Table 10.1. It is assumed that the security's value and its price are equal as of the full disclosure date. The value absent the fraud is then computed backward from the full disclosure date using the predicted return as follows:

$$\text{Security Value}_{t-1} = \text{Security Value}_t / (1 + \text{Predicted Return}_{t-1}) \quad (10.6)$$

Once the security value has been computed, the difference between the "but for" value and the actual price can then be computed.

In this example we assume that the expert is trying to determine a security's value during a ten-day trading period prior to estimate the value line for a nine-day period through day ten. Let us assume that the expert has done some research that shows that the security return can be explained by a combination of the market return and the industry return. Further assume that this research has resulted in the estimation of Equation (10.5).

Table 10.1. Example of Computation of Security Price versus Security Value
(Security Return = .005 + .70 (Mkt Return) + .30 (Industry Return))

Day	Market Return (%)	Industry Return (%)	Predicted Security Return (%)	Security Price	Security Value
1	3.10	2.75	3.50	130.00	89.03
2	-5.00	-2.50	-3.75	135.00	92.14
3	2.50	1.50	2.70	140.00	88.68
4	1.30	5.00	2.91	125.00	91.08
5	-2.00	1.50	-0.45	123.00	93.73
6	-1.50	-2.50	-1.30	119.00	93.31
7	3.20	2.50	3.49	123.00	92.09
8	4.00	3.00	4.20	105.00	95.31
9	-0.15	1.00	0.70	103.00	99.31
10				100.00	100.00

Using this equation we can derive the predicted return for each day. The predicted return is then used to retrospectively estimate the value line. For example, the 0.70% daily return in day nine is "backed out" of the $100 stock price to result in a $99.31 stock value. This value can then be compared to the actual stock price of $103 to result in a daily stock inflation of $103 − $99.31 or $3.69. The stock value for the days prior to day nine can be estimated in a similar manner, as shown in Table 10.1.

Criticism of the Comparable Index Approach

As with any approach that relies on econometric analysis to estimate the best relationship among variables, there are often some disagreements as to whether the expert's estimated relationship is the most accurate one. Some contend that the estimate is made more accurate if more explanatory variables, such as more than one index, are added to the model.[12]

Event Study Approach

The event study approach draws on a methodology that has been extensively used in academia when conducting research on the impact of specific events on shareholder returns. The methodology is an application of econometric analysis

---

[12] William Beaver and James K. Malernee, "Estimating Damages in Securities Fraud Cases," Cornerstone Research, 1990.

to securities markets in a manner that allows the analyst to measure the impact of a particular event on the price and return of a security.[13] The technique was developed jointly by Eugene Fama, Franklin Fisher, Michael Jensen, and Richard Roll.[14] The model itself has come to be known as the FFJR model after its developers. Its application has led to extensive analysis of the effect of a variety of events, such as earnings and new product announcements on shareholder returns. Abundant research was conducted using this model in the 1970s and 1980s to test the efficiency of securities markets.

The event study methodology allows the user to filter out the influence of market forces by constructing a regression model, which includes, as an explanatory variable, market returns. In doing so a security's return is regressed against the market returns. Equation (10.7) shows the mathematical expression of this relationship in what is known as the *market model.*

$$R_{it} = \alpha_i + \beta_i R_{mt} + \varepsilon i \tag{10.7}$$

where α_i = the intercept term of the market model

β_i = security *i*'s beta. Betas measure a security's sensitivity to market returns.

ε_{it} = the model's deviations at time *t*

Figure 10.2 shows a graph of a hypothetical security's return against the market's return which might be measured as the rate of return of some market index such as the Standard & Poor's 500. The graph shows that there is a linear relationship between a security's return and the market's return. The event study methodology uses this relationship, just as the comparable index method utilized it, to compute what the security's return would have been had it not been for the "event" that is the subject of the litigation. However, the event study model computes the relationship between the security's return and the market return to prior to the event and uses the mathematical relationship to forecast the "but for" return of the security. This return can then be compared with the actual postevent return to measure the excess return of the security. This excess return, in the absence of other explanatory factors, can then be used to measure the magnitude of the loss.

---

[13] See A. Craig McKinlay, "Event Studies in Economics and Finance," *Journal of Economics Literature* 35, March 1997, 13–39.

[14] E. F Fama, L. Fisher, M. Jensen, and R. Roll. "The Adjustment of Stock Prices to New Information," *International Economic Review* 10 (1) February 1969, 1–21.

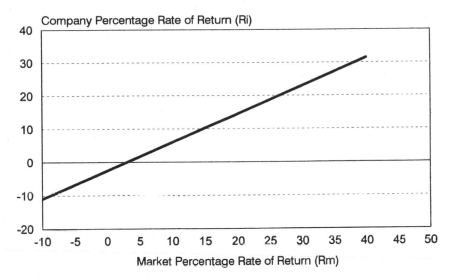

Figure 10.2. Security's return versus market's return.

Abnormal Returns of the Event Study Methodology

The market model allows for the separation of the total return of a security into systematic and unsystematic components. The systematic component is the part that can be explained by the market's return—$\alpha_i + \beta_i R_{mt}$. According to the market model, the part that cannot be explained by the market's influences is attributed to firm-specific effects and is statistically subsumed with the "remainder factor" in the market model's equation—ε_{it}. That is, ε_{it} captures the variety of firm-specific factors including those that are the subject of the litigation—the alleged fraudulently inflated profits of the prior example. The impact of ε_{it} can be more readily discerned by arranging Equation (10.7) as follows:

$$\varepsilon_{it} = R_{it} - (\alpha_i + \beta_i R_{mt}) \qquad (10.8)$$

The historical data on R_{it} and R_{mt} for the period prior to the event in question, which is taken to be $t = 0$, are used to econometrically estimate α and β. The value of these two parameters are then used to compute a predicted return R_{it} and its resulting deviation ε'_{it} which can then be compared to ε_{it}. This latter value represents the deviation of the actual return, inclusive of the effects of the fraudulent behavior, from the predicted return as measured using the market model's estimated parameters α and β. This discussion is sometimes also expressed through the estimation of abnormal returns where abnormal returns are equal to:

$$AR_{it} = R_{it} - \alpha'_i + \beta'_i R_{mt} \qquad\qquad (10.9)$$

where AR_{it} = abnormal returns
$\quad\alpha'_i$ = the estimated alpha
$\quad\beta'_i$ = the estimate of beta

Example of a One-Period Abnormal Return

As an example of a one-period abnormal return, assume that:

$$R_{it} = -9.5\%$$
$$\alpha'_i = -0.15\%$$
$$\beta'_i = 1.40$$
$$R_{mt} = -3.5\%$$

The one-period abnormal return is simply:

$$AR_{it} = -9.5\% - 0.15\% - (1.40 \times -3.5)$$
$$= -4.75\%$$

The abnormal returns computed applies to just one period, i, which may be one day. When the event window being studied is longer, then we need to compute the cumulative abnormal returns, CAR, which is basically a running total of the one-period abnormal returns for the length of the study period. This is mathematically expressed as follows:

$$CAR_T = \prod_{t=1}^{T}(1 + AR_i) - 1 \qquad\qquad (10.10)$$

where T equals the length of the study window. When we compute CAR_T we have a measure of the total impact of the event.

Examining the Variation in Abnormal Returns

Once the security's return has been computed, it may then be useful to examine the variability in the return. In analyzing the variation in a security's return, it may be useful to compute the standard deviation of the return. A security's return does not stay constant but normally varies. One simplifying assumption that is made is to assume that the variation fits a pattern that would be expected if the return were normally distributed. While not perfect, the assumption of normality is commonly made in event studies.[15] The standard deviation of a security's returns can be computed as follows:[16]

$$s = \sqrt{\frac{\sum(R_i - R)^2}{N - 1}} \qquad (10.11)$$

where R equals the mean or average return over the sample period.

The standard deviation can then be used to test the statistical significance of the variation in a return. Using the assumption of a normal distribution, we expect that 68% of the returns will lie within one standard deviation of the mean. Ninety-five percent of the deviations will lie within two standard deviations, while 99.7% will be within three standard deviations. We can take the standard deviations that we have computed to arrive at a Z statistic, which can be applied to a standard normal distribution table that is in every statistics textbook. It is computed as follows:

Z statistic = (actual return value − mean return value)/standard deviation

$$(10.12)$$

Therefore, for each return or abnormal return, we can use the mean and standard deviation to compute that return's Z statistic. This statistic can then be used to determine how likely it is that a given observed return is a certain number of standard deviations from its mean by sheer chance. Given that the average daily return is close to zero for larger capitalization stocks, the application of the Z statistic is tantamount to computing the probability that a given return is different from zero.[17]

Decision Rules in Assessing the Significance of a Particular Return Value

The Z test statistic discussed previously can be used to assess whether a particular return value is as high or low as it is by chance or due to some nonrandom

---

[15] Stephen J. Brown and Jerold B. Warner, "Using Daily Stock Returns: The Case of Event Studies," *Journal of Financial Economics* 14 (1) March 1985, 3–32.

[16] Cheng F. Lee, *Statistics for Business and Financial Economics* (Lexington, Mass.: D.C. Heath) 1993, 98–127.

[17] Johnathan R. Macy and Geoffrey P. Miller, "Lessons From Financial Economics: Materiality, Reliance and the Extended Reach of *Basic v. Levinson, Virginia Law Review* 77, 1991, 1017, 1020.

event. In statistics, this is phrased as saying that the null hypothesis is that the return value is different from some other value by sheer chance. Differences from this selected value, in this case the average daily return of the security, that are so large that they are above a certain threshold value, are then determined to be too large to be a function of normal random movements of the market and must have been caused by some nonrandom process.

A common standard is to use a 5% rule which is, in turn, based on the normal distribution. This rule states that if a certain value is 1.96 standard deviations from the mean (above or below—that is, in absolute value), there is only a 5% chance that such a difference is caused by chance. We can make the decision rule even more stringent by going to a 1% standard, which equates to 2.58 standard deviations, in absolute value, from the mean. We could also relax the decision rule to move to a 10% level of significance, which correspond to 1.65 standard deviations from the mean.

Using an Event Study in a Insider Trading Case

Mark Mitchell and Jeffery Netter, both academic financial economists who were in the employ of the Securities and Exchange Commission, reported the results of an interesting event study analysis in the case of an executive recruiter who was accused of using information he acquired in the search process.[18] The recruiter used the knowledge that the candidate his firm had recommended for the position of chief executive officer of a small fiber optics telecommunication company, Artel Communications, would be appointed to that position on a given day to trade in that stock. On the day he received the insider information, February 9, 1987, the president of the executive search firm purchased 23,500 shares of Artel stock for approximately $72,000, which translates to an average price of $3.06 per share. The purchase was made one day before the announcement of the appointment. Two years after the illegal trades, in April 1989, the SEC charged the president of the management recruiting firm with insider trading.

While managerial appointments tend not to cause as dramatic stock price movements as other important events, such as new product announcements or impressive earnings reports, some research shows relatively small positive stock price effects from these managerial changes.[19] Mitchell and Netter's table, repro-

---

[18] Mark Mitchell and Jeffrey Netter, "The Role of Financial Economics in Securities Fraud cases: Applications at the Securities and Exchange Commission," *Business Lawyer* 2 (2) February 1994, 545–590.

[19] Eugene P.H. Furtado and Vijay Karan, "Causes, Consequences and Shareholder Wealth Effects of Management Turnover: A Review of the Empirical Evidence," *Financial Management* 19, 1990, 60.

Table 10.2. Stock Price Performance for Artel Communications Surrounding the Announcement of Robert Bowman as Chief Executive Officer on 2/10/1987

Date	Artel Price ($)	Artel Volume	Abnormal Return (%)	Z Statistic	Cumulative Abnormal Return (%)	Z Statistic
Feb. 4	2.250	10,100	−6.22	−1.12	−6.22	−1.12
Feb. 5	2.250	4,400	−0.41	−0.07	−6.61	−0.84
Feb. 6	2.250	1,600	0.56	0.10	−6.08	−0.63
Feb. 9	3.250	72,000	45.38	8.20	36.54	3.30
Feb. 10	3.875	68,100	20.53	3.70	64.56	5.22
Feb. 11	3.750	65,200	−3.73	−0.67	58.43	4.31
Feb. 12	3.625	16,300	−2.50	−0.45	54.47	3.72
Feb. 13	3.750	6,800	2.47	0.44	58.28	3.72
Feb. 17	3.750	25,600	−1.39	−0.25	56.09	3.38
Feb. 18	4.500	57,000	20.25	3.67	87.70	5.01
Feb. 19	4.500	23,500	0.17	0.03	88.02	4.79
Feb. 20	4.625	23,600	3.09	0.56	93.83	4.89
Feb. 23	4.250	7,300	−6.92	−1.25	80.42	4.03
Feb. 24	4.250	7,900	0.17	0.03	80.72	3.90
Feb. 25	3.625	24,700	−14.74	−2.67	54.08	2.52
Feb. 26	3.625	6,200	0.61	0.11	55.02	2.49
Feb. 27	3.500	6,200	−3.50	−0.63	49.59	2.17

Source: Mark I. Mitchell and Jeffery M. Netter, "The Role of Financial Economics in Securities Fraud Cases: Applications at the Securities and Exchange Commission," *The Business Lawyer* 49 (2), February 1994, 545–590.
Notes: Returns are expressed in percents. Stock price data is from Center for Research in Security Prices (CRSP) at the University of Chicago. Marked model estimation period is Feb. 4, 1986 through Feb. 3, 1987. Market proxy is CRSP value-weighted index of NYSE, AMEX, and NASDAQ stocks. Beta estimate for Artel Communications is 0.96.

duced here as Table 10.2, shows that the stock price rose sharply the day before and the day of the announcement. They computed abnormal daily returns of 45.38% and 20.53% respectively on these days. The table also shows that trading volume in this relatively thinly traded security was substantially higher during the three-day period starting with one day before and ending one day after the announcement.

Having established that the research studies in the field show that the announcement of an executive appointment can show positive returns, Mitchell and Netter then set about to show that the stock price movement and related change in stock return, was abnormal given the stock price history of this particular company. They computed the standard deviation in the stock price return over a one-year period prior to the event and found it to be 5.57%. Movement of at least two standard deviations, approximately 11%, would allow the researcher to conclude within a 95% level of assurance, that the price movements were unusual and not the product of normal fluctuations in this relatively more volatile stock. They concluded that the abnormal returns during the announcement period were highly statistically significant.

Table 10.2 shows that the stock price remaining at the "announcement level" until news was related in a trade publications that the new CEO would also remain on the board of directors of his former employer, where he was chairman. The article cited certain synergies that might be expected through future dealing between the two companies in the same industry. The stock price remained at that level until a negative quarterly earnings report was released toward the end of February.

The court heard arguments on the magnitude of any disgorgement that would be required. This was ironic in light of the fact that the defendant had actually incurred losses equal to about $17,000 on this investment due to the fact that he held on to the shares for approximately two more years when he sold them at approximately $2 per share. In order to compute the disgorgement amount one needs to compute the *full information price,* the stock price as of the date that the complete effect of the relevant information, the hiring of the new CEO, was internalized into the stock price.

In court, both sides argued about which date should be taken as the one from which to draw the full information price. The defense argued that it was the day after the announcement. The government argued that it extended to February 18, when the story came out about the new CEO remaining as director of his prior employer based on the assumption that he may have also had information about this fact. The court accepted this latter day, and its full information price of $4.50 per share as opposed to $3.75 per share on February 11th. The difference between the purchase price and the full information price, less adjustments for commissions and the bid-asked spread, resulted in a computed disgorgement of $24,663.

Using an Enhanced Market Model

In the Comparable Index model we explicitly included *both* market and industry effects as explanatory factors to come up with a predicted return. This approach has an advantage over the basic market model in that there may be important factors unique to the industry that cannot be captured by the market's variation. These factors can be econometrically filtered by the direct inclusion of an industry return as a separate explanatory variable. This situation is shown in Equation (10.13).

$$R_{it} = \alpha_i + \beta_i R_{Mt} + \beta_j R_{It} + \varepsilon_{it} \qquad (10.13)$$

where β_j = the coefficient of the industry index
R_{It} = the industry index return

The more important industry factors are in explaining the variation in the firm's return, the more important it is to use the industry-enhanced market model. Not doing so can lead to the erroneous conclusion that all of the variation between the predicted and actual return is explained by firm-specific factors including the alleged fraudulent behavior. Including the industry return variable allows us to filter out industry influences and helps better isolate the firm-specific factor factors.

Factors to be Considered in Applying the Event Study Methodology

In using the events study methodology, a number of factors have to be considered. These factors can affect the usefulness of this approach as a tool in measuring damage. One of the most fundamental of these is the availability of the necessary data. Another is the presence of confounding events that may skew the results. Still another is the time period that becomes the event window.

Data Availability

The event study approach works best when there is an abundant history of return data. Having ample return data enhances the statistical reliability of the forecasted "but for" projected return line. When this history is limited, the statistical reliability of the forecasted line may be low, as reflected by relatively high "standard errors," which are a statistical measure of the confidence that one can have that the line lies within a certain range of values above and below the line. The fewer the data points, the wider this range is and the lower statistical reliability of the forecasted values. Moreover, the fewer the data points, the less confidence one can have in the values that are forecasted further into the future. The more data points the further into the future one can confidently project the "but for" return line.

The data availability problem is one of the reasons why it is more difficult to use the event study approach in markets for thinly traded securities. Thinly traded securities are those that have limited trading volume and thus a more sparse data point history. More obscure equities or certain bonds may fall in this category. In contrast, securities traded in more active markets, such as equities that are traded on NASDAQ (National Association of Securities Dealers Automated Quotations) or the major exchanges such as the American and New York Stock Exchanges, are often good candidates for an event study.

Sources of Return Data

Abnormal returns are defined as the ex-post return of the company's securities minus a normal return. Returns data are available from the University of Chicago Center for Security Prices Research database, called the CRSP database. Many universities and some firms subscribe to this database as it is often used in a variety of empirical research studies. When using the CRSP database, one may want to use as a measure of market performance a value-weighted CRSP index of all New York Stock Exchange, American Stock Exchange, and NASDAQ stocks for the market proxy.

Existence of Confounding Events

The event study methodology is easiest to apply when the event in question can be readily isolated and when there are not other events occurring at the same time. In particular, other confounding firm-specific events can make the isolation of the event in question more problematic. For example, in the case of a release of fraudulently inflated earnings information, the task of isolating the impact of this information on the security's return is made more difficult when it occurs at approximately the same time as the company announces the hiring of potentially important members of the management or issues a press release about new product developments. The expert needs to determine whether the security's return increased solely due to fraudulent earnings or did other factors that also might have had an uplifting effect on the security's return cause all or part of the increase. Each case is unique and requires the expert to exercise judgment when considering all relevant information. In the presence of such confounding events, the expert may have to employ more advanced statistical techniques that may enable her to filter out the influence of these confounding factors.

Defining the Event Window

One of the first factors to consider when conducting an event study is to select a time period long enough to include the period covered by the event. Generally, you want to select a time period somewhat longer than the event period so that the returns during the event period can be compared to a period for which the events did not influence the returns. Therefore, you want to include some time before and after the event that are unaffected by the event. For a merger, this should be a period prior to the announcement of the merger and one that is also prior to any improper trading that is the subject of the litigation. In insider trading cases, one needs to identify the dates when the information is used by the illegal trader and the dates when the information reaches the market. Each case is different and requires the expert to use her own judgment to select the proper window. As one can imagine, the window that is selected can be a controversial issue that the plaintiff and defendant may debate, as it can have a significant impact of the amount of monies to be disgorged.

Measuring Damages Per Share

The foregoing discussion presented a model for measuring per-share damages. However, of the number of damaged shares still remains to be explained. Depending on the legal framework of the claims, the number of damaged shares may only include those that traded during the class period. If the number of these shares is known, then the computation becomes a simple one of applying the per-share loss to the number of shares.[20] Unfortunately, it may not be that easy to quantify the exact number of damaged shares and the expert may have to resort to a simplifying process to come up with an estimate of the number of damaged shares. In order to arrive at such an estimate, certain assumptions about the trading behavior of investors needs to be made.

Equal Trading Probability Model

Certain models based on different assumptions about trading behavior have been put forward.[21] These models differ in how they treat the trading behavior of investors. In one version, the *equal trading probability model,* sometimes called the *one-trader model,* it is assumed that shares are only traded one time during the class period. This assumption can lead to a total number of shares traded exceeding the number of shares outstanding. The assumption can be made more realistic by taking into account the fact that shares can be retraded. Under the *one-trader model,* the expert assumes that all shares that enter the class have an equal probability of being traded as a share that has not yet entered the class. This results in the number of shares entering the class being a function of trading volume and the number of remaining shares that are not yet in the class. One of the criticisms of the one-trader model is that it does not differentiate between the types of investors that hold shares in a company. It treats active traders and those who utilize a *buy and hold strategy* the same. This assumption has a significant impact on the damages that result from the use of this model.

Dual-Probability Trading Model

An alternative to the equal probability model is the *dual probability model.* Under the dual probability trading model, sometimes referred to as the *two-trader model,* traders are categorized into two different classes: active traders and traders who utilize a buy and hold strategy. The model requires the expert to assume a certain probability of trading for active traders and inactive traders. The expert may also assume the percent of total shares outstanding held by these two groups of traders. Under this model, shares are retraded among active traders, re-

---

[20] This statement makes the simplifying assumption that the dollar loss is constant throughout the loss period, which may not be the case.

[21] William H. Beaver, James K. Malernee, and Michael C. Keeley, "Stock Trading Behavior and Damage Estimation in Securities Cases," Cornerstone Research, 1993.

sulting in a lower number of shares entering the class. With a lower number of shares in the class, the dual probability trading model results in a lower damage estimate.

The dual probability trading model is more realistic than the equal probability trading model. The latter results in higher losses and thus is more pro-plaintiff. However, the dual probability model is influenced by the different trading probabilities and share percentages assigned to the two groups of traders. The expert may want to draw on research to support these assumptions. One such source of data is depository records which, when combined with trading volume data, may help the expert select the relevant parameters needed to use the dual probability trading model.

Proportional Trading Model

Still another stock trading model is the proportional trading model.[22] In this trading model, the number of shares traded is differentiated from those that were retained. Of the shares traded in the loss period, the model assumes that there is an equal probability that a given share traded on a given day came from a pool of the shares that had already been traded during the loss period and those that were being traded for the first time during the loss period. This assumption is applied on a daily basis throughout the loss period reflecting the retrading of shares, as opposed to shares that enter the class due to being traded for the first time, which is what is assumed in the equal probability model. This differs from the dual probability model in which probabilities that may not be equal are assigned to the two groups of traders.

Impact of the Different Trading Models on the Damage Computation

As we have discussed, measuring the number of damaged shares can be a challenging exercise. One of the ways experts have dealt with this problems has been to incorporate some of the simplifying assumptions embedded in the different trading models that have been discussed. Carleton, Weisbach, and Weiss reported that the total damage amounts can vary very significantly depending on which trading model is used.[23]

---

[22] Dean Furbush and Jeffrey Smith, "Estimating the Number of Shares in Securities Fraud Litigation: An Introduction to Stock Trading Models," *The Business Lawyer* 49 (2) February 1994, 527–543.

[23] Willard T. Carleton, Michael S. Weisbach, and Elliott J. Weiss, "Securities Class Action Lawsuits: A Descriptive Study," *Arizona Law Review,* 1996, 38, 491–511.

Example of Fraud on the Market Computation

In a recent article featuring a case study on measuring an alleged fraud on the market, Edward Dyl demonstrates how losses can be computed.[24] His analysis did not use the market model to estimate the value line but assumed that over a 38-day trading window the value of the stock of Reddi Brake Supply Corporation was the stock price when there was full disclosure. Whether such a simple method of estimating the full disclosure price can be used will depend on the facts of the case. Gross economic damages were measured using Equation (10.14).

$$D_t^g = (P_t - F_t)(V_t)(A_{\text{Nasdaq}}) \qquad (10.14)$$

where D_t^g = gross economic damages

   P_t = stock price on day t

   F_t = full disclosure price

   V_t = raw measure of the number of shares purchased by investors on day t

   A_{Nasdaq} = adjustment factor applied to the raw volume trading values to eliminate intraday trading by dealers

D_t^g measures gross economic damages but the true measure of loss is D_t^n after an adjustment has been made for the fact that some investors who purchased their shares at the start of the loss period may have sold the shares before the end of the loss period. Given that some shares could have been traded several times, an estimate of this trading must be incorporated into the model to adjust D_t^g downward to arrive at D_t^n. The first step in this adjustment process is to compute the daily turnover of shares (T_t). T_t is defined as follows:

$$T_t = (V_t)(A_{\text{Nasdaq}})/S \qquad (10.15)$$

where T_t = the percentage of turnover of shares of the defendant's stock

   S = the number of shares available for trading.

S is also known as the number of float shares. It leaves out the inactive shares that may be held by investors who have a buy and hold strategy such as institu-

---

[24] Edward Dyl, "Estimated Economic Damages in Class Action Securities Fraud Litigation," *Journal of Forensic Economics,* 12 (1) Winter 1999, 1–11.

tional investors.[25] The expert may try to determine what the number of float shares are through publicly available sources. For example, Dyl was able to arrive at an estimate of float shares using investor reports. This information is then used to determine the appropriate adjustment factor A_t which is defined as follows:

$$A_t = \sum_{Z=t+1}^{N} (1 - T_Z) \qquad (10.16)$$

where A_t = the adjustment factor that is applied to the gross economic
damages of day t.

As Table 10.3 shows, A_t is lower at the start of the loss period and increases as we get closer to the end thus reflecting the higher probability that shares purchased closer to the end of the loss period will be held at the end of the period. Dyl shows in Table 10.3 that the total gross economic damages were $14,679,410 while the net economic damages were $11,217,558.

MERGERS-RELATED DAMAGES

Another frequently occurring type of lawsuit involving damages claims related to securities are merger-related suits. These lawsuits became a common occurrence in the 1980s and have continued throughout the 1990s as the pace of mergers reached record highs.

History of Mergers in the United States

The United States is in the midst of another intense period of merger and acquisition activity that gained momentum in 1993. This is the fifth such period, often referred to as *merger waves,* in U.S. economic history.[26] The first started at the turn of the century, with the second occurring in the 1920. The third merger wave occurred at the end of the 1960s. Merger and acquisition activity was relatively

---

[25] Carolyn Brancato and Patrick A. Gaughan, "Institutional Investors and Their Role in Capital Markets," Columbia University School of Law Monograph, 1986.

[26] For a discussion of merger waves see Patrick A. Gaughan, *Mergers, Acquisitions and Corporate Restructuring,* 2nd ed. (New York: Wiley), 1999; and Patrick A. Gaughan, *Mergers and Acquisitions* (New York: Harper Collins) 1990.

Table 10.3. Calculation of Estimated Economic Damages

t	P_t	V_t	D_t	T_t	A_t	D_tA_t
0	4.9375	140,000	95,997.42	0.00786	0.53631	51,484.22
1	5.0000	164,200	117,481.76	0.00919	0.54128	63,591.09
2	5.0313	175,700	128,455.09	0.00984	0.54666	70,221.60
3	5.2188	130,600	107,726.02	0.00731	0.55069	59,323.59
4	5.2813	149,900	128,330.09	0.00839	0.55535	71,268.19
5	5.2500	78,000	65,557.41	0.00437	0.55779	36,567.05
6	5.2500	56,000	47,066.86	0.00314	0.55954	26,335.84
7	5.2500	101,500	85,308.68	0.00568	0.56274	48,006.54
8	5.2500	33,700	28,324.16	0.00189	0.56380	15,969.25
9	5.3125	121,200	105,653.63	0.00679	0.56766	59,974.83
10	5.4375	102,100	95,384.85	0.00572	0.57092	54,457.02
11	6.0000	1,062,400	1,291,325.58	0.05948	0.60703	783,870.68
12	6.1875	560,700	734,085.07	0.03139	0.62670	460,053.12
13	6.0625	312,800	389,977.03	0.01751	0.63787	248,576.39
14	6.0000	119,900	145,736.01	0.00671	0.64219	93,589.58
15	5.9688	177,800	213,334.16	0.00996	0.64864	138,377.72
16	6.1875	294,600	385,699.06	0.01649	0.65952	254,376.95
17	6.1250	204,600	281,474.64	0.01146	0.66716	174,446.65
18	6.0625	223,200	278,270.06	0.01250	0.67561	188,001.46
19	6.0000	123,900	150,597.93	0.00694	0.68033	102,455.92
20	5.8750	124,600	143,661.26	0.00698	0.68511	98,423.37
21	6.0000	306,600	372,666.06	0.01717	0.69707	259,775.73
22	7.0000	1,469,700	2,521,240.44	0.08229	0.75958	1,915,082.76
23	7.0000	920,200	1,578,584.37	0.80084	0.80084	1,264,195.55
24	6.8750	324,000	535,565.41	0.81564	0.81564	436,827.42
25	6.8125	187,800	304,560.83	0.01052	0.82431	251,051.17
26	6.8125	153,800	249,422.02	0.00861	0.83147	207,385.84
27	6.8125	206,800	335,373.69	0.01158	0.84121	282,118.33
28	6.3750	273,100	383,153.74	0.01529	0.85427	327,316.24
29	6.0938	331,100	417,965.62	0.01854	0.87040	363,799.28
30	6.0625	171,600	213,938.81	0.00961	0.87885	188,019.07
31	6.2500	271,800	364,342.37	0.01522	0.89243	325,150.11
32	6.1250	137,000	175,083.21	0.00767	0.89933	157,457.36
33	6.0625	211,800	264,057.34	0.01186	0.91012	240,324.32
34	6.0625	83,000	103,478.56	0.00465	0.91497	90,617.80
35	6.1875	226,700	296,802.36	0.01269	0.92613	274,876.54
36	6.3125	84,600	116,048.22	0.00474	0.93053	107,986.95
37	6.5625	330,000	493,920.78	0.01848	0.64805	468,262.35
38	5.6250	927,800	953,759.52	0.05195	1.00000	953,759.52
			Total = 14,679,410.25			Totals = 11,217,558.16

Source: Edward Dyl, "Estimated Economic Damages in Class Action Securities Fraud Litigation," *Journal of Forensic Economics,* 12 (1) Winter 1999, 1–11.

quiet, with some notable exceptions, until the mid-1980s when corporate America took off in a merger frenzy. This lasted until the end of the 1980s when various events, including the overall economic slowdown and the collapse of the junk bond market, brought about its end. After a comparatively short hiatus, merger and acquisition activity picked up in 1994 and quickly reached unprecedented levels by 1998. This is apparent in both the number of deals and the dollar value of deals (see Figure 10.3 and 10.4).

Merger Laws

Acquisitions of publicly held companies are subject to certain laws that regulate share purchases and takeovers. The most prominent of these is the Williams Act. This law, enacted in 1968, is an amendment to the Securities Exchange Act of 1934. In an effort to regulate hostile takeovers, the law sought to enhance the confidence of investors in securities markets by providing them with certain information and a certain amount of time to deliberate over such information.

Pursuant to Section 13 (d), the Williams Act requires the filing of a Schedule 13D within 10 days of the acquisition of 5% of a public company's outstanding equity securities. The disclosure requires the acquirer of the stock to reveal certain information, such as the identity of the purchaser and the plans the purchaser

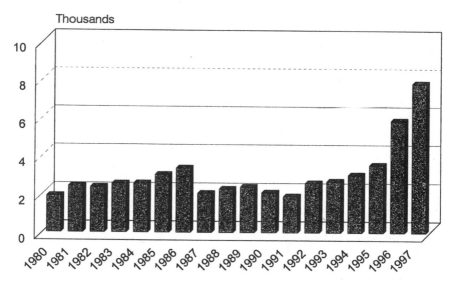

Figure 10.3.   Mergers and acquisitions: number of deals/total dollar value.
Source: Mergerstat Review, 1999.

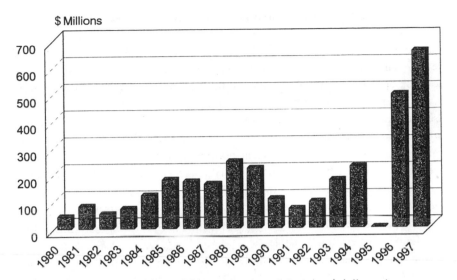

Figure 10.4. Mergers and acquisitions: number of deals/total dollar value.

has for the stock and the issuing company. Section 14 (d) of the law requires the filing of a Schedule 14 D-1 upon the initiation of a *tender offer.* Ironically, the Act did not define what a tender offer is; this was done by a subsequent court decision where a tender offer was defined in terms of the presence of eight factors—called the *Eight Factor Test.*[27] Simply stated, a tender offer is an offer made directly to the shareholders of a public company.

The Schedule 14D-1 requires the disclosure of similar information as Schedule 13D. In addition, the bidder has to reveal such relevant information as the terms of the offer, information on the bidder, and its sources of financing. Due to the fact that target companies tend to receive a takeover premium, a monetary amount in excess of the stock price prior to the announcement, stock prices rise on the announcement of takeovers.[28] For this reason, bidders may try to conceal their plans when making share purchases so that they do not have to pay some component of the takeover premium when they accumulate the target's stock prior to the initiation of a formal bid. When such efforts lead to an evasion of the requirements of securities laws, a lawsuit may be initiated by the SEC or by private parties.

---

[27] *Wellman v. Dickinson,* 475 F. Supp. (SD NY 1979), aff'd 632 F. 2d 355 (CA2 1982), *cert denied* 460 U.S. 1069 (1983).

[28] Asquith Paul, "Merger Bids, Uncertainty, and Stockholder Returns," *Journal of Financial Economics* 11 (1–4), April 1983, 51–83.

Disgorgement in Merger-Related Transactions

Acquirers of stock in targets or potential targets of takeovers may want to avoid the necessary filing of a Schedule 13D. Not filing may allow the purchaser to buy the stock at a lower price than what would have to be paid if the market were aware of the information that it would have been provided with if there had been disclosure pursuant to the Williams Act. There is support in the finance literature for a general positive stock price effect associated with Schedule 13D announcements (although the majority of such purchases were not for the purposes of takeovers).[29] In the 1980s, certain individuals pursued various schemes including *stock parking,* which is the placing of purchased shares in names other than the true purchaser, to avoid the requirements of Section 13D. Various actions were brought against them, including some high profile cases in which the purchasers were found to be criminally liable.

Once again, a methodology similar to what was used in the event study methodology can be applied to determine the purchaser's gains made through the evasion of the disclosure requirements of the Williams Act. The expert needs to compute the full information price—the price that the stock would have traded at had the market been aware of the purchaser's acquisition of the shares. The amount to be disgorged is the difference between the purchase price and the full information price, times the number of shares involved.

Example of Using the Event Study Methodology to Measure the Disgorgement Amount in a Delinquent Schedule 13D Filing

Mark Mitchell and Jeffrey Netter report a case involving the failure to file a Schedule 13D within the time requirements of the Williams Act. On December 18, 1987, the president of Pizza Inn, Francis Spillman, purchased 50,000 shares of a chicken restaurant chain, Winners Corporation, which put his total stake in the company above the 5% threshold. This required him to file a Schedule 13D within 10 calendar days, or on December 28. However, he did not file until January 6, 1988, which was eight days late. He also bought 45,000 more shares between December 28 and January 6. In December 1989, the SEC charged Spillman with vio-

---

[29] Wayne H. Mikkelson and Richard S. Ruback, "An Empirical Analysis of the Interfirm Equity Investment Process," *Journal of Financial Economics* 14 (4), December 1985, 501–523.

lating Section 13 (d) in that the price he paid for the shares he purchased between the required disclosure date and the actual disclosure date failed to reflect the information that would have been contained in the Schedule 13D.

Table 10.4 shows the stock price and return history for the Winners Corporation over a period before and after the trades in question. It shows that the stock price rose from $1.875 on December 28 to $3.00 on January 5—the day before the disclosure. Mitchell and Netter report that during this period Spillman's shares purchased accounted for approximately 45.5% of the trading volume and that his purchases alone during this period often exceeded the historical average trading volume of this security.

One measure of the amount to be disgorged would be the difference between the full disclosure price, $3, and the various prices that Spillman paid for the shares. The SEC, however, took into account the fact that after the filing, which included Spillman's stated intention to initiate a tender offer filing, the stock price fell. They used the average price over a two-week period following the filing—$2.675.

CHURNING[30]

One aspect of the securities industry that seems to be ever present to varying degrees is churning litigation. Churning litigation is an outgrowth of broker-customer holders disputes. While both members and critics of the securities industry would agree that the majority of brokers are honest professionals endeavoring to provide valued services to their clients, there is always a certain percentage of brokers who unscrupulously violate their obligations to their clients. Such violations may take the form of "churning" of customer's accounts. Churning is a fraudulent practice whereby brokers induce customers to excessively trade the securities in their accounts so as to generate greater commission income for the broker without regard to the financial interests of customers. This practice is a violation of a number of laws including the antifraud provisions of the Securities Exchange Act of 1934 as well as specific rules put forward by the Securities and Exchange Commission, the National Association of Securities Dealers, and the New York Stock Exchange. In addition to measuring damages, churning litigation presents another opportunity for the expert with a background in finance to

---

[30]This section is derived from "An Analytical Model of Securities Litigation" by Patrick A. Gaughan, in *Litigation Economics,* Patrick A. Gaughan and Robert Thornton eds. (Greenwich, Conn.: JAI Press) 1993.

Table 10.4. Stock Price Performance for Winners Corporation Surrounding Spillman's Delinquent Schedule 13D Filing on January 6, 1988. (Required filing on December 28, 1987)

Date	Winners Price	Abnormal Return	Z-Statistic	Cumulative Abnormal Return	Z-Statistic	Volume/ Mean Volume	Spillman Volume/ Mean Volume
Dec. 11	1.500	8.71	1.62	8.71	1.62	0.25	
Dec. 14	1.375	−10.92	−1.99	−3.16	−0.41	5.46	1.14
Dec. 15	1.375	−0.06	−0.01	−3.22	−0.34	1.02	0.57
Dec. 16	1.500	7.32	1.35	3.87	0.36	12.54	12.20
Dec. 17	1.500	1.88	0.35	5.82	0.48	1.12	0.57
Dec. 18	2.250	47.96	8.80	56.57	4.26	13.53	5.67
Dec. 21	2.000	−11.22	−2.09	39.01	2.72	4.27	1.14
Dec. 22	2.000	0.21	0.04	39.30	2.57	5.46	0.11
Dec. 23	1.875	−7.29	−1.35	29.15	1.80	2.68	0.23
Dec. 24	2.000	7.15	1.33	38.39	2.25	0.42	0.22
Dec. 28	1.875	−3.58	−0.66	33.43	1.86	1.31	0.57
Dec. 29	1.875	0.65	0.12	34.31	1.83	6.01	2.22
Dec. 30	2.250	19.00	3.52	59.82	3.07	3.42	0.68
Dec. 31	2.250	0.44	0.08	60.53	2.99	0.90	0.90
Jan. 4	2.375	2.16	0.39	63.99	3.05	1.15	0.79
Jan. 5	2.500	4.26	0.79	70.97	3.28	1.12	0.51
Jan. 6	3.000	19.98	3.72	105.14	4.71	4.66	
Jan. 7	3.000	−0.53	−0.10	104.06	4.53	3.95	1.25
Jan. 8	2.875	2.23	0.38	108.6	4.58	0.78	0.34
Jan. 11	2.875	−0.99	−0.18	106.56	4.38	0.70	0.57
Jan. 12	2.750	−3.33	−0.62	99.67	4.00	5.23	3.97
Jan. 13	2.500	−9.05	−1.68	81.60	3.20	1.21	0.57
Jan. 14	2.625	5.20	0.97	91.05	3.50	1.98	0.57
Jan. 15	2.625	−2.23	−0.41	86.78	3.26	0.84	
Jan. 18	2.500	−4.58	−0.85	78.24	2.88	0.06	
Jan. 19	2.500	1.01	0.19	80.04	2.89	0.77	
Jan. 20	2.500	2.73	0.50	84.95	3.01	0.01	
Jan. 21	2.625	5.06	0.94	94.30	3.28	6.13	4.62
Jan. 22	2.750	3.72	0.69	101.53	3.48	0.11	

Source: Mark L. Mitchell and Jeffery M. Netter, "The Role of Financial Economics in Securities Fraud Cases: Applications at the Securities and Exchange Commission," *The Business Lawyer* 49 (2) February 1994, 545–590.

Notes: Returns are expressed in percents. Stock price and volume data is from Center for Research in Security Prices (CRSP) at the University of Chicago. Market model estimation period is December 11, 1986 to December 10, 1987. Marked proxy is CRSP value-weighted index of NYSE, AMEX, and NASDAQ stocks. Beta estimate for Winners is 1.03.

provide useful quantitative analysis that can enable a court or arbitration panel to better analyze the claims of churning.

The execution of a churning claim by a customer generally takes place through the arbitration process. This was underscored by the June 1987 Supreme Court decision, *Shearson American Express v. McMahon,* wherein predispute agreements requiring settlement of disputes through compulsory arbitration were held to be binding.[31] Following this decision, customers no longer had access to the courts and were bound by the arbitration process. Unfortunately for some brokerage customers, many of those with valid claims now find themselves in a less advantageous position relative to their deep-pocket defendants. A customer who pursues a claim against a brokerage firm quickly realizes that the defendant usually has far more resources at its disposal than the claimant. The situation is even more unfortunate when the customer had entrusted most of his financial resources to an unscrupulous broker who then took advantage of this position of trust to deplete the wealth of the customer. The financially weakened customer then discovers that it is most difficult to effectively oppose and challenge a brokerage firm that possesses substantial financial resources and abundant in-house legal and expert talent. A customer first must retain legal counsel who is quite familiar with this area of the law to pursue the available legal remedies. However, legal counsel alone is generally not sufficient to successfully prosecute a churning claim. This is where the role of the experts retained by the attorney comes into play.

Most attorneys seek to retain a former professional in the securities industry who can opine on issues of the suitability of the types of securities that the broker purchased for the client. However, the industry expert's testimony would often be more effective if he were armed with a presentation of a clear quantitative model that measures and summarizes the volume and nature of the trading that took place. A financial economist can play an important role by analyzing the volume and pattern of trades in the account or accounts and presenting a concise and convincing analysis at the arbitration proceedings. The analysis must be cost effective, particularly when the customer possesses only limited resources.

This section presents the framework of a model that can be used to analyze the trading of securities for a churning claim. The model is based on measures that have been found to be indicative of churning in various prior legal decisions. These measures are used to compare the volume of trading in the accounts in question with these accepted legal standards. The measures are used to determine

---

[31] *Shearson American Express v. McMahon,* 107 S.Ct. 2332 (1987); *Perry v. Thomas,* 107 S.Ct. 2520 (1987).

if the trading reached a level that was, according to precedent, clearly excessive. Although the focus of this chapter is on the use of this model in the liability part of a churning case, a brief discussion of the method for computing damages is also included.

Elements of a Churning Claim

There are four elements of a churning claim:

1. Control
2. Suitability
3. Scienter
4. Excessive trading

Control refers to the extent of the customer's involvement in the trading decisions. Control may be clear when the customer had no involvement with the trading decisions and when the broker did not have to consult the customer in order to make trades. Brokers or registered representatives often attempt to acquire such control through a clear written agreement rather than through oral authority. The situation becomes less clear, however, when the customer provides such written authority but also orally instructs the broker to consider this authority limited to certain trades or types of securities. The fact that many customers fail to carefully read a written agreement, but rather place greater weight on the oral representations of brokers makes some churning disputes problematic for arbitrators.

Suitability refers to the recommendation of certain investments that may be suitable for the customer in light of his personal financial circumstances or investment objectives. Broker recommendations to purchase speculative securities for customers who lacked a background in finance or securities trading and who had limited financial resources have been found to be unsuitable. It may be the case that margin trading itself is indicative of unsuitability. In such cases, it may be necessary to present expert testimony on the degree of financial sophistication necessary to fully comprehend the risks of particular types of transactions. For example, such expertise might be useful to demonstrate why buying uncovered call options is a speculative transaction. Expert testimony could be used to explain why a naive investor might have difficulty comprehending the risks and potential for gain in complex option trading strategies, such as the use of butterfly spreads or straddles.

In proving a churning claim, the plaintiff may need to demonstrate *scienter.* Scienter refers to the assertion that the defendant acted either with the intent to defraud the customer or with careless disregard for the financial interests of the client. In 1976, scienter became necessary in order to establish a claim of churning under Section 10(b) of the Securities Exchange Act of 1934. Used in the context of churning, scienter refers to a mental state embracing the intent to deceive, manipulate, or defraud. While scienter may be an integral part of the churning claim, the financial expert may not play an active role in proving this allegation.

The final necessary aspect of a successful churning claim is the demonstration of *excessive trading* in light of the objectives of the account. Such a demonstration might attempt to show that the volume of trading was so excessive that the goal of the trading activity was to generate profits for the broker rather than gains for the customer. Here certain quantitative measures of trading activity can be employed to relate the pattern of trading in the accounts to accepted legal standards of churning.

Quantitative Measures of Churning

There are three main quantitative measures of churning:

1. Turnover ratios
2. Average holding periods
3. Cost of investment services

A successful churning claim may require the combined use of all these measures. High turnover is often associated with a low holding period, which implies high trading costs. These high costs may mean that the trading strategy is required to yield a high rate of return simply to break even.

Turnover Ratios
The most common formulation of turnover ratios is the *Looper formula,* which is defined as follows:

$$\text{Looper Formula} = \frac{\text{total cost of purchases}}{\text{average equity}} \quad (10.17)$$

Average equity is defined as:

$$\text{Average equity} = \frac{\text{beginning period equity} + \text{ending period equity}}{2} \qquad (10.18)$$

For example, an account that had an average equity of $100,000 and purchases of $850,000 in a given year has a turnover ratio of 8.5.

Two of the most commonly used time periods are monthly and annual. Monthly periods can be particularly useful for higher volumes of trading. In the case of margin accounts, the debit balances must be deducted from the equity measure. In addition, it is generally better to include all accounts in the computation of average equity. For example, if the investor has both a cash and a securities account, both should be combined to arrive at total average equity. However, it may be useful to segregate the trading of certain accounts, such as options accounts. If this is the goal of the analyst, a separate turnover analysis can be computed which excludes the options account. Given the inherently short-term nature of options, it may be useful to present a separate analysis in which these trades are excluded. Another ratio, the contract index, which is the ratio of the number of option contracts bought or sold within a given period divided by the average equity, is sometimes used as an alternative to the traditional Looper turnover ratio.

Given the fact that both purchases and sales generate commissions for the broker, it might also be useful to include in the Looper formula both types of transactions in the numerator such as in Equation (10.19).

$$\text{Looper Formula} = \frac{\text{total cost of purchases} + \text{total price of sales}}{\text{average equity}} \qquad (10.19)$$

While Equation (10.19) may be more revealing about the total value of trading and the resulting commission income, which is proportional to the trading volume, it may be counting the same trade twice. If a broker sells one security in order to buy another, this can be considered one transaction. The second security has replaced the first. As far as commission accounting is concerned, each is a separate transaction that generates a commission charge. The debate becomes moot, however, in light of the reasons for the computation of the turnover ratios. The value of the specific turnover ratio utilized is to derive a quantitative measure of trading activity that can be compared with other quantitative measures that have been accepted in prior litigation as being indicative of churning. The standard that is therefore ordinarily relied on is the traditional Looper formula (Equation 10.17), which includes *only purchases* in the numerator. Although the analyst might find it enlightening to compute both measures, the standard Looper is more useful for comparison purchases.

Legal Guidelines for Turnover Ratios

The legal guidelines for turnover ratios as they relate to churning can be grouped into four categories:

1. Turnover ratio less than two
2. Turnover ratio greater than two but less than four
3. Turnover ratio greater than four but less than six
4. Turnover ratio greater than six

Some writers in this area have simply categorized these ratios into those less than two and those greater than two. Goldberg, for example, states that the courts have been reluctant to find that trading that resulted in annualized turnover ratios of less than two was excessive. However, he points out that turnover ratios greater than two have been found to be indicative of active trading and have carried the inference of churning. In cases where the turnover ratio has exceeded four, the courts have found that the volume of trading was such that a conclusion of excessive trading is reasonable. In instances where the turnover ratio is greater than six, the results may be even more conclusive.

It is important for both the expert and legal counsel to consider the turnover ratios in light of the investment objectives of the account. If the account was established as part of a long-term investment strategy that would provide predictable income with little risk of loss of principal for the customer, the higher turnover ratios cited previously would seem to indicate churning. High turnover may be expected for an account that was established along more speculative lines. If the customer has approved an aggressive trading strategy that seeks to frequently trade securities in an attempt to sell at temporary highs while buying at temporary lows, high turnover may be a necessary component of this customer-approved trading strategy. In cases such as this, the courts have failed to find that the account was churned and have indicated higher turnover is expected in such trading accounts.

Holding Periods and In-and-Out Trading

Turnover ratios can be supplemented by other measures that may help reveal the extent of the trading activity in the account. Therefore, it is most useful to combine the computation of the turnover ratios with a measurement of various average holding periods. Holding periods provide an indication of the average length of time that securities are held in a portfolio. This time is useful if one is attempting to determine if there was a systematic pattern of in-and-out trading. In-and-out trading is a pattern of trading in which the broker may sell a security after a short holding period. This sale may even be followed by a series of sales and purchases of the same security. To compute the holding periods the analyst must determine how long each security remained in the portfolio. The securities are then categorized into various holding periods. A common holding period categorization is as follows:

- Less than 30 days
- Less than 90 days
- Less than 180 days
- Less than 360 days

Holding periods can be measured in terms of the dollar value of securities or the total number of securities held. The dollar measure is more revealing than the number of securities, because in effect the nonmonetary measure weights different dollar amounts equally. Nonmonetary measures would treat a $70 share of stock as equal to a $5 share. Because commissions are based on the value of the transaction, a monetary measure is generally more appropriate.

Examples of some of the decisions that have used holding periods as benchmarks are shown in Appendix B. Based on an overview of numerous decisions, the following summary breakdown list is generally considered indicative of excessive trading:

Holding Periods	Excessive
Percent held for less than six months	75% or more
Percent held for less than three months	50% or more
Percent held for less than one month	25% or more

Cost of Investment Services

Brokers charge a commission for each trade executed on behalf of the customer. Herein, of course, lies the potential conflict that sometimes induces brokers to churn their portfolios. Trading is the activity that generates commissions. This sometimes leads brokers to trade simply to increase their income rather than to advance the customer's wealth. This implies there is one level of commission costs that is associated with wealth-enhancing trading and another that is associated with churning. It is, therefore, useful to compute the costs of trading in comparison to both the profits generated as well as to the average equity in the account. The economist's model may, therefore, provide computations of the following:

- Total commissions and fees charged.
- Total margin interest paid by the customer.

- The sum of commissions, fees, and margin interest as a percentage of the total portfolio value on an annual basis. This sum can be referred to as the cost/equity percentage.
- The sum of commissions, fees, and margin interest compared to the income from trading on an annual basis.

The cost/equity percentage is useful because it highlights the rate of return necessary to simply break even. If this rate of return is unreasonably high, the broker's motives must be questioned, particularly if it can be shown that the broker has not generated such a rate of return in any of his or her other accounts.

Measuring Damages

The typical churning case involves a claimant who entrusted funds to a broker with the expectation of achieving rates of return that are consistent with the historical experience in the market. This may involve a diversified portfolio of stocks, bonds, and money market investments. If this is the case, the *expected value* of the portfolio can be measured using a historical weighted average rate of return based on readily available annual return statistics.[32] However, the actual rate of return over the loss period is more relevant. This rate can be computed in the same manner using the actual rates that prevailed for each of the broad categories of stocks, corporate bonds, and Treasuries combined in a manner similar to the composition of the portfolio. The end of the loss period is either the date of the litigation or the date that the claimant ended the relationship with the broker and withdrew the funds. The actual value of the portfolio at the end of this time period can then be deducted from the expected value to determine the damages.

The argument can sometimes be made that broad market statistics are inherently different since they are based on a larger portfolio of securities. However, this argument can be opposed by the abundant research in the field of finance, which shows that as portfolios are diversified they approach the rate of return for the market. That is, as portfolios become increasingly diversified, the unique, unsystematic risk of the portfolio decreases and approaches that of the market. If the investment objective is simply to maintain an original portfolio, or if the broker uses his own judgment to purchase a specific portfolio that differs in performance compared to the market, a specific rate of return for the portfolio in

---

[32] *Stocks, Bills, Bonds and Inflation* (Chicago: Ibbotson & Associates, 1999).

question can be computed using the CRSP monthly return database discussed earlier in this chapter

The loss computation can be complicated by the fact that there may be some withdrawals from or deposits into the account. Deposits can be handled individually using the same rate-of-return computation applied to the original portfolio but with a different starting date. Withdrawals are also handled using the same method but they are given negative values to offset the larger portfolio-compounded values.

Punitive Damages in Securities Litigation

Federal securities laws do not include provisions for the award of punitive damages in civil litigation. Some state laws allow for an award of punitive damages in securities fraud cases. In March 1995 the U.S. Supreme Court upheld an arbitrator's power to award punitive damages in cases where a brokerage agreement contained a New York "choice of law" clause.[33] Prior to this decision, the *Mastrobuono* decision, the Second and Seventh Circuits had held that the *Garrity* rule, which prohibited arbitrators from awarding punitive damages, was the law.[34] Until *Mastrobuono* this ruling was in conflict with the position of the Court of Appeals of the First, Eight, Ninth, and Eleventh Circuits, which supported the award of punitive damages.[35] Given that the Mastrobuono decision led brokerage firms to include a New York choice of law provision, this decision can have far reaching effects depending on the position of the individual courts and how they interpret the brokerage agreements.

Conclusion of Churning Analysis Model

The model and approach described in this chapter are methodologically straightforward, and the computations involve basic mathematics. However, the computations can be a time-consuming and arduous task. The expert should therefore

---

[33] *Mastrobuono v. Shearson Lehman Hutton,* 115 S. Ct. 1212 (1995).

[34] *Garrity v. Lyle Stuart, Inc.,* 40 N.Y.S. 2d 354, 353 N.E. 2d 793, 386 N.Y.S. 2d 831 (1976).

[35] "Carroll E. Nesseman and Maren E. Nelson, "Securities Arbitration Damages," in *Securities Arbitration: 1996,* David E. Robbins, chair, (New York: Practicing Law Institute) 1996.

be able to rely on good spreadsheet or database software to generate the large volume of calculations that are often necessary in active brokerage accounts. While the calculations themselves are basic, their value in litigation can be substantial. Without definitive quantitative evidence, the claimant would have to rely simply on the impressions of the industry expert and the arbitration panel. However, with detailed quantitative analysis, the extent of the trading and its related costs can be precisely demonstrated. Such evidence can also enable the claimant to counter the internally generated analysis often presented by the defendants. In addition, a clear model such as the one presented in this chapter can also be invaluable to defendants in actions where churning has not occurred. The same analysis that a plaintiff might present in cases where there was excessive trading can also be used by defendants to show that the trading was not in excess of the legal standards.

SUMMARY

This chapter discussed the various models used in measuring damages in a fraud on the market case. Such cases often arise from claims having to do with alleged inaccurate disclosure made by publicly held companies. This inadequate or incorrect disclosure may cause a stock's price to trade at a level that is different from its "true value." Damages may then be measured by the difference between these two levels. Certain methods are used to estimate the value of a security. These methods involve taking into account the impact of the market and the industry on the changing value of the company's stock. One of the methods often used is the comparable index method, which attempts to take into account such influences. Other methods may involve conducting events studies in which the circumstances are such that an event study will shed light on the impact of the actions of the defendant.

In measuring damages, the expert also needs to define the loss period as well as the number of damages securities. The loss period is defined by determining the date when there is a complete and accurate disclosure that would eliminate a difference between the stock's price and value. Defining the number of damaged securities can be a challenging exercise. This number is usually arrived at by utilizing models that make different assumptions about the number of securities that were traded during the loss period.

In addition to fraud on the market cases, damage experts are utilized in various cases that arise from mergers and acquisitions. The analysis that the expert may conduct can be similar to the type of analysis that she may do in a fraud on the market case although the set of facts in a merger-related action may be different. Given the feverish pace of mergers and acquisitions in the mid-1990s, this area continues to be a fertile area of work for damage experts.

Churning cases present different opportunities for damage experts. Churning of customer portfolios involves excessive trading designed to generate commissions for brokers that may not be related to maximizing the value of the portfolio. The expert may be able to provide various quantitative measures, such as using the Looper formula and measuring the average holding period. These measures can then be compared to established legal standards to determine if the trading activity was indeed consistent with what has been determined to be churning. The expert can then also compute damages by measuring what the value of the portfolio would have been using a more reasonable investment strategy.

APPENDIX A: CASE STUDY *IN RE COMPUTER ASSOCIATES, INTERNATIONAL, INC.*

This example is derived from a securities case involving allegation of insufficient or inaccurate disclosure by Computer Associates, Inc., a public company that trades on the New York Stock Exchange. The case, which went to trial in the Eastern District of New York, centered around whether Computer Associates, Inc. had made sufficient and timely enough disclosure of performance that was less than expectations. The plaintiff retained an expert who measured a purported amount of the stock price inflation. The company made a disclosure on July 12, 1990, that indicated that performance would be less than expected. The plaintiff contended that these expectation on the part of the market were caused by management's allegedly misleading statements. Following are various excerpts from the direct testimony of the plaintiff's expert.[36] Obviously parts of the testimony are left out to due space consideration. However, the excerpts should give the reader a flavor for the issues that surround this type of expert testimony.

   Q. Did you see any evidence of guidance of future performance as made at that meeting?
   A. Yes, I did. The notes indicated that management in the May 22 meeting indicated that for the year, this is the fiscal year, there would be 20 to 25% revenue growth and that earnings would be higher than that.

---

[36] The excerpts shown are not complete passages and numerous sections are left out. This is necessitated by space limitations. However, the included sections demonstrate some of the concepts that have been covered in this chapter.

> They also indicated that in the first quarter, earnings would be up over the corresponding quarter of a year ago, and that revenue would not be as nearly up for the year, it would be up, but it would be over the corresponding quarter of the year ago. . . .

Q. Do you view whether—what the company said seemed to be affecting the market price of the stock?

A. Yes, because what we saw here is a stock price that was trending upward, to the $16 level, consistent with an expectation of a substantial earnings improvement in fiscal 1991. The statements that were made on January 23, set the groundwork for that and on May 22, those statements were reiterated, and the period after May 22 the stock continued to trade at fairly high levels, relative to what happened, on July 12, which I think we'll get into later. . . .

Figure 10.A1 is a graph of the daily closing stock price of Computer Associates, Inc. over the first seven months of 1990 which includes July 12, 1990, in which the company made an announcement of disappointing results. The depressing effect that such news had on the stock price can be more dramatically seen in Figure 10.A1, which shows the shorter two month period of June and July 1990. In referring to similar graphs that were presented at trial, especially one that featured the first seven months, the expert at trial testified as follows:

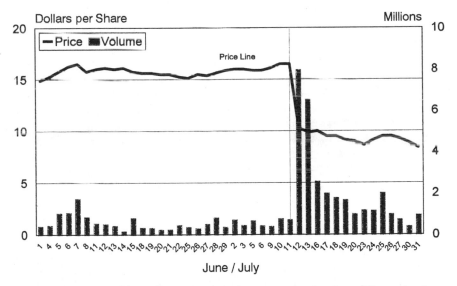

Figure 10.A1. Weekly trading volume and common stock price of Computer Associates, Inc.

Source: Computer Associates International, Inc.

A. . . . It shows the stock price basically prior to July 12, sent three trending upward slightly in the $12, $13 level, up to the $14, $15 level, back down a little
bit and continuing up to the $16 level. Then it shows what occurred on July 12,
when they announced that the earnings for the—that the sales were going to be
off for the quarter and that earnings would be off for the quarter. The stock in
one day went down from the $16 level to the 4.10 level. That was a one day
drop. Very, very substantial drop. Approximately 40 percent. Then in one period after that drop, the stock drifted lower over a period of several months, getting as low as $5 and then by the end of the year it recovered to about $7, $8
level.

In addition to showing the stock price effects, the expert then went on to show
the changes in trading volume that accompanied the July 12, 1990, announcement. The variation in weekly trading volume for the two month period June,
1990 through July 1990 is shown in Figure 10.A1.

A. . . . I added the volume data. This time it's daily volume. You'd have to sum
five days to get a week here, but this shows now on the daily volume, the scale
is in millions of shares per day, from zero to ten million and you could see that
the—in most days, prior to the announcement on July 12, the stock traded less
than a million shares a day. A million shares would be good here.
   There are a couple of dates when it traded up over a million, but at no point
did it get over two million shares a prior to July 12. July 12, it traded up over
seven and a half million shares in one day. July 12 was a Friday—excuse me,
was a Thursday. July 13, which was Friday it again traded over six million on
the 13ᵗʰ and then there was a weekend, and on Monday the 16ᵗʰ it traded over
two and a half million shares. Those three days, you had just enormous trading
volume....

Q. I don't know if you can tell us this. Do you know whether any other stock
traded that many shares as did Computer Associates (CA)?

A. I believe CA was the largest number of shares to the change hands that day.

Q. And, in the same way, did any stock move that much that day on the New York
Stock Exchange?

A. They were down almost 40%, which is an unusually high drop and there was
no other stocks that were down 40% in the New York Stock Exchange.

Q. Have you done any work to see how often a stock might change price 40% in
one day?

A. Yes.

Q. Can you tell the jury what you have done?

A. We've done some research in to just how often stocks change in price at various percentages, and a 40% drop in one day for a stock in the above $10 price
level is extremely unusual. It almost never happens. Less than one in a hundred
thousand chance of that happening. . . .

A. What we've done here is we have constructed a graph to show how CA stock behaved relative to other computer software companies and what we've done here, we've taken the full year 1990, just like we started out with the price graph, and the red line is the price graph, that is CA. This is identical to the first chart that I showed you with the full year.

The red line on the first chart and the red line on this chart are identical. Now, we have added to that an index. I'll tell you what that is. H&Q stands for Hambrecht & Quist. They are a brokerage firm that specializes in technology stocks, and they have their own indices of groups of stocks and they have a software products index and what we've done here is we've slightly modified the index. CA was part of the index.

Well, we want to show what CA did relative to the other companies so we recalculated the index with CA. I don't want to show you how CA did relative to itself, but how it did to the other companies. We recalculated the index taking out CA and what we did is we did something called indexing, which is that we made—we made the index equal to CA stock price to January 2, 1990. . . .

A. . . . It's a little hard to visualize. When the lines are parallel, they are actually doing the same, it's when they are moving apart, when the gap is getting bigger is when the change is occurring. The gap got bigger between March and May and then it stayed about the same until April, then you have the plunge and the other stocks didn't plunge on that day, so this shows that CA going down 40% on July 12 has nothing to do with the other computer companies. They didn't go down 40% that day.

If they had, the blue line would have gone down to here, it didn't. It went down slightly, but it did not go down 40%. Now, all of a sudden you see CA trading below the blue line. It's doing less well relative to starting on January 1. If you bought the average computer software company on January 2 and still held it as of July 12, you would be doing letter than CA, because CA is below the line.

And here you see that after the period of time, the stock drifts down, it's down to the $5 level, the index goes down as well, not quite as much, but then when CA comes back up, it comes up in line with the other software companies.

Essentially after the plunge, it then started at a lower level, lower level, $10 level, acting like the other software companies, so what this tells me is that there was an important event on July 12 that was only to do with CA that pushed that stock from $16 to $10. Otherwise, the stock behaved like other software companies. . . .

A. There is a calculation where we're looking at the price decline on July 12. What I'm trying to do here, I'm trying to determine how much value came out of that press release on July 12. What was it worth, as a negative value, but still a value. One way of doing that is to look at the price of the decline on a one-day basis. On July 11, the stock was 16 and a half, July 12, it was ten and a quarter. That is a loss of $6.25.

The problem with one day declines, there is also a little bit of random movement in the stock prices and may not really tell you, you know, exactly what the loss of value is. One way of being a little more precise on the loss of value is to look at a few days beforehand and a few days afterward and use average guess because sometimes stocks bounce around.

What I have done here, I have taken one trading week, five days before the decline and I have averaged them and that averaged price was $16 and 17 and a half cents. Then I looked at the average price after the decline and the average price after the decline as it continued down through the 18 is $9.82 and a half cents. So the stock price declined, based on a five-day average, before the bad news and a five-day average after the bad news would be $6.35. The difference between the two averages, $6.35.

Q. That is step one of your calculation, Mr. X?

A. Yes.

Q. Could you please explain step two of your calculation, Exhibit 1117?

Now, what I want to do is say, all right, maybe all software companies as measured by an average were going down. We don't want—we know the stock went down $6.35 average price one week before and one week after, but we don't—you can say that is damages, that is the value of the information, you can say the 625 one day decline is the value of it. But, to be a little more refined, you want to take out any drop that was due to a general decline in software companies. If all software companies were going down, I don't want to charge that as damages, I want to take that out of the damages. What I'm doing here, I'm looking at the value of the software index for those same five days. The 5 of July through the 11, and the 12 of July through the 18. And I see that the average was $16 and 17 and a half cents for the index the week before the decline, you have the index decline during that week. You can argue that the index declined because of the shock effect of CA that may have caused other stocks to go down.

That does happen and so you don't have to take this out of the damages, but let's assume that the others went down because it was a change in people's attitudes toward software industry that had nothing to do CA. The index did go down and it went down to $15.34 point two cents. I subtracted the two and said it was down 83.3 cents. That's what I have done here. Even though that index may have gone down because of the shock of what happened to CA.

Q. If you could tell the jury the third step?

A. Now, what I have done, I have combined the two, this step three shows the previous two charts, which is the CA calculation of the decline, the software products calculation, and its decline and I subtract from the $6.35 decline, the equivalent decline of the software, which is 83.3 cents and that's how I reached at the damage number, $5.51 point seven cents for approximately $5.52.

If you take out of the decline the entire—the entire decline of the other software companies, and just remove that and say that's not damages, that may be an economic condition, I come up with $5 and 51 point seven or 552.

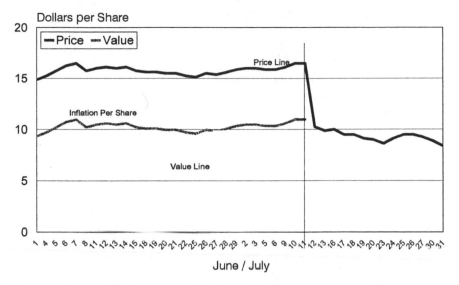

Figure 10.A2. Daily common stock price and value.
Source: Computer Associates International, Inc.

The expert in this trial included certain graphical illustrations as part of his testimony. A similar graph to that which he presented is shown in Figure 10.A2 which is a price-value graph similar to that shown in Figure 10.A1

APPENDIX B: CASES SETTING HOLDING PERIODS

Holding Period Percentages within an Eight-Month Period

Percentage Case

67% *Matter of R H. Johnson & Company,* 36 S.E.C. 467, 477 (1955), affirmed 231 F.2d 523 (D.C. Cir. 1956).

77% *Matter of R. H. Johnson & Company,* 33 S.E.C. 180. 182 (1952), affirmed 198 F.2d 690 (2d Cir. 1952).

79% *Matter of R. H. Johnson & Company,* 36 S.E.C. 467, 471 (1955), affirmed 231 F.2d 523 (D.C. Cir. 1956).

86% *Matter of Behel, Johnson & Company,* 26 S.E.C. 163, 165-66, 167 (1947).

88% *Matter of R. H. Johnson & Company,* 36 S.E.C. 467, 480 (1955), affirmed 231 F.2d 523 (D.C. Cir. 1956).

Holding Period Percentages within a Six-Month Period

21%   *Matter of Logan & Company,* 41 S.E.C. 88, 94 (1962), affirmed *Hersh v. S.E.C.* 325 F.2d 147 (9 Cir. 1963).

56%   *Matter of Behel, Johnson* & Company, 26 S.E.C. 163, 167 (1947).

Holding Period Percentages within a Thirty-Day Period

39%   *Stevens v. Abbot, Proctor & Paine,* 88 F. Supp. 836, 840 (E.D. Va. 1968).

REFERENCES

Asquith, Paul, "Merger Bids, Uncertainty, and Stockholder Returns," *Journal of Financial Economics* 11 (1–4), April 1983.

Banz, R.W., "The Relationship Between Return and Market Value of Common Stocks," *Journal of Financial Economics* 9 (1) March 1981.

Basu, S., "The Relationship Between Earnings Yield, Market Value and Return to NYSE Common Stocks," *Journal of Financial Economics* 12 (1) June 1983.

Beaver, William H., James K. Malernee, and Michael C. Keeley, "Stock Trading Behavior and Damage Estimation in Securities Cases," Cornerstone Research, 1993.

Branch, Ben, "A Tax Loss Trading Rule," *Journal of Business* 50 (2) (April 1977).

Brown, Stephen J., and Jerold B. Warner, "Using Daily Stock Returns: The Case of Event Studies," *Journal of Financial Economics* 14, 1985.

Carleton, Willard, T., Michael S. Weisbach, and Elliott J. Weiss, "Securities Class Action Lawsuits: A Descriptive Study," *Arizona Law Review,* 1996, 38, 491–511.

Carolyn Brancato and Patrick A. Gaughan, "Institutional Investors and Their Role in Capital Markets," Columbia University School of Law Monograph, 1986.

Cornell, Bradford, and Gregory R. Morgan, "Using Finance Theory to Measure Damages in Fraud on the Market Cases," *UCLA Law Review* 37, 883.

Dyl, Edward, "Estimated Economic Damages in Class Action Securities Fraud Litigation," *Journal of Forensic Economics,* 12 (1) Winter 1999, 1–11.

Fama, Eugene F., *The Theory of Finance* (New York: Holt, Rinehart and Winston, 1972).

Fama, Eugene F. "Efficient Capital Markets II," *Journal of Finance* 46 (5), December 1991.

Fama, Eugene F., L. Fisher, M. Jensen, and R. Roll, "The Adjustment of Stock Prices to New Information," *International Economic Review* 10 (1) February 1969.

Furbush, Dean, and Jeffrey Smith, "Estimating the Number of Shares in Securities Fraud Litigation: an Introduction to Stock Trading Modes," *The Business Lawyer* 49 (2), February 1994.

Furtado, Eugene P. H., and Vijay Karan, "Causes, Consequences and Shareholder Wealth Effects of Management Turnover: A Review of the Empirical Evidence," *Financial Management* 19, 1990, 60.

Garrity v. Lyle Stuart, Inc., 40 N.Y.S. 2d 354, 353 N.E. 2d 793, 386 N.Y.S. 2d 831 (1976).

Gaughan, Patrick A., *Mergers and Acquisitions* (New York: Harper Collins, 1990).

Gaughan, Patrick A., *Mergers, Acquisitions and Corporate Restructuring* (New York: Wiley, 2nd ed. 1999).

Gaughan, Patrick A., "An Analytical Model of Securities Litigation," in *Litigation Economics,* Patrick A. Gaughan and Robert Thornton eds. (Greenwich Conn.: JAI Press, 1993).

Green v. Occidental Petroleum Corp., 541 F. 2d 1335.

Johnathan, Mary R., and Geoffrey P. Miller, "Lessons From Financial Economics: Materality, Reliance and the Extended Reach of *Basic v. Levinson, Virginia Law Review* 77, 1991.

Keim, Donald B., "Size Related Anomalies and Stock Return Seasonality," *Journal of Financial Economics* 12 (1) June 1983.

Lee, Cheng F., *Statistics for Business and Financial Economics* (Lexington, Mass.: D. C. Heath, 1993).

Johnathan R. Macy and Geoffrey P. Miller, "Lessons From Financial Economics: Materiality, Reliance and the Extended Reach of *Basic v. Levinson, Virginia Law Review* 77, 1991, 1017, 1020.

Malkiel, Burton, *Random Walk Down Wall Street,* 6th ed. (New York: W. W. Norton & Co., 1997).

Mastrobuono v. Shearson Lehman Hutton, 115 S. Ct. 1212 (1995).

McKinlay, Craig A., "Event Studies in Economics and Finance," *Journal of Economic Literature* 35, March 1997.

Mikkelson, Wayne H., and Richard S. Ruback, "An Empirical Analysis of the Interfirm Equity Investment Process," *Journal of Financial Economics* 14 (4), December 1985.

Mitchell, Mark, and Jeffrey Netter, "The Role of Financial Economics in Securities Fraud Cases: Applications at the Securities Commission," *Business Lawyer* 2 (2) February 1994.

Nesseman, Carrol E., and Maren E. Nelson, "Securities Arbitration Damages," in *Securities Arbitration: 1996,* David E. Robbins, Chair (New York: Practicing Law Institute, 1996).

Perry v. Thomas, 107 S.Ct. 2520 (1987).

Posner, Norman, "Options Account Fraud: Securities Churning in a New Context," *Business Lawyer* 39 (2) February 1984.

Reinganum, Marc R., "Misspecification of Capital Asset Pricing: Empirical Anomalies Based On Earnings Yield and Market Values," *Journal of Financial Economics* 9 (1) March 1981.

Rielly, Frank, *Investment Analysis and Portfolio Management* (Fort Worth, Tex.: Dryden Press, 1994).

Ritchken, Peter, *Options: Theory, Strategy and Applications* (Glenview, Ill.: Scott Foresman,1987).

Robbins, David E., *Securities Arbitration: 1996,* (New York: Practicing Law Institute, 1996).

Ross, Stephen, Randolph, Westerfield, and Bradford D. Jordan, *Fundamentals of Corporate Finance,* 2nd ed. (Homewood, Ill.: Richard D. Irwin, 1993).

SEC v. Texas Gulf Sulphur Co., 401 F. 2d 1301 (2nd Cir.), *cert denied,* 404 U.S. 1005 (1971).

Shearson American Express v. McMahon, 107 S.Ct. 2332 (1987).

Stocks, Bills, Bonds and Inflation (Chicago, Ill.: Ibbotson Associates, 1999).

Van Horne, James C., *Financial Management and* Policy, 9th ed. (Englewood Cliffs, N.J.: Prentice Hall, 1992).

Wellman v. Dickinson, 475 F. Supp. (SD NY 1979), aff'd 632 F. 2d 355 (CA2 1982), *cert. denied* 460 U.S. 1069 (1983).

11

ANTITRUST CONCERNS

Antitrust enforcement has changed dramatically over the past century. It started at the end of the 1800s with the passage of the Sherman Antitrust Act and has moved along a winding path that featured periods of more and less antitrust enforcement. Ppresently, we see relatively mild antitrust enforcement compared to prior periods such as the 1950s and 1960s. However, over the past few years the antitrust enforcement authorities have given signs that they are pursuing such enforcement with a somewhat greater vigor.

Antitrust cases present opportunities for experts to express opinions on both the liability and the damages sides of the case. The cases generally are larger projects than the usual commercial damages case. Although economists typically are the experts working on antitrust cases, there are also opportunities for accountants to work on important aspects of the analysis.

ANTITRUST LAWS

The main antitrust laws are the

- Sherman Antitrust Act
- Federal Trade Commission Act
- Clayton Act
- Celler Kefauver Act
- Hart-Scott-Rodino Act

The Sherman Act, being the most important, is discussed first.

Sherman Act

The Sherman Act is the cornerstone of U.S. antitrust laws. Named after Senator John Sherman, it was passed in 1890 as part of an effort to control the anti-competitive activities of large trusts that started to exercise growing influence over corporate America of that time. The trusts were often under the control of the major banks such as Morgan Bank. These trusts gained voting power over large amounts of equities of various companies and then used the voting rights associated with these shares to merge and combine various companies. The goal of these transactions was to try to create larger and more economically viable entities.

It is ironic that just after the passage of the country's first major piece of antitrust legislation, the first merger wave took place. Between 1898 and 1904 a wave of mergers and acquisitions occurred that featured many horizontal combinations that resulted in a markedly increased concentration in many industries. There are several reasons why the Sherman Act did little to influence the large number of horizontal combinations. Among them was the difficulty that the enforcers at the Justice Department had in interpreting a law that they wrongly believed was so broad that it could be applied to any commercial transaction. That, combined with the limited resources of the department, led them to put the Sherman Act to little use during the merger wave.

The two main sections of the Sherman Act are:

Section 1   This section outlawed all contracts and combinations that restrain trade.

Section 2   This section made monopolization and attempts to monopolize illegal. It did not necessarily make monopolies illegal, but made actions a person or firm might take to monopolize a market illegal.

Given the uncertainty on the part of the courts and the Justice Department about how the Sherman Act should be used to foster competition, legislators passed two other laws in 1914 to facilitate antitrust enforcement, the Clayton Act and the Federal Trade Commission Act.

Clayton Act of 1914

The four main components of the Clayton Act and the section of the Act to which they apply are described in the following list:

Section 2   Section Two prevents price discrimination except that which can be justified by costs economies. This was further clarified and enhanced by the Robinson-Patman Act of 1936.

Section 3   Tying contracts, which tie the purchase of one product to the purchase of another, as well as exclusive dealing, which results in the impairment of competition, are illegal under this section.

Section 7   This section, under its original wording, made the purchase of stock of competing corporations, which result in reduced competition, illegal. This section was amended under the Celler-Kefauver Act of 1950, which closed the asset loophole and made the law apply to both stock and asset acquisitions. The Celler-Kefauver Act of 1950 also made vertical and conglomerate mergers and acquisitions illegal if they have an adverse effect on competition.

Section 8   Interlocking directorates of competing corporations were made illegal by this section of the Clayton Act.

Federal Trade Commission Act

The Federal Trade Commission Act was passed at the same time as the Clayton Act. Among its purposes was to establish an agency that would be charged with enforcing antitrust laws and preventing other unfair business practices. Included in these practices is false advertising. The Act also established the Federal Trade Commission to enforce this law and other antitrust laws.

Hart-Scott-Rodino Antitrust Enforcement Act of 1976

The Hart-Scott-Rodino Act was designed to prevent the completion of mergers and acquisitions that regulatory authorities might find objectionable and must try to undo well after the deal has been completed. Under Hart-Scott-Rodino, a merger or acquisition cannot be completed until either the Justice Department or the Federal Trade Commission gives its approval. This approval process requires that the merging firms submit a 16-page form that includes various business data broken down by standard industrial classification (SIC) codes. The Justice Department and the Federal Trade Commission decide between themselves which has jurisdiction.

Following the submission of the required forms, the regulatory authorities respond within a certain stipulated time, which varies depending on whether the deal is a cash or securities offer. The authorities can extend the response period to a certain stipulated additional amount of days, which is usually taken as a sign that they have problems with the deal. Given the more relaxed pattern of antitrust enforcement in recent years, merging companies have been asking for an early termination of the Hart-Scott-Rodino waiting periods based on a lack of antitrust concerns.[1]

ANTITRUST ENFORCEMENT

Antitrust enforcement is the joint responsibility of both the Justice Department and the Federal Trade Commission. When the Justice Department wants to take action it can bring a civil suit in federal court. Among the tools at its disposal are the power of an injunction that it can wield to halt the objectionable activities. It can also pursue criminal proceedings against the targeted individuals or companies.

The Federal Trade Commission can take action that is brought to an administrative law judge whose decision is then reviewed by the Federal Trade Commissioners. The Federal Trade Commission may get a cease and desist order to halt the illegal activities.

In addition to antitrust actions being pursued by the Justice Department and the Federal Trade Commission, individuals also have the right to file suits alleging antitrust violation. If successful, such suits can result in an award of treble damages.

Economics of Monopoly in Antitrust Actions

Antitrust laws are based on the principle that certain benefits of competition are reduced when markets are monopolized. To understand these benefits, we must explore the microeconomics of market structures.

In microeconomics we have several different broad forms of market structure. At one extreme is pure competition, which is a market structure characterized by many independent sellers each selling a small fraction of total market output. Being so small, their impact on the market is insignificant and they cannot do any-

---

[1] For a more detailed discussion of this law and its impact on mergers and acquisitions see Patrick A. Gaughan, *Mergers, Acquisitions and Corporate Restructuring,* 2nd ed. (New York: Wiley), 1999, 89–98.

thing to influence market price. That is, the market price does not change when they vary their output. In addition, pure competition assumes that the products produced in the competitive market are homogeneous and undifferentiated. Based on these assumptions, the firms in the industry are price taker, which means that they cannot do anything to influence market price. The assumption of being a price taker means that the demand curve is a flat, horizontal line. This line also becomes the firm's marginal revenue curve. The marginal revenue function is the function that shows the additional revenue a firm receives when it sells another unit of output.

The profit-maximizing output of the firm is shown in Figure 11.1 as q_c. As with all types of firms, the profit-maximizing output is selected as the point where marginal revenue equals marginal costs The difference in the case of pure competition is that the marginal revenue curve is flat and is the same as the demand curve.

In a monopoly, the only seller in the market is the monopolist. Therefore, the demand curve that the monopolist faces is the demand curve for the product itself. Like all firms, even purely competitive ones, the monopolist selects its profit-maximizing output by where marginal revenue and marginal costs are equal. The difference between this market structure and pure competition is that with the demand curve having the usual downward sloping structure given by the inverse relationship between quantity demanded and price, the marginal revenue is also downward sloping and below the demand curve. The intersection of the upward sloping marginal cost curve with the downward sloping marginal revenue function gives us the profit maximizing output Q_m shown in Figure 11.2.

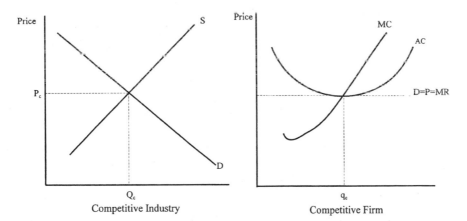

Figure 11.1. Perfectly competitive industry and firm.

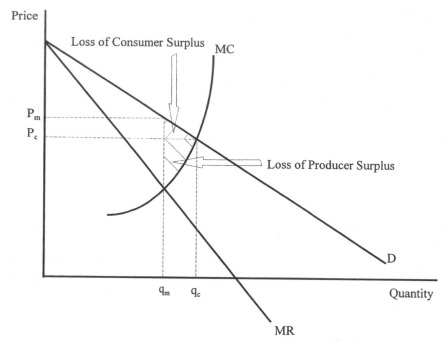

Figure 11.2. Monopoly versus pure competition.

It is possible for us to compare this monopolistic output with that of pure competition by trying to hypothesize what output this monopolist would produce if it were to act as though it were operating under pure competition. Figure 11.2 shows that the purely competitive industry structure results in a larger market output which, in turn, causes market price to be lower. These fewer units traded in monopoly result in a welfare loss which is the loss of consumer and producer surplus as shown in Figure 11.2.

Fact versus Amount of Damages in Antitrust Cases

Economic analysis in antitrust cases can be divided into a two-part process that has much in common with other types of cases, such as employment and even personal injury analysis. First, it must be established that the plaintiff incurred measurable damages that were *caused* by the actions of the defendant. Some courts have referred to this process as establishing the fact and the amount of damages. The fact of damages itself has two parts: proving that the plaintiff was damaged and that these damages were caused by the defendant.[2] Establishing the fact of the damages is the key first hurdle that an antitrust plaintiff must traverse. Courts have used words such as *reasonable probability* (*Knutson v. Daily Review, Inc.*) and *reasonable certainty* (*Sunkist Growers v. Winkler & Smith Citrus Products Co.*) when describing the standard to be used in establishing the fact of damages and the causal relationship between the defendant's actions and the damages incurred by the plaintiff.

The strict requirements in establishing the fact of the damages present many opportunities for defendants to find other factors that could have caused the plaintiff's damages. These factors vary from case to case, but often they may be found in the economic and industry analysis that was covered in Chapters 3 and 4. The defendant may accomplish its goals even if it cannot conclusively prove that such other factors caused the plaintiff's damages. The defendant may be able to accomplish its goal by making the waters murky and raising doubts about the causal linkage put forward by the plaintiff. For example, in the *United States Football League v. National Football League,* the defendant was able to establish that factors such as mismanagement were important explanatory variables.[3]

Once the fact of the damages has been established, courts tends to apply a more relaxed standard to measuring the amount of the plaintiff's damages,[4] partially because once the world has been changed by the defendant's conduct, it is difficult to reconstruct the position of plaintiff. As with other types of damages analysis, while the burden of proof may be less for measuring damages, the analysis still must be nonspeculative. If the defendant can show that the plaintiff's damages analysis is speculative, then such damages may not be recoverable.

Interpretation of Antitrust Violations: Structure versus Conduct

There are two opposing schools of thought in antitrust enforcement. The structure school of antitrust sees that the mere possession of monopoly power is by itself an antitrust violation. Under this view, a firm is guilty of an antitrust violation even if it did not engage in conduct that would otherwise be considered a

---

[2] *Bogosian v. Gulf Oil Corp.*, 561 F.2d 434, 454 (3rd Cir. 1977), *cert denied*, 434 U.S. 1086 (1987).

[3] *United States Football League v. National Football League*, 842 F. 2d 1335 (2d cir. 1988).

[4] *Van Dyk Research Corp. v. Xerox Corp.*, 631 F. 2d 251, 255 (3rd Cir. 1980).

violation of antitrust laws. Mere size alone would be enough to be found guilty of antitrust violations. Such would be the case even if the firm did not do anything to limit the ability of other firms to enter the market and to compete.

Under the conduct view, the mere possession of monopoly power is not a per se violation. The firm would have to engage in other unacceptable conduct in order for it to be guilty of antitrust violations. It is even possible that one firm that had a large market share but did not engage in any anticompetitive behavior could be innocent of antitrust violations, whereas a firm with a smaller market share that took actions to try to limit competition would be found guilty.

Changing Pattern of Antitrust Enforcement

In the early part of the century, the courts focused on a combination of structure and conduct. It went after companies that clearly had very large market shares but it also considered their anticompetitive conduct. These decisions quickly evolved into the *Rule of Reason* where behavior became the main focus of the court.

Early Cases

In 1911, two major antitrust cases were brought against two companies that held dominant positions which they achieved through the use of various forms of anticompetitive behavior. The first of these is the *Standard Oil* case in which the court focused on the many anticompetitive acts engaged in by the company to garner a 90% market share of the petroleum industry.[5] Although the court was impressed with the large market share, it was even more concerned with the variety of anticompetitive behavior the company engaged in to drive out competitors in order to achieve this market share. Such behavior included industrial espionage and local price wars. The court's solution was to require dissolution of the company, which was dissembled into 34 separate companies.

In the same year, the U.S. Supreme Court ruled against American Tobacco for similar reasons.[6] American Tobacco's market share was even greater than Standard Oil's with American Tobacco dominating over 90% of the market. American Tobacco achieved this market share through a variety of questionable marketing and promotional tactics that were used in large-scale predatory campaigns designed to drive competitors out of existence. The company invested a large

---

[5] *Standard Oil Company of New Jersey v. U.S.*, 221 U.S. 1 (1911).
[6] *U.S. v. American Tobacco Co.*, 221 U.S. 106 (1911).

percent of revenues in advertising and marketing and used these resources in selective markets to eliminate competitors. This predatory behavior also included the establishment of "fighting brands," which were sold at predatory prices until the competitors acquiesced and sold out to American Tobacco and its CEO James Duke. Once again, the court focused on the objectionable behavior and required dissolution of the company. An oligopolistic market structure resulted.

Rule of Reason and the U.S. Steel Case

The evolution of the rule of reason took a major step with the *U.S. Steel* case.[7] Here U.S. Steel was shown to have a dominant position as evidenced by its market share, which was far greater than that of any of its competitors. The firm was formed through a consolidation of many different plants and competitors, leaving it with most of the market's production. This process was part of an overall consolidation that was occurring throughout the U.S. economy and constituted the first merger wave in U.S. economic history. However, the court concluded that even though U.S. Steel did possess market power, it did not engage in any offensive conduct. The court found that even though the company accounted for approximately one-half of the market, its market share actually had fallen from as high as 66%.

In the *U.S. Steel* case the court focused on the fact that the company did not make any attempt to price its products in a manner that would drive out competitors. In its decision, the court stated that size alone was not anticompetitive and U.S. Steel did not use its dominant position to limit competition.

Structure and the Alcoa Case

The position of the Court shifted in 1945 when it moved away from the Rule of Reason and began to consider size by itself to be objectionable. In his decision, Judge Learned Hand found that Alcoa had built up its bauxite reserves with the intention to monopolize the aluminum industry.[8] He was particularly impressed by the dominant position of Alcoa and was concerned that even if the company had not used its market power to engage in anticompetitive conduct, the mere possession of such power and the clear ability of a firm who possessed such power to dominate markets was sufficient to constitute an antitrust violation. Judge Hand's solution was to force Alcoa to sell off parts of the company to competitors Reynolds Metals and Kaiser Aluminum and to not build any more plants for a period of time.

---

[7] *U.S. v. U.S. Steel Corporation*, 251 U.S. 417 (1920).

[8] *U.S. v. Aluminum Company of America et al.*, 148 F. 2d 416, 424 (1945).

It is noteworthy that the Alcoa decision was followed by another major antitrust decision in the following year. In 1946, the court continued a pattern of more intensive antitrust enforcement when it found the management of A&P guilty of anticompetitive behavior.[9]

The Fifties and Sixties

Following the *Alcoa* and the *A&P* decisions, antitrust enforcement grew very intense. Antitrust laws were buttressed by the passage of the Celler-Kefauver Act in 1950 which strengthened the Clayton Act. Combined with the decisions of the 1940s, it created an environment in which the Justice Department and the Federal Trade Commission wielded considerable power. There were not as many landmark decisions in this period but this was not indicative of the intensity of antitrust enforcement. Companies were often reluctant to pursue a case through trial and ended up settling and entering into agreements with the Justice Department.

When companies wanted to expand in the 1960s they ran into a veritable wall of antitrust enforcement that limited their ability to expand within their own markets or even outside of their usual industries. The intense antitrust enforcement of this period combined with the desire of companies to expand following the longest recovery on modern U.S. economic history caused the unique characteristics of the third merger wave. This wave, which took place at the end of the 1960s, featured conglomerate mergers, which are mergers outside of the company's industry.[10] Companies were reluctant to expand within their own industries because they knew that such mergers were often challenged. The antitrust enforcement became so intense that even conglomerate mergers were questioned.

The Seventies and Eighties

The 1970s and the 1980s were periods of more relaxed antitrust enforcement. More pro-business administrations in Washington, D.C. came to power and placed similarly minded individuals in positions of power at the Justice Department. These individuals believed that even in oligopolistic market structures there can be significant competition among the participants of the industry. Broader definitions of markets were applied while consideration was given to factors such as global competitiveness.

---

[9] *U.S. v. New York Great Atlantic and Pacific Tea Company et al.*, 67 F. Supp. 626 (1946), 173 F. 2d (1949).

[10] Patrick A. Gaughan, *Mergers, Acquisitions and Corporate Restructuring*, 2nd ed. (New York: Wiley) 1999, 30–38.

The Nineties

The 1990s marked somewhat of a shift away from the more relaxed posture of antitrust enforcement that was the norm during the 1980s. Mergers that may not have been questioned in the 1980s were given somewhat closer scrutiny by the Justice Department. Certain major firms that held dominant positions in markets, such as Microsoft and Intel, were watched carefully and challenged when they attempted acquisitions within their broadly defined industry category or when they tried to market products that could be construed as giving their products an unfair advantage over competitors. The government's challenge to Microsoft's efforts to market its web browser within its operating system is an example of this sterner posture.

MONOPOLIZATION AND ATTEMPTS AT MONOPOLIZATION

As noted earlier in this chapter, Section 2 of the Sherman Act prohibits a company from monopolizing an industry or taking actions designed to achieve this goal. As part of the process of making a judgment regarding whether a firm has a monopoly position, various quantitative microeconomic measures can be employed. One of the first steps in this process is to define the relevant market.

Market Definition

The definition of a market determines the products and services that are competing with the product in question as well as the geographical area within which such competition occurs. Therefore, a market can be defined in two broad ways—geographic markets and product markets. Each way to define markets has its own quantitative measures that can be employed.

Geographic Market Definitions

Geographic definitions of markets have varied considerably over time as the intensity of antitrust has varied. As markets have become broader and more internationalized, the definition of the relevant markets in some instances has widened. The degree to which increased internationalization is relevant to the case clearly depends on the industry and the facts of the case.

Economists usually define the geographic boundaries of a market by judging whether an increase in the price in one market affects the price in another market.[11] Other factors related to the definition of the geographic market are variables such as transportation costs that would be incurred to move the products from one market to the other. The more significant the transportation costs in the total costs of the product, the more likely that such costs might serve to segregate the markets into separate markets. However, the expert needs to consider factors that could offset these costs, such as the existence of storage or distribution facilities.

Regulatory factors may play a role in the geographic definition of a market. For example, if there are governmental regulations that prohibit selling the product or service outside of certain boundaries, these regulations may help define the geographical boundaries. Such factors have played an important role in the banking industry, although their importance has declined significantly as the industry has undergone deregulation.

If marketing and advertising play a major role in the generation of the demand for the product or service, then the geographic limitations of the often used advertising media may also help define the geographic market. However, as the marketing and advertising industry has itself undergone major changes, the role of this factor may vary considerably.

Product Market Definitions

The broader the market, the less likely it is that a given firm is found to have monopolized it. Competitive products are those which are substitutes for one another. Products X and Y are *demand substitutes* for each other if an increase in the product X causes an increase in the quantity demanded of product Y. Products A and B are *supply substitutes* if an increase in the price of product A causes companies that are producing B to alter their production mix and increase their production of A.

Price and Substitutability

The degree of substitutability between two products is not a constant but rather may vary as the price changes. At a low price two products, X and Y, may not be substitutable but at higher prices they may become substitutes. There tends to be some price, which if the seller sets it at a certain level, that will cause consumers to look for substitutes. The fact that at a higher price of good X its

---

[11] Dennis Carlton and Jeffrey M. Perloff, *Modern Industrial Organization* (New York: Harper Collins) 1994, 807.

seller faces competition from substitutes does not mean that the company selling X lacks market power. Its market power may lie in the fact that it has the ability to sell the products at a price as high as can be before it faces significant competition.

Determining the Existence of Substitutes

A simple method of determining the degree to which products are considered substitutes is to survey the marketing and sales professionals in the industry. Sales people who may not have any knowledge of economics may know very well who their competition is as they try to sell their products. Marketing professionals who develop marketing campaigns may also have intimate knowledge of who their major competitors are.

Using Correlation Analysis

If two products are substitutes, then presumably their prices move together as they engage in price competition. The degree to which these prices move together may be measured using correlation analysis. Correlation analysis was discussed in Chapter 2 in the context of causality in commercial litigation. High correlation coefficients would be one indicator that the products are substitutes. Low correlations would not support the assertion that products are substitutes. However, this is not to imply that correlation analysis alone is conclusive.

Another method of determining whether a particular product Y may be a substitute for another one, X, is to find still another product, Z, which is accepted as a substitute for X. Correlations of the movements in the prices of X and Z could be computed to measure their degree of association. This value is used as a benchmark.[12] This correlation would then be compared to the correlation between the prices of X and Y. Very different correlation coefficients fail to support the assertion that X and Y are in the same market. However, this statement is very general, and each case may have other factors that may offset this difference in the correlation coefficients.

Cross Price Elasticity of Demand

A quantitative measure that may be useful in assessing the extent to which two products are substitutes is the cross price elasticity of demand. This cross price elasticity of demand measures the percent change in quantity demanded of good X in response to a given percent change in the price of good Y. This measure is

---

[12] *Id.*, p. 806.

expressed as follows:

$$\varepsilon_{xy} = \%\Delta Q_x / \%\Delta P_y = \Delta Q_x / Q_x / \Delta P_y / P_y = P_y / Q_x \Delta Q_x / \Delta P_y \qquad (11.1)$$

Two goods can have three different values of the cross elasticity of demand. The values can be positive, negative, or zero. Such values reflect the extent to which they are substitutes, complements, or have no interrelation in consumption. Substitutes are goods that can be used in place of the good in question, presumably because they have some similar characteristics in the eyes of consumers. Complements are goods that must be used together. Many consider tea and lemon complements, whereas some consider Coca Cola and Pepsi Cola to be substitutes.

When the price of good Y increases and the quantity demanded of X increases, X and Y are said to be substitutes in consumption. When the price of Y rises and the quantity demanded of X decreases, the two goods are said to be complements. If there is no change in the quantity demanded of X when the price of Y changes, the consumption of the two goods may not be interrelated. This relationship is summarized as follows:

$$\varepsilon_{xy} > 0 \qquad \text{X and Y are substitutes}$$

$$\varepsilon_{xy} < 0 \qquad \text{X and Y are complements}$$

$$\varepsilon_{xy} = 0 \qquad \text{X and Y have no relationship in consumption}$$

Own Price Elasticity of Demand versus Cross Price Elasticity of Demand

The own price elasticity of demand, that is the percent change in the quantity of X that occurs as a result of the percent change in the price of X, is different from the cross price elasticity of demand, which is the percent change in the quantity of X in response to a percent change in the price of Y. Both elasticity measures are relevant to antitrust analysis and a firm's market power. The own price elasticity of demand is relevant to understanding the ability of the firm to raise price above marginal costs and enjoy extranormal profits, whereas the cross price elasticity of demand is also relevant in assessing competitive effects.

Barriers to Entry

A monopoly has two important features:

- Lack of close substitutes
- Barriers to entry

We have already discussed the process of determining whether close substitutes for the product of an alleged monopolist exists. Another factor that can insulate a company from competition is barriers to entry. Such barriers prevent competitors from entering the industry and competing. These can arise for several reasons. Legal barriers occur when a company is given a legal right to be the only marketer of a product such as in the case of a patent or copyright. Another legal barrier would be a franchise which may be awarded in cases where the government believes that there are significant economies of scale and society would benefit by having one company producing a higher output and realizing cost economies. Such a company would be what is referred to as a natural monopoly. Barriers to entry that are more relevant to antitrust litigation occur when a company takes actions that are tantamount to erecting a barrier to prevent potential entrants from competing with it. Professor Schmalensee, dean of the Sloan School of the Massachusetts Institute of Technology, in his direct testimony as an expert witness for Microsoft contrasted a noneconomist's view of barriers to entry to that of an economist's:

> People who are not trained in economics tend to think of barriers as obstacles that entrants face—for example, scraping together the money to start a business and developing a reputation with customers—and high barriers as obstacles that are large in some absolute sense. Economists, however, apply a more rigorous approach and consider a cost or obstacle to be a barrier to entry if and only if it can prevent a more efficient entrant (More efficient in the sense of having a better product or a lower cost of production) from competing effectively with (and perhaps displacing) a less efficient incumbent.[13] That refined definition confines the use of the pejorative term "barrier" to those instances in which the barrier prevents an entrant from making consumers better off. Although there is no generally accepted definition of what a high barrier to entry is, I define high as a barrier that is larger relative to the expected gains from entry.[14]

---

[13] In his paper "Diagnosing Monopoly," Professor Fisher has noted, "A barrier to entry would be socially beneficial but is somehow prevented." [in Franklin Fisher, *Industrial Organization, Economics and the Law* (Cambridge, MA: Massachusetts Institute of Technology), 1991, 22.] Also see Franklin Fisher, John McGowan, and Joen Greenwood, *Folded Spindled and Mutilated* (Cambridge: MIT Press), 1985, 165.

[14] Direct testimony of Dean Richard Schmalensee, *United States v. Microsoft Corporation et al.,* January 14, 1999.

MARKET POWER

In microeconomics, market power is measured by the ability of the seller to charge a price above marginal costs. Marginal costs are taken to be the price that would prevail in a purely competitive market. Sellers set price equal to marginal cost. However, few industries correspond to the exact characteristics of a purely competitive market. These characteristics are as follows:

- Many independent sellers
- Perfect information
- Homogeneous, undifferentiated products
- No barriers to entry

Clearly most firms have some element of market power while others possess significant market power. To the extent that a given firm has some market power, its price exceeds marginal costs. One of the problems of applying a concept such as marginal cost is that it is difficult to measure. If, however, a reasonable approximation can be made, then market power may be measured using the *Lerner Index*. This index, named after the economist Abba Lerner, may be expressed as follows:

$$(P - MC)/P = 1/\varepsilon \tag{11.2}$$

The left-hand side of this equation is called the *price-cost margin*. This margin is a function of the price elasticity of demand, ϵ. Specifically, the magnitude of the margin is inversely related to the price elasticity of demand. That is, when the price elasticity of demand is low, price is significantly greater than marginal costs. On the other hand, when the price elasticity of demand is high, marginal costs are very close to price.

The Lerner Index is useful in that it enables us to see how a monopolist's market power is related to its ability to set price above marginal costs. The more inelastic demand is, the greater the monopolist's ability to widen the price-marginal costs gap.

However, merely having monopoly power, as measured by the ability to set price above *marginal* costs, does not mean that a firm makes a profit.[15] It could be that the firm has fixed costs, for example, that make a positive profit at its op-

---

[15] Economists define profit differently from accountants. Economic profit may include opportunity costs, which can create a situation where an accountant can say that there are profits where an economist might not agree.

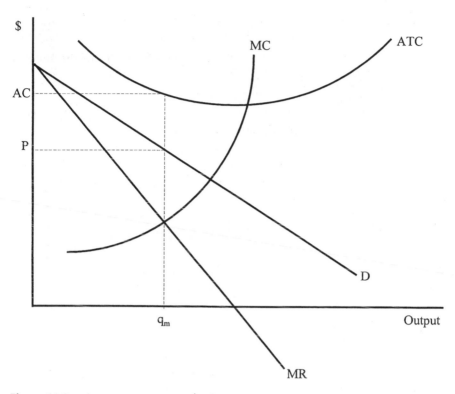

Figure 11.3. Average costs exceed price.

timal output, the output where marginal revenue equals marginal costs, impossible. This condition is shown in Figure 11.3 where average costs (*AC*) are always above the demand curve, which means that in this example price (*P*) is always less than average costs, even at the optimal output $-q_m$.

Market Power versus Monopoly Power

Market power is not the same as monopoly power. As described earlier, market power is a departure from competitive conditions. Firms with market power can maintain prices above the level that would have prevailed in a competitive environment. However, just because a company has some market power does not mean that it is a monopolist. Monopoly power implies an even greater degree of market power. The distinction between these two concepts is described in the direct testimony of Dr. Franklin Fisher in the *U.S. v. Microsoft* trial.

Market power is a matter of degree. The possession of a small degree of market power is common in the real world. For example, a corner grocery store may possess a small degree of market power. When present only to a small degree, market power should not be of antitrust concern.

Monopoly power is a substantial degree of market power. While a firm with a slight degree of market power may find it profitable to charge supra-normal prices for a short time or to charge prices that are only slightly supra-normal, a firm with monopoly power will find it profitable (a) to charge a price significantly in excess of competitive levels and (b) to do so over a significant period of time. I believe this definition is consistent with the often cited legal definition of monopoly power as "the power to control prices or to exclude competition." [16]

Measures of Market Concentration

In economics there are two opposite types of market structure—pure competition and monopoly. In pure competition, the firms lack market power, whereas in monopoly the monopolist has some degree of market power. In reality, most industries are neither monopolists or purely competitive. However, depending on how close they are to either end of the industry spectrum, some of the characteristics of either form of industry structure may apply. Towards that end, it is useful to measure the degree of concentration in an industry. This can be done in different ways. One of the most basic is simply concentration ratios.

Concentration Ratios

Concentration ratios measure the amount of total market output that is accounted for by the top four, top eight or possibly other groupings, such as the top 12 companies in the industry. The greater the market share accounted for by a smaller grouping of firms, the closer to monopoly an industry is. Industries where the top four or eight account for most of the industry output usually are considered oligopolies. An example of the wide ranges of concentration ratios in different industries can be found in the Census Bureau's reports.[17] It is important to keep in mind that one cannot judge the degree of competition in an industry by simply looking at concentration ratios alone. An industry can have a significant degree of competition, even when the number of competitors is relatively small.

---

[16] Direct testimony of Dr. Franklin Fisher, *United States of America v. Microsoft Corporation et al.*

[17] U.S. Bureau of the Census, 1982 Census of Manufactures, "Concentration Ratios in Manufacturing," April 1986, Washington, D.C.

Herfindahl-Hirshman Index

Concentration ratios are not that sensitive to changes in industry concentration caused by mergers among firms in the same size category. For example, if the top firms constitute 98% of total industry output and there is a merger between the number six and number seven companies in the industry, the top eight concentration ratio will shed little light on the competitive effects of this change in control. To remedy such problems, regulatory authorities rely on the Herfindahl-Hirshman Index, which is expressed as follows:

$$\text{HHI} = \sum_{i=1}^{n} S_i^2 \qquad (11.3)$$

where s_i equals the market share of the ith firm.

Given that the market shares of the firms are squared, the index places disproportionately greater weight on larger firms. In Equation (11.4), the merger between the sixth and seventh largest firms has little impact on the top eight concentration ratio other than to admit the relatively small previously ninth firm into the number eight spot. However, the HHI index may rise significantly when the number six and seven firms merge. In an effort to set guidelines on the types of mergers and acquisitions that would be opposed by the Justice Department, it has set forth merger guidelines in terms of the Herfindahl-Hirshman Index.

COMMON TYPES OF ANTITRUST CASES

Overview

With the dramatic increase in mergers and acquisitions that occurred in the 1980s and 1990s, lawsuits involving alleged increases in market power resulting from such transactions may require antitrust analysis. However, in addition to allegations of basic monopolization of markets, certain other types of antitrust violations arise: predatory pricing and tying contracts. Predatory pricing is a violation of Section 2 of the Sherman Act, whereas tying contracts violates Section 3 of the Clayton Act. There is an abundant literature on each of these types of violations that is well beyond the scope of this chapter. We provide an introduction to some of the issues and tools that may be employed in a litigation environment.

Mergers and Acquisitions Antitrust Analysis

The 1980s featured a dramatic increase in both the number and size of mergers and acquisitions. This period was the fourth merger wave that occurred in U.S. economic history. It ended in the late 1980s with the collapse of the junk bond market, which helped fuel the many hostile deals that occurred then, and the overall slowdown in the economy. However, after a relatively short hiatus, the pace of mergers and acquisitions picked up around 1993 and the resulting merger frenzy surpassed even the lofty levels reached in the 1980s.

Regulatory Framework

Mergers and acquisitions are highly regulated. Purchases of stock beyond the 5% threshold requires the filing of a Schedule 13D disclosure statement pursuant to the Williams Act or Section 13 (d) of the Securities Exchange Act, while tender offers require the filing of a Schedule 14D-1 pursuant to Section 14(d) of the same law. However, in addition to these securities laws, a special disclosure-related law, the Hart-Scott-Rodino Antitrust Improvement Act, exists for the antitrust ramifications of mergers and acquisitions.

Horizontal Mergers and Acquisitions

Section 7 of the Clayton Act, which was amended in 1950 by the Celler-Kefauver Act to include asset transactions, makes deals in "any area of commerce" or in "any section of the country" that lessens competition or tends to create an illegal monopoly. The wording of these excerpts from the law is revealing. The term "any area of commerce" implies that the industry definition may be flexible. In addition, regional concentration becomes an issue under the wording "any section of the country." The phrase "tend to create a monopoly" makes the law applicable even if the deal did not result in a clear monopoly. Given its broad wording, this section of the Clayton Act, along with the Sherman Act, are potent weapons in the hands of regulators who are predisposed to oppose such deals.

One of the most common antitrust complaints in mergers and acquisitions has to do with increases in market power caused by horizontal transactions, such as a merger between rivals. This claim began to be asserted more often in the mid-1990s as the industry consolidations of the fifth merger started to have an effect on the degree of concentration in some industries. This led the Justice Department to play a more active role in examining the mergers that took place.

Predatory Pricing

Predatory pricing refers to the use of price competition to drive rivals out of business and to prevent the entry of competitors into the firm's market. Obviously, one of the key tasks in a predatory pricing analysis is to determine whether the price competition was the result of ordinary competitive actions or was part of a predatory process. One of the problems of predatory pricing economic analysis is distinguishing predatory pricing from ordinary competition.[18] Courts have recognized that cutting prices is one of the main forms of competition.[19] In order to determine if the prices were predatory one must compare price to some measure of the alleged predators costs, which usually involves showing that the predators incurred losses, usually short-run losses, in order to generate longer term gains.

Predation may be more possible in markets where the predator has certain advantages over current or potential rivals. The advantages may come in the form of larger size or lower costs. Certain game-theoretic issues can arise when the competitors do not know the other firm's cost structure but can merely formulate guesses based on a variety of observable variables such as the rival's prices and responses to the prices of competitors.

Areeda and Turner's Marginal Cost Rule of Predatory Pricing

One of the leading treatises in the area of predatory pricing was the 1975 article by Philip Areeda and Donald Turner.[20] Under the Areeda and Turner standard, pricing is predatory if it falls below the alleged predator's short-run marginal cost. This implies that costs above short-run marginal costs are lawful. However, given the difficulty in measuring marginal costs, Areeda and Turner suggest that average *variable* costs be used as a proxy for marginal costs. Alternatives to the Areeda and Turner average variable costs rule have been put forward, which include using long-run marginal costs as well as average total costs. Given that average variable costs are generally below average total costs, it may not be necessary to look at *both* average variable and average total, because prices that are below average variable should also be below average total costs.[21]

The courts have not put forward one accepted measure of costs. For example, this issue was sidestepped in both *Cargill, Inc. v. Monfort of Colorado* and *Matsushita Electrical Industrial Corp. v. Zenith Radio Corp. et al.* Even in *Brooke Group Ltd. v. Brown & Williamson Tobacco Corp.*, the court did not have to deal with this issue as both parties to the suit agreed that the appropriate cost measure

---

[18] Frank Easterbrook, "Predatory Strategies and Counterstrategies," *University of Chicago Law Review,* 48 (2), Spring 1981, 263–337.

[19] *Eastman Kodak Co. v. Image Tech. Services.,* 112 S. Ct. 2072, 2088 (1992).

[20] Philip E. Areeda and Donald F. Turner, "Predatory Pricing and Related Practices Under Section Two of the Sherman Act," *Harvard Law Review* 86, 697–733.

[21] Paul L. Joskow and Alvin K. Klevorick, "A Framework for Analyzing Predatory Pricing Policy," *The Yale Law Journal* 89 (2) December 1979, 213–270.

was average variable cost. Other unresolved cost issues are how to treat fixed versus variable cost. This issue includes how one treats costs that are fixed over one time period but that vary as the time period expands.

Recoupment of Losses

One important result that one can derive from *Brooke Group v. Brown & Williamson Tobacco* is that the plaintiff must demonstrate that the defendant has a reasonable probability of recouping the losses it incurred by allegedly pricing below costs. This process involves showing that over some reasonable time period the defendant would be able to increase price above the competitive level.[22] The present value of these future profits must offset the present value of the costs incurred through the losses caused by the below cost prices.

Criticisms of the Economics of Predatory Pricing Claims

There has been much criticism of the appropriateness of predatory pricing claims, much of which revolves around whether predatory pricing can be an effective means of acquiring monopoly power.[23] Some question the reasonableness of a rational competitor pricing at a level where it incurs losses simply to impose losses on other firms.[24] John McGee, a famous critic of reasonableness of predatory pricing claims, has emphasized that there are much less costly ways to obtain the same advantages that predators are seeking, such as mergers.[25] In addition, he points out that once competitors perceive that the predator's actions are temporary, they may also wait out the loss period with the predator. If the actions force them to leave, McGee states that they may reenter. Others have questioned the reasonableness of McGee's criticisms, which may seem accurate in theory but when confronted with the realities of certain market situations may not hold up.[26] Rivals may not be able to wait out the losses as well as a predator with larger financial resources. In addition, rivals who were once forced out by losses

---

[22] Michael Denger and John A. Herfort, "Predatory Pricing Claims After Brooke Group," *Antitrust Law Journal* 62 (3) Spring 1994, 541–558.

[23] B. S. Yamey, "Predatory Price Cutting: Notes and Comments," 15, *Journal of Law and Economics,* 129, 1972.

[24] Richard Posner, *Antitrust Law: An Economic Perspective* (Chicago: University of Chicago Press) 187.

[25] John S. McGee, "Predatory Price Cutting: The Standard Oil Case," *Journal of Law and Economics* October 1958, 137–169; John S. McGee, "Predatory Pricing Revisited," Journal of Law and Economics October 1980, 289–330.

[26] Douglas Greer, *Industrial Organization and Public Policy,* 3rd ed., (New York: MacMillian), 1992, 453–455.

incurred at the hands of a predator may think twice before devoting capital to an industry that has dealt such unpleasant experiences while other more attractive opportunities may exist.

Credibility and Alleged Predation Over Time
In *Matsushita Electrical Co. Ltd. v. Zenith Radio Corporation et al.,* the Supreme Court questioned the reasonableness of claims of predatory pricing that extended two decades. The court concluded that it is not reasonable that any competitor would incur losses over such a long time period in the hope of recouping these gains at some indeterminate time in the future. Such a plan implies that the alleged predator is using a rather unreasonable discount rate in its competitive strategy. Ruling out such a strategy, the court concluded that the prices must be the product of normal competition. One lesson that arises from this case is that the time period over which the alleged predatory pricing occurred must be of a reasonable length and cannot be so long as to make the claims lack credibility.

Predatory "Costing"
An interesting variant of predatory behavior is where a firm seeks to drive out rivals not by lowering their revenues through predatory pricing but by taking actions that will increase their costs. Competitors who have their costs increased may reduce output, which may allow the predator to increase its market share.[27]

Price Fixing

Price fixing is a violation of Section 1 of the Sherman Act. The law makes collusive behavior among competitors who seek to establish certain market prices per se illegal. This type of price fixing is called *horizontal price fixing*. Price fixing can also be vertical, such as when a firm at one stage of the production-distribution chain seeks to change prices at another stage. An example would be if a manufacturer wanted to require distributors or retailers to maintain prices above certain levels.

Damages in Horizontal Price Fixing
In cases of horizontal price fixing, plaintiffs may pay higher prices that what they would have paid in the absence of price fixing. This difference in prices

---

[27] Steven C. Salop and David T. Scheffman, "Recent Advances in the Theory of Industrial Structure," *Recent Advances in the Theory of Industrial Structure* 73 (2), May 1983, 267–271.

may be a measure of the plaintiff's per-unit damages. The price difference can then be applied to a quantity measure to arrive at a cumulative damages value. One of the difficult tasks facing the economist is to determine what prices would have been without the collusive behavior. One method that is used to determine such prices is the *Before and After method* which was discussed in Chapter 2. This method looks to find a period of time where there was no price fixing. Depending on the facts of the case, this time period could either be before or after the price fixing. The difference in prices between the "no-price fixing" time and the price-fixed period are then computed to measure the per-unit damages. One important analytical element of the Before and After method is to establish the economic comparability of the two time periods to rule out any other economic factors that may have been responsible for the price difference. Defendants may want to explore this area. One issue that is often not considered by courts is the quantity variation that might have occurred in response to the varying prices.

If there are no time periods without the presence of price fixing then an alternative to the Before and After method would be to find some proxy firms who are very similar but who are not involved in the price fixing. As discussed in Chapter 2, this method is referred to as the *Yardstick method*.[28]

Measuring Damages in Vertical Price Fixing Cases

The measurement of damages in a vertical price fixing case involves establishing the per-unit damages as measured by the difference between the fixed price and unaffected prices. The expert may be able to find examples of both prices when there are marketers who sell under the fixed as well as the unfixed price policy. An example would be if a manufacturer of a product requires its distributors to sell at certain minimum prices. If the distributors try to sell at lower prices and the manufacturer responds by taking certain actions such as cutting off the distributors' supplies, there may be readily available evidence of both sets of prices in the market.

One important component of the analysis is to show that there actually are damages. It could be the case that the manufacturer is trying to extract economic rent by imposing its fixed prices. If the defendant can establish that the plaintiff would have sold at the disputed prices even without the actions of the defendant, then no damages will be found.

---

[28] *Fishman v. Estate of Wirtz,* 807 F. 2d 520, 551 (7th Cir. 1986).

Tying Contracts

Another common type of antitrust case is one where there is an allegation of a *tying contract*. Tying contracts can occur when a seller requires a buyer to purchase products from it at certain prices which the buyer would otherwise not purchase. Such contracts are illegal pursuant to Section 3 of the Clayton Act. Tying contracts can occur when the defendant is trying to extend market power it may possess in one market into another market where its lacks such power. This could occur, for example, if the defendant has a monopoly in one market but faces competition from several other sellers in the other market. If the plaintiff needs both products for its production process, it be forced to acquiesce to the seller's requirements.

A famous tying contract case was *International Business Machines v. U.S.*[29] The Supreme Court concluded that IBM's requirement that buyers of its machines purchase their computer cards from them as well was an example of IBM using its market power, derived from its preeminent position in the computer industry, to engage in price discrimination. The more intensive users of the machines would purchase more cards and would, therefore, pay more in total than those who used the machines less intensively and order fewer cards. Here tying contracts were the means whereby IBM became what is referred to as a *price discriminating monopolist*.

Determining If Products Are Truly Separate

One of the tasks before the economic expert in a tying contracts case is to determine if the products are truly separate or if they are naturally bundled together. If the latter is the case, it may be a costly task to unbundle them and this process may work to raise the ultimate price to the consumer. For example, in *Jefferson Parish Hospital District No. 2 v. Hyde*, the court determined that the services of anesthesiologists were separate from the services that a hospital offers.[30]

A classic example of goods that are often tied together but that do not necessarily have to be offered together are products that require service. The manufacturer may want to require buyers to purchase the service from it. One argument made by defendants in these types of actions is that substandard service may damage the product and affect the warranty.[31] This argument can be weakened if the plain-

---

[29] *International Business Machines v. United States*, 298 U.S. (1936).

[30] *Jefferson Parish Hospital No. 2 v. Hyde*, 466 U.S. 2 (1984).

[31] *Jerrold Electronics Corp. v. United States*, 187 F. Supp. 545 (1961).

tiff service organization can demonstrate that it is capable of offering similar quality services. Such cases have arisen when former service employees of a defendant leave its employ after having provided service to the defendant's consumers and after having been trained by the defendant and enter into competition with the defendant in the services business. In such circumstances, the defendant needs to show why, in spite of these factors, there is a quality control issue.

One of the ways that manufacturers try to make it difficult for third party service organizations to enter the services market is to refuse to sell parts to such organizations. Faced with such a shortage of parts essential to provide timely service, these companies often resort to purchasing used equipment and taking it apart for parts. Even here the manufacturer may have an advantage in that it may be able to claim that only it has new parts while competing services companies offer used parts that may not perform as well. Probably the most well-known case in this area is *Eastman Kodak Co. v. Image Technical Services.*[32] In a case of this type the definition of market can be crucial. The independent services organizations (ISOs) conceded that Kodak, which had less than a 25% market share, did not have power in the market for the copiers that they sold and which were being serviced by the ISOs. However, the ISOs asserted that Kodak had a monopoly in the market for the parts for Kodak's own products. A divided Supreme Court concluded, however, that the absence of market power at the initial product level did not necessarily preclude the exercise of anticompetitive market power in the aftermarket.[33] Kodak had argued that assertions that Kodak would raise prices in the aftermarket above competitive levels would not make sense as they would raise the total cost of the product, which would hurt Kodak's competitive position in the equipment market. This view is put forward by some economists who assert that the market power for these interrelated products or systems, is very interdependent.[34] While some see this as a rejection of pure economic theory, the court did conclude that markets may not work perfectly and these imperfections may make the simplistic theory of equipment market competition fail to prevent aftermarket anticompetitive activities.[35] Others do not see this as a rejection of pure economic theory, or what some refer to as Chicago economic theory, but rather see the courts moving to a more modern, or post-

---

[32] *Eastman Kodak Co. v. Image Technical Services,* 112 S. Ct. 2072 (1992).

[33] *Image Technical Services, Inc. v. Eastman Kodak Co.,* 903 F. 2d, 612, 617 (9th Cir. 1990).

[34] Carl Shapiro and David Teece, "Systems Competition and Aftermarkets: An Economic Analysis of *Kodak*," *Antitrust Bulletin* 39 (1), Spring 1994, 135–162.

[35] Benjamin Klein, "Market Power in Antitrust: Economic Analysis After *Kodak*," *Supreme Court Economic Review* 3 (0), 1993, 43–92.

Chicago stance, in which a variety of economic factors, which include more recent developments in the field of industrial organization, are taken into account in reaching modern antitrust decisions.[36] Other economists do not think that the Court went far enough and assert that the competition in the equipment market may have little effect on a manufacturer's attempt to monopolize its after-market.[37] As of this writing, this issue remains hotly debated in the economics profession.

Measuring Damages from Tying Arrangements

Damages analysis for tied products is similar to the analytical process used for horizontal price fixing. The expert may measure the difference between the price that would have been paid had there not been tying and the price that was actually paid.[38] This price difference can be applied to a measure of quantity to arrive at an amount of damages.

Part of the damages investigation process may be to try to determine if, but for the tying, there were other substitute products available at lower prices. If this cannot be done, then there may not be a basis for a damages claim. The expert's research needs to establish that the products were comparable in their features and characteristics.

Distributor Termination and Antitrust

Termination of distributors is a common type of case where there are antitrust allegations along with possible other claims such as breach of contract. In order to seek relief under antitrust laws, the plaintiff ex-distributor needs to show a conspiracy on the part of the defendant to terminate the distributor as part of a process to reduce competition or monopolize a given market.

The methods used to measure damages from a termination of a distributor's agreement are similar to those discussed at length earlier in this book. They often involve a measurement of reduced sales and application of a relevant profit mar-

---

[36] Steven C. Salop, "Kodak as Post-Chicago Law and Economics," Charles River Associates, April 1993.

[37] Severin Borenstein, Jeffery MacKieMason, and Janet S. Netz, "The Economics of Customer Lock-In and Market Power in Services," *The Service Productivity and Quality Challenge,* Patrick T. Harker, ed., International Studies in The Service Economy, Vol. 5 (Dordrecht, Boston and London: Kluwer Academic) 1995, 225–250.

[38] *Northern v. McGraw-Edison Co.,* 542 F. 2d 1336, 1347 (8th Cir. 1976), cert. denied, 429 U.S. 1097 (1977).

gin that is applied to the amount of lost sales. One of the differences with the analysis that the expert may do in an antitrust case compared to another type of business interruption claim may be in the additional economic analysis done to establish the economic effects of the anticompetitive behavior. This analysis may be done to establish liability while the traditional damage measurement methods may be used to quantify the damages.

In cases where the terminated distributor has gone out of business, it may be necessary to do a business valuation. This may be done for the entire business in cases where it has closed, or it may be done for a component of the business that may have ceased operating. If the plaintiff can establish that this segment of its overall operation could have been sold separately in a market for such entities, then the valuation may be easier to perform. The valuation may either show a diminished value or a loss of the entire value in cases where the entity no longer exists. Business valuation is discussed at length in Chapter 8.

Just as in other types of damages analysis, the terminated distributor needs to take steps to mitigate its damages. This may involve locating alternative sources of supply. If the plaintiff fails to take such reasonable steps, the court may find that the defendant is not liable for the plaintiff's damages that could have been avoided.[39]

However, changing suppliers may impose additional and unique costs on the plaintiff, which may add to its damage claim. For example, the plaintiff may have incurred a variety of additional costs, ranging from a changeover of marketing materials to sales support items. These costs may be added to the total damages.

SUMMARY

Antitrust enforcement is increasingly presenting more opportunities for experts to present economic damages testimony. Such work calls for experts to potentially present testimony on both the liability and the damages side of the case.

This work often calls for the experts to possess a strong background in microeconomics. However, both economists and accountants may provide valuable testimony on the damage-related issues of an antitrust action.

Several key laws provide the regulatory framework for antitrust enforcement. Primary among these is the Sherman Antitrust Act. This law is the cornerstone of U.S. antitrust laws. Other important laws include the Clayton Act, Federal Trade

---

[39] *Golf City, Inc. v. Wilson Sporting Goods Co.,* 555 F.2d 426, 436 (5th Cir. 1977)

Commission Act, Celler-Kefauver Act, and the Hart-Scott-Rodino Antitrust Improvements Act. These laws have been interpreted, sometimes in conflicting ways, by many court decisions.

Antitrust laws are designed to prevent the formation of a monopoly, a market structure in which there is only one seller. Because of a more competitive market structure, there will be more output placed on the market and the product will be sold for a lower price. As a market moves toward a more competitive structure, societal welfare may be increased.

Various quantitative methods can be employed to analyze the degree of competition in a given market. These methods may be used to assess the extent of any monopoly power that a firm may possess. Using tools that are mainstays in the world of industrial organization, the expert may be able to provide valuable assistance to the court in an antitrust proceeding.

REFERENCES

Areeda, Phillip E., and Donald F. Turner, "Predatory Pricing and Related Practices Under Section Two of the Sherman Act," *Harvard Law Review* 86.

Bogosian v. Gulf Oil Corp., 561 F.2d 434, 454 (3rd Cir. 1977), *cert denied*, 434 U.S. 1086 (1987).

Borenstein, Severin, Jeffrey K. MacKie-Mason, and Janet S. Netz, "The Economics of Customer Lock-In and Market Power in Services," *The Service Productivity and Quality Challenge*, Patrick T. Harker., ed., International Studies in the Service Economy, Vol. 5 (Dordrecht, Boston, and London: Kluwer Academic, 1995).

Carlton, Dennis, and Jeffrey M. Perloff, *Modern Industrial Organization*, 3rd ed. (New York: Harper Collins, 1994).

Denger, Michael L., and John A. Herfort, "Predatory Pricing Claims After Brooke Group," *Antitrust Law Journal* 62 (3), Spring 1994.

Easterbrook, Frank, "Predatory Strategies and Counterstrategies," *University of Chicago Law Review* 48 (2), Spring 1981.

Eastman Kodak Co. v. Image Tech. Services., 112 S. Ct. 2072, 2088 (1992).

Fishe, Franklin, Diagnosing Monopoly, (in Franklin Fisher, *Industrial Organization, Economics and the Law*, Massachusetts Institute of Technology: Cambridge, MA, 1991)

Fishman v. Estate of Wirtz, 807 F. 2d 520, 551 (7th Cir. 1986).

Gaughan, Patrick A., *Mergers, Acquisitions and Corporate Restructuring* (New York: Wiley, 1996).

Golf City, Inc. v. Wilson Sporting Goods Co., 555 F.2d 426, 436 (5th Cir. 1977).

Greer, Douglas, *Industrial Organization and Public Policy,* 3rd ed. (New York: MacMillan, 1992).

Image Technical Services, Inc. v. Eastman Kodak Co., 903 F. 2d, 612, 617 (9th Cir. 1990).

International Business Machines v. United States, 298 U.S. (1936).

Jefferson Parish Hospital No. 2 v. Hyde, 466 U.S. 2 (1984).

Jerrold Electronics Corp. v. United States, 187 F. Supp. 545 (1961).

Joskow, Paul L., and Alvin K. Klevorick, "A Framework for Analyzing Predatory Pricing Policy," *The Yale Law Journal* 89 (2), December 1979.

Klein, Benjamin, "Market Power in Antitrust: Economic Analysis After Kodak," *Supreme Court Economic Review* 3 (0), 1993.

McGee, John S., "Predatory Price Cutting: The Standard Oil Case," *Journal of Law and Economics,* October 1958.

McGee, John S., "Predatory Pricing Revisited," *Journal of Law and Economics,* October 1980.

Posner, Richard, *Antitrust Law: An Economic Perspective* (Chicago: University of Chicago Press, 1987).

Salop, Steven C., "Kodak as Post-Chicago Law and Economics," (Boston, MA: CRA Research Review), April 1993.

Salop, Steven C., and David T. Scheffman, "Recent Advances in the Theory of Industrial Structure," *Recent Advances in the Theory of Industrial Structure* 73 (2), May 1983.

Shapiro, Carl, and David J. Teece, "Systems Competition and Aftermarkets: An Economic Analysis of Kodak," *Antitrust Bulletin* 39 (1), Spring 1994.

Standard Oil Company of New Jersey v. U.S., 221 U.S. 1 (1911).

U.S. Bureau of the Census, 1982 Census of Manufactures, " Concentration Ratios in Manufacturing," April 1986, Washington, D.C.

United States Football League v. National Football League, 842 F. 2d 1335 (2d Cir. 1988).

U.S. v. Aluminum Company of America et al., 148 F. 2d 416, 424 (1945).

U.S. v. American Tobacco Co., 221 U.S. 106 (1911).

U.S. v. New York Great Atlantic and Pacific Tea Company et al., 67 F. Supp. 626 (1946), 173 F. 2d (1949).

U.S. v. U.S. Steel Corporation, 251 U.S. 417 (1920).

Van Dyk Research Corp. v. Xerox Corp., 631 F. 2d 251, 255 (3rd Cir. 1980).

Yamey, B.S., " Predatory Price Cutting: Notes and Comments," 15, *Journal of Law and Economics,* 1972, 129–142.

GLOSSARY

Abnormal returns The excess of a security's return beyond what can be explained by the variation in the market's return.

Autocorrelation Another name for serial correlation.

Base damages The amount of damages upon which prejudgment interest may be computed.

Before and after method A method of measuring damages that involves measuring the plaintiff's performance before an event, such as a business interruption, and using this to estimate what the plaintiff's performance would have been over the loss period.

Beta Measure derived from the capital asset pricing model that quantifies the risk as it compares the variation in the overall securities market.

Business cycles The up-and-down movement of the overall economy.

Capital asset pricing model Financial technique that analyzes a securities rate of return as a function of certain components of its risk.

Capitalization Process of determining the present value of a stream of monies of indefinite length (a perpetuity)

Capital market Securities with a maturity of greater than 270 days. It contains such long-term securities as corporate bonds and common stock.

Churning A fraudulent practice whereby brokers induce customers to excessively trade the securities in their accounts so as to generate greater commission income for the broker without regard to the financial interests of customers.

Cointegration A phenomena that occurs when two time series move together.

Collateral transaction A transaction contingent upon another transaction.

Comparable index approach This method of measuring securities market damages attempts to predict the security's return using explanatory variables such as the market return and the industry return.

Concentration ratio A measure of market concentration used in the field of industrial organization. It measures the market shares of certain groups of larger firms in an industry, such as the Top 4 or Top 8.

Conduct school of antitrust A view of antitrust enforcement that the possession of monopoly power alone is not sufficient to have an antitrust violation. Rather, the company would have to engage in anticompetitive conduct.

Confidence interval Statistical bands in which projected values are expected to lie within a certain degree of certainty.

Copyright   A copyright protects the expression of an idea such as a literary or musical work. Copyright protection lasts for 75 years after the date of publication or 100 years after the date of creation.

Correlation   Statistical technique that measures the strength of association between two economic variables.

Demand substitutes   Two products are demand substitutes for each other if an increase in the price of one product causes an increase in the quantity demanded of the other product.

Dual probability trading model   Sometimes referred to as the *two-trader model,* this model of securities trading activity is categorized into two different classes: active traders and traders who utilize a buy-and-hold strategy.

Durbin-Watson statistic   Statistical test designed to detect the presence of serial correlation (first order serial correlation). If its value is close to 2, there probably is no serial correlation. Values close to 0 usually imply positive serial correlation while values close to 4 imply that there may be negative serial correlation.

Econometrics   The field of economics that applies statistical analysis to economic issues.

Efficient markets hypothesis   The theory of financial markets that considers the speed or efficiency with which financial markets internalize new information into the prices that securities trade at. There are three versions of the efficient markets hypothesis: strong form, semi-strong form, and weak form.

Elasticity   A measure of the sensitivity of a change in a dependent variable, such as quantity demanded, to changes in another variable, such as price.

Equal trading probability model   Sometimes called the one-trader model, this model of securities trading activity assumes that shares are only traded one time during the class period.

Event study   An econometric analysis of the returns of a security which, after filtering out the component of the return attributable to the market, allows the researcher to compute abnormal returns, which are those returns that cannot be explained by the market's variation.

Fixed costs   Costs that do not vary with output.

Fraud on the market   The sale of securities pursuant to some material misrepresentation that investors may or may not have relied upon. It is an example of a violation of Rule 10b-5.

Goldfeld test   Econometric technique used when dealing with the statistical problem of heteroskedasticity.

Gross domestic product   The broad economic measure that reflects the performance of the overall economy. Specifically, it measures the market values of all final sales of goods and services within an economy.

Gross net product   The value of a country's total income in a given year. GNP differs from GDP in that GNP includes income received from work or investments in other countries.

Industrial organization   The study of the structure of an industry and the interaction of companies in that industry.

January anomaly *See* Turn-of-the-year effect.

Lerner index This index reflects the difference between price and marginal costs as compared to price.

Lespeyres index A type of index used to compute rates of inflation in prices.

Looper formula A quantitative measure of trading activity used in churning litigation.

Macroeconomics The field of economics that analyzes the overall economy.

Merger waves Periods of intense merger and acquisition activity. There have been four such waves in U.S. economic history prior to the current period of merger and acquisition activity, which may be considered a fifth wave.

Microeconomics The field of economics that analyzes specific subunits of the overall economy, such as specific firms and industries.

Money market This very liquid market contains short-term, low-risk securities. Examples of securities included in this market are Treasury bills and federal funds.

Monopoly A type of market structure in which there is only one seller.

Multicollinearity Where certain of the explanatory variables in the model are correlated. A violation of some of the assumptions of the standard regression analysis model.

Nominal interest rate The amount of dollar interest expressed as a percentage of the amount of dollars that are lent

Nominal values Economic values that have not been adjusted for the impact of inflation.

One-trader model Another name for the equal probability model.

Paper profits In securities litigation, the amount that may be defined as the difference between what the defendant paid for the shares and the value that the court may assess.

Park test Econometric technique used when dealing with the statistical problem of heteroskedasicity.

Patent A grant of a property right that is extended by the Patent and Trademarks Office of the U.S. Department of Commerce. The right bestows upon the owner of the patent the right to exclude others from using the patent without permission from the holder of the patent.

Price discriminating monopolist A monopolist who sets different prices for different consumers based on their different elasticities of demand.

Price theory Another name for microeconomics.

Pure competition A type of market structure in which there are many, independent sellers producing an undifferentiated product with each having such a small market share that they are price takers .

Real interest rate The inflation-adjusted interest rate that reflects the buying power of the interest.

Real values The value of economic variables after the influence of inflation has been removed.

Rule of reason Where behavior or conduct, as opposed to structure, is the main focus of the court. Under this policy, monopoly power alone is not per se illegal.

Semistrong form market efficiency The version of the efficient markets hypothesis which asserts that stock prices internalize all public information.

Serial correlation   Also referred to as autocorrelation. It sometimes occurs in time series analysis where there is some systematic relationship between the error terms or residuals of a regression model.

Service marks   Trademarks for service providers.

Size effect   Also called the neglected firm effect, this securities market phenomena occurs when smaller firms or companies that are not as closely followed can be a source of above-normal gains.

Spurious regression   Regressions that provide some superficially impressive results when under closer examination that regression is flawed.

Strong form market efficiency   The version of the efficient markets hypothesis which asserts that stock prices internalize all information including public and private information.

Structure school of antitrust   A view of antitrust enforcement that the possession of monopoly power is not sufficient to have an antitrust violation.

Supply substitutes   Products A and B are *supply substitutes* if an increase in the price of product A causes companies that are producing B to alter their production mix and increase their production of A.

Tender offer   A share purchase offer made directly to the shareholders of a company.

Time series analysis   The field of econometrics that analyzes economic variables over various economic time periods.

Total offset method   A method of inflation-adjusting and discounting future amounts by simply assuming that the downward impact of discounting will be exactly offset by the upward influence of inflation. The method has been the target of much criticism within the economics profession and in the courts.

Trade dress   Refers to the physical features of the product that have become known in the marketplace to be associated with a particular marketer of that product.

Trademarks   Used to certify the authenticity of a product which, in turn, comes with the expectation on the part of a consumer of the quality of the product or services.

Treasury bills   U.S. government securities with a maturity of one year or less.

Treasury bonds   Long-term U.S. government securities.

Turn-of-the-year effect   Also called the *January anomaly,* this is the tax-loss motivated change in trading activity that occurs at the turn of the year.

Two-trader model   Another name for the dual probability trading model.

Unit root test   Test to determine if a time series is stationary. It examines the relationship between successive values in the time series.

Variable costs   Costs that vary with output.

Vertical integration   Where companies operate at more than one level in the structure of industry. Backward vertical integration can occur if a company moves back toward the source of supply by, for example, buying a supplier. Forward vertical integration can occur if, for example, a company buys a retailer, thereby moving toward the ultimate consumer.

Weak form market efficiency   This is the version of the efficient markets hypothesis that asserts that stock prices reflect all information of past stock price trends.

Worklife expectancy   A period of time in which a worker may remain in the workforce. It is a concept used in personal injury litigation to establish the end of a lost earnings projection.

Yardstick approach   A method of measuring damages that involves finding comparable firms, sometimes called *proxy firms,* which are similar in most relevant respects except for the fact that the proxy firms were not affected by the actions of the defendant. The performance of these firms is used to estimate the performance of the plaintiff.

INDEX

ABC Trans National Transport Inc. v.
Aeronautics Forwarders, Inc., 148
Abnormal returns, 319–321
A.C. Neilsen, 112
Accountants, 169
economists contrasted to, 5, 6–7
Accounting book value, 239
Accounting firms, as source of experts,
9–10
Accounting Horizons, 12
Accounting income, 240, 250–251
Accounting Review, 12
Activity ratios, 198
Adverse publicity, damages from, 54–55
Advertising, corrective, 302
Akaike Information Criterion, 146
Alcan Aluminum v. Carlton Aluminum of
New England, 23
Alcoa, 362–364
Aluminum Products Enterprises v.
Fuhrmann Tooling, 17
American List Corp. v. U.S. News and
World Report, 230
American Tobacco Company, 362–363
Amoco *Cadiz, see In re Oil Spill by*
Amoco Cadiz
Annual reports, 113
Annual Survey of Manufactures, 100
Antitrust concerns, 219, 355
common case types, 373–382
distributor termination, 381–382
mergers and acquisitions, 374
predatory pricing, 374–377

price fixing, 377–378
tying contracts, 357, 379–381
enforcement, 358–362
changes in, 362–365
laws, 355–358
market power, 370–373
monopolization, 365–369
structure versus conduct school of,
361–362
Areeda, Philip, 375
Artel Communications, 322
Asset valuation models, 267–268
Associated Indemnity Co. v. CAT Con-
tracting Inc., 22
Associations, data of, 110, 124–126
Assumptions, role of, 38–39
Attrition, customer, 51
Autotrol Corp. v. Continental Water Sys-
tems Corp., 173
Average costs, defined, 171

Baker, Gary, 4
Barbee, William C., 266
Barriers to market entry, 368–369
Base damages, 225
Basic, Inc., 310–311
Basic, Inc. v. Levinson, 310–311
Baumol, Dr. William, 149
Before and after method of proof, 40, 44
challenges to, 41–42
failure to consider, 40–41
macroeconomic analysis with, 93–94
price fixing and, 378

Bendix Corp. v. Balax, Inc., 57–58
Beta Book, 220
Betas, 219–220, 259
Billingsley, Randall S., 239, 255
Bob Willow Motors, Inc. v. General Motors Corp., 122–123
Bogdanski, John A., 254, 262
Bond Guide, 275
Bonding capacity, loss of, 223–225
Boskin Commission, 82–83
Boskin, Dr. Michael, 82
Brandon & Tibbs v. George Kevorkian Accountancy Corporation, 188
Breach of contract, 61–62
Brigham, Eugene F., 263
Brooke Group Ltd. v. Brown & Williamson Tobacco Corp., 376
Brookshire, Michael, 4
Buildup method, risk premia, 228
Bureau of Economic Analysis, 238
Bureau of Labor Statistics, 238
Business cycles, 67, 81
    economic damages and, 73–74
    firms' reactions to, 74–75
Business Damage Forum, 2
Business Data Analysts, 110
Business Statistics of the United States, 97, 100
Business valuations, *see* Valuations
"But for" revenues, *see* Revenue projection

Capacity analysis, 151–152
    fixed versus variable costs, 181–182
Capital, *see* Time value of money, cost of capital
Capital asset pricing model (CAPM), 219, 258–259
Capital market, 205–209
Capitalization, 60–61, 230–231
Capitalization rate, 231
Carleton, Willard T., 328

Carter Products, Inc. v. Colgate Palmolive Company, 305
Causality, 44–45
    adverse publicity and, 54–55
    client understanding of, 50
    correlation analysis and, 45–46
    correlation scale and, 46–49
    customer loss and, 51
    sales analysis and, 52–53
Celler-Kefauver Act, 357, 364, 374
Center for Security Prices Research (CRSP) database, 325–326
Central Trust Co. v. United States, 269
Cerillo, William, 24
Chained real GDP, 69
Chicago, University of, 325
Churning, 335, 337–338, 344–345
    elements of, 338–339
    measuring damages from, 343–344
    punitive damages for, 344
    quantitative measures of, 339–343
Clayton Act of 1914, 356–357, 364, 379
Client, understanding of losses by, 50
Closed loss period, 55–56
Closely-held companies, valuation, *see* Valuations
Coefficient of determination, 79
Collateral transaction, 28
Combustion Engineering, Inc., 310–311
Commercial damages, 23–24. *See also* Commercial damage analysis
    from business torts, 32
    case law, 24
    contract-related, 28–30
    legal principles of, 24–28
    in personal injury, 30–31
    proving
        before and after method, 40–42, 44
        yardstick method, 42–44
    punitive damages, 32–33
Commercial damage analysis
    causality and, 44–55

compared to personal injury/employment litigation, 2–4
loss period determination and, 55–62
methodology for measuring, 62–65
team approach to, 5–7
testimony about, 37–40
Common stock, 208
Comparability, *see* Yardstick method
Comparable Index Approach, to measuring damages, 314–317, 324
Compensation studies, 253
Competition, changing level of, 120–121
Computer Associates, Inc., 346–351
Computer software, 293
Concentration ratios, 372–373
Conduct school of antitrust, 362
Confidence interval, 144–145
Consequential damages, 28
Construction litigation, 30, 155–156, 223–225
Consultants, as experts, 9, 17
Consumer Price Index (CPI), 82–83
Contract-related damages, 28
  construction-related, 30
  distributor/manufacturer's representative/ franchisee relationships, 29
  liability limitations of, 28
  noncompete agreements, 30
  service provision, 30
  warranty-related damages, 28–29
Contracts, *see also* Contract-related damages
  breach of, 61–62
  cost-plus, 185
Contributory infringement, 283
Control, churning claim and, 338
Control premium, 272
Cooper Liquor v. Adolph Coors Co., 59–60
Copyrights, 293–294, 306
  legal economics of, 294–296
  lost profits and, 296–298

remedies for infringement of, 294
statutory damages for, 298–299
Corporate bonds, 208
Correlation analysis, 45–46
  economic aggregates, 78–79
  on product substitutes, 367
Correlation scale, 46–49
Cost analysis/profitability, 4, 169
  burden of proof for, 173
  case study, 195
  cash flow versus net income, 190–192
  financial statements and, 170–171
  fixed versus variable costs, 173–175
  measures of costs, 171
  mitigation of damages and, 187–190
  overhead costs and, 183–186
  profit margins and, 172–173
  recast profits, 192–194
  regression analysis and, 174–181
  unadjusted accounting data and, 182–183
Cost of capital
  as prejudgment rate, 216–218
  as source of discount rate, 227
Cost of Capital Quarterly, 221
Cost-plus contracts, 185
Courts
  econometric use and, 147–148
  experts and, 4, 5, 7, 10, 15–22
  industry association data/averages and, 122–126
  risk premium and, 229–230
Cover, 28
Credentials, of damage expert
  evaluating, 10–13
  versus experience, 13–14
Cross-sectional analysis, 201
Currency conversion, 93
Curriculum vitae (CV), of damage expert, 9, 12–13
  academic degrees, 10–11
  presentations, 12

Curriculum vitae *(cont.)*
  published books, 11
  refereed journal articles, 11–12
  testimony lists, 12
    Customers
  loss of, 51
  misappropriation of lists of, 305

Damage analysis, *see* Commercial damage analysis
Damages expert
  credentials versus experience, 13–14
  CV of, 10–13
  early need for, 15–16
  finding, 8–10
  management as, 17–18
  qualifications of, 4–5
  reports of, 20–21, 39–40
  from specific industry, 114–115
  testimony of, 18–23, 156
Daubert v. Merrill Dow, 19–20
Debt rate, 216, 218–219
Debt valuation, 274–275
Deltak, Inc. v. Advanced Systems, Inc., 298
Demand substitutes, 366
Desmond, Glenn, 253, 263
Determining Economic Damages (Martin), 4
Determining Economic Loss in Personal Injury and Death Cases (Baker and Seck), 4
Dicky Fuller test, 142
Digital & Analog Design Corporation v. North Supply Company, 7
Direct infringement, 283
Disaggregating revenues
  causality and, 58–59
  spillover losses and, 59–60
Discount rate, 207, 226–228
  versus capitalization rate, 231
  court's position on, 229–230
  nominal versus real rates, 228–229

Discounted cash flow (DCF) valuation model, 242–248
Discounts, valuation and, 270–274
Disgorgement
  for fraud on the market, 312–313
  for merger-related transactions, 334–335
Distributors
  relationships with, 30
  termination of, 381–382
Dual-probability trading model, 327–328
Duke, James, 363
Dunn, Robert, 24, 61, 184, 189, 229
Durbin-Watson Statistic, defined, 140
Dyl, Edward, 329–330

Earnings before interest and taxes (EBIT), 241
Eastman Kodak Co. v. Image Technical Services, 380
Econometrica, 12
Econometrics, 48, 143
Economic aggregates, 75–78
  firm performance and, 78–82
  sources of, 78
Economic expert, *see* Damages expert
Economic Expert Testimony: A Guide for Judges and Attorneys, 3
Economic/financial assumptions, 38
Economic/Hedonic Damages (Brookshire and Smith), 4
Economic income, 240
Economic Indicators, 87
Economic Report of the President, 237
Economics, 44–55. *See also* Macroeconomic analysis
Economist, 239–240
Economists
  causality role and, 53–54
  versus accountants, 5, 6–7
  versus finance specialists, 7–8
Efficient market hypothesis, 310

Eichleay formula, 185
Eight Factor Test, 333
Elasticity of demand, 367–368, 370
Emory, John D., 273, 274
Empire Gas Company v. American Bakeries Co., 22–23
Employment data, 87
Employment litigation, 147
  compared to commercial damage analysis, 3–4
  economists and, 44–45
Encyclopedia of Associations, 110
Entire market value theory, 292–293
Equal trading probability model, 327
Equity, return on, 219–220
Event study approach, to measuring damages, 311–312, 317–330
  data and, 325–326
  delinquent Schedule 13D filing and, 334–335
Excessive stock trading, 339
Expert, *see* Damages expert
Exponential smoothing technique, 151
Express warranty, 29–30

F score, defined, 140
Factual assumptions, 38
Fair market value, *see* Valuations
Fama, Eugene F., 220, 318
Federal funds rate, 207
Federal Reserve Bank, 88
  website of, 78
Federal Reserve Board, 75n
  website of, 238
Federal Reserve Bulletin, 238
Federal Rules of Civil Procedure
  Rule 26(a)(2), 21
Federal Rules of Evidence
  Rule 702, 17, 19
  Rule 703, 37
Federal Tax Valuation Digest, 272
Federal Trade Commission Act, 357
FFJR model, 318

Financial Analysts Journal, 12
Financial Management, 12
Financial ratio analysis, 195, 198–199
Financial statements, costs presented on, 170–171
Find/SVP, 111
Firm-specific financial analysis, 62, 63, 195, 198–199
First differencing process, 143
Fisher Equation, 210–211
Fisher, Franklin, 318, 371
Fisher, Irving, 210
Fisher, Lawrence, 260
Fixed costs
  capacity analysis and, 181–182
  defined, 171
  versus variable costs, 173–175
Forecasts, economic versus accounting terminology in, 128–129
Forensic economics, 1
Foreseeability rule, 26–27
Foster, Carroll B., 235
Franchises, 29, 153, 154–155, 157
Fraud on the market, 310–312
  disgorgement for, 312–313
  measuring damages from, 313–315, 326–330
    comparable index approach, 314–317
    event study approach, 311–312, 317–330
    per share, 326–328
Free cash flow, 253–255
Fredonia Group, 110
French, Kenneth, 220
Frye test, 18–20
Frye v. United States, 18
Fuentes, Henry, 253
Full information price, 312
Funk and Scott Index, 110

Gallinger, George W., 240
Gaughan, Patrick A., 253, 255

General acceptance, testimony and, 19–20

Geographical market definitions, 365–366

Georgia Pacific Corp. v. U.S. Plywood-Champion Papers, Inc, 285, 290

Georgia Pacific royalty factors, 290–292

Gilbert, Gregory A., 266

Goldfield test, 141

Goodwill, 248–250, 268–269, 277

Gordon valuation model, 245, 263, 265

Granger Causality, 48*n*

Graphic Directions, Inc. v. Robert L. Bush, 53–54

Graphical analysis
  forecasting and, 129–131
  sales and, 52–53

Green v. Occidental Petroleum Corp., 313

Gross domestic product (GDP), 68–69, 75
  business cycles and, 73–74, 81
  components of, 69–70
  data release on, 70–72

Gross margin, 172

Growth, post/preinterruption, 57–58

Growth rate extrapolation, 133–136

Growth rate, of industry
  macroeconomic analysis and, 68–75
  for specific industry, 115–118

Hadley v. Baxendale, 27

Hall v. Commissioner, 274

Hand, Learned, 363

Hansen v. Alpine Valley Ski Area, Inc., 292

Hart-Scott-Rodino Antitrust Enforcement Act of 1976, 357–358, 374

Hartness International, Inc. v. Simplimatic Engineering Company, 292

Healey, Basil P., 240

Hearsay, 39

Hedonic damages, 20

Hemphill, C.L., 269

Herfindahl-Hirshman Index, 372

Heteroskedasticity, defined, 140–141

Hickman, Kent, 262

H.K. Porter Co. v. Goodyear Tire and Rubber Co., 289

Holding periods, churning and, 341–342
  case study, 351–352

Holt-Winters exponential smoothing technique, 151

Horizontal price fixing, 377–378

Ibbotson Associates, 214, 220, 221, 247, 261–262

Ibbotson, Roger, 214, 260

Implied warranty, 29

In-and-out trading, *see* Holding periods

In re Computer Associates, International, Inc., case study, 346–351

In re Oil Spill by Amoco Cadiz, 148, 215, 222–223

Incidental damages, 28

Income
  accounting, 240, 250–251
  economic, 240
  minimization, tax issues, 193–194
  net operating, 241
  net, versus cash flow, 190–192

Incremental costs, defined, 171

Incremental profits, 285

Industrial organization, 96

Industry analysis, 62, 63, 96, 126
  conducting, 115–118
  data sources, government, 96–107
  data sources, private, 107–114
  versus firm, 120–122
  relating to plaintiff's growth, 118–119
  retaining expert for, 114–115
  yardstick approach to, 122–126

Infinite loss period, 60–61

Inflation
  interest rates and, 209–211
  overstatement of statistics and, 82–84

Infringement, *see* Copyrights; Patents;
    Trademarks
Injunction, 283
Insider trading case, event study in,
    322–324
Intangible asset valuation, 276–278
Intel, 365
Intellectual property
    copyrights, 293–299, 306
    patents, 282–293, 306
    trade secrets, 303–305, 306
    trademarks, 299–303, 306
Interest rates, 204
    inflation and, 209–211
    loanable funds and, 211
    real versus nominal, 209–211
    risk and return and, 211, 213–214
    types of, 204–209
Internal Revenue Service (IRS)
    Revenue Ruling 59-60, 268–269
    Revenue Ruling 68-609, 248
    Revenue Ruling 74-456, 277
    Revenue Ruling 77-298, 273
    Revenue Ruling 81-253, 272
International Business Machines v. U.S.,
    379
International economic analysis, 91–93
Internet, *see* On-line resources
Investment services, cost of, 342–343

Jefferson Parish Hospital District No. 2
    v. Hyde, 379
Jensen, Michael, 318
Jet Spray, Inc. v. Crampton, 305
Journal of Accountancy, 12
Journal of Accounting and Economics,
    12
Journal of Applied Corporate Finance,
    12
Journal of Econometrics, 12
Journal of Finance, 11
Journal of Financial Economics, 11–12
Journal of Forensic Economics, 2, 11

Journal of Law and Economics, 11
Journal of Law, Economics and Organi-
    zation, 11
Journal of Legal Economics, 2, 11
Journal of Legal Studies, 11
Journal of the American Statistical Asso-
    ciation, 12
Juengel Construction Co., Inc. v. Mt.
    Etna Inc., 184

Katskee v. Nevada Bob's Golf, 40–41
Kaufman Co. v. Lantech, Inc., 286–287
Kelley, Richard E., 263
Key man, loss of, 32
Known rate of error, testimony and, 19
Knutson v. Daily Review, Inc., 361

Landes, William M., 294, 295, 300
Laro, Judge, 268, 270
Larsen v. Walton Plywood Company,
    16–17, 156
Laspeyres Index, 82
Lee v. Durango Music, 172
Legal damage principles
    collateral transactions, 28–29
    foreseeability, 27–28
    occurrence of versus amount of dam-
        ages, 26–27
    proximate causation/reasonable cer-
        tainty, 25–26
    reasonable basis for calculation, 27
Lerner, Abba, 370
Lerner Index, 370
Leverage ratios, 198–199
Liebowitz, Martin L., 267
Life cycles, of specific industry,
    117–118
Life expectancy basis, 3
Lightning Lube, Inc. v. Witco Corp.,
    154–155
    case study of, 158–159
Liquidation value, 239
Liquidity discount, 271–272, 273

Liquidity ratios, 198
Litigation economics, 1–2
Litigation Economics Digest, 2, 11
Loanable funds, 211
Looper formula, 339–340
Lorie, James, 260
Loss period, length of
    breach of contract, 61–62
    business interruption, 55–57
    going out of business, 60–61
Lost asset value, 23–24
Lost profits, *see* Commercial damage
    analysis
Lost revenues, *see* Revenue projection
Lucas, Dr. Robert, 13–14
Lump sum royalties, 289

Macroeconomic analysis, 62, 63, 67–68,
    94
    with before and after method, 93–94
    with economic aggregates, 75–82
    with GDP, 68–75
    inflation statistics and, 82–84
    international, 91–93
    regional trends and, 84–88
Management, as expert witnesses, 17–18
Manufacturer's representative relation-
    ships, 29
Markets, barriers to entry, 368–369
Marginal costs, defined, 171
Market/book valuation models, 265–266
Market definitions, 365–366
Market model, 318–319
Market power, 370–373
Market value, 239
Marketability, lack of, 271–274
Martin, Gerald, 4
Mastrobuono v. Shearson Lehman Hut-
    ton, 344n
Matsushita Electrical Co. Ltd. v. Zenith
    Radio Corporation et al, 377
McGee, John, 376
Mercer, Christopher Z., 273

Mergers
    antitrust analysis of, 374
    disgorgement for, 334–335
    history and laws of, 330, 332–333
Michel Cosmetics v. Tsirklas, 305
Micro Motion Inc. v. Exac Corp.,
    180–181
Microsoft, 365, 371–372
Midland Hotel Corp. v. Reuben H. Don-
    nelly Corp., 123–124
Miles, Raymond C., 239
Minority discount, 271
Mitchell, Mark, 322–323, 334, 335
Mitigation of damages, 187
    burden of proof for, 187–188
    offsetting profits, 188
    tax-related, 189–190
Money market, interest rates and,
    205–209
Monopolies
    barriers to entry, 368–369
    economics of, 358–360
    market definition and, 365–366
    price and suitability issues, 366–368
Monthly Labor Review, 238
Moving average process, 150–151
Mukherji, Sandip, 266
Multicollinearity, defined, 141

NAFE-L, 2
NASDAQ National Market, 261
National Association of Forensic Eco-
    nomics (NAFE), 1–2
National Bureau of Economic Research
    (NBER), 68
Net income, cash flow versus, 190–192
Net margin, 172
Net operating income (NOI), 241
Netter, Jeffrey, 322–323, 334, 335
New England Economic Indicators, 88
New Jersey, 87–88
Newly established businesses
    case study of, 158–159

revenue projection and, 153–156
  yardstick approach to, 43–44
Nexis, 112
Nicholas, David W., 267
Nominal GDP, 68
Nominal versus real interest rates,
    209–211, 228–229
Nominal versus real values, 79, 81–82
Noncompete agreements, 30
North American Industry Classification
    System (NAICS), 106

Offsetting profits, 188
Oligopoly, 120
Omitted variables, defined, 141
On-line resources, 2, 78, 110, 113, 238
One-trader model, 327
Open loss period, 55–56
Operating margin, 172
Opinions, of experts, 38
Out of business loss period, 60–61
Out-of-pocket costs, defined, 171
Overhead, 183–184
  deduction of, 184–185
  as recoverable component of damages,
    185
  unabsorbed, 186

Pabst Brewing Co. v. Commissioner, 269
*Pacific Mutual Life Insurance Co. v.
    Haslip,* 33
Packaged Facts, 110–111
*Palmer v. Connecticut Railway & Light-
    ing Co.,* 61–62
*Panduit Corp. v. Stahlin Brothers Fibre
    Works, Inc.,* 284, 290
Panduit factors, 284–285, 306
Paper profits, 312
Park test, 141
Parr, Russell L., 277
Parts market, 379–381
Patents, 282, 306
  changing legal framework of, 283

direct versus contributory infringe-
    ment and, 283–284
  lost profits damages, 284–288
  prejudgment interest computation, 225
  royalties and, 284, 288–293
Peer review, testimony and, 19
Percentage of sales forecasting, 170, 175
Performance ratios, 199
Perpetuities, 231
Personal injury litigation, 31–32
  compared to commercial damage
    analysis, 2–4
  loss of key man, 32
Petry, Glenn H., 262
Pierce v. Ramsey Winch Company, 44,
    58–59
Polaris Industries v. Plastics, Inc., 125
*Polaroid Corporation v. Eastman Kodak
    Company,* 149, 189
Posner, Richard A., 294, 295, 300
Pratt, Shannon P., 239, 259, 262, 266
Predatory costing, 377
Predatory pricing, 374–377
Predicasts Basebook, 107, 110
Preferred stock
  cost of capital and, 219
  valuation and, 274–276
Prejudgment rate of return, 214–215
  impairment of capital losses and,
    223–225
  risk adjustment of past losses and,
    225–226
  sample computation, 223, 225
  time period of, 222
Present value, *see* Time value of money
Price/earnings valuation model, 263–265
Price elasticity of demand, 367–368, 370
Price fixing, 377–378
Price line, of stocks, 313, 314
Price, monopoly and, 366–368
Price/revenue valuation models,
    266–267
Pricing, predatory, 374–377

Prime rate, 207
PRN of Denver v. A.J. Gallagher, 43
Producer Price Index (PPI), 82, 84
Product market definitions, 366
Profitability, *see* Cost analysis/profitabil-
    ity
Profits
    lost, *see* Commercial damage analysis
    offsetting, 188
    paper, 312
    recasted, 192–194
Proportional trading model, 328
Proving Business Damages (Cerillo), 24
Proximate causation, 24–25
Proxy firms, 153, 156, 219
Public utilities, 222
Publications, of experts, 11–12, 18
Publicity, damages from adverse, 54–54
Publicly-held companies, valuation of,
    235–236
Punitive damages, 33–34, 344
Pure competition, 120

R_, defined, 139
Raines, Gary, 266
*Rancho Pascado v. Northwestern Mutual
    Life Insurance Co.,* 158
Rate of return
    data sources for, 214
    risk and return and, 211, 213–214
Rational standard, 26
Real Business Cycle Theory, 73
Real GDP, 68–69
Real versus nominal interest rates,
    209–211, 228–229
Real versus nominal values, 79, 81–82
Reasonable basis, for damages, 26
Reasonable certainty, of damages, 24–25
Recasted profits, 192–193
    professional corporations, 194
    public versus private corporations,
        193–194

Recessions, 68, 73–75
*Recovery For Personal Injury and
    Wrongful Death* (Speiser), 4
Recovery of Damages for Lost Profits
    (Dunn), 24
References, of experts, 8
Regional Economic Digest, 88
Regional economic trends analysis, 62,
    63, 84–85, 88
    before and after method and, 93–94
    sources of data for, 87–88, 116–117
    timeliness of data and, 85, 87
Regression analysis
    cost analysis and, 174–181
    event study methodology and, 318
    revenue projection and, 136–144, 147
Reports, of experts, 21–22, 39–40
Restructuring, within industry, 121–122
Return on equity (ROE), 264, 264n
Revenue base selection, 133–135
Revenue projection, 128
    capacity constraints and, 151–152
    confidence in, 144–147
    econometrics used in, 147–149
    forecasts contrasted, 126–127
    graphical analysis of, 128–131
    methods of, 131, 133
        basic growth rate extrapolation,
            133–136
        curve fitting methods, econometric
            models, 136–144
    for new business, 153–156
    seasonality and, 149–151
    sensibility check for, 152–153
    for unestablished business, 156–158
Revenues, disaggregating, 58–60
Reverse engineering, 304
Risk adjustment discount rate, 226–228
Risk and return, 211, 213–214, 257–258
Robert Morris Associates, 253
Robinson-Patman Act of 1936, 357
Roll, Rachael, 318

Royalties, patent infringement and, 284, 288–293
  determining, 290–292
  entire market value theory and, 293–294
  versus lost profits, 292
  reasonable, 288–290
  types of, 289

S. Jon. Kreedman & Co. v. Meyers Bros. Parking-Western Corp., 155–156
Sales analysis, 52–53
Sandler v. Lawn-a-Mat Chemical & Equipment Corp., 62
S.C. Anderson v. Bank of America, 224
Scatter diagrams, 49
Schmalensee, Richard, 369
Schwartz Information Criterion, 146–147
Scienter, 339
Scullin Steel Co. v. PACCAR, Inc., 184–185
Seasonal decomposition technique, 150
Seasonality, 149–151
SEC v. Texas Gulf Sulphur Co., 312
Seck, Michael, 4
Securities Exchange Act of 1934, 207, 310
  Schedule 13D, 332, 334–335
  Schedule 14D-1, 333–334, 374
  Section 10(b), 339
  Section 13(d), 374
  Section 14(d), 374
  Williams Act of, 332, 335
Securities losses
  case study in, 346–351
  churning, 335, 337–345
  fraud on the market, 310–330
  mergers-related damages, 330–335
Securities markets reports, 113–114
Serial correlation, defined, 140
Service marks, 299

Services, contacts to provide, 31
Shearson American Express v. McMahon, 337
Sherman Antitrust Act, 355–356, 365, 377
Sherman, John, 356
Sierra Wine & Liquor Co. v. Heublein, Inc., 188
Sinquefeld, Rex, 214, 260
Smith Development Corp. v. Bilow, 157
Smith, Gordon V., 277
Smith, Stan, 4
Software, 293
South Carolina Federal Savings Bank v. Thornton-Crosby Development Co., 155
Speiser, Stuart, 4
Spillman, Francis, 334–335
Spreadsheet regression programs, weakness of, 144
Spurious regression, 142
Standard Industrial Classification (CID) Codes, 100, 106, 221, 357
Standard Oil Company of New Jersey v. U.S., 362
Stationarity, lack of, 141–143
Statistical Abstract of the United States, 97, 238
Stocks
  common, 208
  parking of, 334
  preferred, 273, 274–276
Stocks, Bills, Bonds, and Inflation, 214
Story Parchment Co. v. Paterson Parchment Paper Co., 25–26
Structure school of antitrust, 361–362
Substitutes, of products, 366–367
Suitability, churning claim and, 338
Sunk costs, defined, 171
Sunkist Growers v. Winkler & Smith Citrus Products Co., 361
Supply substitutes, 366

Survey of Current Business, 238
Systematic risk, 206*n,* 219

t scores, defined, 139–140
Tau test, 142
Tax issues, 189–190. *See also* Internal
    Revenue Service (IRS)
    debt rate and, 218–219
    income minimization and, 193–194
    of valuation, 268–270
Taylor, Dr. Larry, 144
    testimony of, 160–166
Taylor v. Meirick, 296
"Ten Most Frequent Errors in Litigating
    Business Damages, The," 114
Testimony
    admissibility standards, 18–20
    of defense expert, 21–23
    foundations for, 37–38
        assumptions, 38–39
        expert reports, 39–40
        hearsay, 39
Testimony lists, of experts, 12
Testing, testimony and, 19
Texaco v. Pennzoil, 22
Texas Gulf Sulphur, 312
Time series analysis, 48, 137
    versus cross-sectional, 199
Time value of money, 62, 203–204,
    231–232
    background of, 204–214
    cost of capital and, 216–222
        components of, 218–220
        as element of damages, 221
        public utilities and, 222
    discount rate and, 203, 226–232
    prejudgment rate of return and,
        214–218, 222–226, 231
Todd, J.F., 269
Torts, 33
Total costs, defined, 171
Total offset method, 229
Trade dress, 300, 306

Trade secrets, 303–304, 306
    customer list losses, 305
    damages for misappropriation of,
        304–305
Trademarks, 299, 306
    damages for infringement of, 301–302
    defendant's profits and, 302–303
    economics of, 300
    royalties and, 302
Trading models, 327–328
Treasury bill rate, 207
Treasury bonds, 208
Treasury Bulletin, 238
*Trio Process Corp. v. L. Goldstein's
    Sons, Inc.,* 289
Trout, Robert B., 23, 235, 270
Troy, Leo, 253
Turner, Donald, 375
Turnover ratios, churning and, 339–341
Two-trader model, 327–328
*TXO Production Corp. v. Alliance Re-
    sources Corp.,* 33
Tying contracts, 357, 379–381

Unestablished business, 156–158
Unit root test, 142
*United States Football League v. Na-
    tional Football League,* 361
*Universal Power Systems, Inc. v. God-
    father's Pizza, Inc.,* 184, 185
Universities, as source of experts, 9
Unprofitable businesses, 186–187
Urban economics, *see* Regional econom-
    ics trend analysis
U.S. Bureau of the Census, 94, 100
U.S. Department of Commerce
    as data source, 96–100
    website of, 78
U.S. Department of Labor website, 78
U.S. Industrial Outlook, 97
*U.S. v. Aluminum Company of America et
    al,* 363–364
U.S. v. American Tobacco Co., 362*n*

U.S. v. Microsoft, 371–372
U.S. v. New York Great Atlantic and Pacific Tea Company et al, 364
U.S. v. U.S. Steel Corporation, 363

Valuations, 235–239, 268–270
  asset models, 267–268
  cash flow estimation, 250–256
  discount rate estimation, 257
    capital asset pricing model, 258–259
    historic returns, 260–262
    risk and return, 257–258
  discounts and premiums, 270–274
  earnings-based models, 243
    discounted cash flow (DCF), 242–248
    excess earnings method, 248–250
  equity models, 240–243
  market comparable models, 262–263
    market/book, 265–266
    price-earnings, 263–265
    price/revenue, 266–267
  measures of, 239–240
  of other financial assets
    debt, 274–275
    intangible assets, 276–278
    preferred stock, 275–276
Value Line Investment Survey, 220
Value line, of stocks, 313, 314
VanHorne, James C., 241
Variable costs
  capacity analysis and, 181–182
  defined, 171

versus fixed costs, 173–175
Venuto, Ralph, 158, 159
Vertical price fixing, 378
Vickers v. Wichita State University, 26
Vuyanich v. Republic National Bank of Dallas, 147

Wachowicz, John M., 241
Wade, William W., 270
Warranty-related damages, 29–30
Weighted average, 134
Weisbach, Michael S., 328
Weiss, Elliott J., 328
White v. Southwestern Bell Telephone Co., 147–148
Willamette Management Associates, 273, 274
Williams Enterprises, Inc. v. The Sherman R. Smoot Company, 221n
Winners Corporation, 334–335
Worldcom, Inc. v. Automated Communications, Inc. et al, 144
  testimony excerpts from, 160–166
Wrongful death litigation, *see* Personal Injury litigation

Yardstick method of proof, 42
  challenges to, 42–43
  industry analysis and, 122–126
  for newly established businesses, 43–44

Zukin, James, 239